EXPEDITIONARY ANTHROPOLOGY

Methodology and History in Anthropology
Series Editors:
David Parkin, Fellow of All Souls College, University of Oxford
David Gellner, Fellow of All Souls College, University of Oxford

Just as anthropology has had a significant influence on many other disciplines in recent years, so too have its methods been challenged by new intellectual and technical developments. This series is designed to offer a forum for debate on the interrelationship between anthropology and other academic fields but also on the challenge to anthropological methods of new intellectual and technological developments, and the role of anthropological thought in a general history of concepts.

For a full volume listing, please see back matter

EXPEDITIONARY ANTHROPOLOGY

Teamwork, Travel and the 'Science of Man'

Edited by
Martin Thomas and Amanda Harris

berghahn
NEW YORK • OXFORD
www.berghahnbooks.com

First published in 2018 by
Berghahn Books
www.berghahnbooks.com

© 2018, 2021 Martin (Edward) Thomas and Amanda Harris
First paperback edition published in 2021

All rights reserved. Except for the quotation of short passages for the purpose of criticism and review, no part of this book may be reproduced in any form or by any means, electronic or mechanical, including photocopying, recording, or any information storage and retrieval system now known or to be invented, without written permission of the publisher.

Library of Congress Cataloging-in-Publication Data

A C.I.P. cataloging record for this book
is available from the Library of Congress

British Library Cataloguing in Publication Data

A catalogue record for this book is available from the British Library

ORCID:
Martin (Edward) Thomas: 0000-0002-2261-5888
Amanda Harris: 0000-0002-9858-2568

ISBN 978-1-78533-772-7 hardback
ISBN 978-1-80073-018-2 paperback
ISBN 978-1-78533-773-4 ebook

CONTENTS

List of Illustrations   vii

Anthropology and the Expeditionary Imaginary: An Introduction to the Volume   1
    Martin Thomas and Amanda Harris

Part I. Anthropology and the Field: Intermediaries and Exchange

Chapter 1. Assembling the Ethnographic Field: The 1901–02 Expedition of Baldwin Spencer and Francis Gillen   37
    Philip Batty

Chapter 2. Receiving Guests: The Cambridge Anthropological Expedition to Torres Straits 1898   64
    Jude Philp

Chapter 3. Donald Thomson's Hybrid Expeditions: Anthropology, Biology and Narrative in Northern Australia and England   95
    Saskia Beudel

Part II. Exploration, Archaeology, Race and Emergent Anthropology

Chapter 4. Looking at Culture through an Artist's Eyes: William Henry Holmes and the Exploration of Native American Archaeology   127
    Pamela M. Henson

Chapter 5. The Anomalous Blonds of the Maghreb: Carleton Coon Invents the African Nordics   150
    Warwick Anderson

Chapter 6. Medium, Genre, Indigenous Presence: Spanish Expeditionary Encounters in the Mar del Sur, 1606   175
    Bronwen Douglas

Chapter 7. Ethnographic Inquiry on Phillip Parker King's
Hydrographic Survey   205
  Tiffany Shellam

Part III. The Question of Gender

Chapter 8. Gender and the Expedition: Feminist
Anthropologist Elsie Clews Parsons and the Politics of
Fieldwork in the Americas in the 1920s and 1930s   235
  Desley Deacon

Chapter 9. What Has Been Forgotten? The Discourses of
Margaret Mead and the American Museum of Natural History
Sepik Expedition   263
  Diane Losche

Chapter 10. Gender, Science and Imperial Drive: Margaret
McArthur on Two Expeditions in the 1940s   290
  Amanda Harris

Index   313

ILLUSTRATIONS

Figure 1.1 Senior Arrernte men overseeing the Engwura ceremony, Alice Springs. Photograph by Baldwin Spencer, 1896. 44

Figure 1.2 Members of the 1901–02 expedition, Alice Springs. Unknown photographer, 1901. 47

Figure 1.3 An Atninga ('revenge') party of Arrernte men, Alice Springs. Photograph by Baldwin Spencer, 1901. 50

Figure 1.4 Women crawl through the legs of decorated men towards the end of a Warumungu burial ritual, Tennant Creek. Photograph by Baldwin Spencer, 1901. 52

Figure 2.1 William Rivers, Charles Seligman, Sidney Ray, Anthony Wilkin, Alfred Haddon. Mabuyag, 1898. 65

Figure 2.2 Waria, Papi, Noboa, Gizu. Mabuyag Island, 1898. 66

Figure 2.3 Jimmy Rice, Debe Wali, Alfred Haddon, Charlie Ongtong, Anthony Wilkin, William Rivers, Sidney Ray, William McDougall, Charles Myers, Charles Seligman, at Mer, 1898. 71

Figure 2.4 'Singing at Las', Gasu, Enoka, Ulai and Wano. Gadodo standing at centre with John Bruce, William Rivers, Sidney Ray, 1898. 76

Figure 2.5 *Mai*, worn only by *giri-giri le* (bird clan men) at the conclusion of the Malu ceremonies. 77

Figure 3.1 Photograph published in Donald F. Thomson, 'The Story of Arnhem Land', *Walkabout*, 1 August 1946. 99

Figure 3.2 *Herald and Weekly Times*, 'Prof. [Professor] Donald Thomson' with family, 1936. 101

Figure 3.3 'Portrait of Dr. Donald Thomson'. Unknown photographer, circa 1937. 110

Figure 4.1 Sketch of participants in the Hayden Survey (United States Geological and Geographical Survey of the Territories, 1871–77), 1874. 130

Figure 4.2 'Panorama from Point Sublime', illustration by William H. Holmes, 1882. 131

Figure 4.3 Topographic sketch of the Mayan city at Copan, Honduras. Drawing by William H. Holmes, 1916. 137

Figure 5.1 Carleton S. Coon with others in Morocco, late 1920s. 154

Figure 5.2 Warrior on horseback. Photograph by Carleton S. Coon, late 1920s. 156

Figure 5.3 Hunting in the Rif. Photograph by Carleton S. Coon, late 1920s. 162

Figure 6.1 Spanish–Chamorro encounter, Guam, Anon., c. 1590. 179

Figure 6.2 *La gran baya d. S. Philippe y S. Santiago*, Diego de Prado y Tovar, 1606. 182

Figure 6.3 *Esta xente es d'esta baia st felipe y st tiago ...*, Diego de Prado y Tovar, 1607. 183

Figure 6.4 *Puertos i bayas de Tiera de San Buenaventura*, Diego de Prado y Tovar, 1606. 184

Figure 6.5 *Esta xente es desta baya de san millan ...*, Diego de Prado y Tovar, 1607. 185

Figure 6.6 *La gran baya d. S. Lorenço y puerto d. Monterei*, Diego de Prado y Tovar, 1606. 186

Figure 6.7 *Esta xente delas yslas questan alaparte del sur de la Nueva Guinea ...*, Diego de Prado y Tovar, 1607. 187

Figure 6.8 *Baya de Sanct Pedro de Arlança, Tiera de S. Santiago de los Papuas*, Diego de Prado y Tovar, 1606. 188

Figure 6.9 *Esta xente es del rremate dela nueva guinea ...*, Diego de Prado y Tovar, 1607. 189

Figure 7.1 Sketch of the spear in Phillip Parker King's Remark Book, April 1818. 207

Figure 7.2 Sketch of the basket with ironhoop handles, by Allan Cunningham. 217

Figure 7.3 Sketch of a spearhead by John Septimus Roe, September 1821. 218

Figure 7.4 'Weapons & c., of the Natives of Hanover Bay'. Drawing by Francis Chantrey. 219

Figure 7.5 Title page of Phillip Parker King, *Narrative of a Survey of the Intertropical and Western Coasts of Australia, Performed between the Years 1818 and 1822*, 1826. 220

Figure 8.1 Elsie Clews Parsons in the Southwest, 1920. 236

Figure 8.2 Professor Henry Fairfield Osborn shares his package of 'Pirates' cigarettes with man on camel, Mongolia, 1923. Photograph by Roy Chapman Andrews. 240

Figure 8.3   Alfred Kidder in his hairy-chinned period in
1912. Photograph by Jesse Nusbaum. 249
Figure 9.1   Conducting Public Flutes, Alitoa Village,
Arapesh. Photograph by Reo Fortune, 1932. 269
Figure 9.2   Gregory Bateson, Margaret Mead, Reo Fortune,
captioned as 'Group of Anthropologists Who Arrived on
Macdhui'. Unknown photographer, July 1933. 275
Figure 10.1   David Cameron, Margaret McArthur and
Doreen Langley with an unidentified group in New Guinea.
Photograph by James (Jim) Fitzpatrick, 1947. 293
Figure 10.2   The American-Australian Scientific Expedition
to Arnhem Land at Oenpelli. Photograph by Howell Walker,
1948. 301

ANTHROPOLOGY AND THE EXPEDITIONARY IMAGINARY

AN INTRODUCTION TO THE VOLUME

Martin Thomas and Amanda Harris

Anthropologists as Explorers

Felix Driver opens *Geography Militant* (2001), his foundational study of exploration and empire, by quoting Claude Lévi-Strauss on the hubris of explorers. For the doyen of structural anthropology, exploration had by the twentieth century degenerated into 'a trade' where the object was not to discover unknown facts but to cover as much distance as possible and assemble 'lantern-slides or motion pictures, preferably in colour, so as to fill a hall with an audience for several days in succession'.[1] Driver observes that for Lévi-Strauss, 'the calling of the anthropologist was something altogether more noble' than that of the explorer. The former pursued a course of disciplined observation while the latter disseminated 'superficial stories'.[2] The scientifically trained Lévi-Strauss felt duty-bound to differentiate himself from these commercial travellers.

The proposition that anthropology is antithetical to the ethos of adventurism raises questions that are investigated in the pages ahead. Why this insistence upon a dichotomy so flimsy? Why discount the call of adventure when it acted as a siren for countless anthropologists? To understand the concerns voiced by Lévi-Strauss, we need to acknowledge that they are more than an assertion of academic superiority. The anxieties from which they stem reveal much about anthropology's formation as a discipline; they are the residue of a complex and at times quarrelsome nexus between exploration, imperial expansion and the 'science of man'. Anthropology in its early life was enabled by the systemized observation and reporting that a codified practice of exploration had first projected into putatively uncharted spaces. The expeditions of Cook and other Enlightenment voyagers are paradigmatic in this regard, but they had important progenitors (see Douglas, this volume, for a discussion of some Iberian precedents). Anthropology and ethnology, as defined in the guides and rulebooks of the specialist societies created for their promotion in the nineteenth century, absorbed many of the codes and procedures that explorers were expected to follow.[3] Anthropology developed in tandem with the blossoming of exploration, which it ultimately outlived, for exploration came to be thought of as an imperial conceit, while anthropology became institutionally entrenched in universities and museums.

By 1948, Evelyn Waugh was having great fun with the vanities of exploration in his novel *A Handful of Dust*. Nine years later, Patrick White in *Voss* would render the explorer's mission an existential folly. In Werner Herzog's *Fitzcarraldo* (1982), it is something decidedly more ludicrous. Bathos is a trait of many depictions of expeditionary journeys from the postwar period. The extent to which explorers became objects of mirth and parody in twentieth-century culture is an indication of how their stocks fell as the world began to decolonize. The once hallowed figure of the explorer could now be safely laughed at, even if, as Simon Naylor and James R. Ryan have pointed out in an illuminating volume of essays, exploration *did* enjoy an afterlife through the twentieth century and beyond, albeit in modified and often derivative forms.[4] Space travel was the most paradigm-shifting manifestation of twentieth-century exploration, yet the cost, the connectedness with the Cold War, and a plethora of other military associations made it anything but unproblematic. The progressivist mythology that legitimized nineteenth-century exploration had by this time worn thin. That exploration survived at all in the latter part of the twentieth century is due, on one hand, to the plasticity of the concept, and, on the other, to the continuing power of the tropes around race, gender and nation that had always underlain it.[5] Various sorts of re-versioning of the exploratory impulse continue in the twenty-first century, with re-enactments of explorers' routes or voyages being quite common.[6] Here is evidence that despite being the butt of jokes, explorers have not entirely lost their place in the pantheon of Western nations. To former imperial powers, they embody the global spread of European values; in settler societies, they are often foundational figures. In narrative, if no longer in person, they continue to straddle the divide between 'centre' and 'periphery'. They bridge the 'new' world and the 'old'. That role of bridging helps explain why so much cultural processing, in cinema, television, literature and especially on the internet, goes about the work of keeping alive the expeditionary imaginary.

In this book, we demonstrate that anthropology's association with exploration has been far more enduring than is usually acknowledged. We do this by providing a survey – a historical journey – through a range of expeditions that collected data that were in some way anthropological. The period covered begins in the seventeenth century and extends through to the twentieth. In choosing this starting date, we acknowledge that the recorded observation of manners, customs and traditions has an older provenance, extending back to at least the Middle Ages.[7] But that is more than we can deal with here. Our earliest case study is Douglas's chapter on the Quirós and Torres voyage to Vanuatu, New Guinea and the Torres Strait Islands. That journey occurred in 1606, less than fifteen years after the astrologer and polemicist Richard Harvey made the first recorded use of the word 'anthropology' in his book *Philadelphus, or a Defence of Brutes and the Brutans History* (1593).[8] By this time, many of the arguments and developments that we now know as the Scientific Revolution were having impact. In an unprecedented way, nature had become an object of formal inquiry. This prompted new forms of travel and data collection, as is evident in the many exploratory ventures dating from the 1600s. Naval and commercial seafaring established protocols that would culminate in the famed scientific voyages of the Enlightenment. Throughout the period of imperial expansion, opportunities for observing and describing the panorama of humanity were steadily increasing. This ultimately resulted in the more rigorously theorized notion of anthropology that took root in the second half of the nineteenth century.

We consider it timely to excavate this history because anthropology's connection with exploration has been rendered peripheral in many accounts of the discipline. The reasons why the long and formative tradition of expeditionary anthropology has been eclipsed are perhaps obvious. The preference for immersive fieldwork by a sole investigator had, by the mid twentieth century, become the dominant mode of cross-cultural observation, especially for social anthropologists. Our argument is that anthropology never entirely disconnected itself from its genealogy in scientific voyaging and formalized geographic travel. On the contrary, it *drew* from expeditionary models, replicating them on some occasions and channelling them in new directions on others.

George W. Stocking, the best-known historian of anthropology, was alert to the pervasive effects of exploration upon the anthropological enterprise. He too was convinced that fieldwork by an individual researcher retained vestiges of discovery into the 'unknown'. He found evidence of this in – of all places – the Trobriand diary of Bronisław Malinowski, which notes: 'This island, though not "discovered" by me, is for the first time experienced artistically and mastered intellectually'.[9] For Malinowski to be quoted as evidence of anthropology's indebtedness to exploratory expeditions is curious, given his catalytic role in encouraging the departure from group expeditions such as the one led by his mentor, A.C. Haddon, to the Torres Strait (see Batty and Philp, this volume).[10] As Malinowski's model of cultural 'immersion' became prevalent in social anthropology, large-scale expeditions were increasingly regarded as archaic and inauthentic (see Deacon, this volume). Yet in spite of their diminishing reputation, grand ethnological expeditions *did* continue. We will shortly cast a spotlight on one that was both influential and controversial.

Firstly, however, we need to emphasize that the desire to travel, discover and convey information about exotic locales to an audience back home – the fundamental driver for geographical exploration – was by no means at odds with anthropological inquiry. The two had a symbiotic relationship, with metropolitan anthropologists often revelling in the role of veteran adventurer. Consequently, it is not surprising that the authors of a recent study of Frederick Rose, who was based for many years at Humboldt University, tell us that his students 'responded with a sense of wonderment to Rose's accounts of a universe they could never witness themselves. For them he was not just the dedicated, groundbreaking scientist but the intrepid explorer …'.[11] Comments such as this appear often in biographies of ethnographers, many of whom actively cultivated the persona of explorer-scientist. In her essay 'Science as Adventure' (2015), Henrika Kuklick argued that the mantle of explorer lent credibility to anthropologists who, like other field scientists, considered it imperative to consolidate their authority as observers. In this tradition of scientific inquiry, the veracity of the investigator's subjective impressions was open to question in a way that was never the case for the experimenter in the lab. Naturalists and anthropologists, according to Kuklick, 'used their heroism in the field as proof that they were persons of fine character, mobilizing agreement that their judgements were sound'.[12]

We should bear in mind that by the time Fred Rose was wowing his students in East Berlin, the concept of geographic exploration was essentially obsolete. Yet this did surprisingly little to derail the anthropological project. The residual power of exploratory narratives, and the ease with which they could be transferred to an anthropological context, is especially apparent in the discipline's more popular guises. *National Geographic*, in both its articles and film productions, provides innumerable examples;[13] time-honoured tropes, such as the search for 'unknown tribes', are a regular refrain. Ignoring or even eschewing narratives of geographical conquest, popular anthropology was nonetheless infused with motifs of expeditionary heroism and romance. Anthropology could enact the urge to discover, even if it openly disavowed it. Humanity in its bewildering diversity became surrogate geography for anthropologists.

Among the host of connections between anthropology and geographical exploration, the role of expeditionary practices in cultivating a public audience was highly formative. Professorial pooh-poohing of the popular lecture circuit ignores the reality that anthropology is itself hardly innocent of entertaining the masses. Largely banished from the discipline's corporate memory is a long and remarkable – if sometimes decidedly problematic – tradition of anthropology finding a broad public for its ideas. Admittedly, some of this was shamelessly opportunistic. P.T. Barnum infamously claimed an interest in the discipline, to the extent that his circus of the 1880s, billed 'The Greatest Show on Earth', boasted an 'Ethnological Congress of Strange and Savage Tribes' where ensembles of 'cannibals' and 'primitives', some abducted from their homelands, were savagely paraded.[14] Of course, not all attempts to gratify the public appetite for anthropological content were so lacking in sobriety. As Diane Losche points out in this volume, during her many years of being the world's best-known anthropologist, Margaret Mead was based in a museum. Producing gallery displays, magazine articles, documentary films and other 'non-academic' outputs was part of her job description, as it was for so many of her contemporaries. Lévi-Strauss bemoaned the banality of explorers, yet forgot to acknowledge the long and rich tradition of *anthropologists* giving public lectures that were often illustrated by lantern slides or films. To ignore these and other 'low-brow' outputs is to overlook their role in the shaping of anthropology, both as a public spectacle that anticipated what we now call 'infotainment', and as a disciplinary formation. Of course, popular anthropology generated excitement in a way that learned articles could not. Yet as the public face of the discipline, it was a prime vehicle for the recruitment of students. Just as importantly, it brought access to money.

In its popular and in many of its academic manifestations, anthropology was enabled by an intricate circuitry that connected 'the field', the auditorium, the museum, the press and sources of funding. Here is evidence that far from being antithetical to exploration, anthropology and the larger project of geographical 'discovery' have not only a common intellectual lineage but, in certain phases of their history, a common business model. The observations of exploratory voyagers and reports by missionaries or officials on colonial frontiers are the progenitors of what we now call 'fieldwork data'. The practice of raising public interest and finance by publishing and lecturing was standard procedure for geographical travellers. Henry Morton Stanley, who came to exploration from journalism, is a paradigmatic example of the Victorian explorer-showman.[15] While Stanley blurred the boundaries between discovery and the generation of copy – much to the irritation of the Royal Geographical Society (RGS) and others who tried to police the exploration business – many of the heroic explorers officially endorsed by the RGS or kindred organizations were themselves popular authors and speakers. A number of the anthropologists discussed in this book (Margaret Mead and Donald Thomson are key examples) consistently sought popular outlets in addition to scholarly publishing, sometimes to the detriment of their academic reputations (see Losche and Beudel, this volume). Notably, Claude Lévi-Strauss himself was supremely talented as a public communicator. Indeed, his jeremiad about the commercial crassness of explorers appears in *Tristes Tropiques* (1954), a classic memoir that remains in print after sixty years precisely *because*, as Patrick Wilcken has written, it consisted of a 'genre-bending mix of confessional, travelogue, philosophy and science...'. So writerly was the text that the judges of the Prix Goncourt expressed regret that as a work of non-fiction it could not be considered for France's highest literary honour. In 1956, *Tristes Tropiques* was selected for the Gold Pen, an award for travel writing. But Lévi-Strauss, perhaps mindful of what he had said about the evils of explorers, turned it down.[16]

Driver points out that the concerns voiced by Lévi-Strauss were not novel to his epoch. 'Anxieties about the relationship between sober science and sensational discovery, "professional" fieldwork and "popular" travel, have characterised writings on anthropology (and geography) for at least two hundred years.'[17] When, in the early to mid twentieth century, anthropology became firmly established as a field of academic inquiry, it was naturally keen to assert its maturity by distinguishing itself from that all-too-recent epoch when armchair theorists and amateur fieldworkers were a prevailing force. Part of this agenda involved severing links with geographical exploration. Yet the campaign to exorcise the ghosts of expeditions past was only partially successful. Roy MacLeod points out that exploratory logic came to function as an organizing principle across the sciences. As the blank spaces on maps turned into a thing of the past, 'the representation of science itself' became 'a symbolic act of perpetual exploration'.[18]

Spotlight on an Anthropological Expedition

This volume acknowledges and interprets the defining influence of exploration upon the anthropological enterprise. From this premise, we have pursued the specific agenda of examining the structural effects of expeditionary culture upon the discipline. As the book makes plain, expeditions reveal a very different face of the anthropological project. In contrast to the labour of an independent fieldworker, an expedition is at heart a *collective* enterprise. Team-based research can provide companionship, security and support for members of an investigative party. It can also be a theatre for internal competition and conflict. For the people being investigated, the expedition presents a very different experience to a visit from a lone investigator. Solo fieldworkers are, by definition, disconnected from their own societies. Expeditions, in contrast, present a spectacle where scientists appear in something resembling their own social context. As the pages ahead make clear, the collectivity of expeditions shaped the discipline in a multitude of ways.

Expeditions, by their very nature, transplant a structured social environment into a new and often jarring cultural context. The expeditionary team forms a subculture of the society that produced it. These teams arose out of professional and institutional networks that often perpetuated colonial relationships between the knowledge seekers and their subjects. Publicly and privately sponsored, and often supported by major collecting institutions, expeditions were enmeshed in imperial politics and agendas. While the relationship between explorers and the institutions of empire is widely acknowledged, recent scholarship has begun to explore how networks innate to indigenous societies interacted with scientific, exploratory and anthropological expeditions.[19] Several chapters in *Expeditionary Anthropology* specifically address this issue (see Douglas, Shellam and Philp, this volume).

Recognition that local people, whether they acted as guides, interviewees, interpreters or in other roles, could be active *shapers* of expeditions is but one example of how this subject dovetails with current research in the humanities and social sciences. The digital turn has been pivotal to reassessment of the meaning and significance of expeditionary legacies. Photographic and other forms of copying have greatly increased access to the often vast collections of artefacts or specimens amassed by expeditions, which for years were hidden in museum storage. Digital preservation of sound recordings and photography has generated new audiences for such material, especially among the communities visited by anthropologists and explorers.

This explains why the expedition as a specific mode of knowledge production is at last getting the attention it deserves. In *Expeditions as Experiments* (2016), an edited volume that examines the significance of expeditions to the history of science, the editors Marianne Klemun and Ulrike Spring describe the expedition as a locale where 'individuals discover and create their own professional identity within this metaphorical constellation of space'.[20] Their volume examines the relationship between the laboratory and the field, paying attention to the communitarian aspects of the expeditionary experience. For contributors to *Expeditionary Anthropology*, the formation of 'professional identity' through team-based fieldwork is also an abiding concern. However, for contributors to our volume, the professional identities of both male and female expeditionary anthropologists are indelibly connected with the politics of gender, which we interrogate in some detail. One thread linking this volume and Klemun and Spring's is recognition of the interdisciplinary potential of expeditions – a subject explored at length by Saskia Beudel in her discussion of the Australian anthropologist Donald Thomson.

For both editors of this volume, the dispatch of knowledge-gathering *parties* to far-flung locations is a source of particular fascination.[21] Although expeditions are remarkably varied, they have common features. The hierarchical organization with a leader at the top and lesser functionaries at the bottom is almost a constant. For Martin Thomas, writing in 2011, the fact that expeditions are severed from their social context renders them a form of human 'time capsule'. In their representation of personnel, equipment, methods and ideas, they form a curated bricolage of their host society.[22] In introducing the edited volume *Expedition into Empire* (2015), Thomas describes expeditions as 'machines for producing discourse'. There he argued that modern expeditions exhibit a preoccupation with technological display and a strong interest in self-representation through engagement with diverse media.[23] That expeditions come equipped with a range of perceptual antennae – human and technological – led James Clifford to describe them as 'a sensorium moving through extended space'.[24] While not in disagreement with this eloquent formulation, Thomas has emphasized the military provenance of expeditionary travel, concurring with Michael Taussig's observation that 'science and war' are conceptually amalgamated in such journeys.[25] Pointing to the naval and military roots of Western exploration, Thomas noted that 'the infrastructure of violence lies buried in the DNA of the expedition ...'.[26] This martial pedigree must be borne in mind as we examine the relationship between exploration and the putatively peaceful expeditions conducted under the aegis of the 'science of man'.

Expeditions, whether they claim to be exploratory, scientific or specifically anthropological (demarcations that are often blurry), represent a specific form of social organization. A benefit of studying an expedition's complex and at times conflicted internal politics is that they provide a highly revealing portal for observing the observers and understanding the powers they represent. Although relatively few anthropologists have explored the cultural properties of expeditions in great detail, Johannes Fabian is a noteworthy exception. His book *Out of Our Minds* (2000) is a significant investigation of the institutions and social practices that enabled the exploration of Central Africa by Europeans. In his account, an expedition functions as a cultural buffer between the travellers and the polities they traverse. He points out that expeditions bear similarities to, and sometimes model themselves on, localized modes of travel, common through much of Africa, such as the caravan. Drawing on his earlier investigations of temporality, race and ethnicity, Fabian attends to the time-based rituals of expeditionary parties: their celebrations of royal birthdays and other ritual occasions. Honouring the familiar calendar allowed the expedition to maintain an 'umbilical' connection with home.[27]

Fabian makes much of the performative tendencies of expeditions: the fondness for music and dancing among exploratory parties, for example. The expression of communitarianism, which consolidates the data-gathering mission of expeditions, is indicative of the ways in which the culture of exploration straddles science and ritual. The 'chores of knowledge production', writes Fabian, the taking of 'regular observations and measurements, collecting zoological, botanical, and geological specimens and ethnographic objects, drawing maps, gathering information, and keeping logs and diaries' constituted 'a form of hygiene', often linked to the survival of the party.[28] Fabian's scholarship on inland Africa complements Greg Dening's earlier ethnohistorical analysis of naval hierarchies and rituals.[29] Both writers have contributed to what is now identifiable as a gradual shift in scholarship on travel and exploration, resulting in the increasing recognition of group formations and their importance. Thus, to cite a recent example, a volume titled *Indigenous Intermediaries: New Perspectives on*

Exploration Archives (2015) opens with the assertion that by 'working against a conventional emphasis on the exploits and achievements of the singular heroic explorer, imperial and colonial exploration is recast as a collective enterprise involving a diverse labour force and upon which expeditions were dependent for their progress and success'.[30]

To further elucidate the challenges and opportunities of investigating expeditionary anthropology, we will now shine a spotlight on an expedition that occurred in 1948. Both editors have studied this venture from various perspectives. Known as the American-Australian Scientific Expedition to Arnhem Land or, more concisely, the Arnhem Land Expedition, it reappears later in this volume as one of two formative journeys in which the Australian anthropologist Margaret McArthur participated (see Harris, this volume). As an international expedition with ethnological and natural science agendas, the Arnhem Land Expedition exemplifies the entwinement of science, anthropology and exploration in a mid-twentieth-century context.

The 1948 expedition was a collaboration involving the National Geographic Society, the Smithsonian Institution and the Australian Government. The leader was Charles P. Mountford, a self-taught photographer and ethnologist, who attracted seed funding from the National Geographic Society while on a lecture tour of the United States in 1945. The expedition travelled widely through the extensive Aboriginal reserve of Arnhem Land in northern Australia. As a twentieth-century journey, sponsored by the publisher of *National Geographic Magazine*, it resulted in a vast cache of media including many hours of colour film footage, thousands of photographs and audio documentation of Aboriginal music and ceremony made on electronic wire recorders. Aboriginal men and women displayed aspects of their lives and culture to the camera, as did the expeditionaries themselves. News of the expedition was communicated around the world.[31]

In addition to the more popular outputs, the expedition did 'serious' scientific work by gathering vast quantities of plant, animal and ethnographic collections. The fieldwork was reported in four large volumes.[32] The expedition's most famous contribution to anthropological theory resulted from its study of Aboriginal food gathering and nutrition.[33] These data were employed by Marshall Sahlins to support his theory of the original affluence of hunter-gatherers.[34] More infamously, the expedition was responsible for the removal of Aboriginal human remains from mortuary sites and their export to the Smithsonian Institution in Washington. Decades later, they became subject to a repatriation campaign that was ultimately successful, despite fierce resistance from some Smithsonian curators.[35]

An image of the social world created by the expedition is conveyed in a radio documentary by Colin Simpson, a journalist and later a well-known travel writer, who at that time was working for the Australian Broadcasting Commission (now Corporation) (ABC). He met with the expedition at the mission station, Oenpelli (now known as Gunbalanya), its final base. Simpson's radio feature, *Expedition to Arnhem Land* (1948), begins with some artful scene setting. A page of reflective travelogue, recorded by the author in the Sydney studios of ABC, primes the listener for the novelty of the 'actuality recordings' that lie ahead.

> COLIN SIMPSON: Arnhem Land is like no other part of Australia I've seen. At Oenpelli the expedition was camped in green canvas tents beside a beautiful inland lagoon – a big boomerang of shining blue water fringed with emerald green grass and decorated right down the middle with waterlilies. On the other side of this lovely lagoon or billabong rose Injalak, a great hill of rugged sandstone and quartzite, full of caves of Aboriginal rock paintings in ochre colours and kangaroo blood. Back on this side, up past the tents, the expedition's cookhouse butted onto the stockyards of Oenpelli Mission. Beyond the tin gunyahs of some mission Natives, up past the small airstrip where we landed in from Darwin, lie plains: savannahs of wild rice and spear grass where the buffaloes graze. It is late afternoon of a burningly hot day. To the east a plateau of stone country has softened with purple haze. Down at the far end of the lagoon natives are gathering lily roots to eat and hand netting fish. And in the middle foreground of this picture are fourteen male members of the expedition, bathing. From wearing only shorts in the sun, they are copper brown to the waist. But here they are wearing nothing except beards. I am going to pick out the expedition leader, he is one of the clean-shaven minority, and go with Mr C.P. Mountford back to his tent. Now he is dressed in khaki shirt and long trousers this time against the evening's mosquitoes. His white solar topee is set aside for the day. And I am asking Mr Mountford how this expedition to Arnhem Land came about.
> CHARLES MOUNTFORD: Well it happened this way . . .[36]

This is the point where the broadcast cuts from scripted narration to an interview with Mountford, recorded in the field. For what must have been the umpteenth time, Mountford told the story about the favourable reception of his lectures and film screenings in the United States and the largess of the National Geographic Society, who offered him a research grant. When that formality was dispensed with, Simpson rebounded with a trickier question.

SIMPSON: And the nature of this expedition, Mr Mountford, it's not an exploring expedition is it, going into darkest Arnhem Land to contact savages who don't exist any more? It is a scientific expedition, is that right?
MOUNTFORD: That is so. This is not an exploring party, its objects are purely scientific and that is to increase our knowledge of the natural history and the Aborigines of Arnhem Land.[37]

Admittedly, Simpson prompted his interviewee with a possible defence for his 'unexploratory' expedition. Yet Mountford's naturalness in running with this argument suggests that it was not the first time someone had insinuated to him that expeditions had exceeded their design life. In Australia in that period, the notion of acquiring 'new' knowledge within Aboriginal territory was not inherently suspect in the way it is today. But Mountford still had to tread carefully in claiming 'discoveries'. An adept publicist, he knew that salesmanship of the expedition had to be credible to be effective.

White Australia in the 1940s knew little about Aboriginal life in general or Arnhem Land in particular. That said, the terrain of the expedition was hardly terra incognita – at least to the extent that Mountford may have wished. Maps of his day usually identified it. If the actual boundaries of the reserve were marked, it appeared as a great trapezium of country in the northeast of the Northern Territory. Major rivers were usually marked and named; a few other toponyms were inscribed, all foreign imports. Even to this day, the vast network of Aboriginal place names is only partially recorded. In terms of Western cartography, sections of the coastline had been known for centuries. That is how the toponym 'Arnhem', originally the city in the Netherlands, found its home-away-from-home in the southern hemisphere. *Arnhem* and its sister vessel *Pera* were the names of Dutch pinnaces that sailed from Batavia on an exploratory expedition in 1623.[38]

The potent combination of distance and ignorance was conducive to the more baroque imaginings of the reserve that circulated in the United States around the time of the expedition. For the most part, of course, Arnhem Land was too obscure to intrude upon the consciousness of Americans. Once or twice a decade the press referred to it, usually in a short novelty item where familiar clichés to do with savagery and cannibalism were invoked.[39] When the time came to promote the American-Australian adventure, the American publicists enjoyed a licence that their counterparts 'down under' might have envied. We see this in the official announcement of the expedition, written by press officers at the National Geographic Society and published verbatim by the *Washington Post*. To give some extracts:

> Its purpose ... is to fill in the blank space in human knowledge represented by this Maine-size aboriginal reserve east of Darwin...
>
> Named for the yacht of its Dutch discoverers in 1623, the region remains virtually unmapped and unexplored except from the air. Although a few exploring parties have penetrated inland, their reports are meagre, scientifically...
>
> Only in recent years have the aboriginal tribes been absolved to some degree of a mythical reputation as bad men, killers and cannibals. They can be warlike on slight provocation, but are now described as generally friendly, extremely wary and difficult to approach except by persons they know...
>
> True stone-age wild men, they have lived the same primitive life down the centuries amid stone-age birds, beasts and reptiles. Mixed blood is evident only on coasts where equally wild Papuans have come across from nearby New Guinea...
>
> A succession of dense scrub forests, deep watercourses and low ranges often rising in sheer, rocky bluffs thwart inland progress...[40]

The *Post* article, a swirl of hogwash in which a few sediments of truth are improbably suspended, is easily dismissible. Certainly, as an insight into the world encountered by the expedition, it is useless – but that is not why we quote it. The value of this text lies in the transparency with which it reveals the logic underlying the 1948 expedition: the imaginary geography that it imposed upon the world it purported to 'discover'. That fantasized topos is the habitat most natural to expeditions. You could say that it is their 'native territory'. Recognition of this is fundamental to any understanding of how an expedition works. To explain by analogy: we know that the instruments carried by expeditions – cameras or telescopes, for example – process an environment in particular ways. They reduce it; enlarge it; frame it. They sever details from a greater totality and render the three-dimensional in two-dimensional form. That same transformational logic is a feature of the expedition – itself an invention – albeit more complex than the instruments named. In light of this, Mountford's suggestion to Simpson that his modern and 'innocently' scientific expedition was a world apart from its nineteenth-century forebears is at best naive and at worst deliberately deceptive. If only historical baggage could be so easily discarded! Expeditions were of course as inextricably involved in imperial conquest as science itself.

That the 1948 expedition involved researchers from one of the world's largest museums is hardly incidental. Many in the museum world remained wedded to the concept of the expedition, which was extremely conducive to the wholesale gathering of specimens.[41] For the first half of the twentieth century, expeditions were an endemic feature of professional life for the Smithsonian curator, often to the despair of families who were expected to endure their extended absences. 'Join the Smithsonian and see the world', was the adage.[42] The Arnhem Land journey was part of a century-long tradition of Smithsonian expeditions.[43] Indeed, the institution's museum status is inextricably connected with one of the most prominent expeditionary ventures of the Antebellum period. When the English chemist James Smithson bequeathed his fortune to the United States government to found an institution in Washington 'for the increase and diffusion of knowledge', his likely model was the Royal Society in London (of which he had been a fellow). There was nothing in the will that required it to be a collecting institution, and certainly no hint that it would become the great repository of cultural and scientific treasures – the 'attic of the nation' – that we know today.[44] The Smithsonian's museological turn was a by-product of the 1838–42 United States Exploring Expedition. Commanded by Lieutenant Charles Wilkes, this was a wide-ranging cruise through the Pacific that surveyed waterways for strategic and mercantile opportunities and pursued more general scientific objectives, including ethnographic investigation. In 1858, the many artefacts and specimens it acquired were lodged with the Smithsonian, to the annoyance of some officials who saw the warehousing of collections as a distraction from the 'pure' science they wished to pursue.[45]

Four Smithsonian curators and a National Geographic Society writer/photographer comprised the United States delegation on the 1948 Arnhem Land Expedition. Occurring at a time when the nature of the postwar American–Australian relationship was still being hammered out, this exercise in soft diplomacy was calculated to generate as much publicity as possible, much to the irritation of local academics who were excluded from its ranks.[46] Even Donald Thomson, a zoologist-cum-anthropologist who had previously worked in Arnhem Land and sympathized with expeditionary modes of inquiry, thought too much attention was given to Mountford and his party, to the detriment of his own reputation (see Beudel, this volume). Here is evidence that as late as 1948, the expeditionary project retained lustre in the eyes of the public, who were blissfully unaware of its facility for exposing disciplinary factions and fault-lines. Perhaps the most pertinent indicator of this expedition's capacity to capture the imagination of the public is a cache of letters in Mountford's archive, written by young men who had seen early press announcements of the venture. In the rush to volunteer their services, they adhered to a fairly standard formula:

I am eighteen years old and as I have been looking forward to such an expedition all my life I thought you might be needing a lad like myself. I have had experience on board boats, and as a cook in the galley also years of experience in the boy scouts and otherwise having three badges of great importance to the backwoods-man, the Campers, Cooks, Pioneers.[47]

The author of this missive, a resident of suburban Brisbane, noted in his cheery sign-off that he was 'waiting for a favourable reply'. He did not receive one. Nor did Bill Smith from New York State, who, upon reading of the Arnhem Land Expedition in the American press, wrote directly to the National Geographic Society, asking if they 'might be able to find a place somewhere for a strong, healthy American boy who has for a long time seriously considered the life of an Explorer but who was always told that you must know someone in the trade to get a start'.[48] As these letters show, expeditions had their supplicants, the vast majority of whom would do no more than participate vicariously by reading the press or watching the films. Yet these files of letters are important, for they reveal the extent to which an expedition's audience might project themselves into the privileged space of the journey.

With its troupe of actors at large in the field, an expedition is both an ideal and a reality. It is underwritten by common codes and bound by often unspoken rules. Simpson evoked this little universe with his description of the tents and cookhouse at Oenpelli, beyond which the expedition members performed their ablutions in the lagoon 'wearing nothing but beards'. This was playful writing on his part. A newspaperman by training, Simpson was on one of his first assignments as a broadcaster when he went to Arnhem Land.[49] He went there determined to explore the radio medium to its full potential.[50] Later, when writing about the experience, Simpson explained that because *National Geographic* retained the photographic rights, print journalists had been precluded from visiting the expedition. He won admission only because radio 'is non-pictorial and so was considered near enough to being non-competitive, and, by permission, we could go in and do a "feature" on the expedition and gather whatever else seemed interesting to describe and record in sound, such as aboriginal corroboree'.[51] Communicating 'non-pictorially', he boldly revealed the expeditionaries in their nakedness, telling the radio audience what a camera could never show. Now one thing that *is* shown in this tableau of scientists parading their manhood is the deeply gendered character of expeditionary anthropology. Where, we might ask, in that scene of expeditionary hygiene are Margaret McArthur and Bessie Mountford, the two female members of the party?

Mountford had had no easy time in getting even this amount of female representation on his expedition, despite a belated acceptance among Australian ethnographers, influenced by the prewar findings of anthropologists such as Ursula McConnel and Phyllis Kaberry, that the gendered nature of Aboriginal society produced a domain of women's knowledge that was largely impervious to male researchers.[52] The Director-General of the Department of Information (the government agency that oversaw the expedition from the Australian side) was convinced that it would be 'most unwise to have a woman attached to a party that will be living among the natives'. He urged Arthur Calwell, the Minister for Information, to veto the idea. That the presence of women would cramp the very freedom described by Simpson is implied in the director-general's letter.

> One would imagine that natural modesty would make a man reluctant to take his wife on such an expedition but there are other considerations. Only recently, we had an unhappy experience in Queensland when Mr. Foster permitted the producer to take his wife on the Barrier Reef Expedition. The party had to live on a launch and husband and wife occupied practically the whole of the living accommodation, compelling the six men in the party to sleep on deck or wherever else they could find room to spread a blanket.
>
> It is a human characteristic that men living under such conditions submit chivalrously to inconvenience at the time, but later moan to all and sundry about the bad management that made such living conditions necessary.[53]

For most of its history, expeditionary society has been predominantly male. Yet for all the hairy-chested ruggedness that goes with the genre, the keepers who patrol this patch invariably paint their expeditions as delicate flowers, bound to wither if exposed to the pollution of femininity. As Tom Griffiths writes in his study of Antarctic science, the excuses used to exclude women from scientific travel could be pathetically lame. Lack of toilet facilities was an old favourite. The disasters that beset any expedition leader so careless as to mix the sexes were knowingly chronicled by commentators, themselves part of the brotherhood. Griffiths writes: 'The French explorer-historian, Paul-Emile Victor, in his book *Man and the Conquest of the Poles*, summarised the Ronn expedition in one line: "The expedition ran into all the difficulties ordinarily caused by the presence of women in such circumstances"'.[54]

The politics of gender are omnipresent in expeditions. The 'presence of women' on the Arnhem Land Expedition was certainly a complicating factor in terms of management of personnel. The matronly

Bessie Mountford carved out for herself a maternal role in the expeditionary family, while Margaret McArthur became an object of attraction to more than one of her companions.[55] Gossip began to circulate and Mountford, to McArthur's indignation, began to think of ways in which she might be chaperoned.[56] As an experiment in sexual mixing, the Arnhem Land Expedition was an extremely unequal one. Numerically, the expedition was a male enterprise with two female extras. Inevitably, masculine values shaped the image of the expedition, enabling the proliferation of certain narratives and allowing the enforcement of certain silences. These are issues that are taken up in detail in the course of this book.

The Journey Ahead

As we have suggested, there is no clear linear march away from imperial exploration and towards expeditionary anthropology. Rather, explorers have often found themselves engaged with the study of human others as a necessary side project to the exploration of foreign shores. Both in clearing paths into unknown territories and in approaching human unknowns, cultural intermediaries have acted as go-betweens in the process of exchange. Scholarship in North America in particular, dating from the 1990s, has increasingly brought such people into focus as the subjects of scholarly research into the culture of exploration.[57] Their role in influencing the course of expeditions, and the alternative window they provide onto the activities of investigative parties, is a major theme of *Expeditionary Anthropology*, especially in 'Anthropology and the Field: Intermediaries and Exchange', the first of our three thematic sections.

This section is comprised of a trio of essays by scholars long immersed in the activities of the anthropologists discussed. In Philip Batty's case, a deep understanding of the literature is combined with personal knowledge of territory and communities traversed by the expedition he describes. Batty lived for many years in the Northern Territory where he worked closely with desert communities and co-founded the Central Australian Aboriginal Media Association. Later, as a curator at Museum Victoria in Melbourne (a position he still occupies), he acquired an insider's perspective on the massive cache of material culture, visual records and other data concerning Central Australia that was deposited by Sir Baldwin Spencer. Batty opens the volume with an intriguing examination of the notion of 'the field', a key conceptual construct of expeditionary anthropology.

Batty's lens on this subject is the pioneering 1901–02 anthropological expedition of Spencer, a zoologist-cum-anthropologist and professor at the University of Melbourne, and his close collaborator, Francis Gillen, a post and telegraph master at the desert settlement of Alice Springs who was closely connected with the Aboriginal communities of the region. Commencing at the inland settlement of Oodnadatta, their expedition took a roughly northward trajectory through Central Australia, terminating at the town of Borroloola near the Gulf of Carpentaria. Batty's chapter is both an account of the expedition and an interpretation of how the anthropological field was defined and composed. He regards it as a composite spatial formation, brought into being by the expedition's interaction with the locations visited, the objects collected and the local intermediaries who opened facets of their culture to the investigators. The equipment, animals, personnel and funds – the daily necessities of expeditionary life – also contributed to the making of the field, which was of course the product of anthropological intervention, although the researchers purported to 'discover' it.

Batty suggests that the shaping of this objectified field as a privileged site of anthropological meaning occurred in parallel with the establishment of the expedition as a key means of acquiring anthropological expertise. He points out that the fields created by expeditions are highly dynamic and that they morph and resurface over time. Indeed, he suggests that the semiotic richness of the expeditionary field tends to increase as the original subjects of study, or more often their descendants, draw upon expeditionary legacies in projects aimed at cultural revitalization. The use of historical collections to make land claims or assert cultural identity provides examples of how the anthropological field continues to be reinvented.

The 1898 Cambridge Anthropological Expedition to Torres Straits occurred just a few years earlier than Spencer and Gillen's mission. This is the subject of the chapter by Jude Philp, a museum curator who, like Batty, has close personal ties with communities studied by this expedition. One of Philp's key contributions to our discussion is her argument that the lines between intermediaries and expedition members were surprisingly blurry. She questions the idea that nineteenth-century expeditions were necessarily disengaged from the lived realities of their research subjects. On the contrary, Philp shows that the visitors from Cambridge were cognizant of the hierarchies and lines of authority that existed in Meriam communities, and that their results – documented traditions, collections of cultural objects, studies of performance traditions and other ancestral heritage – were irrevocably affected by the decisions of Islanders. The expedition members actively named and profiled their Islander participants and consultants. These data are detailed in both the field notes *and* the expedition's publications – in contrast to the practice of many of their successors (Malinowski and A.R. Radcliffe-Brown among them). As a result of these clear attributions and the publication of large sections of text in the local Island creole, the practices and knowledge stores of nineteenth-century Meriam-le can be retrieved by contemporary communities. The expedition's publications continue to be used in the Torres Strait.

Donald Thomson's Arnhem Land journeys of the 1930s were directly influenced by the Cambridge expedition and his travels resonate with nineteenth-century explorer journeys more broadly. Saskia Beudel, who previously engaged with Thomson's desert expeditions in her landscape memoir, *A Country in Mind* (2013), here turns her eye to his work in Arnhem Land (which preceded by more than a decade the large expedition of Charles Mountford). In this chapter, Beudel argues that recognition of long-standing 'cultures of exploration' is essential to understanding Thomson's multimodal expeditionary style, in which anthropological research was just one among a suite of objectives that also included photojournalism, narratives of adventure travel and deep immersion in Australian Aboriginal lifestyles.

The fluidity with which Thomson moved between academic and more popular, journalistic modes of expression resulted in an uneasy relationship with dominant anthropological institutions and caused him problems when he sought funding from the Australian National Research Council. Unconventionally for an Australian anthropologist, he developed a close relationship with the Royal Geographical Society who supported his work. Thomson's idiosyncratic views on what constituted serious anthropological fieldwork placed him in conflict with Radcliffe-Brown, who at the time was Professor of Anthropology at Sydney, and then with A.P. Elkin who succeeded Radcliffe-Brown to the chair, the first in an Australian university. Beudel provides an intriguing discussion of Thomson's affinity with expeditionary modes of travel. He formed parties composed not of white men but of Arnhem Landers, with whom he formed genuinely collegial relationships and co-habited on egalitarian terms.

Beudel, Batty and Philp are all deeply concerned with the formation and potentialities of expeditions. They deal specifically with anthropological journeys, but the insights they provide are an important contribution to present-day conversations about geographical exploration, which is now feeling the benefit of comparative approaches. This is apparent in Dane Kennedy's study of inland journeys in Africa and Australia, which alerts us to the different conventions of expedition making that developed in the two continents.[58] Whereas in Africa it was common for a European explorer to recruit his entire (often extensive) entourage from local labourers, his counterpart in Australia preferred a party composed of Europeans, with the possible exception of native guides who seldom numbered more than one or two. Beudel's discussion suggests that Donald Thomson was bending the conventions of expeditionary practice, especially as they had developed in his own country.

The book's second section, titled 'Exploration, Archaeology, Race and Emergent Anthropology', deals with some of the less benign aspects of the expeditionary imaginary. From very varied perspectives, the four chapters investigate racial categorization and its impacts. The discussion is opened by Pamela M. Henson, who gives a close reading of the late nineteenth-century expeditions of the artist, geologist, archaeologist and museum director William Henry Holmes, a prominent figure at the Smithsonian Institution where Henson herself is Director of Institutional History. Holmes held positions in two newly formed organizations. From 1879, he worked with the United States Geological Survey. Then, in 1889, he began his long involvement with the Smithsonian's Bureau of American Ethnology. Holmes' movement between these organizations – one focused on documentation of the landscape of the United States and the other on the history and traditions of people who occupied that landscape – is indicative of the short distance that then existed between the fields of geology, archaeology and anthropology.

Holmes used physical anthropology research to show that contemporary Native Americans were the descendants of the civilizations who had built advanced structures throughout North America – a corrective to the thinking of other researchers in this period. Henson argues that Holmes played a major role in the shift from geological and topographical exploration to expeditionary research that focused on the human occupants of ancient cities.

Warwick Anderson's chapter on Carleton S. Coon's voyages to the Maghreb in the 1920s explores the complicity of expeditionary activities in the survival of social evolutionary thinking. A student of Earnest Hooton at Harvard, Coon was sent to Africa to study racial mixing. The race-based 'human biology' study then in vogue set many of Coon's peers on a trajectory that would lead them, post-Second World War, to robustly critique the very notion of racial classification. Not so for Coon, who remained completely unreconstructed on questions of race

– a position that Anderson explores by excavating the archival record. In so doing, he reveals the inner workings of a physical anthropology expedition in exquisite detail. In a gesture that touches on the long tradition of connecting with, or re-enacting, expeditionary journeys, Anderson's historical narrative is interwoven with an account of his journey, eighty years later, to the site of Coon's adventures.

Anderson is a historian of medicine and a former physician. His celebrated work on Papua New Guinea has delved into the triangulated relationship of science, adventurism and the inscription of human difference.[59] His account of Coon's colourful career reveals not only the prejudices embedded in the expeditionary paradigm but again the potentialities and contradictions. Coon's research took place in the Maghreb region of North Africa. He performed anthropometrical observations that convinced him that the fair-skinned Berber people whom he was studying were not the 'degenerate half-castes' he expected, but 'African Nordics' whom he stridently defended because of their racial 'superiority'. Adopting an anti-colonial position, Coon remonstrated against their oppression and degradation by their Spanish colonizers.

The relationship between expeditionary adventure and the way maritime voyaging opened observational opportunities for the inscription of human differences is explored in the chapter by Bronwen Douglas, whose polyglot inquiries into the cartographic history and maritime exploration of Oceania have exposed the genealogy of racial theorizing.[60] Here she embarks on a fine-grained analysis of cross-cultural encounters, drawing extensively from the records of Iberian explorers who were ostensibly focused on charting land and ocean, but who found themselves involved in an increasingly detailed classification of the people they observed in various clashes and encounters. Through an investigation of the Spanish expedition of Quirós and Torres across the Mar del Sur in 1606, Douglas shows that voyagers' representations of these encounters are enormously significant for charting European ideas about human difference. In the process, she suggests methods and vocabulary for reading the agency of the indigenous communities described in expeditionary texts.

Like the Spanish voyagers of the seventeenth century, early explorers of Australia's coastline were focused chiefly on cartography and geography. In a chapter about Phillip Parker King's hydrographic surveys, Australian historian Tiffany Shellam shows that although expeditions like King's aimed to chart the coastline, the inevitability of encounter between the travellers and occupants of country where an expedition might seek refuge or potable water meant that some form of ethnographic observation became essential to the expedition's daily business. Shellam makes her argument by drilling deeply into events dating from 1821 when King's party was stationed at Hanover Bay on the Western Australian coast. An encounter between crew and indigenes spiralled out of control, resulting in the spearing of the ship's surgeon and the shooting of at least one Aboriginal man from the Worora group. Like Douglas, Shellam is interested in unpacking the motivations of the local people involved in such episodes. She finds keys to the cipher in a spearhead and other objects, collected by the British in the wake of the skirmish, and in the enigmatic figure of Bundle, an indigenous man from the Sydney area. He travelled on board and mediated interactions with a great succession of Aboriginal groups, showing extraordinary facility for overcoming the linguistic and other cultural differences between himself and the people encountered.

The third part of the book, 'The Question of Gender', extends the discussion, begun in the present chapter, about the contested roles of men and women in the masculinized world of expeditions. The contributors survey a variety of sites and polities, touching on both the theory and pedagogy of anthropology. The conflicts and entanglements of male and female anthropologists, working in a range of university, museum and government contexts, are examined in detail. The three chapters rove widely in scope and perspective, migrating from the nitty-gritty micro-politics of life in the field to broader social and political contexts.

The first offering in this section is by Desley Deacon, a cultural historian and author of the definitive biography of Elsie Clews Parsons.[61] Born into high society in New York, Parsons broke the social mould by becoming a pioneering feminist and anthropologist. In the 1920s, she used her personal wealth to set up the Southwest Society, an organization that funded innovative anthropological fieldwork, supporting – among others – many of the students of Franz Boas who were coming through Columbia University. An intriguing aspect of Parsons' initiative was that the Southwest Society was deliberately set up in resistance to the American Museum of Natural History, still continuing its policy of financing expensive expeditions led by adventurer-scientists. Through her own investigations and through her funding of fellow ethnographers, Parsons encouraged the rise of the woman fieldworker, a development she linked to a larger feminist project. Deacon shows that in countering the heroic and self-serving ethos of those who led large and lavishly funded group expeditions, Parsons encouraged modern modes of anthropological research that would alter the shape of American anthropology.

The second chapter in this section is by anthropologist-cum-art historian Diane Losche, whose work on Margaret Mead complements the discussion of Parsons. Losche takes us inside the American Museum of Natural History, the base from which Mead, too often unsupported and continually unpromoted, made her rise to anthropological stardom. The chapter demonstrates how the framework of the expedition provides an avenue for rethinking the Mead legacy, which has been obscured by misogynistic attacks on Mead's character and her accuracy as an ethnographer. Losche roams widely through Mead's long career, but her case study is the American Museum of Natural History Sepik Expedition of the early 1930s. The chapter shows that Mead's focus on Melanesian women and girls and her investigation of female sexuality posed significant challenges to patriarchal forces within the anthropological establishment.

Mead's Sepik journey won fame for the romantic interests and estrangements that took place *within* the expedition party. This resulted in some uncanny mirrorings between the researchers and the researched. Mead arrived at the Sepik with her first husband, anthropologist Reo Fortune who, in a strange inversion of the usual gender hierarchy, was presented in the press as Mead's consort. While in the field, they met Gregory Bateson, doing ethnographic fieldwork of his own. Mead and Fortune's marriage splintered during the course of the expedition. She and Bateson became romantically involved and eventually married. Losche playfully juxtaposes the anthropologist's interest in the sex lives of others with the often bizarre way in which Mead's own sexual adventurism has been chronicled.

In the third chapter in this section (the last in the volume), Amanda Harris examines some key events in the career of Margaret McArthur, previously mentioned as one of just two women on the Arnhem Land Expedition of 1948. McArthur was a nutritionist and biochemist before she retrained in London as an anthropologist. She belonged to a succeeding generation of women who benefited from the pioneering leadership of figures such as Mead and Parsons. Harris examines McArthur's participation in both the 1948 expedition and another in Papua New Guinea the year before. She documents McArthur's pathway from the female-dominated field of nutritional research into the masculine space of the scientific expedition. Food and the domestic sphere provided a gateway to a broader expeditionary anthropology that was both formative and enabling in terms of her professional aspirations. Not only did she produce field-expanding work in her collaborative publications with Frederick McCarthy, but she laid the groundwork for a future career as an academic anthropologist. In tracing the shift in women's roles in post-Second World War nation building, Harris argues that women could create opportunities for themselves in twentieth-century expeditions, despite the stubbornness of patriarchal dominance. Certainly, the minority presence of women illuminates the larger culture of masculinity that is such an integral element of the expeditionary imaginary.

Final Words

This book is not unique in arguing that expeditions deserve fresh and critical attention. In addition to the many studies, historical and biographical, that continue to appear on particular expeditions, anthropologists or explorers, there has in recent years been a spate of publications on the popular impact of exploratory narratives, many of them concerned with the dissemination of film and still photography.[62] The release of an edited volume titled *The Anthropology of Expeditions* (2015) is further evidence of how the expedition has become a site for re-exploration in a postcolonial context.[63] The emphasis there is the connection between the collecting function of expeditions and the institution of the museum. The chapters focus on the hybrid composition of expeditions and are underwritten by a general ambition to investigate the expedition's relationship with the colonial project.

With editors and contributors who are enmeshed in the curatorial world, it is unsurprising that material culture lies at the heart of *The Anthropology of Expeditions*. Indeed, the emphasis on collectors and collecting is so embedded that the book's title turns out to be something of a misnomer. Expeditions are treated as phenomena that ipso facto perform the work of anthropological collection; seldom are they recognized as social phenomena that anthropological analysis might illuminate. Inevitably, this brings some limitations. The realities of gender politics go almost unnoticed, as do the controversies surrounding human remains collection and the claims for repatriation that have resulted.

The contributors to *Expeditionary Anthropology* are hardly indifferent to material culture or the materiality of expeditions themselves. Cultures of collecting, regimes of exchange and broader questions of funding and economy are dealt with in various ways in the pages ahead. But the overall thrust of our argument is that the generation of university and museum collections – certainly an integral aspect of expeditionary anthropology – cannot be adequately contextualized without a history of the sociopolitical formations embedded in and around the notion of the expedition.

Hence the trajectory of this chapter, an introductory foray into expeditions and the imaginary that underlies them. We began with Lévi-Strauss and his denunciation of twentieth-century explorers. Drawing insight from Johannes Fabian and other thinkers along the way, we queried the alleged demarcation between exploration and anthropology, and in the process journeyed into the social space of the Arnhem Land Expedition, led by the intrepid Charles Mountford. That 1948 journey revealed a set of embedded traits, endemic to expeditionary travel. With its arrangement of tents around the billabong, the expedition had its own architectural layout and its distinctive hierarchical structure in the organization of personnel. Through its relationship with diverse media, the expedition members – and especially the publicity-hungry leader – could channel their fondness for self-representation. Like so many expeditions, it was heavily charged with internal divisions, influenced in part by its gender politics and the under-representation of women scientists. Conforming to such patterns, expeditions have gone about their business of documenting, representing and collecting. As the chapters ahead show, there are many differences between individual expeditions. But they are bound by commonalities. Being mobile organizations that move between cultural spaces, they are specially designed for the documentation and production of difference.

Martin Thomas is Professor of History at the Australian National University and Co-Director of the Menzies Australia Institute at King's College London. His publications include *The Many Worlds of R. H. Mathews: In Search of an Australian Anthropologist* (2011) and *Expedition into Empire: Exploratory Journeys and the Making of the Modern World* (2015), with the former winning the National Biography Award of Australia.

Amanda Harris is Senior Research Fellow at Sydney Conservatorium of Music, University of Sydney and Director of the Sydney Unit of the digital archive PARADISEC (Pacific and Regional Archive for Digital Sources in Endangered Cultures). Her book *Representing Australian Aboriginal Music and Dance 1930-70* was published by Bloomsbury

Academic in 2020. Her edited book *Circulating Cultures: Exchanges of Australian Indigenous Music, Dance and Media* was published in 2014.

Notes

1. Claude Lévi-Strauss, *Tristes Tropiques*, trans. John and Doreen Weightman (Harmondsworth: Penguin, 1992), 17–18.
2. Felix Driver, *Geography Militant: Cultures of Exploration and Empire* (Oxford: Blackwell, 2001), 1.
3. British Association for the Advancement of Science, *Notes and Queries on Anthropology, for the Use of Travellers and Residents in Uncivilized Lands* (London: Council of the Anthropological Institute, 1874) was the most influential manual for the anthropological fieldworker. See George W. Stocking Jr, *After Tylor: British Social Anthropology 1888–1951* (Madison, WI: University of Wisconsin Press, 1995) for extended discussion of its publication and influence.
4. Simon Naylor and James R. Ryan (eds), *New Spaces of Exploration: Geographies of Discovery in the Twentieth Century* (London: I.B. Tauris, 2010).
5. Mary Louise Pratt, *Imperial Eyes: Travel Writing and Transculturation* (London/New York: Routledge, 1992) and Clare Pettitt, *Dr. Livingstone, I Presume? Missionaries, Journalists, Explorers, and Empire* (Cambridge, MA: Harvard University Press, 2007).
6. For discussions of re-enactment, see 'Extreme and Sentimental History', a special issue of *Criticism* 46(1) (2004); Iain McCalman and Paul Pickering (eds), *Historical Reenactment: From Realism to the Affective Turn* (Basingstoke: Palgrave Macmillan, 2010); and Christy Collis, 'Walking in Your Footsteps: "Footsteps of the Explorers" Expeditions and the Contest for Australian Desert Space', in Naylor and Ryan, *New Spaces of Exploration*, 222–40.
7. Margaret T. Hodgen, *Early Anthropology in the Sixteenth and Seventeenth Centuries* (Philadelphia, PA: University of Pennsylvania Press, 1964).
8. Martin Thomas, 'Anthropology and the British Empire', in Robert Aldrich and Kirsten McKenzie (eds), *The Routledge History of Western Empires* (London/New York: Routledge, 2013), 612.
9. George W. Stocking, 'The Ethnographer's Magic: Fieldwork in British Anthropology from Tylor to Malinowski', in George W. Stocking, *The Ethnographer's Magic and Other Essays in the History of Anthropology* (Madison, WI: University of Wisconsin Press, 1992), 39.
10. Henrika Kuklick, 'Personal Equations: Reflections on the History of Fieldwork, with Special Reference to Sociocultural Anthropology', *Isis* 102(1) (2011), 1–33.
11. Peter Monteath and Valerie Munt, *Red Professor: The Cold War Life of Fred Rose* (Mile End, South Australia: Wakefield Press, 2015), 186.

12. Henrika Kuklick, 'Science as Adventure', in Joshua A. Bell and Erin L. Hisinoff (eds), *The Anthropology of Expeditions: Travel, Visualities, Afterlives* (New York: Bard Graduate Center, 2015), 40.
13. For discussion of *National Geographic* and race, see Catherine A. Lutz and Jane L. Collins, *Reading National Geographic* (Chicago, IL: University of Chicago Press, 1993); and Tamar Y. Rothenberg, *Presenting America's World: Strategies of Innocence in National Geographic Magazine* (Aldershot, UK: Ashgate, 2007).
14. Roslyn Poignant, *Professional Savages: Captive Lives and Western Spectacle* (Sydney: UNSW Press, 2004), ch. 4.
15. Pettitt, *Dr. Livingstone, I Presume?* and Driver, *Geography Militant*, ch. 6.
16. Patrick Wilcken, *Claude Lévi-Strauss: The Poet in the Laboratory* (London: Bloomsbury, 2010), 206.
17. Driver, *Geography Militant*, 1–2.
18. Roy MacLeod, 'Discovery and Exploration', in Peter J. Bowler and John V. Pickstone (eds), *The Modern Biological and Earth Sciences: The Cambridge History of Science* (Cambridge: Cambridge University Press, 2009), Vol. 6, 38.
19. See, for example, Jane Carey and Jane Lydon (eds) *Indigenous Networks: Mobility, Connections and Exchange* (London/New York: Routledge, 2015); Shino Konishi, Maria Nugent and Tiffany Shellam (eds), *Indigenous Intermediaries: New Perspectives on Exploration Archives* (Canberra: ANU Press and Aboriginal History Inc., 2015).
20. Marianne Klemun and Ulrike Spring, 'Expeditions as Experiments: An Introduction', in Marianne Klemun and Ulrike Spring (eds), *Expeditions as Experiments: Practising Observation and Documentation* (London: Palgrave Macmillan, 2016), 8.
21. Examples of our scholarship on this subject include Martin Thomas and Margo Neale (eds), *Exploring the Legacy of the 1948 Arnhem Land Expedition* (Canberra: ANU E Press, 2011), especially ch. 1, 'Expedition as Time Capsule: Introducing the American–Australian Scientific Expedition to Arnhem Land'; and Amanda Harris, 'Food, Feeding and Consumption (or the Cook, the Wife and the Nutritionist): The Politics of Gender and Class in a 1948 Australian Expedition', *History and Anthropology* 24(3) (2013), 363–79. Thomas convened and Harris participated in a 2012 symposium titled 'What Is an Expedition?', an inspiration for this volume. See http://historynet.anu.edu.au/exhibitions (accessed 20 December 2015).
22. Thomas, 'Expedition as Time Capsule', ch. 1 in Thomas and Neale, *Exploring the Legacy*, 1–30.
23. Martin Thomas, 'What Is an Expedition? An Introduction', in Martin Thomas (ed.), *Expedition into Empire: Exploratory Journeys and the Making of the Modern World* (New York/London: Routledge, 2015), 12–17.
24. Cited in Laurel Kendall, 'A Most Singular and Solitary Expeditionist: Berthold Laufer Collecting China', in Bell and Hisinoff, *The Anthropology of Expeditions*, 68.

25. Michael Taussig, *Mimesis and Alterity: A Particular History of the Senses* (New York: Routledge, 1993).
26. Thomas, 'What Is an Expedition?', 21.
27. Johannes Fabian, *Out of Our Minds: Reason and Madness in the Exploration of Central Africa* (Berkeley/Los Angeles, CA: University of California Press, 2000), 55–56.
28. Ibid., 60.
29. Examples include Greg Dening, *Mr Bligh's Bad Language: Passion, Power and Theatre on the Bounty* (Cambridge: Cambridge University Press, 1992) and Greg Dening, *Readings/Writings* (Melbourne: Melbourne University Press, 1998).
30. Shino Konishi, Maria Nugent and Tiffany Shellam, 'Exploration Archives and Indigenous Histories: An Introduction', in Konishi, Nugent and Shellam, *Indigenous Intermediaries*, 1.
31. Thomas and Neale, *Exploring the Legacy*.
32. Charles P. Mountford (ed.), *Records of the American-Australian Scientific Expedition to Arnhem Land* (Melbourne: Melbourne University Press, 1956–64), 4 Vols.
33. Frederick D. McCarthy and Margaret McArthur, 'The Food Quest and the Time Factor in Aboriginal Economic Life', in Mountford, *Records of the American-Australian Scientific Expedition*, Vol. 2, 145–94.
34. Marshall Sahlins, *Stone Age Economics* (Chicago, IL: Aldine Atherton, 1972). For further discussion of the Arnhem Land Expedition's influence on Sahlins, see Jon Altman, 'From Kunanj, Fish Creek, to Mumeka, Mann River: Hunter-Gatherer Tradition and Transformation in Western Arnhem Land, 1948–2009', in Thomas and Neale, *Exploring the Legacy*, 113–34.
35. Martin Thomas, 'Bones as a Bridge between Worlds: Repatriation and Reconciliation between Australia and the United States', in Kate Darian-Smith and Penelope Edmonds (eds), *Conciliation on Colonial Frontiers: Conflict, Performance, and Commemoration in Australia and the Pacific Rim* (New York/London: Routledge, 2015), 150–68; Martin Thomas, 'Turning Subjects into Objects and Objects into Subjects: Collecting Human Remains on the 1948 Arnhem Land Expedition', in Amanda Harris (ed.), *Circulating Cultures: Exchanges of Australian Indigenous Music, Dance and Media* (Canberra: ANU Press, 2014), 129–66; and Martin Thomas, 'Because It's Your Country: Death and Its Meanings in West Arnhem Land', *Life Writing* 12(2) (2015), 203–23.
36. Colin Simpson (writer/producer), *Expedition to Arnhem Land*, ABC radio documentary, first broadcast on 30 November 1948, Australian Broadcasting Commission, Sydney.
37. Ibid.
38. Alan Powell, *Northern Voyagers: Australia's Monsoon Coast in Maritime History* (North Melbourne: Australian Scholarly Publishing, 2013), ch. 1.

39. 'Cannibals in Australia Are Studied by Scientist', *New York Times*, 17 May 1936, 38.
40. 'Science to Study Wild Region of Northern Australia Corner', *Washington Post*, 8 February 1948, L6.
41. MacLeod, 'Discovery and Exploration', 52; and Joshua A. Bell and Erin L. Hisinoff, 'Introduction: The Anthropology of Expeditions', in Bell and Hisinoff, *The Anthropology of Expeditions*, 4. See also Deacon, this volume.
42. Cited in Gifford Hubbs Miller and Robert Charles Cashner, 'Beneath the Billabongs: The Scientific Legacy of Robert Rush Miller', in Thomas and Neale, *Exploring the Legacy*, 272.
43. Paul Michael Taylor, 'Transformations of the Expeditionary Enterprise: Perspectives on the Smithsonian's Expeditionary History before 1948', *reCollections* 9(2) (2014).
44. Heather Ewing, *The Lost World of James Smithson: Science, Revolution, and the Birth of the Smithsonian* (New York: Bloomsbury, 2007), 317.
45. Nathaniel Philbrick, 'The Scientific Legacy of the U.S. Exploring Expedition', http://www.sil.si.edu/digitalcollections/usexex/learn/Philbrick.htm (accessed 10 December 2014).
46. On the academic fault-lines, see Thomas, 'Expedition as Time Capsule', ch. 1 in Thomas and Neale, *Exploring the Legacy*, 1–30; Martin Thomas, 'A Short History of the 1948 Arnhem Land Expedition', *Aboriginal History* 34 (2010), 143–69; and Philip Jones, 'Inside Mountford's Tent: Paint, Politics and Paperwork', in Thomas and Neale, *Exploring the Legacy*, 33–54. For a reading of the expedition's significance to the US–Australian relationship, see Kim Beazley, 'Nation Building or Cold War: Political Settings for the Arnhem Land Expedition', in Thomas and Neale, *Exploring the Legacy*, 55–71.
47. W.A. Dack to C.P. Mountford, 28 August 1945, American/Australian Scientific Expedition to Arnhem Land 1948: Correspondence Vol. 2, Mountford-Sheard Collection, PRG 1218/17/5, State Library of South Australia, Adelaide.
48. William Smith to Gilbert Grosvenor, C.P. Mountford-Gilbert Grosvenor correspondence file, National Geographic Society Archives.
49. Richard White, 'Simpson, Edwin Colin (1908–1983)', *Australian Dictionary of Biography*, National Centre of Biography, Australian National University, http://adb.anu.edu.au/biography/simpson-edwin-colin-15926/text27127, published first in hardcopy 2012, accessed online 12 December 2015.
50. Martin Thomas, 'The Rush to Record: Transmitting the Sound of Aboriginal Culture', *Journal of Australian Studies* 90 (2007), 105–21.
51. Colin Simpson, *Adam in Ochre: Inside Aboriginal Australia* (Sydney: Angus & Robertson, 1962), 5.
52. For discussion of McConnel and Kaberry, see Geoffrey Gray, *A Cautious Silence: The Politics of Australian Anthropology* (Canberra: Aboriginal Studies Press, 2007), chs 5–6. For an overview of early Australian

women anthropologists, see Julie Marcus (ed.), *First in Their Field: Women and Australian Anthropology* (Carlton, Vic.: Melbourne University Press, 1993).
53. Bonney to Calwell, 30 January 1947, Publicity – Arnhem Land Expedition – C.P. Mountford, General correspondence files, two number series, Department of Information, CP815/1, Item 005.87 Part 1, National Archives of Australia, Canberra.
54. Tom Griffiths, *Slicing the Silence: Voyaging to Antarctica* (Sydney: New South, 2007), 210.
55. Frederick McCarthy claimed that the expedition's deputy leader, Frank Setzler, frequently made sexual innuendoes to McArthur: Diary 1: Field Notes Groote Eylandt 1, Papers of Frederick David McCarthy, MS 3513/14/1, Australian Institute of Aboriginal and Torres Strait Islander Studies, Canberra, entry for 18 April 1948. Other observers suspected a relationship between McArthur and Frederick Rose, who was an advisor to the expedition at its first base. See Harney to Elkin, 18 April 1948, Correspondence Files, A.P. Elkin Papers, P. 130, Series 8, File 1/8/3, University of Sydney Archives, Sydney; and Elkin to Harney, 19 and 22 April 1948, ibid.
56. Amanda Harris, 'Chaperoned into Arnhem Land: Margaret McArthur and the Politics of Nutrition and Fieldwork in 1948', *Lilith: A Feminist History Journal* 20 (2014), 62–75.
57. Significant examples include Richard White, *The Middle Ground: Indians, Empires, and Republics in the Great Lakes Region, 1650–1815* (New York: Cambridge University Press, 1992) and Margaret Connell Szasz (ed.), *Between Indian and White Worlds: The Cultural Broker* (Norman, OK: University of Oklahoma Press, 1994).
58. Dane Kennedy, *The Last Blank Spaces: Exploring Africa and Australia* (Cambridge, MA: Harvard University Press, 2013).
59. Warwick Anderson, 'Objectivity and Its Discontents', *Social Studies of Science* 43(4) (2012), 557–76.
60. Examples include Bronwen Douglas and Chris Ballard (eds), *Foreign Bodies: Oceania and the Science of Race 1750–1940* (Canberra: ANU E Press, 2008) and Bronwen Douglas, *Science, Voyages, and Encounters in Oceania, 1511–1850* (Basingstoke: Palgrave Macmillan, 2014).
61. Desley Deacon, *Elsie Clews Parsons: Inventing Modern Life* (Chicago, IL: Chicago University Press, 1997).
62. Examples include: Nicolas Peterson, Lindy Allen and Louise Hamby (eds), *The Makers and Making of Indigenous Australian Museum Collections* (Carlton, Vic.: Melbourne University Publishing, 2008); Joshua A. Bell, Alison K. Brown and Robert J. Gordon (eds), *Recreating First Contact: Expeditions, Anthropology, and Popular Culture* (Washington, DC: Smithsonian Institution Scholarly Press, 2013); Gregg Mitman and Paul Erickson, 'Latex and Blood: Science, Markets, and American Empire', *Radical History Review* 107 (2010), 45–73; Robert Dixon, *Photography,*

Early Cinema and Colonial Modernity: Frank Hurley's Synchronized Lecture Entertainments (Herndon, VA: Anthem, 2013); and Prue Ahrens, Lamont Lindstrom and Fiona Paisley, *Across the World with the Johnsons: Visual Culture and American Empire in the Twentieth Century* (Burlington: Ashgate, 2013).
63. Bell and Hisinoff, *The Anthropology of Expeditions*.

Bibliography

Ahrens, Prue, Lamont Lindstrom and Fiona Paisley. *Across the World with the Johnsons: Visual Culture and American Empire in the Twentieth Century.* Burlington: Ashgate, 2013.

Altman, Jon. 'From Kunanj, Fish Creek, to Mumeka, Mann River: Hunter-Gatherer Tradition and Transformation in Western Arnhem Land, 1948–2009', in Martin Thomas and Margo Neale (eds), *Exploring the Legacy of the 1948 Arnhem Land Expedition* (Canberra: ANU E Press, 2011), 113–34.

Anderson, Warwick. 'Objectivity and Its Discontents'. *Social Studies of Science* 43(4) (2012), 557–76.

Bell, Joshua A., Alison K. Brown and Robert J. Gordon (eds). *Recreating First Contact: Expeditions, Anthropology, and Popular Culture.* Washington, DC: Smithsonian Institution Scholarly Press, 2013.

Bell, Joshua A., and Erin L. Hisinoff (eds). *The Anthropology of Expeditions: Travel, Visualities, Afterlives.* New York: Bard Graduate Center, 2015.

Beazley, Kim. 'Nation Building or Cold War: Political Settings for the Arnhem Land Expedition', in Martin Thomas and Margo Neale (eds), *Exploring the Legacy of the 1948 Arnhem Land Expedition* (Canberra: ANU E Press, 2011), 55–71.

British Association for the Advancement of Science. *Notes and Queries on Anthropology, for the Use of Travellers and Residents in Uncivilized Lands.* London: Council of the Anthropological Institute, 1874.

Carey, Jane, and Jane Lydon (eds). *Indigenous Networks: Mobility, Connections and Exchange.* London/New York: Routledge, 2015.

Collis, Christy. 'Walking in Your Footsteps: "Footsteps of the Explorers" Expeditions and the Contest for Australian Desert Space', in Simon Naylor and James R. Ryan (eds), *New Spaces of Exploration: Geographies of Discovery in the Twentieth Century* (London: I.B. Tauris, 2010), 222–40.

Connell Szasz, Margaret (ed.). *Between Indian and White Worlds: The Cultural Broker.* Norman, OK: University of Oklahoma Press, 1994.

Deacon, Desley. *Elsie Clews Parsons: Inventing Modern Life.* Chicago, IL: Chicago University Press, 1997.

Dening, Greg. *Mr Bligh's Bad Language: Passion, Power and Theatre on the Bounty.* Cambridge: Cambridge University Press, 1992.

———. *Readings/Writings.* Melbourne: Melbourne University Press, 1998.

Dixon, Robert. *Photography, Early Cinema and Colonial Modernity: Frank Hurley's Synchronized Lecture Entertainments*. Herndon, VA: Anthem, 2013.

Douglas, Bronwen. *Science, Voyages, and Encounters in Oceania, 1511–1850*. Basingstoke: Palgrave Macmillan, 2014.

Douglas, Bronwen, and Chris Ballard (eds). *Foreign Bodies: Oceania and the Science of Race 1750–1940*. Canberra: ANU E Press, 2008.

Driver, Felix. *Geography Militant: Cultures of Exploration and Empire*. Oxford: Blackwell, 2001.

Ewing, Heather. *The Lost World of James Smithson: Science, Revolution, and the Birth of the Smithsonian*. New York: Bloomsbury, 2007.

Fabian, Johannes. *Out of Our Minds: Reason and Madness in the Exploration of Central Africa*. Berkeley/Los Angeles, CA: University of California Press, 2000.

Gray, Geoffrey. *A Cautious Silence: The Politics of Australian Anthropology*. Canberra: Aboriginal Studies Press, 2007.

Griffiths, Tom. *Slicing the Silence: Voyaging to Antarctica*. Sydney: New South, 2007.

Harris, Amanda. 'Chaperoned into Arnhem Land: Margaret McArthur and the Politics of Nutrition and Fieldwork in 1948'. *Lilith: A Feminist History Journal* 20 (2014), 62–75.

———. 'Food, Feeding and Consumption (or the Cook, the Wife and the Nutritionist): The Politics of Gender and Class in a 1948 Australian Expedition'. *History and Anthropology* 24(3) (2013), 363–79.

Hodgen, Margaret T. *Early Anthropology in the Sixteenth and Seventeenth Centuries*. Philadelphia, PA: University of Pennsylvania Press, 1964.

Jones, Philip. 'Inside Mountford's Tent: Paint, Politics and Paperwork', in Martin Thomas and Margo Neale (eds), *Exploring the Legacy of the 1948 Arnhem Land Expedition* (Canberra: ANU E Press, 2011), 33–54.

Kendall, Laurel. 'A Most Singular and Solitary Expeditionist: Berthold Laufer Collecting China', in Joshua A. Bell and Erin L. Hisinoff (eds), *The Anthropology of Expeditions: Travel, Visualities, Afterlives* (New York: Bard Graduate Center, 2015), 61–90.

Kennedy, Dane. *The Last Blank Spaces: Exploring Africa and Australia*. Cambridge, MA: Harvard University Press, 2013.

Klemun, Marianne, and Ulrike Spring. 'Expeditions as Experiments: An Introduction', in Marianne Klemun and Ulrike Spring (eds), *Expeditions as Experiments: Practising Observation and Documentation* (London: Palgrave Macmillan, 2016), 1–25.

Konishi, Shino, Maria Nugent and Tiffany Shellam (eds). *Indigenous Intermediaries: New Perspectives on Exploration Archives*. Canberra: ANU Press and Aboriginal History Inc., 2015.

Kuklick, Henrika. 'Personal Equations: Reflections on the History of Fieldwork, with Special Reference to Sociocultural Anthropology'. *Isis* 102(1) (2011), 1–33.

———. 'Science as Adventure', in Joshua A. Bell and Erin L. Hisinoff (eds), *The Anthropology of Expeditions: Travel, Visualities, Afterlives* (New York: Bard Graduate Center, 2015), 33–57.

Lévi-Strauss, Claude. *Tristes Tropiques*. Trans. John and Doreen Weightman. Harmondsworth: Penguin, 1992.

Lutz, Catherine A., and Jane L. Collins. *Reading National Geographic*. Chicago, IL: University of Chicago Press, 1993.

MacLeod, Roy. 'Discovery and Exploration', in Peter J. Bowler and John V. Pickstone (eds), *The Modern Biological and Earth Sciences: The Cambridge History of Science* (Cambridge: Cambridge University Press, 2009), Vol. 6, 34–59.

Marcus, Julie (ed.). *First in Their Field: Women and Australian Anthropology*. Carlton, Vic.: Melbourne University Press, 1993.

McCalman, Iain, and Paul Pickering (eds). *Historical Reenactment: From Realism to the Affective Turn*. Basingstoke: Palgrave Macmillan, 2010.

McCarthy, Frederick D., and Margaret McArthur. 'The Food Quest and the Time Factor in Aboriginal Economic Life', in Charles P. Mountford (ed.), *Records of the American-Australian Scientific Expedition to Arnhem Land* (Melbourne: Melbourne University Press, 1956–64), Vol. 2, 145–94.

Miller, Gifford Hubbs, and Robert Charles Cashner. 'Beneath the Billabongs: The Scientific Legacy of Robert Rush Miller', in Martin Thomas and Margo Neale (eds), *Exploring the Legacy of the 1948 Arnhem Land Expedition* (Canberra: ANU E Press, 2011), 271–82.

Mitman, Gregg, and Paul Erickson. 'Latex and Blood: Science, Markets, and American Empire'. *Radical History Review* 107 (2010), 45–73.

Monteath, Peter, and Valerie Munt. *Red Professor: The Cold War Life of Fred Rose*. Mile End, South Australia: Wakefield Press, 2015.

Mountford, Charles P. (ed.). *Records of the American-Australian Scientific Expedition to Arnhem Land*. Melbourne: Melbourne University Press, 1956–64.

Naylor, Simon, and James R. Ryan (eds). *New Spaces of Exploration: Geographies of Discovery in the Twentieth Century*. London: I.B. Tauris, 2010.

Peterson, Nicolas, Lindy Allen and Louise Hamby (eds). *The Makers and Making of Indigenous Australian Museum Collections*. Carlton, Vic.: Melbourne University Publishing, 2008.

Pettitt, Clare. *Dr. Livingstone, I Presume? Missionaries, Journalists, Explorers, and Empire*. Cambridge, MA: Harvard University Press, 2007.

Poignant, Roslyn. *Professional Savages: Captive Lives and Western Spectacle*. Sydney: UNSW Press, 2004.

Powell, Alan. *Northern Voyagers: Australia's Monsoon Coast in Maritime History*. North Melbourne: Australian Scholarly Publishing, 2013.

Pratt, Mary Louise. *Imperial Eyes: Travel Writing and Transculturation*. London/New York: Routledge, 1992.

Rothenberg, Tamar Y. *Presenting America's World: Strategies of Innocence in National Geographic Magazine*. Aldershot, UK: Ashgate, 2007.

Sahlins, Marshall. *Stone Age Economics*. Chicago, IL: Aldine Atherton, 1972.
Simpson, Colin. *Adam in Ochre: Inside Aboriginal Australia*. Sydney: Angus & Robertson, 1962.
Stocking, George W. 'The Ethnographer's Magic: Fieldwork in British Anthropology from Tylor to Malinowski', in George W. Stocking, *The Ethnographer's Magic and Other Essays in the History of Anthropology* (Madison, WI: University of Wisconsin Press, 1992), 12–59.
——. *After Tylor: British Social Anthropology 1888–1951*. Madison, WI: University of Wisconsin Press, 1995.
Taussig Michael. *Mimesis and Alterity: A Particular History of the Senses*. New York: Routledge, 1993.
Taylor, Paul Michael. 'Transformations of the Expeditionary Enterprise: Perspectives on the Smithsonian's Expeditionary History before 1948'. *reCollections* 9(2) (2014).
Thomas, Martin. 'Anthropology and the British Empire', in Robert Aldrich and Kirsten McKenzie (eds), *The Routledge History of Western Empires* (London/New York: Routledge, 2013), 255–69.
——. 'Because It's Your Country: Death and Its Meanings in West Arnhem Land'. *Life Writing* 12(2) (2015), 203–23.
——. 'Bones as a Bridge between Worlds: Repatriation and Reconciliation between Australia and the United States', in Kate Darian-Smith and Penelope Edmonds (eds), *Conciliation on Colonial Frontiers: Conflict, Performance, and Commemoration in Australia and the Pacific Rim* (New York/London: Routledge, 2015), 105–68.
—— (ed.). *Expedition into Empire: Exploratory Journeys and the Making of the Modern World*. New York/London: Routledge, 2015.
——. 'The Rush to Record: Transmitting the Sound of Aboriginal Culture'. *Journal of Australian Studies* 90 (2007), 105–21.
——. 'A Short History of the 1948 Arnhem Land Expedition. *Aboriginal History* 34 (2010), 143–69.
——. 'Turning Subjects into Objects and Objects into Subjects: Collecting Human Remains on the 1948 Arnhem Land Expedition', in Amanda Harris (ed.), *Circulating Cultures: Exchanges of Australian Indigenous Music, Dance and Media* (Canberra: ANU Press, 2014), 129–66.
Thomas, Martin, and Margo Neale (eds). *Exploring the Legacy of the 1948 Arnhem Land Expedition*. Canberra: ANU E Press, 2011.
White, Richard. *The Middle Ground: Indians, Empires, and Republics in the Great Lakes Region, 1650–1815*. New York: Cambridge University Press, 1992.
Wilcken, Patrick. *Claude Lévi-Strauss: The Poet in the Laboratory*. London: Bloomsbury, 2010.

PART I

Anthropology and the Field: Intermediaries and Exchange

Chapter 1

ASSEMBLING THE ETHNOGRAPHIC FIELD

THE 1901–02 EXPEDITION OF BALDWIN SPENCER AND FRANCIS GILLEN

Philip Batty

The Australian anthropologist James Wafer has argued that 'most definitions of "ethnography" are premised on the notion of "the field"; conceived as a clearly delimited area of the anthropologist's experience, with neat geographical and temporal boundaries'.[1] Ethnography can thus be seen as 'an exercise in containing the social world of the field, in subjecting it to the kind of logic that renders it controllable'.[2] While there may be any number of factors implicated in rendering the ethnographic field 'controllable', I wish to focus here on the 'anthropological expedition', and the extent to which the logic and logistics of such ventures shaped and continue to shape the field. Indeed, if fieldwork is the 'central ritual' of the anthropological 'tribe', as George W. Stocking suggests, then one could say that the anthropological expedition plays the role of ritual leader.[3]

The progression of an anthropological expedition sets not only the geographical and temporal boundaries of the field, but the type, quality and availability of the ethnographic information that may or may not be made discoverable. The mundane practicalities and events of the expedition also shape the parameters of the field. This might include: the means of transport (horses, wagons, porters, boats, motor vehicles, buses, aeroplanes, helicopters); unintended events (accidents, misdirection, loss of supplies, deaths, vehicle failure); communications ('native runners', translators, 'informants', the telegraph, radio, satellite phone, the internet); and a host of other expeditionary logistics. Moreover, I will suggest that the formation of the ethnographic field as an object of scientific enquiry went hand in hand with the emergence of the anthropological expedition during the nineteenth century.

The ethnographic field can also be considered a conceptual object shaped just as assuredly by considerations of a more intangible nature that are as complex and variable as the physical constraints imposed by the expedition. The theoretical framework through which ethnologists construct their proposed investigations (totemism, social evolutionism, functionalism, structuralism, poststructuralism, for example) plays a central role in determining the choice of geographical and/or social space in which the investigation occurs. It will also guide the kind of questions to be asked of the field and thereby delineate the field itself. The deployment of an anthropological expedition may be motivated by a desire to prove or disprove a particular theoretical position, which may result in a reshaping of the field to accommodate the theory, or vice versa. Other factors will further influence the approach to the field and its configuration. These include research methodologies; the results of previous expeditions; the kind of technologies used to record ethnographic information; related literature; knowledge of local languages; and personal relationships with informants. In other words, the 'ethnographic field' is not something that is simply 'out there', awaiting the arrival of the anthropologist. Rather, it is assembled through a complex array of variable relations of both a conceptual and physical nature, including the expedition.

In a more speculative sense, I would also suggest that the things acquired during an expedition and assembled in a collection that might include artefacts, photographs, films, recordings, notes, sketches, diaries and other items can themselves be likened to an ethnographic field with certain regions, borders and histories. This post-expedition field – assembled in multiple configurations – becomes, over time, a place open to exploration by other anthropologists, historians, theorists, political activists, museum curators and artists, all of whom may employ it as a resource for their own intellectual, social, cultural and political ends. This does not necessarily mean that this new, reassembled field becomes irrelevant or detached from the physical region where the original expedition was conducted, or from the people who were the subjects of investigation. On the contrary, it may assume a position of authority in the interpretation and representation of that region and its people. In fact, they might claim ownership of the collection and use it as a critical field of ethnographic information to revive cultural traditions, to construct new identities or to make claims to lands upon which the expedition was undertaken and the collection acquired. In a similar vein, the field notes, documentation and diary entries included in a collection may become the final arbiter in verifying the 'authenticity' of a particular tradition or object, and the means by which an individual or group claims ownership of that tradition or object. Furthermore, the expedition that made the collection possible will also assume a level of authority, or iconic status, as it played an instrumental role in fixing the temporal, geographical and material limits of this new, reassembled field of ethnographic information.

Given these considerations, there are two questions I wish to pose in this chapter. Firstly, I will investigate how the social world of a specific geographical space was transformed into an ethnographic field, focusing on the role of the expedition in shaping that field. Secondly, I will examine the ways in which ethnographic material was acquired on an expedition and assembled as a single collection in order to explore whether the collection was transformed into an ethnographic field in its own right.

In attempting to answer these queries, I will use as a case study the 1901–02 anthropological expedition led by Walter Baldwin Spencer (1860–1929), professor of biology at the University of Melbourne, and Francis James Gillen (1855–1912), an ethnographer as well as the post and telegraph station master who was based for many years in the desert township of Alice Springs. The expedition traversed the centre of Australia, from Oodnadatta in South Australia, to Borroloola, a coastal town in the Gulf of Carpentaria in the Northern Territory. In covering a distance of almost two thousand kilometres, the expedition circumscribed an extensive ethnographic field encompassing more than ten different Aboriginal cultural groups with whom Spencer and Gillen conducted intensive fieldwork over a period of eleven months. How, then, was the geographical space through which Spencer and Gillen travelled – and the social world of that space – transformed into an ethnographic field? I will begin by examining the rise of the 'ethnographic field' as an object of intellectual and scientific interest in Britain, for it was there that Spencer and Gillen's expedition had its origins.

The Ethnographic Field as an Object of Scientific Enquiry

The notion that all societies evolved unilaterally through stages – from 'savage' to 'civilized' states through a process of social evolution – was a pervasive view in nineteenth-century thought. Although Darwin's theory of biological evolution gave such notions a certain scientific legitimacy, the essential ideas underlying social evolutionary theory had a long history, going as far back as the Roman philosopher Lucretius.[4] However, social evolutionism gained a more theoretical formulation through the work of Victorian scientists and thinkers such as the anthropologist Edward Burnett Tylor (1832–1917) and the philosopher Herbert Spencer (1820–1903). This led to the notion that reliable knowledge concerning the origins of social structures and institutions could be obtained by gathering ethnographic information from societies that still survived in a 'savage' state and were therefore positioned at the lower end of the evolutionary ladder. The more 'primitive' such people were considered to be, the greater the chance of extracting from them what Gillen later termed 'bedrock' data concerning the evolution of human society. This helped to facilitate not only the invention of 'primitive' societies, as Adam Kuper has argued, but the invention of an 'ethnographic field' where such societies were imagined to exist and from whom answers concerning the evolution of the most fundamental social institutions could be found.[5] Inevitably, this led to the rise of a new kind of scientific venture. Expeditions were dispatched to locate and study societies that represented the early stages of social development.

Certainly, expeditions that incorporated a scientific component, including the collection of ethnographic materials, had been under way at least since the eighteenth century. James Cook's first Pacific voyage (1768–71) was jointly sponsored by the Royal Society. Apart from undertaking astronomical observations, acquiring botanical specimens and conducting other scientific activities, it returned with an impressive collection of ethnographic artefacts. Nonetheless, expeditions with the sole purpose of conducting anthropological research did not occur with any frequency until the end of the nineteenth century – at least in the British tradition. Moreover, the deployment of such expeditions only occurred as the notion of an 'ethnographic field' came into sharper focus as a specific object of scientific enquiry, constructed through the theoretical prism of social evolutionism. The anthropological expedition and the ethnographic field were therefore mutually constitutive. Yet the formation of the ethnographic field as a fully articulated arena of investigation, bound by certain geographical borders and encompassing a particular cultural group, was a relatively slow process.

Before serious consideration was given to sending trained anthropologists on expeditions, British anthropologists initially relied on reports from explorers, missionaries and traders on the colonial frontier. This was not so much due to the practical difficulties of obtaining first-hand data; rather, collecting ethnographic information was considered to be separate from the more cerebral, theoretically oriented work of university-bound anthropologists. For these stay-at-home academics – who had little if any direct contact with the peoples they wrote about – the ethnographic field was a distant realm of imagined possibilities. The near-total lack of personal engagement with the field gave the 'armchair' anthropologist a much freer hand to invest it with a particular shape and structure that could support his theoretical concerns. James Frazer, who had no experience of fieldwork, relied on many untrained collectors when producing his vast compilation of myths from around the world. They provided the substance for Frazer's famous twelve-volume book, *The Golden Bough: A Study in Magic and Religion* (1890–1915).

One of the problems that troubled Tylor and his contemporaries about this method of acquiring primary data was their poor quality. Much of the material was not only second-hand, but filtered through the prejudicial perceptions of individuals without training in ethnology. In an attempt to resolve these difficulties, Tylor and other members of the British Association for the Advancement of Science published *Notes and Queries on Anthropology, for the Use of Travellers and Residents in Uncivilised Lands* (1874 and later editions).[6] This extensive guide offered highly detailed advice on how to do ethnography in the field. The variety of topics covered was encyclopaedic: 'Marital Relations', 'Body Temperature', 'Insanity', 'Dietary Laws', 'Personal Ornaments', 'Cannibalism', 'Tribal Marks', 'Infanticide', 'Games' and more. With the publication of this guide in 1874, the notion of the 'ethnographic field' became much more precise. Now it had carefully delineated categories and a framework through which ethnographic knowledge could be constructed.

Attempts to regularize the collection of ethnographic data were not, however, confined to Britain. An approach approximating the 'Notes and Queries' methodology had also been developed in the United States. Indeed, it would have a significant, if indirect influence on the constitution of an ethnographic field in Australia.

The renowned pioneer of American anthropology, Lewis H. Morgan (1818–81), had developed an ethnographic data collection method that entailed sending questionnaires to colonial residents in remote regions in the hope of obtaining information on local indigenous kinship systems, marriage customs and other social structures. In 1869, Lorimer Fison (1832–1907), a missionary based in Fiji, responded to Morgan and not only provided him with data on the Fijians, but acquired an enduring interest in anthropology through continued correspondence with Morgan. During a four-year sojourn in Australia, Fison subsequently set out to collect ethnographic data on Aboriginal customs by placing notices in newspapers that called on interested parties to provide information via questionnaires based on the Morgan model. One of those who responded was Alfred William Howitt (1830–1908), an explorer, natural scientist and magistrate who had gained fame in Victoria after rescuing John King, the only surviving member of the doomed Bourke and Wills exploration party. During this venture, he had made close observations of Aboriginal groups, which led to further studies of Aboriginal people in south eastern Australia. He was personally acquainted with the Kurnai people of Victoria as he was, for a time, one of their official 'guardians' and thus well positioned to acquire first-hand accounts of their social structures. From 1872, Fison and Howitt worked together, gathering and compiling ethnographic information on Aboriginal groups, both through questionnaires and direct engagement with Aboriginal people on missions and settlements. In 1880, they published *Kamilaroi and Kurnai*, a work that W.E.H. Stanner later described as 'a landmark in the new "anthropology" replacing "ethnology"'.[7]

Fison was initially positioned on the periphery of the anthropological enterprise as a 'fieldworker', gathering ethnographic information on behalf of Morgan. However, he effectively broke with the 'periphery-centre' model and subsequently claimed his own ethnographic ground in Australia. Of course, this was accomplished through his partnership with Howitt, who undermined the old model even further by partly collapsing the division between fieldworker and anthropologist by combining an active engagement with Aboriginal people with the production of anthropological texts. Here, the intellectual distance separating collectors in the field and university-bound theorists began to diminish.

Among those impressed with the work of Fison and Howitt was Edward Tylor, who entered into regular correspondence with them both. Although Tylor had remained at the 'centre' of the British anthropological enterprise, and at a distance from ethnographic fieldworkers, the activities of Fison and Howitt indicated that the prospect of sending trained scientists into the field was a viable proposition. Even so, some twenty years would pass from the publication of *Kamilaroi and Kurnai* to the departure of Spencer and Gillen's expedition in 1901 – an early example of a scientist, trained at the 'centre' in Oxford, going into the field. What were the circumstances that led to this event?

Spencer and Gillen, Haddon and Rivers

Seven years after the publication of *Kamilaroi and Kurnai*, Baldwin Spencer arrived in Australia to take up the position of Foundation Chair of Biology at the University of Melbourne.[8] He had studied biology at Oxford under Henry Moseley, the Professor of Anatomy and a committed social evolutionist. Following his graduation, Spencer remained in Oxford where he audited Tylor's undergraduate lectures and assisted him in organizing anthropological exhibits in the university's Pitt Rivers Museum. Although he developed a general interest in anthropology through his engagement with Tylor, Spencer's primary academic focus remained on biology. Before leaving Britain, Tylor suggested that if he 'ever chanced to come into contact' with native peoples in Australia, he 'might be able to do some work of value'.[9] Perhaps with this in mind, he made a point of reading *Kamilaroi and Kurnai* after taking up residence in Melbourne and then went on to establish a warm relationship with its authors, from whom he gained a sound understanding of the current state of Australian ethnography. While the influence of Howitt and Fison was formative, Spencer's meeting with Gillen some years later made, in his own words, 'all the difference'.[10]

Spencer first met Gillen in 1894 as a member of the Horn Expedition, a research venture funded by a pastoralist-cum-mining magnate that studied the natural history of Central Australia. Gillen was then in charge of the overland telegraph station in Alice Springs; he was also the local magistrate and sub-protector of Aborigines. After working in the region for some twenty-five years, Gillen had developed an abiding interest in the Arrernte people and acquired a remarkable understanding of their traditions and, to some extent, their language. He had also acquired a collection of artefacts and tried his hand at ethnographic photography and the compilation of Aboriginal vocabulary. The two men hit it off almost immediately and their friendship quickly evolved into one of the most influential partnerships in the history of Australian anthropology. Gillen brought to the collaboration his extensive, if undisciplined, ethnographic knowledge and, more importantly, his ready access to Aboriginal people in Central Australia. As Grafton Elliot Smith suggested, Gillen was Spencer's 'most important discovery'.[11]

Two years after that first meeting, the two men engaged in an intensive research project in Alice Springs. Gillen had persuaded local Arrernte groups to perform a major cycle of secret-sacred men's ceremonies, the Engwura. The entire event ran for more than four months, during which time they took several hundred photographs and recorded detailed information about the ceremonies. Extensive information was also gathered regarding social organization and kinship systems; totemic affiliations; initiation rites; burial rituals; 'song lines'; magic; childbirth; food restrictions and other areas of Arrernte life. The results of this extensive project were published in a 670-page book, *The Native Tribes of Central Australia* (1899). Thanks in part to Frazer's high praise of the work (and his initial help in getting it published), *Native Tribes* had a significant impact on intellectual circles throughout Europe and the United States. As a result, the geographic and social space of Central Australia became a highly elaborated ethnographic field, around which the current debates in anthropological theory were played out. As Malinowski noted in a 1913 article on Spencer and Gillen, 'half the total production of anthropological literature has been based on their work and nine tenths affected or modified by it'.[12]

Figure 1.1 Senior Arrernte men overseeing the Engwura ceremony, Alice Springs, 1896. From right to left: Erlikintera, Erpolingarinia, Ingelilba, Eruramunga, Arai-iga, Ingapaila and Intwailiuka. Photograph by Baldwin Spencer. By permission of Museum Victoria.

Was the 1896 fieldwork Spencer and Gillen conducted in Central Australia undertaken as part of an 'anthropological expedition'? Yes and no. Their research with the Arrernte was largely confined to areas located less than a few kilometres from Alice Springs. Nonetheless, Spencer had to conduct what could be described as an expedition when he made what was then the arduous journey from Melbourne to Central Australia. Moreover, their investigations facilitated the formation of an ethnographic field that attracted worldwide attention, while also paving the way for their 1901–02 journey, a project that clearly had all the attributes of an *expedition*. Their work in Alice Springs was also an important precursor to a project that is now considered to be the first major British expedition with an anthropological purpose: the 1898 Cambridge Anthropological Expedition to Torres Straits (see Philp, this volume).

The Torres Strait venture – conducted over a period of seven months – was organized and led by the biologist Alfred Cort Haddon (1855–1940). Other researchers included the physician and ethnologist Charles G. Seligman, the psychologist Charles S. Myers and, most notably, the psychiatrist and ethnologist William H.R. Rivers (1864–1922). In most respects, the innovative methodologies used by the expedition in acquiring ethnographic information were similar to those employed by Spencer and Gillen, although there is little evidence of direct influence. Their commonalities included the use of genealogies to ascertain social systems and structures; the re-enactment and documentation of sacred ceremonies; and the double-checking of data obtained from different informants. The Cambridge Expedition's capture of wax-cylinder recordings and motion-picture film for ethnographic purposes was pioneering. Spencer and Gillen employed the same technologies on their 1901–02 expedition.

The most important developments to emerge from the Torres Strait expedition were threefold. First, it undermined, perhaps fatally, the long accepted 'armchair' approach to anthropological research. Instead of the university-based theorist relying on ethnographic material sent in from the field, the theorist was now in the field undertaking the hands-on research. Second, the expedition was primarily concerned with questions of an anthropological nature, rather than being a more general scientific venture that might have an ethnographic component attached. Third, and most importantly, the research and observations of Rivers led to the development of what eventually became the standard methodological model for ethnographic fieldwork. As Kuklick shows in her assessment of his work, Rivers stressed the importance of conducting research on a limited cultural group within a defined geographical area and insisted that anthropologists must live alone among their subjects for at least a year in order to master their language and develop personal relationships with all members of the group under investigation. As Kuklick indicates, Rivers' experiences with the Cambridge team convinced him that large, multidisciplinary expeditions, conducted over a short period, were counterproductive because they had the effect of disturbing the normal life patterns of the subject group and therefore skewing attempts to gain accurate ethnographic information. For Rivers, sole 'participant-observers', living discreetly among their ethnographic subjects, offered the most effective way of producing quality ethnographic work.

The approach advocated by Rivers was later adopted by professional anthropologists well into the twentieth century, including Bronisław Malinowski.[13] Yet, despite Rivers' criticisms of large anthropological expeditions, they continued to form a significant component of ethnographic research up until the 1950s, in parallel with the lone 'participant-observer' approach. One could cite here the expeditions conducted by the University of Adelaide's Board of Anthropological Research throughout the 1930s, or the 1948 National Geographic Society-sponsored American-Australian Scientific Expedition to Arnhem Land, led by Charles Mountford (see Harris, this volume). Although the 'anthropological expedition' had become a thing of the past by the 1960s, it had nevertheless played a central role in the formation of the ethnographic field, which if anything had become a more stable arena for the production of ethnographic knowledge under the, by then, dominant 'participant-observer' method.

Through the work of Spencer, Gillen and Rivers, the ethnographic field had gained a greater structural coherence, with parameters that were both recognizable and practicable. Indeed, it acquired a place in the Western intellectual imagination that endures up to the present. With the basic elements of the anthropological expedition in place – and the ethnographic field a well-established object of scientific enquiry – Spencer and Gillen's 1901–02 expedition could almost be described as inevitable. I will now turn to a closer examination of this venture.

The Spencer and Gillen Expedition

In an 1899 letter to Fison, Spencer noted that he wished to conduct a fully equipped twelve-month expedition in Central Australia. Fison subsequently sent the letter to James Frazer in Cambridge, who immediately organized a petition to support Spencer's project, addressed to the 'Government of Victoria'. In a concise summation of social evolutionist thought, Frazer noted that Australia offered 'the most interesting field of observation now open to students of primitive man', since it was there, 'more perhaps than in any other part of the globe', that 'solutions to ... problems of great moment in the early history of society and religion' would be found.[14] The seventy-seven signatures attached to the petition constitute a veritable rollcall of the major British anthropologists of the late nineteenth century: Edward Tylor, Alfred Haddon, William Rivers, Andrew Lang, Henry Balfour, Henry Sidgwick and, of course, Frazer himself. Other signatories included Charles Darwin's sons, Francis and George Darwin, and Henry Asquith, the future prime minister. The petition had a positive effect; Spencer and Gillen were both given twelve months' leave by their employers to undertake the expedition. Thanks to Spencer's charm and talent for public promotion, David Syme, the proprietor of *The Age* newspaper in Melbourne, offered him £1,000 towards the expedition. In return, Spencer would be required to contribute regular reports from the field. With further assistance from the South

Figure 1.2 Members of the 1901–02 expedition, Alice Springs, 1901. Left to right: Purunda (Warwick), Francis Gillen, Harry Chance, Baldwin Spencer and Erlikilyika (Jim Kite). Unknown photographer. Permission of Museum Victoria.

Australian government and Spencer's own contribution of £400, sufficient finances were finally secured to launch the expedition.

The party consisted of three core members: Spencer, Gillen and mounted constable Harry Chance, who was employed to manage the general logistics of the journey. Numerous Aboriginal men were also recruited at various points along the route, acting as guides, horse wranglers and interpreters. Most prominent among them were two Arrernte men, Erlikilyika (also known as Jim Kite) and Purunda (also known as Warwick). Both travelled with the team from Charlotte Waters, on the South Australia–Northern Territory border, through to Borroloola. Inspired perhaps by his employers, Erlikilyika produced a collection of drawings during the expedition that depict members of the team as well as stylized sketches of various ceremonies. He later mounted a solo exhibition of his work in Adelaide in 1913.

The route of the expedition, and thus the geographic field in which they conducted their work, was largely defined by the overland telegraph line. Completed in 1872, it ran 3,200 kilometres through the centre of Australia from Port Augusta to Darwin. For the first two-thirds of the journey, the party rarely strayed from the line as arrangements had been made to have essential supplies deposited at repeater stations along its length. These included four tons of flour, seven hundred pounds of sugar, four hundred pounds of fruit and vegetables, six hundred tins of meat and jam, and numerous bags of sweets, tobacco and other consumables.[15] Apart from these supplies, several hundred axes, knives, mirrors, spectacles, clothing, pipes and, curiously, several toy dolls were shipped north and strategically placed at telegraph stations along the line where they were exchanged with Aboriginal people in reward for ethnographic information and the performance of ceremonies. As Gillen informed Spencer in a letter prior to the expedition:

> It is imperative that we start with a flourish of trumpets and attract the natives to us ... to do this we must have liberal supplies, and the word must go forth that the great white *oknirabati* [wise elders] have come with lavish hoards so that [they] may be ready to take us to their bosoms.[16]

Telegraphic messages were also delivered to the chief officers at the stations, instructing them to tell the local Aborigines of the imminent arrival of the anthropologists. The audiovisual technology with which they would record and document Aboriginal life and customs included both still- and motion-picture cameras and a wax-cylinder recorder, along with packets of photographic glass plates, chemicals and paper, allowing the anthropologists to process photographs in the field.

Leaving Oodnadatta in late summer on 19 March 1901, the party travelled north with a team of horses, a buggy and a heavy supply wagon. For two weeks, they journeyed through a particularly arid region of South Australia, dotted with salt lakes, spindly vegetation and dry riverbeds. Both Spencer and Gillen suffered severe eye infections on this first leg of the journey, brought on by the heat and ever-present swarms of flies. It was only after reaching Alice Springs on 2 April that their eyesight began to recover.

The telegraphic messages sent ahead about Spencer and Gillen's forthcoming appearance played a role in facilitating the formation of a readily available ethnographic field, as well as preparing the ethnographic subjects for the visitors. Indeed, this particular field had been well established during the earlier fieldwork around Alice Springs in 1896. A group of senior Arrernte men were waiting to greet the two anthropologists with a special welcoming ceremony, replete with elaborate iconographic designs painted on their bodies.

There was also a certain ritual duty implied in the welcome. According to their own testimony, Spencer and Gillen were considered by the Arrernte to be initiated men and the descendants of a sacred caterpillar ancestor (the *utnerrengatye* or 'emu bush' caterpillar).[17] Gillen had been given this totemic status during his residence in the region.[18] It was subsequently accorded to Spencer, whom the Arrernte viewed as Gillen's classificatory brother.[19] The senior men who had arranged the welcome were thus paying due customary respect to both Spencer and, particularly, Gillen, whom they believed was an outstanding descendant of the *utnerrengatye*. Indeed, the Arrernte had cast Spencer and Gillen as real actors within their religious system and found a recognizable place for them in what they perceived to be the cosmological order of things. Gillen actively encouraged this understanding, especially the notion that he was an *akngerrepate* or 'wise elder' possessing supernatural powers. On at least one occasion, he played the part of a traditional Arrernte healer, tending to the sick with a medicinal chant.[20] As Spencer noted, it was a way of 'getting into their beliefs and thinking'.[21]

Neither Gillen nor Spencer had any qualms about allowing themselves to be culturally assimilated in this way, despite having no personal faith in such religious beliefs. For them, it was an effective methodological procedure in their attempts to penetrate the ethnographic field. As we have seen, Rivers later endorsed this approach as a legitimate method in anthropological research. He argued that if

Figure 1.3 An Atninga ('revenge') party of Arrernte men, Alice Springs, 1901. Photograph by Baldwin Spencer. By permission of Museum Victoria.

anthropologists were to acquire accurate ethnographic information, they must immerse themselves in the culture of their indigenous subjects in such a way as to ensure that they were active participants in that culture – the instruments of research.

Not long after arriving in Alice Springs, a spontaneous incident involving preparations for a revenge party attack, known as an Atninga, erupted near Spencer and Gillen's camp. The anthropologists had to move quickly to photograph and document it. To capture this incident, they used the innovative Goertz-Anschutz camera, which had an extremely fast shutter speed (one thousandth of a second). This allowed split-second exposures that eliminated the blur of moving figures. Until the invention of such technology, photography of human subjects required much more stage management, with subjects being required to remain as still as possible.

The Goertz-Anschutz gave the anthropologists the ability to create sharp images of unexpected events and to move in and around the day-to-day activities of camp life, almost as participants. On the other hand, their motion-picture camera, a cinematograph, had the opposite effect. Unlike the Goertz-Anschutz, it had to be attached to a tripod, with the lens pointing in a single, pre-determined direction, without the possibility of movement.

While in Alice Springs, they made arrangements to film a solemn Aboriginal ritual, but things did not go according to plan. Apart from problems with the cumbersome cinema camera, the Aboriginal men performing the ritual did not act as expected. Spencer had tried to explain that the camera's field of vision was fixed in one position and that consequently the men would have to change the ritual in order to stay in frame. These instructions had little effect. As Spencer complained in his diary,

> I got my cinematograph all fixed up, but ... the performers who were supposed to be coming in a certain direction ... suddenly skipped behind some bushes ... so as I ground on and on at the handle hoping every second that they would come into the field I secured a good deal of scenery but very little performance.[22]

Spencer felt that this mishap was not 'the native's fault'. He understood that they were bound by strict protocols to perform the ritual as they believed their ancestors had once performed it. He noted that it 'was not that they did not want us to [film the ritual], but quite naturally they could not do such a special thing except in the proper way [and] I much respected them for this'.[23]

Nonetheless, Spencer and especially Gillen could not help feeling put out. From their point of view, the men could have made some small adjustments to the ritual to accommodate the technical limitations of their documentation methods. They were particularly annoyed at the waste of expensive film stock. More galling was the fact that they had agreed to give the performers several bags of flour, a good quantity of tobacco and several knives if they conducted the ritual as requested. But after several reruns, the performers continued to move out of frame. In frustration, the anthropologists refused to give the Aboriginal men the promised goods. Spencer wrote:

> Gillen and I were so disgusted with their ancestral stupidity that we packed our things up and departed in wrath, leaving the natives sad and supper-less and hoping that they would – which they doubtless did – regret that their ancestors had not known of the existence of a cinematograph and arranged their ceremonies to suit.[24]

Obviously, the Goertz-Anschutz and the motion-picture cameras dramatically affected the extent to which Spencer and Gillen could document Arrernte ritual activity and, therefore, the constitution of the ethnographic field. The Goertz-Anschutz seemingly extended their ethnographic vision, doing away with the need for stage management, while the motion-picture camera necessitated a careful orchestration of events. The cinematograph not only produced a far more limited ethnographic field, but gave the anthropologists, albeit reluctantly, a greater role in shaping it.

With fresh supplies of water and extra horses purchased in Alice Springs, they continued north on 24 May to Barrow Creek where they worked for six weeks, collecting information on the Kaytej people, a northern Arrernte group on whose traditional lands the Barrow Creek telegraph station had been built. Twenty-seven years earlier, in 1874, a band of Kaytej warriors had attacked the station, mortally wounding two staff members including the stationmaster, John Stapleton. It was Gillen (then a junior telegraph operator based in Adelaide) who relayed Stapleton's last telegraphic conversation with his wife. Remarkably, one of the Kaytej men who had participated in the attack – and survived the brutal police reprisals – met Spencer and Gillen when they arrived at the station and become a willing and valuable informant.

Their next destination was Tennant Creek, where they stayed for two months working with Warumungu people. It would be the most productive location of the entire expedition. More than twenty-five separate ceremonies were photographed and documented; lists of totemic ancestors were compiled and described; kinship systems

Figure 1.4 Women crawl through the legs of decorated men towards the end of a Warumungu burial ritual, Tennant Creek, 1901. Photograph by Baldwin Spencer. By permission of Museum Victoria.

and terms were recorded; and a large collection of artefacts was assembled.

They made a side expedition to Thapauerlu, a totemic site in the Murchison Range, believed by the Warumungu to be the home of Wollunqua, a sacred snake ancestor. They were also able to record the complete cycle of Warumungu mortuary rituals, occasioned by the actual death of an older Warumungu man. Like the revenge party they documented in Alice Springs, these rituals were not stage managed, but rapidly captured with the Goertz-Anschutz camera as they unfolded. The inherent spontaneity of the resulting images was perhaps one of the reasons why they so fascinated Durkheim, who explored and exploited Spencer and Gillen's representation of them in *Elementary Forms of the Religious Life* (1912).

On 19 July, the party departed Tennant Creek and travelled some two hundred kilometres further north to the telegraph station at Powell Creek, arriving on 23 September, just before the onset of the monsoonal season. The semi-arid country through which they had been travelling changed to savannah plains with warmer temperatures. Here they focused their ethnographic attention on the Jingili people, whose ceremonial life, social structure and religious belief system were similar to that of the Warumungu with whom they were in regular contact.

The expedition now took a new course to the east – travelling towards the remote outpost of Borroloola, on the Gulf of Carpentaria, their final destination. Up until this moment they had been able to 'tap' into the telegraph line using a special device operated by Gillen. They had used this not only to alert telegraph station staff of their approach, but to communicate with their colleagues and families in the southern states. Henceforth, such communication would cease and they would rely on what Spencer described in his diary as 'paper yabbers' to communicate with the outside world.[25] This was a pidgin term referring to a mail system that involved Aboriginal men carrying letters on foot for Europeans over distances of up to several hundred kilometres.

Spencer and Gillen's reliance on Aboriginal people throughout their expedition cannot be overestimated. They tended to the horses, packed and unpacked equipment and, most significantly, worked as interpreters and cultural go-betweens. They spoke their own languages as well as some English, having occasionally worked on cattle stations. Most had spent time in prison where they endured a crash-course in the ways of Europeans, which no doubt improved their English – a point that Spencer cheerfully acknowledged. Much of what Spencer and Gillen recorded to the north of Alice Springs – particularly around Barrow Creek – was only made possible as a result of the bilingual skills of their main Aboriginal assistant, Erlikilyika, or Jim Kite as they usually called him. After arriving in Tennant Creek, where the predominant language was Warumangu, Spencer noted in his diary: 'luckily there are one or two men who can speak a little English [here] so we will probably do well...'[26]

Like Jim Kite, the Aboriginal men who worked for Spencer and Gillen had come of age in the intercultural world that had arisen in Central Australia following the construction of the overland telegraph line, thirty years before the commencement of the expedition. It was their expert knowledge of this cross-cultural environment and their ability to navigate its complexities that made them such indispensable components of the anthropologists' research programme. But it was not just a matter of their operating as intercultural go-betweens. Their intimate involvement in these research events, and their interpretative skills (both linguistic and cultural), played a fundamental role in shaping the ethnographic field that the anthropologists carefully constructed.

Of all the terrain they covered during their expedition, the two hundred kilometres between Powell Creek and Borroloola was the most difficult. It alternated between wet marshlands, chest-high 'grass forests', mud flats, waterholes and rivers infested with crocodiles. Moreover, the elevated heat and humidity left the expedition members in a perpetual state of exhaustion. Coupled with these difficulties was the lack of familiarity with the languages and traditions of the Aboriginal people in the area. Gillen had spent some twenty-five years working between Charlotte Waters and Tennant Creek – the heart of Central Australia – and had acquired a good knowledge of the Aboriginal groups in the region. Here, however, both Gillen and the Arrernte guides were complete strangers. Indeed, Erlikilyika was so concerned about attacks from local Aboriginal people that he once used a revolver – given to him by Gillen – to frighten away what he erroneously thought was an *artwe inentye* (a traditional executioner, also known as a *kurdaitcha*).

Despite these problems, they managed to record, if only to a moderate degree, some of the rituals and kinship systems in the region between Powell Creek and Borroloola, including those of the Ngandji, Alawa and Bingbinga groups. Most notably, a detailed examination was made of the mortuary rituals of the Bingbinga, from whom they acquired, after exchanging large quantities of trade items, grave goods and the bones of a deceased person. After the expedition, this material was reassembled and put on display in the National Museum of Victoria in Melbourne (now Museum Victoria) where it remained for over sixty years. In the mid 1970s, the bones and funerary objects were locked away in a restricted storeroom, where they still await repatriation. This assemblage of Bingbinga grave goods – redeployed in a radically different context by museum curators – took on a life of its own with the meanings attached to it changing over time, from an object of scientific enquiry through to an object of shame, to be returned to the Bingbinga who may yet use it to revive lost traditions.

On 2 November, the expedition reached the dilapidated town of Borroloola. From here they were expecting to take passage on a coastal steamer and return south via Darwin. However, the steamer had been wrecked in a storm a few months prior to their arrival and they were now stranded in Borroloola until other arrangements could be made. Although frustrated and somewhat dispirited, this nonetheless allowed Spencer and Gillen to study in greater detail the coastal Aboriginal groups in the area surrounding Borroloola: the Yanuwa, Mara and Garawa. Although there was a certain resonance in the cultural traditions of these groups with those that Spencer and Gillen had recorded in Central Australia, the differences allowed them to produce valuable comparative studies of a range of ceremonies, including, perhaps most significantly, rituals associated with the initiation of young boys. As elsewhere, they also documented local social structures and concluded that the Mara in particular possessed an exceedingly complex kinship system that took weeks of painstaking research to unlock.

In January 1902, Spencer managed to have a letter sent out – probably to Powell Creek via the 'paper yabber' system – to a friend in Melbourne, alerting him to their dire situation and indicating that both he and Gillen were suffering from fever. This sparked a flurry of newspaper reports in the southern press, with one headline reading: 'The Spencer-Gillen Expedition. Leaders in Danger. Suffering from Malaria'.[27] As a result, the Queensland government agreed to send a small steamer, the *Vigilant*, from Thursday Island to Borroloola. Oblivious to this urgent activity, the two men were surprised when one night they were woken by the captain of the vessel, telling them he had come to their 'rescue'. Two days later, they were on their way – much relieved – to Normanton, Queensland, where they boarded a passenger ship for Brisbane. By this time, the news surrounding their 'evacuation' from the subtropics of the Northern Territory had filtered south. On arriving in Brisbane, they were given a special mayoral reception attended by numerous dignitaries including the president of the Royal Society of Queensland and fellow anthropologist Walter Roth. A number of full-page newspaper features were also published on the expedition, replete with long interviews with both men. A few days later, they were heading south – Spencer to his opulent home in Melbourne, and Gillen to his modest dwelling at the telegraph station in Moonta, South Australia.

Two years after returning from their eleven-month venture, Spencer and Gillen published the results in *The Northern Tribes of Central Australia* (1904), which they described as a 'sequel' to their earlier *Native Tribes*. In the course of the expedition, they amassed a collection of more than one thousand objects: over eight hundred glass plate photographs, sixteen films, twenty-seven audio recordings and some five thousand pages of sketches, field notes, diary entries and correspondence. To this can be added almost the same quantity of material of a similar nature gathered during their previous work in Alice Springs. More than eight thousand museum objects result from their partnership, which ended with the death of Gillen in 1912. Although the major part of this collection is housed in Museum Victoria and the South Australian Museum, a significant proportion was distributed, through exchanges and sales, to more than thirty institutions across the world: the Museum of Natural History in New York, the Pitt Rivers Museum in Oxford, the Pigorini Museum of Ethnography in Rome, to name a few. Spencer and Gillen's two books, *The Native Tribes of Central Australia* and *The Northern Tribes of Central Australia* (totalling 1,454 pages with 448 photographs) were widely distributed, becoming anthropological classics. Spencer produced three further publications based on their work: *Across Australia* (1912), *The Arunta* (1927) and *Wanderings in Wild Australia* (1928). Kuklick has noted that between 1931 and 1976, no fewer than nine standard textbooks on anthropology refer to the work of Spencer and Gillen.[28]

As suggested at the outset, this extensive corpus of materials can be likened to an ethnographic field with its own borders, prohibited areas, distinct regions and particular histories. I now turn to some of the ways in which this field has been explored, studied and used.

The Post-Expedition Field

Up until the late 1920s, the vast ethnographic field constructed by Spencer and Gillen was zealously mined by contending parties in what was considered to be a major theoretical issue of the day, the problem of 'totemism'. Briefly, totemism referred to a 'spiritual relationship' between an individual and an animal, plant or natural phenomenon that served as the 'totem' of that person; it could also refer to a clan or other social group. Such totems were believed to be the ancestors of living individuals, delineating their ritual and social obligations. Nonetheless, no fixed agreement existed between anthropologists and social scientists over the meaning of totemism and, as Kuklick shows, many of the combatants employed Spencer and Gillen's ethnography to support their respective positions. This included Frazer, who used their work to substantiate his social evolutionist viewpoint in *The Golden Bough*, and Emile Durkheim, whose *Elementary Forms of the Religious Life* owed much to Spencer and Gillen's representation of Arrernte 'totemic beliefs'. Indeed, the original French title of Durkheim's book was subtitled *Le système totémique en Australie* (The Totemic System in Australia). Similarly, Sigmund Freud's *Totem and Taboo* (1913) borrowed elements from their work. Conversely, Franz Boas repudiated the kind of unilinear notions of human development associated with totemism. One of his acolytes, Alexander Goldenweiser, dismissed the debates around totemism as simply 'hazy theorizing'.[29]

Although social evolutionist ideas associated with totemism played a central role in propelling Spencer and Gillen to fame, the gap between theory and what they observed in regard to totems became ever more pronounced as they penetrated further into the intricate social world of their Aboriginal informants. They came to believe that some of the fundamental notions of totemism as promulgated by leading antagonists in these debates were 'quite inapplicable to our tribes'.[30] Nevertheless, the ethnographic field they had constructed, which included detailed accounts of 'Arrernte totems', served as a source of authority in both framing and legitimizing such debates, shaping the notion of totemism itself.

Just as the somewhat arcane arguments surrounding totemism were reaching their apogee, Spencer and Gillen's ethnography was employed for entirely different purposes. In 1925, the Australian artist Margaret Preston published a series of striking woodcut prints in a special edition of *Art in Australia*, based in part on Spencer and Gillen's photographs of Aboriginal artefacts.[31] Preston was the first in a long line of artists, designers, composers and writers to use Spencer and Gillen's rich ethnographic quarry. During the 1930s, architect Gert Sellheim incorporated Arrernte designs taken from Spencer and Gillen in his buildings, glassware and fabrics.[32] In 1941, the artist Nancy Mackenzie reinterpreted ground-painting designs, taken from

Spencer and Gillen's photographs of the Warumungu burial ceremony, for a work in the 'Exhibition of Australian Aboriginal Art and Its Application'. In 1951, the composer John Antill employed their photographs of Arrernte headdresses in staging his ballet *Corroboree*. The author Rex Ingamells recast their work in fictional form in his novel *Aranda Boy* (1952).[33]

Spencer and Gillen's ethnography has also served in recent times as an abundant source of ammunition for scholars working in the field of postcolonial theory, albeit in a strictly negative sense. Indeed, it has been studiously recruited to attack Spencer and Gillen themselves – and the project of anthropology in general.[34] Perhaps the most outstanding instance of this trend can be found in the work of Patrick Wolfe.[35] Focusing on Spencer and Gillen's support for the contentious notion that the Arrernte were unaware of the physiological cause of conception, Wolfe traces what he views as the theoretical and ideological roots of this notion and, further, how it informed the subsequent government policies of assimilation and child removal. Exploiting and analysing Spencer and Gillen's ethnography to an almost forensic degree, Wolfe concludes with a not particularly innovative proposition, that 'Australian Aboriginal policies have consistently been informed by anthropological representations of Aboriginal society'.[36]

Wolfe argues that anthropology is 'a kind of soliloquy – a Western discourse talking to itself'.[37] In other words, anthropological accounts of indigenous cultures are, for Wolfe, essentially Western constructs, informed by a theoretical framework that is 'overdetermined by its own internal conversation'.[38] I have similarly suggested that ethnographic accounts and collections are 'constructed' assemblages that operate as ethnographic fields in their own right. However, contrary to Wolfe's position, I have also suggested that while these assemblages are in part the product of Western theoretical imaginings, they are not necessarily detached from the originating field, or indeed from the ethnographic subjects. Rather, the material collected by anthropologists – including accounts of their ethnographic subjects – can, with the passage of time, assume a position of authority in the interpretation of the field and its indigenous peoples. Moreover, these peoples may themselves claim ownership of such material and incorporate it into projects of self-reconstruction. Indeed, the descendants of the Aboriginal groups Spencer and Gillen documented are perhaps the most avid excavators of their ethnography.

Several land claims under the *Aboriginal Land Rights (Northern Territory) Act 1976* were mounted with the assistance of Spencer and Gillen's work, including a successful claim by the Warumungu, whose traditions were documented during the 1901–02 expedition.[39] A native title case, successfully pursued by Arrernte peoples in relation to lands surrounding Alice Springs, also employed Spencer and Gillen's ethnography. A celebration of Arrernte culture, held at the Mbantua Festival in Alice Springs in 2013, used a wide range of material amassed by the anthropologists, including a Gillen portrait of an Aboriginal man that served as the festival's logo. Films shot by Spencer of the Titjingala ceremony in 1900 were carefully studied by local Aboriginal people and recreated in several performances during the festival. Secret-sacred objects (*tywerenge*) collected and documented by Spencer and Gillen – and stored in museums for over a century – have not only figured in claims to traditional lands, but are finding a place in the originating communities in projects of 'religious revival'.

Conclusion

In this chapter, I have argued that the 'ethnographic field' is not simply a given entity awaiting discovery; rather, it needs to be understood as an object that is assembled – intentionally and accidentally – through a complex array of variable relations of a conceptual, temporal and physical nature. I have also proposed that one of the primary variables in this constitutive process is the 'anthropological expedition', since it plays a central role in setting the temporal and physical limits of the field. Moreover, by sketching the emergence of the ethnographic field as an object of scientific enquiry during the latter half of the nineteenth century, and therefore as a site for the production of ethnographic knowledge, I have also tried to show that the ethnographic expedition and field were mutually constitutive. Here I have outlined how these developments collimated in the 1901–02 expedition of Spencer and Gillen, which I have used as a case study on the formation of a particular ethnographic field, physically located in Central Australia.

I have also suggested that the things acquired during an expedition and assembled in a single collection can be likened in themselves to an ethnographic field, with certain regions, borders and histories. Subsequently assembled in various configurations, this post-expedition 'field' becomes a resource for others in a multiplicity of projects. It may also assume a position of authority in the interpretation of the social world in which the expedition was originally undertaken. As I have attempted to demonstrate in the case of the Warumungu, Arrernte and other groups, the post-expedition field of ethnographic information may be adopted by the peoples subject to the original anthropological study and employed to revitalize their cultural sense of self. The complex connections between anthropological expeditions, the formation of ethnographic fields and the role of post-expedition fields in cultural formation have only been touched upon here. They demand further examination and development.

Philip Batty is Senior Curator in Anthropology at Museum Victoria. Formerly the director of the Central Australian Aboriginal Media Association, he has published three edited books and directed several documentary films.

Notes

1. James Wafer, 'After the Field', in Michael Jackson (ed.), *Things As They Are: New Directions in Phenomenological Anthropology* (Bloomington/Indianapolis, IN: Indiana University Press, 1996), 260.
2. Ibid.
3. George W. Stocking, *After Tylor: British Social Anthropology, 1888–1951* (Madison, WI: University of Wisconsin Press, 1995), 70, 96.
4. Lucretius, *De rerum natura* (Cambridge: Cambridge University Press, 1937).
5. See Adam Kuper, *The Invention of Primitive Society: Transformations of an Illusion* (London/New York: Routledge, 1988).
6. British Association for the Advancement of Science, *Notes and Queries on Anthropology, for the Use of Travellers and Residents in Uncivilized Lands* (London: E. Stanford, 1874).
7. William Edward Hanley Stanner, 'Howitt, Alfred William (1830–1908)', in *Australian Dictionary of Biography*, National Centre of Biography, Australian National University, http://adb.anu.edu.au/biography/howitt-alfred-william-510/text6037, published first in hardcopy in 1972, accessed online 12 December 2015.
8. See D. J. Mulvaney and J. H. Calaby, *So Much That Is New Baldwin Spencer 1860–1929* (Melbourne: University of Melbourne Press, 1985).
9. Baldwin Spencer, *Wanderings in Wild Australia*, Vol. 1 (London: Macmillan, 1912), 185.
10. John Mulvaney, Howard Morphy and Alison Petch, *My Dear Spencer: The Letters of F.J. Gillen to Baldwin Spencer* (Melbourne: Hyland House, 1997), 484.
11. Cited in Mulvaney and Calaby, *So Much That Is New*, 117.
12. Bronisław Malinowski, 'Review of "Across Australia" by Baldwin Spencer and F.J. Gillen', *Folk-Lore* 24 (1913), 278.

13. Henrika Kuklick, 'Personal Equations: Reflections on the History of Fieldwork, with Special Reference to Sociocultural Anthropology', *Isis* 102(1) (2011), 1.
14. University of Melbourne, Council Minutes, 1900–01, 165.
15. Mulvaney, Morphy and Petch, *My Dear Spencer*, 323.
16. Ibid., 284.
17. Baldwin Spencer and F. J. Gillen, *The Native Tribes of Central Australia* (New York: Dover Publications, 1968), 8.
18. Gillen's main informant, Unchalka ('King Charley') gave Gillen both his totemic affiliation and kinship name.
19. See Jason Gibson, 'Addressing the Arrernte: F.J. Gillen's Engwura Speech', *Australian Aboriginal Studies* 1 (2013), 57.
20. See Philip Batty, 'Cameras, Campfires and Sorcery: Spencer and Gillen in the Field', in Philip Batty, Lindy Allen and John Morton (eds), *The Photographs of Baldwin Spencer* (Melbourne: The Miegunyah Press, 2005), 124.
21. Spencer to Fison, 6 August 1901, Spencer manuscript collection, Museum Victoria Archives, xm 5867.
22. Baldwin Spencer, unpublished manuscript, Spencer's Personal Diary: Spencer and Gillen Expedition 1901–1902, Mitchell Library, Sydney, Sir Walter Baldwin Spencer Papers, 1880–1929, Call Number MLMSS 29, p. 17.
23. Ibid.
24. Ibid.
25. Robert Foster, 'Paper Yabber: The Messenger and the Message', *Aboriginal History* 22 (1998), 105.
26. Baldwin Spencer, unpublished manuscript, Spencer's Personal Diary: Spencer and Gillen Expedition 1901–1902, Mitchell Library, Sydney, Sir Walter Baldwin Spencer Papers, 1880–1929, Call Number MLMSS 29, p. 132.
27. *Chronicle* (Adelaide, South Australia), 25 January 1902, 30.
28. Henrika Kuklick, '"Humanity in the Chrysalis Stage": Indigenous Australians in the Anthropological Imagination', *British Journal for the History of Science* 39(4) (2006), 537n.
29. Ibid., 550.
30. Mulvaney, Morphy and Petch, *My Dear Spencer*, 419.
31. *Art in Australia*, Series 3, no. 11, March 1925.
32. Nicolas Peterson, 'The Use of Spencer and Gillen's Photography', in Batty, Allen and Morton, *The Photographs of Baldwin Spencer*, 154.
33. See Rex Ingamells, *Aranda Boy* (London: Longmans Green, 1952).
34. See Russell McGregor, 'The Idea of Racial Degeneration: Baldwin Spencer and the Aborigines of the Northern Territory', in Roy MacLeod and Donald Denoon (eds), *Health and Healing in Tropical Australia and Papua New Guinea* (Townsville: James Cook University Press, 1991), 23; and Colin Tatz, 'Genocide in Australia', AIATSIS Research Discussion Paper no. 8, 1999.

35. See Patrick Wolfe, *Settler Colonialism and the Transformation of Anthropology: The Politics and Poetics of an Ethnographic Event* (London: Cassell, 1999).
36. Ibid., 7.
37. Ibid., 4.
38. Ibid.
39. See Warumungu Land Claim in Report by the Aboriginal Land Commissioner to the Minister for Aboriginal Affairs and to the Administrator of the Northern Territory, 1991. Report no. 31. The report is publically available at the National Library of Australia (1259459; N 346.94290432 A938; NL 346.94290432 A938).

Bibliography

Batty, Philip. 'Cameras, Campfires and Sorcery: Spencer and Gillen in the Field', in Philip Batty, Lindy Allen and John Morton (eds), *The Photographs of Baldwin Spencer* (Melbourne: The Miegunyah Press, 2005), 124–29.

British Association for the Advancement of Science. *Notes and Queries on Anthropology, for the Use of Travellers and Residents in Uncivilized Lands.* London: E. Stanford, 1874.

Durkheim, Emile. *The Elementary Forms of the Religious Life.* Oxford: Oxford University Press, 2001.

Fison, Lorimer, and William Howitt. *Kamilaroi and Kurnai: Group-Marriage and Relationship, and Marriage by Elopement; Drawn Chiefly from the Usage of the Australian Aborigines; Also the Kurnai Tribe, Their Customs in Peace and War.* New York: Oosterhout N.B.: Anthropological Publications, 1967.

Foster, Robert. 'Paper Yabber: The Messenger and the Message'. *Aboriginal History* 22 (1998), 105–15.

Frazer, James. *The Golden Bough: A Study in Magic and Religion.* Abridged edition. London: Macmillan, 1922.

Freud, Sigmund. *Totem and Taboo: Resemblances Between the Psychic Lives of Savages and Neurotics.* New York: Moffat Yard and Company, 1918.

Gibson, Jason. 'Addressing the Arrernte: F.J. Gillen's Engwura Speech'. *Australian Aboriginal Studies* 1 (2013), 57–72.

Ingamells, Rex. *Aranda Boy.* London: Longmans Green, 1952.

Kuklick, Henrika. '"Humanity in the Chrysalis Stage": Indigenous Australians in the Anthropological Imagination'. *British Journal for the History of Science* 39(4) (2006), 535–67.

———. 'Personal Equations: Reflections on the History of Fieldwork, with Special Reference to Sociocultural Anthropology'. *Isis* 102(1) (2011), 1–33.

Kuper, Adam. *The Invention of Primitive Society: Transformations of an Illusion.* London/New York: Routledge, 1988.

Lucretius. *De rerum natura.* Cambridge: Cambridge University Press, 1937.

Malinowski, Bronisław. 'Review of "Across Australia" by Baldwin Spencer and F.J. Gillen'. *Folk-Lore* 24 (1913), 278–79.

McGregor, Russell. 'The Idea of Racial Degeneration: Baldwin Spencer and the Aborigines of the Northern Territory', in Roy MacLeod and Donald Denoon (eds), *Health and Healing in Tropical Australia and Papua New Guinea* (Townsville: James Cook University Press, 1991), 23–34.

Mulvaney, D.J., and J.H. Calaby. *So Much That Is New: Baldwin Spencer 1860–1929.* Melbourne: University of Melbourne Press, 1985.

Mulvaney, John, Howard Morphy and Alison Petch. *My Dear Spencer: The Letters of F.J. Gillen to Baldwin Spencer.* Melbourne: Hyland House, 1997.

Peterson, Nicolas. 'The Use of Spencer and Gillen's Photography', in Philip Batty, Lindy Allen and John Morton (eds), *The Photographs of Baldwin Spencer* (Melbourne: The Miegunyah Press, 2005), 154–90.

Spencer, Baldwin and F.J. Gillen. *Across Australia.* 2 Vols. London: Macmillan, 1912.

———. *The Arunta.* 2 Vols. London: Macmillan, 1927.

———. *The Native Tribes of Central Australia.* New York: Dover Publications, 1968.

———. *The Northern Tribes of Central Australia.* London: Macmillan, 1904.

Spencer, Sir Baldwin. *Wanderings in Wild Australia.* Vol. 1. London: Macmillan, 1928.

Stanner, William Edward Hanley. 'Howitt, Alfred William (1830–1908)', in *Australian Dictionary of Biography*, National Centre of Biography, Australian National University, http://adb.anu.edu.au/biography/howitt-alfred-william-510/text6037, published first in hardcopy in 1972, accessed online 12 December 2015.

Stocking, George W. *After Tylor: British Social Anthropology, 1888–1951.* Madison, WI: University of Wisconsin Press, 1995.

Tatz, Colin. 'Genocide in Australia'. AIATSIS Research Discussion Paper no. 8, 1999.

Wafer, James. 'After the Field', in Michael Jackson (ed.), *Things As They Are: New Directions in Phenomenological Anthropology.* (Bloomington/Indianapolis, IN: Indiana University Press, 1996), 260–72.

Wolfe, Patrick. *Settler Colonialism and the Transformation of Anthropology: The Politics and Poetics of an Ethnographic Event.* London: Cassell, 1999.

Chapter 2

RECEIVING GUESTS

THE CAMBRIDGE ANTHROPOLOGICAL EXPEDITION TO TORRES STRAITS 1898

Jude Philp

The Expedition and the *Reports*

In 1898, seven Englishmen travelled to the Torres Strait to conduct fieldwork. Although their research centred on the people of Torres Strait, the men also conducted comparative work in three British colonies: Queensland, British New Guinea and British North Borneo. Their expedition results were principally disseminated through six volumes, *The Reports of the Cambridge Anthropological Expedition to Torres Straits* (hereafter *Reports*), published between 1901 and 1935.[1] Some scholars view the expedition as a forerunner to the new age of anthropology, while others regard it as the definitive nineteenth-century 'salvage' expedition.[2]

The expedition leader, ethnologist Alfred C. Haddon (1855–1940), had first been to Torres Strait in 1888 as a zoologist. Focusing on Actiniaria (sea anemone) of Mer and Mabuyag, two islands with differing geological foundations, he worked for six months but was distracted by a growing interest in his Islander companions during his daily dredges. He determined to return with an expedition that could fully document the psychological capacities and physical appearances of the region's people and to salvage their precolonial forms of language, arts, technology and science. Ethnography, the description of a particular people, would be at the core of this expedition. In 1896, Haddon began to select his ideal team.

Haddon chose William Rivers to lead the comparative anthropology team's work in physiology and psychology, which included medical doctors Charles Myers, Charles Seligman and William McDougall. Haddon and his student Anthony Wilkin would concentrate on ethnography, with Myers also documenting music and Seligman conducting comparative ethnographic and anthropological studies in British New Guinea. The self-taught Pacific linguist, schoolteacher Sidney Ray, led the work on languages.

Subsequent anthropologists have been drawn to thinking about the expedition for its ground-breaking inclusion of psychology, broad anthropological framework and the prominence and academic influence of its members.[3] Haddon, Rivers and Seligman had an immense impact on anthropology, while Rivers, McDougall and Myers were equally significant in the fields of psychology and sociology.[4] However, the scale of the investigation and the composition of information in the *Reports* have led some to dismiss the expedition as antiquated. One such dismissal comes from anthropologist Michael Taussig in his discussion of a photograph of five of the expedition's members (see Figure 2.1).

Figure 2.1 Back row, left to right: William Rivers, Charles Seligman, Sidney Ray, Anthony Wilkin. Seated: Alfred Haddon. Mabuyag, 1898. Museum of Archaeology and Anthropology, University of Cambridge (MAA) (N.23035.ACH2). With permission of MAA.

... Truly mischievous, even camp, certainly playful, this image shows five happy men, unkempt, barefoot, trousers rolled to the calf, posing for the camera not in pith helmets but in crazy-looking felt hats...

They are having fun with the camera, for sure, but they are far from staging ethnographers-at-work. And there is not a native in sight. Certainly not any naked ones. This is not parody. This is not a worked-out theatricalization of colonial realism. After all, these are self-confident Englishmen who fit right in. These guys are pre-Copernican in the sense that they precede the Great Revolution in Anthropology credited to Malinowski of 'participant observation', and they boast no effort to fraternize with the natives, only with themselves.[5]

The photograph that caught Taussig's eye was one of several hundred made by the team during their seven months in Torres Strait. Another (see Figure 2.2) directly refutes and subverts his reading that the expedition was about these self-confident Englishmen. In the second image, four men from Mabuyag Island sit in positions matching those of the Cambridge team, with a nod to the skills and positions of each. Gizu, for example, seated in the same position as expedition leader Haddon, was recognized as the most senior and knowledgeable of the people who assisted the expedition at Mabuyag. The relationship expressed through the twin images transforms Taussig's pre-Copernican colonial jokers into proto-anthropologists. The 'natives'

Figure 2.2 Waria, Papi, Noboa. Seated: Gizu. Mabuyag Island, 1898 (MAA N.22988.ACH2). With permission of MAA.

are not just entwined in the photographic frame; they are partners in the laughter shared between the expedition members and an audience who is none too distant. Both images were taken at the same time, smack bang in the middle of the village for all to see.[6]

This chapter mimics the juxtaposition of these two images. I argue that the Englishmen and the Islanders were part of a shared project to document Islander history. My focus is on the unfolding of events at Mer, in the eastern Torres Strait, where a great deal of time and resources were spent in the documentation of Malu ceremonies. The period of the expedition's work at Mer has been much studied.[7] Anthropologist Jeremy Beckett, for example, has observed the nuances of Haddon's writing that substantiate his authoritative account, interleaving the terms 'friends' and 'savages' and moving deftly between 'the present' and 'the past'.[8] As Taussig wrote (above), the Englishmen predate the 'participant observation' revolution of twentieth-century anthropology – they did not immerse themselves in Islanders' worlds. But Haddon did leave space for Islanders to immerse themselves in the work of the Englishmen. I argue that individual Islanders took up the opportunity to be 'observers' of their own culture. As I will demonstrate, specific Islanders had critical roles in the direction of the fieldwork and in the composition of the *Reports*.

It is easy to 'lose' the Islander presence in the expedition texts. The *Reports* are a dry, disjointed and archaic publication, partly because Haddon maintained many of the divisions of the 'Notes and Queries' format that he had used in his first ethnography of the Torres Strait, written when still a zoologist.[9] Educationalist Martin Nakata has scrutinized the *Reports* for the effect such science had on Islanders during colonial and neocolonial governance (1903–2000s). His study makes plain the constructions that worked to present the lives of Islanders as 'data' supporting a Victorian British model of the world, albeit one with a humanist intellectual tinge.[10] Both the structure and the content of the *Reports* are criticized by anthropologist Fredrik Barth, who described them as being of 'no great consequence'.[11] For Barth (as for Philip Batty writing in this volume), it was the change effected in anthropology that marks the expedition's significance. Barth narrows these changes down to four: taking the discipline from 'armchair' to 'field'; changing the subject matter from the selection of 'facts' to the cacophony of life; the development of the genealogical method; and the conversion of Seligman and Rivers to anthropology, which enabled the rise of a new generation of 'modern' anthropologists.[12] Barth ignores the expedition's technological innovations, yet their use of photography and film both as documentary devices and methodological tools would become standard. He does, however, recognize that Islanders had a critical part in the 'conversion' of Seligman and Rivers. Barth's recognition of Islanders as contributors to the discipline is important for understanding the *Reports*. For while the *Reports* conform to nineteenth-century salvage ethnography texts in the copious accumulation and ordering of ethnographic 'facts', the anchoring of such 'facts' to named individuals creates an altogether purposeful document for its Islander contributors.[13] The Meriam-le (people of Mer) who background and foreground the sixth volume, *Sociology, Magic and Religion of the Eastern Islanders*, are the focus of this chapter.

The Plan: Salvaging the Past through Ethnography

'Now is the time to record', wrote Haddon just prior to the expedition. 'The change that has come over the uttermost parts of the world during the last fifty years is almost incredible.'[14] Haddon's anxiety was mediated by his faith in 'salvage' ethnography, the ability to retrieve the past through the memories of older men such as those he had talked with in 1888. He defined anthropology as 'what man is, what he thinks, what he aspires after, what he does', whereas 'salvage' ethnography was the historical description of a particular group of people, obtained through a study of the memories and folklore of the living.[15] The time period Haddon hoped to 'salvage' largely predated the extensive commercialization of pearl-shell fishing that swept the region from 1864.[16]

The underlying conceptual frame of historical transformation was evidently understood differently by the expedition's English and Islander participants. Haddon's history was dominated by his background in biology.[17] James Urry defines Haddon's ethnological model as 'the reconstruction of the evolutionary and historical relationship between groups located within specific geographical and historical settings, based in evidence drawn from the analysis of "racial" types, languages, customs and material culture'.[18] Through the excavation of Islanders' oral histories, along with their customs, Haddon and Rivers hoped to understand the pattern of migration and movement that joined and separated the peoples of the region. Physiology and psychology were additional methods to see into the biological past.

An indication of the Islander understanding of history is the large number of compositions from oral histories, or 'myths and legends' as they are often titled, authored by Islanders in the *Reports*. This style of history continues today. 'The Muiar' is a modern example of this kind of text, including discussion of geographic features and social behavioural models. Such texts are related as stories to young people, but reveal deeper spiritual meanings to initiated or older members of a community.[19]

> Four men, known as the Muiar felled a cotton-tree (kob) and made a canoe from it by hollowing out its trunk. They dragged it down towards Las, blazing a trail of cleared ground which can still be seen. The Muiar did not put their canoe into the water, however, because branches of sem, the yellow flowering hibiscus, had been hung at the boundary of Las. These were recognized and respected as a sign of gelar (taboo), the people of Las having shown in that manner that 'outside people' – people who did not belong to Las – must not set foot in Las territory until the branches of sem had been removed. The Muiar turned back: they were men who belonged to Piad. On the way, all four turned to stone, one at Sager, one at Zeum, one at Pairmed, and the fourth at Korkor.[20]

This kind of history was eagerly captured in numerous nineteenth-century studies, but it should not be confused with European interpretations of such material. For Islanders, these stories contain symbolic and more obvious histories of the orator and their island(s). The same format of 'mythic' storytelling also envelops stories that Europeans recognize as 'history', such as the arrival of missionaries known as 'The Coming of the Light'.[21]

The Expedition Teams

Across Torres Strait communities, age plays an important part in the rights and duties of individuals. Older people are generally deferred to, respected for their knowledge, experience and position in society. First and second cousins grow up together as 'cousin-brothers' and 'cousin-sisters', forming a life-long bond that is often closer than a sibling relationship. The Englishmen could be termed 'age-mates': unrelated men who shared experiences on a personal as well as a professional level. All had associations with the University of Cambridge except for Ray and Seligman. Seligman and McDougall worked together at St Thomas' Hospital in London and they, like Myers and Wilkin, were young unmarried men in their twenties. Rivers was in his thirties, Haddon and Ray in their early forties. It is significant that many of the Englishmen were Freemasons, a secret society that shared similarities with Meriam-le's own fraternities.[22]

Of those people who worked closely with the Englishmen on Mer, Pasi is the most prominent. It is useful to relate something of his background.[23] Pasi's parents had probably seen the officers from HMS *Fly* land at Mer in April 1845, part of the trickle of foreigners who visited in the decades before commercial pearling began in 1864. Pasi's generation experienced the changes to social life brought about by the subsequent years of colonization. This had involved extensive social and geographical reorganization as the people from the twenty-seven or so villages across Mer, Dauar and Waier were encouraged to move to the western side of the island to be nearer to the church and school. Meriam-le were also encouraged to nominate leaders who would be responsible to the colonial government. A court was established to meet the needs of local dispute settlement, which also relied upon locally nominated councillors. Men and women of Pasi's generation, schooled at the missionary school, became pioneer missionaries to coastal communities in British New Guinea and northern Australia.[24]

The first years of the 1870s saw the London Missionary Society (LMS) established in the Strait. Pioneer Reverend Samuel McFarlane determined that Mer was the most suitable site for the principal mission station.[25] He established a school and industrial college for men and women across the region (including those from British New Guinea). Pasi went to this school and was serving as a policeman in 1888. In this capacity, he spent time with Haddon over the five months of his first visit, contributing to the dredging and collecting work. Along with Baton and Mamai, Pasi spent long days in the hot sun, chatting with and assisting the young zoologist.[26] In 1888 (and in 1898), Haddon stayed in the LMS mission house, situated slightly up the hill from the school. By 1898, Pasi was no longer a policeman but one of two leaders given the title '*mamoose*'. Ostensibly, the paid positions of police officer and *mamoose* were government appointed. In reality, the local systems of leadership were folded into the enforced system of colonial governance.[27]

Pasi's position as *mamoose* of Dauar was not, therefore, just a factor of his being a bright and talented member of the Meriam community. He had inherited a position of some importance within a central and spiritually potent fraternity that the expedition labelled the 'Cult of Malu-Bomai'. When the expedition arrived, it was Pasi, now in his forties, who assisted them most. Arei (or Harry), the *mamoose* of Mer, was older, frail and spoke less Creole, the trade English fast becoming the principal language of the whole region.[28] In what Myers assumed to be bragging, but was more likely a straightforward assertion of fact, Pasi told him one evening over dinner that when 'the old man died', he would be *mamoose* of both Mer and Dauar, which in due course happened.²⁹

Along with Pasi, other Meriam men of his generation became closely involved in the expedition. First cousins Debe Wali and Jimmy Rice of Dauar were paid as cooks and assistants to the psychology team at one pound a month. They predominantly supplied extensive 'data' about the social structure of Meriam life.³⁰ Haddon described them in his popular expedition account *Head-Hunters: Black, White and Brown*: 'they afforded us much amusement, no little instruction, and a very fair amount of moral discipline'.³¹ They were photographed with the entire English team and Haddon's domestic assistant Ontong (see Figure 2.3). Police sergeant Jimmy Dei's role was slightly more

Figure 2.3 At Mer 1889, (left to right) seated: Jimmy Rice, Debe Wali; second row: Alfred Haddon, Charlie Ontong, Anthony Wilkin; third row: William Rivers, Sidney Ray; back row: William McDougall, Charles Myers, Charles Seligman (MAA N.22900.ACH2). With permission of MAA.

ambiguous; he assisted in the documentation of garden knowledge, and was one of the few invited for dinner with Haddon and the others. Haddon certainly had respect for him, singling him out as 'a very intelligent man'.[32] Three older men of Arei's generation, Enoka, Wanu and Ulai, were prominent sources of information about the past, and makers of cultural items collected during the expedition.[33]

Haddon partly attributed the cooperation of the Islanders with the Englishmen to their position as some of the few white people interested in 'them' at all.[34] Ron Day, a descendant of Pasi and of Jimmy Dei ('the two kings' as Haddon called them),[35] has argued that his ancestors were likely to have involved themselves because of concerns over how their spirituality would be rendered through the Englishmen's work. For this reason, Day suggests, individual Meriam-le put great effort into guiding the focus of the Englishmen, and in ensuring that interviews were with the most relevant owners of particular knowledge.[36] In their research on Haddon's archive, Day and linguist and elder Ephraim Bani (from Mabuyag) looked into the knowledge that Meriam-le directed into the expedition's research and scrutinized the relationships forged between particular Islanders and Englishmen.[37] I will follow their lead here, through the *Reports* and the journals of Haddon and Myers in particular. The fieldwork at Mer was the only time the Englishmen worked together in one location, and part of their time was spent working through methods and practicalities. This was also the period when, to paraphrase Haddon, they were most at the mercy of their informants.[38]

Arrival

The Murray Islands of Mer, Dauar and Waier are the most eastern islands of the Torres Strait, situated just inside the tip of the Great Barrier Reef. To approach from the northwest by sea, as the expedition members did, is to see the form of Gelum, the boy from Moa island who turned into a dugong to escape his mother before finding a home at Mer. No doubt the Englishmen had been alerted to this history by Haddon during their 'homework' on the journey out.[39]

Piloted by Spear, the pearling schooner *Freya* had taken two days to battle the Sager seasonal winds from the nearby island of Erub. On board were Haddon, Seligman, Ray and Rivers along with Ontong, Haddon's domestic assistant, and Finau, the Samoan LMS resident teacher. Landing on 6 May, they were received by Pasi and Arei at the house of John (Jack) Bruce, another expedition collaborator, long-term resident and quasi-colonial government representative. Pasi and Haddon took time to talk over old times while they walked up and down the sand beach at Baur.[40] The following day, the Englishmen moved to the old LMS mission house that would be their home and laboratory for the next four months. At the end of the church service the following day, many waited to shake hands with Haddon, and accepted his invitation to go up to the 'laboratory' to see his lantern slides from 1888. They overwhelmed Haddon with their delight and enthusiasm. It was, he later wrote, both jolly and gratifying 'to take up our friendship where we left it'.[41]

Throughout the expedition, photographs mediated relationships.[42] Indeed, when men and women in ones and twos returned to see the images again the next day, Arei explained to Haddon that the produce they brought with them – thirty-six bunches of bananas and over fifty coconuts – were gifts to him.[43] In return, Haddon commemorated the gifts with a photograph that included five men: police sergeant and noted horticulturalist Jimmy Dei; policemen Baton and Basser (or Barsa); and the cousins Debe Wali and Jimmy Rice. This photograph, which captured both friendships and the bounty of this fertile island, was then incorporated into subsequent lantern slide shows.

By 10 May, Haddon's former students Myers, McDougall and Wilkin arrived and quickly fell into the established pattern of work. Often at Pasi's invitation, Haddon spent his time visiting significant sites and the people connected to them. McDougall and Myers worked with Seligman at the impromptu surgery to treat the sick. Rivers conducted colour and other psychological tests on the surgery patients. Ray had hourly morning sessions with Arei, recording the older style of Meriam-mir language with the younger Pasi translating.[44]

Noted in his diary and occasionally in *Head-Hunters*, but not in the *Reports*, are events like the evening 'play' on 10 May, one of a series of seasonal dances and songs given and received between the villagers across the island during the Sager season.

On Saturday 14 May, Pasi invited all the Englishmen to Dauar for a picnic, although only Haddon, Seligman and Ray took up the invitation. The party visited and documented a number of story sites at Dauar, including at Giar Pit where Pasi was from. A few days later, Pasi invited Haddon to Las, the other place of significance to his identity and responsibilities, the village of his ancestor Koit, on the northeastern coast of Mer. Haddon had recorded details of the Malu 'cult' at Las in 1888, and had organized and photographed a 're-enactment' of some of the associated dances, but he was keen to see what else he might find out. They set off on the long walk in company with Pasi's cousin-brother Gadodo and Rivers, who was eager to see how easy it would be to take the scientific equipment over to that side of the island from their residence.[45] That night, Haddon and Rivers were introduced to the church deacon Enoka during the evening Christian service led by Pasi. Enoka was one of the Zagareb-le men responsible for beating Malu's sacred drums (Wasikor and Namau) and singing Malu's songs. The following day, Rivers returned to the surgery and so missed the 'beautifully mournful couplet' of Malu sung by Enoka that morning.[46] Haddon, keen to 'pick up some information of which I had previously gained clues',[47] then accompanied Pasi to Mamai's house a little further along the beach. Pasi, Gadodo and Mamai had posed for Haddon's camera in 1888 as young smiling men, their fathers were all *zogo-le* (officiates) in the Malu ceremonies. When Haddon had asked young men about their history in 1888, he had often received the reply, 'me young man, me no savvy [know], old man he savvy'. He interpreted this to mean that the younger men were ignorant of their past.[48] It is more likely that it was only in 1898 that men such as Pasi, Gadodo and Mamai were in a sufficiently senior position to talk about their knowledge.

For the next two-and-a-half weeks, the expedition members went through their scientific paces, carefully inscribing the things they were told and the results of their measurements.[49] Money and trade goods were paid for people's involvement, which for Myers and Haddon explained the Meriam-le's preparedness to involve themselves in the work. The medical team had the assistance of Debe Wali and Jimmy Rice, while Pasi and Haddon (with Ray, Seligman or Wilkin) talked with older men and organized things for photography and purchase. From the Englishmen's view, the psychological tests were seemingly boring and repetitive, and quite often required pauses to fix equipment or settle a fundamental technical problem.[50] For Haddon, the ethnological work was plagued by people's reticence to give information about Malu and *doiom*, the *zogo* (spiritually active) stones used to control weather, influence garden produce and fishing, and manipulate the futures of individual lives.

Still, a good pace was made. Haddon managed to get some of the details of the Malu ceremonies that he had missed in 1888. Rivers, Myers and McDougall resolved the problems of their experimental equipment in the bright and windy conditions. Then Seligman, Wilkin, Ray and Haddon left for British New Guinea. Myers noted his relief at the relative quiet: '[I] look forward to a glorious six weeks of uninterrupted research'.[51] No sooner was this written than the psychology team was pulled back to their ethnographic work as Islanders celebrated Queen Victoria's birthday with a day of dancing, play and singing. Rivers, Myers and McDougall did eventually get to their psychological testing but, of the people who presented themselves as test subjects, more seemed to be interested in having their photographs taken than in deciding if they could hear a faint sound through a tube, identify the colour of a wool strand or describe the relative weight of objects.[52]

By the time Haddon, Wilkin and Ray returned (Seligman continued his comparative studies in British New Guinea), two months had passed and Rivers had become interested in genealogy. At first, he had collected family trees to understand how certain characteristics, like colour-blindness, may be inherited. But he was soon consumed with their complexity and detail, sometimes extending back five generations, and the way they hinted at ceremonial and property divisions across Meriam society.[53]

Within two days of their return, Haddon was excited to learn that everything for the 'revival' of ceremonies relating to Malu was finally ready to go. Myers, who later co-authored the Malu chapter with Haddon, had predominantly been working on psychology and medicine, so Pasi had probably been the one to work towards this goal during Haddon's absence.

> All was supposed to be ready on Thursday aft. (July 28th) so we walked over but found nothing ready ... We all had an evening meal in Gadodo's house, potted meat, yams & coconut water. We spent the evening in yarning & we got some songs in the phonograph. We were all fairly disappointed & it looked as if we were to be thoroughly sold.[54]

It was, by Myers and Haddon's account, a close-run thing that the ceremonies happened at all. Finau, the LMS mission worker, had rallied a number of deacons, possibly including Enoka, against the performances. Haddon wrote that he and a number of others had spoken 'sternly' to all concerned so that the ceremonies could go ahead.[55]

The next morning, Haddon borrowed Wasikor, the named drum associated with Malu, from its custodian at Ulag to try and force the beginning of the performances.[56] That lunchtime at Gadodo's house, they were given a soup of octopus, which was possibly a ceremonial act in reference to a significant point in the stories of Malu-Bomai. Shortly after lunch, 'it was soon evident that something was about to happen'.[57] That 'something' was several performances connected to

Figure 2.4 'Singing at Las', 1898: note the presence of Malu's two *seri-seri* feathered clubs in the foreground and, to the left, Kilerup in an attitude of religious ecstasy. Men in the central group include initiates with feathered ornaments, and with painted bodies, the singers Gasu, Enoka, Ulai and Wanu. Gadodo standing at centre with John Bruce, William Rivers, Sidney Ray in the crowd (MAA N.22988.ACH2). With permission of MAA.

initiation into Malu ceremonies, with numerous participants at the two main ceremonial grounds (Figure 2.4). All of the Englishmen came together to watch and to assist in documenting the event.

That Pasi and others had been busy negotiating this performance during Haddon, Ray and Wilkin's absence is evident in the photographs and recordings from the day. Performers appeared ochred and with the appropriate hair ornaments, particular exotic and seasonal bird feathers depending on their clan. The participants knew their parts in the dances and songs essential to the ceremonies. Around fifteen senior men and a few dozen bystanders were witness to the performances at the *au kop* (sacred ground) at Gazir where (in pantomime) the masks were 'revealed', and at Las where larger groups of men, women and children watched the public dances at the sand beach. Despite Haddon having documented Malu ceremonies in 1888, and despite his repeated questioning in May, it was only at this moment that 'Bomai' – the *zogo* (sacred) name for Malu – was revealed to him, and to the Western world.

Figure 2.5 *Mai*, worn only by *giri-giri le* (bird clan men) at the conclusion of the Malu ceremonies (MAA Z.9443). With permission of MAA.

Over the next month, as Haddon chased further details about Malu, Myers worked with singers and the phonograph to make wax cylinder recordings, while Ray worked with Pasi and Arei on the esoteric language used in Malu's songs. 'Though this particular custom may have died out many years ago, the memory of it was green', wrote Haddon.[58]

Around forty objects associated with Malu were commissioned and collected. Of the Malu heirlooms, the *mai* (pearl-shell) once worn by the *giri-giri le* (parrot men) was exceptional (Figure 2.5), the only remaining one on Mer, but Haddon was unsuccessful in buying either the *seri-seri* (Malu's star-shaped clubs) or the drum Wasikor. Commissioned replicas included the initiates' belts, and the *zogo-le kadik* (arm guards). Presumably decisions about what to give and what to withhold had been a part of the closed discussions and negotiations between Meriam-le. It was only after great deliberation that Wanu and Enoka had agreed to make replica masks of Bomai and Malu. They requested as payment gold coins for the church donation plate, and determined to make them out of cardboard. Neither felt it appropriate to make such powerful masks from the original material of turtle-shell.[59] The finished products brought a number of men to the mission house to see them. Gododo, Kilerup and 'another man' wore them at the *au kop* at Kiam for the cinematograph, filmed the day before Haddon, Rivers, Ray and Wilkin's departure.[60] It was the first act of cinematic documentation in an anthropological context.[61]

All the while Haddon did not lose his interest in *zogo* stones and was particularly excited by one even Bruce did not know of, 'Tomog Zogo', of which Jimmy Dei was part custodian. It was used to good effect to predict the arrival of the *Olive Branch* that would take the Englishmen away from Mer for good.

Thanks to Pasi, Debe Wali, Jimmy Rice, Arei, Kilerup, Wanu, Ulai, Enoka and Jimmy Dei, the expedition documented parts of what Islanders call 'deep history'. Deep history includes the spirituality of actions, the purposes and meanings of stories, songs and particular pieces of material culture. Haddon was unable to fully appreciate the spirituality of what he saw and heard, expressing disappointment at the literal meaning of one chant despite being witness to the effect this and other chants had on the singers and audience.[62] He did, however, appreciate the purpose of what he was told. Years later, writing to Bruce about the Meriam reception of Volume 6, he asked, 'Did they mind the Bomai mask being published? And do they object to women now seeing it?'[63]

The continuing importance and purposefulness of Malu in Meriam life and for people's identity is one reason that Haddon's *Reports* are still read by Meriam-le. It joins people of the present day to those who, by 1898, were long dead. Despite Haddon's anxieties that such ceremonial spiritual practices were disappearing, Malu continues to exert its importance in acts of law, ceremony and dance, and has had the capacity to embrace Christianity and modern life.[64]

A Time and a Place

In a place where things are not understood to happen casually or coincidentally, it is important to recognize the possibility that if the expedition had arrived in a different season they may not have witnessed Malu dances, but rather turtle hunting or other vital aspects of cultural life. The Sager season when the Englishmen arrived was a time of both secular and spiritually powerful dances, a time appropriate for Malu performances.[65] From the end of May to September, days of dancing were witnessed, mostly explained by the Englishmen as sporadic or 'the fashion' of the moment. These activities were seldom treated as chapters like Malu or prohibited acts like warfare; rather, the seasonal performances were segregated as footnotes or anecdotal asides. The seasonal corpus documented in the diaries and photographs of the expedition included two competitive kinds of performances with games, quizzes and novel choreography and singing between villages. On the night of Myers, MacDougall and Wilkin's arrival, one dance depicted the movements of the Thursday Island carousel ride.[66] At Las, one song was based around a popular and rollicking 1860s American spiritual.[67] Along with these innovative dances between villages, there were days spent by men in competitive top spinning. Four feasts were given. One commemorated the end of a period of mourning; ceremonial feasting gifts by women included two *kakatut* (gifts acknowledging relations). On 24 May, a full day and night of dances and games were performed under the 'flag' of Queen Victoria's birthday. As these included formal dances from the Meriam canon, they became useful to Myers in his descriptions of former times, and some are described in the *Reports* as 'funeral dances' and 'harvest dances'. The Englishmen, of course, also presented entertainments. Their portable photographic studio, their attempts to introduce a competitive game element to the psychological tests, the numerous lantern slide shows and the long talks of past times seem to have been neatly incorporated into this time of community festivity.

The Sager season signalled an appropriate time for Malu ceremonies and, I argue, was the rationale for the participation of particular Meriam-le with the appropriate positions to perform. Pasi, Gadodo and Mamai introduced Haddon to those who were custodians of Malu's objects, and they facilitated Haddon's access to sacred grounds connected to the performances. Pasi and his cousins may have also made it possible for the psychologists to do their work. To explore this possibility, it is necessary to turn to that one thing academics agree was truly remarkable about the expedition – the genealogical method.

Every Man's Place Is Known

> The Murray Islands were so small that everything was strictly regulated, every man's position was perfectly well known, and his social and religious duties were fixed by the mere fact of parentage (real or by adoption)...
> —Alfred C. Haddon, *Reports of the Cambridge Anthropological Expedition to Torres Straits*

The period of the expedition was characterized by extraordinary disruption to the 'strictly regulated' system described in the *Reports* quoted above. From the 1860s, bullying and violent attacks by foreign fishermen had forced some residents from their villages.[68] By the 1880s, many had migrated to Mer's western coast.

Rivers' genealogies created further problems for the people of this 'strictly regulated' place because of the way they were acquired and composed. Meriam-le only agreed to give their family details in one-to-one meetings with Rivers. Each subject was asked who their 'true' mother, father and siblings were. Rivers claimed to have kept out error by continuously cross-checking, but it is evident that because the Englishman was confused by the multiple names an individual may use in his or her lifetime, this cross-checking was prone to error. Because he was originally looking at bloodlines ('pedigrees') that could indicate inherited traits picked up in the psychological work, Rivers deliberately excluded adoptions, a common practice but one kept secret from the adoptee's generation. By the time he reached Mabuyag in October, Rivers recognized the greater purpose of the pedigrees for charting people's social relations. He attempted to fill the gaps, but in making his genealogical charts Rivers achieved neither the bloodlines he wanted, nor the kinship data that revealed the essential nature of Meriam society as he understood it.[69]

The twenty-seven numbered genealogies were used rigorously by Haddon throughout *Reports* Volume 6, devoted to the Eastern Islanders. Pasi, for example, is usually identified as 'Pasi (27)', this being the number allocated to his family line at Giar Pit. By systematically cross-referencing people with their genealogies, Haddon inadvertently created maps of who did and who did not involve themselves in the expedition project. For Meriam-le today, this is also a map of the veracity of particular information.[70] Two men from the village of Er serve as an example. 'Joe Brown/Poloaii (18c)' was an older man, a choreographer and a person at the centre of the Queen Victoria birthday dances; he appears also in the background of photographs of feasts. But he is not an author of information in the *Reports* and this distance from the expedition's work is reflected in the minimal genealogy that accounts for him. The short genealogy not only reflects his lack of direct involvement but also indicates that his inherited information and knowledge were not part of the Englishmen's document of Meriam-le past. In contrast, 'Enoka (18a)' was directly involved in the expedition's work; he authored stories, was central to the Malu performance documentation and contributed intangible and tangible heritage items. His direct involvement is reflected in his genealogy, which covers four generations, and includes his siblings' children and his paternal aunts' children. He also ensured that his connection to

Dawita, his adopted son, was recorded (although in a footnote rather than in the genealogies).

In their accounts, Rivers and Myers claim that their test subjects were drawn from across Mer's population of four hundred or so. Throughout the expedition's work, this 'even-ness' was drawn almost exclusively from adult men. By cross-referencing individual names in the *Reports* psychology volume with those of Volume 6, it is possible to further investigate this claim. Myers tested fifty-two men, McDougall fifty and Rivers thirty-nine.[71] Many men did tests with all three, so in all there were around seventy men who consented to be tested. Myers was most successful in engaging people to do more than one test, and a great many did three or four tests each. From Myers' perspective, 'his' fifty men came for tobacco and a photograph; Rivers believed that they came out of consideration for Haddon. McDougall, it would seem, got on with the job at hand without too many words to say.

So where did these seventy men come from? The population of two particular areas was most committed to the studies: people with affiliations to Dauar and to Samsep (which includes Las), with nineteen and thirteen men respectively. These are areas of importance within Malu's ceremonies and histories, and they were also areas in which Pasi had influence. In Komet, the district nearest to their 'laboratory', only nine men came but they agreed to participate in the highest number of tests, fifty in all. Three of their names should now be familiar to the reader because of their role in the expedition: Arei, Jimmy Dei and Ulai.

Of the three cousins who assisted with Malu's ceremonies, only Pasi submitted himself to tests (two with Rivers on colour, three with Myers on hearing and one with McDougall). Pasi's three sons, Poi, George and Charlie, also consented to be tested. Mamai and Gododo evidently refused but did work on a variety of expedition activities, including knowledge about *zogo* stones and the staging of the Malu ceremonies. Mamai patiently related those stories he had the authority to tell to Ray and Haddon, along with information on those ceremonial occasions, such as the *Dogaira wetpur* (harvest ceremony), connected to him. Gadodo apparently preferred to talk with Jack Bruce, and his information in the *Reports* comes via Bruce's translation. It is unlikely that dislike of Haddon accounted for Gadodo's preference for Bruce. He repeatedly hosted the Englishmen at his own house and delighted in seeing the pictures of Haddon's family. More likely, he either lacked confidence in his own ability to explain complex and vital religious meanings and purposes in another language, or lacked confidence in the Englishman's ability to understand him. Bruce, unlike Haddon, spoke Meriam-mir.

The psychologists' results, and Rivers' most complete genealogical records for Mer, came from men who were invested in the expedition, and generally it seems Pasi organized these people together for the Englishmen. Following the Malu performances, the Englishmen had the opportunity to do tests on the Samsep men, such as Enoka, who lived on that side of the island.

For all of his assistance and coordination of Meriam for the Englishmen, Pasi may have had some reservations about the work – not about the project to document the past, but rather about the cultural bias he must have perceived. I have come to this conclusion from seeing the document made by Pasi in his own language – a document with significant overlap with the records penned by the Englishmen.

Following July's Malu performances, Pasi wrote a fifty-nine-page book in mission-school Meriam, a written version of the language created by the LMS for bible translation and instruction. The content of the book was detailed within the 'Linguistics' volume of the *Reports*. It included a number of stories, including the history of Malu and a variety of nouns such as the names of reefs, islands, body parts and different animals, along with place names in Dauar. There were transcripts of three songs, and short compositions titled 'Way people read', 'These are right words' and 'People's words'.[72] Some of these Pasi had already told to Haddon in the local Creole; others he had recited to Ray in Meriam-mir. Despite the overlaps, it was evidently important for Pasi to make a record in his own order and fashion for inclusion in their work. Ray only published part of the manuscript, partly because he was dismissive of the modern Meriam-mir in which the document was written. The fact that he did not publish some sections, such as the intriguingly titled 'These are right words', may also have been because Ray lacked the ability to translate without assistance. He admitted that he did not have the chance to go through Pasi's manuscript with him before they left Mer.[73]

The Cambridge team were not the only ones publishing local languages at the time. Ray had first learnt Meriam-mir from the pamphlets published by the LMS pioneer Samuel McFarlane in the 1870s. Finau was in the process of translating the gospels of Matthew and Mark.[74] The school and the court also used written local language. But uniquely, the expedition offered Islanders a way to record their own vision of Meriam life.

The Inclusive Encounter

In 1888, Haddon had been excited to meet people who remembered J. Beete Jukes, officer on the HMS *Fly* expedition, and to meet members of families mentioned by the author, Duppa, Sewai, Dudegab, Wati and Daras.[75] Jukes in turn had sought out these individuals, for they had been mentioned by name in the 1836 reports of the rescue of the *Charles Eaton* shipwreck survivors. This had inspired the LMS to come to the Torres Strait, which they eventually did in 1871. In one of Haddon's four lantern slide shows at Mer, the first slide showed the 'Murray Islanders eager for barter' illustration in Juke's narrative of *Fly*'s voyage. Haddon followed this with his own picture of Jimmy Dei and other men with the gift of bananas. In this, Haddon consciously connected himself to past voyages and incorporated contemporary Meriam-le into his English arc of Meriam history.

The maritime expedition tradition of naming people became an outdated practice for the 'new anthropologists' of the twentieth century – those men of the 'Great Revolution' in anthropology to which Taussig referred, A.R. Radcliffe-Brown and Bronislaw Malinowski.[76] Though each anthropologist acknowledged his teacher – Radcliffe-Brown's first monograph was dedicated to Rivers and Haddon and Malinowski's first Trobriand Island study was dedicated to Seligman – they did not extend the same courtesy to their subjects.[77] Both Malinowski and Radcliffe-Brown effectively excised individuals from their record. The worlds they observed have remained solidly their creation, perhaps because so few other individuals occupy the space of their books. While Haddon's practice of including individual voices in the *Reports* is a throwback to the practice of earlier voyagers, it became something different in combination with Rivers' genealogies. By publishing the names of individuals who gave information, those who participated in an action or who described a particular feature of their culture, Haddon, consciously or not, made it possible for this large, frustrating and complex document to be useful beyond anthropology. It is only possible to retrieve Meriam-le's vision of their cultural life because of this practice.

For Nakata, the Englishmen were hunters after a certain kind of information for European knowledge systems. While the Englishmen certainly sought to capture all they saw, they were continually limited by the frame of view that was offered to them.

Pasi and many others who assisted also directed the Englishmen's attention to particular activities and introduced them to people who had the authority to talk about certain aspects of cultural knowledge. That Pasi and Waria (Figure 2.2) were independently compelled to write their own histories for the expedition demonstrates that these two understood the potential of the work to uniquely document their vision. The *Reports* are a record of the history they wanted their descendants to have.[78] From the 'facts' they presented in the *Reports* through the Englishmen, Meriam-le seem to have desired a future for their children based on older styles of knowledge side by side with Christianity and modern governance.

This chapter began with two photographs, one of Englishmen, characterized by Taussig as five men acting wholly within their own cultural-academic boundaries. The second image of men from Mabuyag showed that this was not the case; indeed, Islander and Englishman joined to produce photographs positioning the 'self' with the 'other'. If one agrees with Taussig that the expedition did little for anthropology beyond changing the course of study for its students, then, as Barth argues, Islanders should at least be given recognition for 'civilizing' the Englishmen to other sensibilities. Islanders' impact is evident in their persistence in asserting their genealogies, in directing the gaze of the Englishmen towards what they wanted documented and their assistance in getting others to participate as subjects. Haddon enabled Islanders to author their own histories and created space through the *Reports* for individuals to direct their messages to their descendants.

Undoubtedly, through the editing of a large scientific text, the Englishmen had ultimate control over what was included. Much of the Christian context and political negotiations for governance were pushed to the side in the *Reports*, while aspects of pre-Christian spiritual life were promoted. Regardless of their many cultural and intellectual biases, Haddon allowed for the inclusion of great chunks of texts written in the Creole and in indigenous languages. This created space for some Islanders to preserve and detail parts of their knowledge for future Torres Strait Islander readers. Waria's text begins: 'I am writing this so that those who come after will know'.[79]

Observers Observed

> A small crowd assembled to bid us farewell & I know many of the natives were genuinely sorry that we were going. We have spent such a happy, profitable time that we will always have a soft corner in our hearts for this beautiful island.
> —1898 Journal of Alfred C. Haddon

Thirty-six cases contained the various goods and chattels of the Englishmen. Four local men were recruited and paid in stick tobacco and shillings for the landing and carrying the boxes (and Rivers and Ray) up to the old mission house. Luggage and equipment were carried back and forth another five times as the Englishmen divided their goods for journeys to British New Guinea and then Borneo. Haddon ultimately sent back nineteen cases of unwanted equipment and forty cases of objects from the Strait. Over five hundred objects from Meriam-le were included.[80]

The correspondence between people at Mer and those in Cambridge continued for many years after the expedition left the Torres Strait. Haddon was evidently nervous at the reception of the *Reports* on Mer in 1908 (it was a success).[81] Haddon wasn't able to return to Mer because of the Great War, but he and his daughter got to meet Pasi's daughter, if only briefly, in 1914 on a boat to British New Guinea. Haddon remained close to his friends at Mer, Mabuyag and Tudu over the years the *Reports* were slowly written up. Letters sent to Jack Bruce contained continuous questions for further information and on one occasion included two photographic albums, one for Pasi and one for Arei. Those from Bruce to Haddon carried news of friends, answers to questions and requests for photographs.[82]

The photographs, objects, journals, drawings and great variety of products of the expedition have been of increasing interest for Torres Strait Islanders in the twenty-first century.[83] Today they draw similar numbers of people of Torres Strait heritage to Cambridge as they do non-Islander observers, intrigued by Meriam-le's remarkable history and Haddon's composition of it.

Following fieldwork in the Torres Strait in 1995–96, **Jude Philp** gained a PhD in anthropology from the University of Cambridge. For the last ten years she has been Senior Curator of the Macleay Museum at the University of Sydney, where she continues to research the continuing importance of collections acquired from Torres Strait and southeast coastal Papua New Guinea in the colonial period.

Notes

1. Alfred C. Haddon (ed.), *The Reports of the Cambridge Anthropological Expedition to Torres Straits* (Cambridge: Cambridge University Press, 1901–35).
2. A comprehensive account of the expedition is given in Anita Herle and Sandra Rouse (eds), *Cambridge and the Torres Strait: Centenary Essays on*

the *1898 Anthropological Expedition* (Cambridge: Cambridge University Press, 1998). See also Martin Nakata, *Disciplining the Savages, Savaging the Disciplines* (Canberra: Aboriginal Studies Press, 2007). On Haddon's nineteenth-century expedition style, see George W. Stocking, 'The Ethnographer's Magic: Fieldwork in British Anthropology from Tylor to Malinowski', in George W. Stocking (ed.), *Observers Observed: Essays on Ethnographic Fieldwork* (Madison, WI: University of Wisconsin Press, 1983), 75–76.

3. Graham Richards, *'Race', Racism and Psychology: Towards a Reflexive History* (London: Routledge, 1997), 41; Jack Goody, 'The Isnad of the Cambridge Expedition to the Torres Strait 1898', *The Cambridge Journal of Anthropology* 21(1) (1999), 39.
4. Keith Hart, 'The Place of the 1898 Cambridge Anthropological Expedition to the Torres Strait (CAETS) in the History of British Social Anthropology', opening session of St John's College, Cambridge centenary conference, August 1998, http://human-nature.com/science-as-culture/hart.html (accessed 25 July 2017).
5. Michael Taussig, *What Colour Is the Sacred?* (Chicago, IL: University of Chicago Press, 2009), 124.
6. Anita Herle, Jude Philp and Jocelyne Dudding, 'Reactivating Visual Histories: Alfred Haddon's Photographs from Mabuyag 1888, 1898', in I.J. McNiven and G. Hitchock (eds), *Goemulgal: Natural and Cultural Histories of the Mabuyag Islands, Zenadth Kes (Torres Strait), Memoirs of the Queensland Museum – Cultural Heritage Series* 8(1) (Brisbane: Queensland Museum, 2015), 270–71.
7. Jeremy Beckett, *Torres Strait Islanders: Custom and Colonialism* (Cambridge: Cambridge University Press, 1987), 110–47; Herle and Rouse, *Cambridge and the Torres Strait*; and Nonie Sharp, *Stars of Tagai: The Torres Strait Islanders* (Canberra: Aboriginal Studies Press, 1993).
8. Jeremy Beckett, 'Haddon Attends a Funeral: Fieldwork in Torres Strait, 1888, 1898', in Herle and Rouse, *Cambridge and the Torres Strait*, 23–49.
9. James Urry, 'Notes and Queries on Anthropology and the Development of Field Methods in British Anthropology, 1870–1920', *Proceedings of the Royal Anthropological Institute of Great Britain and Ireland* 1 (1972), 45–57; Alfred C. Haddon, 'Ethnography of the Western Tribes of the Torres Straits', *Journal of the Royal Anthropological Institute of Great Britain and Ireland* 19 (1890), 297–442.
10. Nakata, *Disciplining the Savages*, chs 3 to 6.
11. Fredrik Barth, 'From the Torres Straits to the Argonauts, 1898–1922', in Fredrik Barth, Andre Gingrich, Robert Parkin and Sydel Silverman (eds), *One Discipline, Four Ways: British, German, French and American Anthropology* (Chicago, IL: University of Chicago Press, 2005), 12–13.
12. Ibid.
13. Jacob Gruber, 'Ethnographic Salvage and the Shaping of Anthropology', *American Anthropologist* 6 (1970), 1290, http://onlinelibrary.wiley.

com/doi/10.1525/aa.1970.72.6.02a00040/epdf (accessed 26 June 2015).
14. Alfred C. Haddon, *The Study of Man* (London: John Murray, 1898), xxiii.
15. Ibid., xvi, xx.
16. For pearl-shelling history, see Steve Mullins, *Torres Strait: A History of Colonial Occupation and Culture Contact, 1864–1897* (Rockhampton: Central Queensland University Press, 1995).
17. Only Sidney Ray did not study biology. Arturo Roldán, 'Looking at Anthropology from a Biological Point of View: A.C. Haddon's Metaphors on Anthropology', *History of the Human Sciences* 5(4) (1992), 21–32; Henrika Kuklick, 'The Color Blue: From Research in the Torres Strait to an Ecology of Human Behavior', in Roy MacLeod and Philip Rehbock (eds), *Darwin's Laboratory: Evolutionary Theory and Natural History in the Pacific* (Honolulu, HI: University of Hawaii Press, 1994), 347.
18. James Urry, 'Making Sense of Diversity and Complexity: The Ethnological Context and Consequences of the Torres Strait Expedition and the Oceanic Phase in British Anthropology, 1890–1935', in Herle and Rouse, *Cambridge and the Torres Strait*, 201.
19. Jude Philp, 'Resonance: Torres Strait Islander Material Culture and History', PhD dissertation (Cambridge: Darwin College, University of Cambridge, 1999), ch. 6.
20. Benny Mabo, 1968, quoted in Margaret Lawrie, *Myths and Legends of the Torres Strait* (Brisbane: University of Queensland Press, 1970), 319.
21. Philp, 'Resonance', ch. 6; David Lawrence, 'Shared Space: Papuan Perspectives of the Torres Strait', in Richard Davis (ed.), *Woven Histories, Dancing Lives* (Canberra: Australian Institute of Aboriginal and Torres Strait Islander Studies, 2004), 190–206.
22. Bruce Hogg, 'Freemasons and the Royal Society', The Library and Museum of Freemasonary, http://freemasonry.london.museum/resources-information/freemason-fellows-royal-society/ (accessed 26 July 2017). Anthony Wilkin and William McDougall were possibly not Freemasons.
23. Pasi's name is now internationally known, through the *Reports* and because two of his descendants, Sam Passi and David Passi, were plaintiffs in the Murray Island Land Case (1992), the judgement that changed Australia's land laws in relation to Native Title.
24. Steve Mullins and David Wetherall, 'LMS Teachers and Colonialism in Torres Strait and New Guinea 1871–1915', in D. Munro and A. Thornley (eds), *The Covenant Makers: Islander Missionaries in the Pacific* (Suva, Fiji: Pacific Islands Theological College and the Institute of Pacific Studies at the University of the South Pacific, 1996), 186–207.
25. Samuel McFarlane, *Among the Cannibals of New Guinea* (Philadelphia, PA: Presbyterian Board of Publication, 1888), 87. McFarlane advised Haddon to go to the Strait in 1887.

26. Alfred C. Haddon, 'Journal 1898', Haddon Papers 1030, Cambridge University Library, 203 [hereafter 'Journal 1898'].
27. The addition of extra government councillors in 1899 indicates some tension within the *mamoose* system. Haddon, *Reports*, Vol. 6, 179.
28. Anna Shnukal, *A Dictionary of Torres Strait Creole* (Kuranda, Qld: Rams Skull Press, 2004).
29. Charles Myers, 'Journal 1898', MS Add.8073, Cambridge University Library, 10 [hereafter 'Journal 1898'].
30. For example the emerging love story and land cases in Haddon, *Reports*, Vol. 6, 103, 117.
31. Alfred C. Haddon, *Head-Hunters: Black, White and Brown* (London: Methuen, 1901), 42.
32. Ibid., 34.
33. Anita Herle, 'The Life Histories of Objects: Collections of the Cambridge Anthropological Expedition to the Torres Strait', in Herle and Rouse, *Cambridge and the Torres Strait*, 77–105.
34. Haddon, *Reports*, Vol. 1, xi.
35. Haddon, 'Journal 1898', 207.
36. Ron Day, 'Meriam-Le, Anthropologists and the Idea of Logical Understanding', unpublished paper for the Sydney Sawyer Seminar *The Impact of the Antipodes on Anthropological Thought: Histories of Human Order*, 27 March 2009.
37. See Anita Herle, 'Objects, Agency and Museums: Continuing Dialogues between the Torres Strait and Cambridge', in Anita Herle et al. (eds), *Pacific Art: Persistence, Change and Meaning* (Hindmarsh, South Australia: Crawford House Publishing, 2002), 231–48. Personal notes taken by the author during visits of Islanders to Cambridge University Museum of Archaeology and Anthropology, including Ron Day and Terrence Whap (June–July 1998) and Ephraim Bani (June 1999).
38. The exact quote is: 'That error has crept into my accounts I do not doubt. I have done my best to keep it out, but one is necessarily at the mercy of one's informants'. Haddon, 'Ethnography of the Western Tribes', 298.
39. Haddon, 'Journal 1898', 8.
40. Haddon, *Head-Hunters*, 8.
41. Haddon, 'Journal 1898', 64.
42. Elizabeth Edwards, 'Performing Science: Still Photography and the Torres Strait Expedition', in Herle and Rouse, *Cambridge and the Torres Strait*, 124.
43. Haddon, 'Journal 1898', 64.
44. Ibid., 65; Simon Schaffer, 'From Physics to Anthropology and Back Again', *Prickly Pear Pamphlet No. 3* (Cambridge: Prickly Pear Press, 1994), 36.
45. Haddon, 'Journal 1898', 71–72.
46. Ibid., 80.
47. Ibid., 74.

48. Alfred C. Haddon, 'The Saving of Vanishing Data', *The Popular Science Monthly* 62(13) (1903), 227.
49. See Nakata, *Disciplining the Savages*, chs 4 and 5; Herle and Rouse, *Cambridge and the Torres Strait* includes images documenting recording styles.
50. William Rivers, 'Physiology and Psychology' (1901) *Reports*, Vol. 2, 31 is one example of difficulty with the E tests. See also Richards, *'Race', Racism and Psychology*, 47–53.
51. Myers, 'Journal 1898', 23 May.
52. Myers, 'Journal 1898'.
53. Haddon, 'Journal 1898', 202; Rivers, 'Genealogies', in Haddon, *Reports*, Vol. 6, 64–66.
54. Haddon, 'Journal 1898', 193.
55. See Beckett, 'Haddon Attends a Funeral', 42–43.
56. Myers, 'Journal 1898', 105. In Haddon's account, he gets the *seri-seri* clubs and organizes the other sacred things of Malu to be brought over. Haddon, 'Journal 1898', 93.
57. Ibid.
58. Haddon, 'Introduction', in *Reports*, Vol. 6, 23.
59. See Leah Lui-Chivizhe, 'Le op: An Islander's History of Torres Strait Turtle-Shell Masks', PhD dissertation (Sydney: University of Sydney, 2017), ch. 5.
60. Haddon, *Head-Hunters*, 47
61. Haddon, *Reports*, Vol. 6, 306. Original film held and digitized by British Film Institute. See http://aso.gov.au/titles/historical/torres-strait-islanders/clip1/ (accessed 5 June 2015). See also Elizabeth Edwards, 'Making Histories: The Torres Strait Expedition of 1898', *Pacific Studies* 20(4) (1997), 18–19.
62. My thanks to Ron Day for alerting me to this, and to the continuing significance of this omission. Day, 'Meriam-Le'.
63. Letter from Haddon to Bruce dated 27 February 1909, Haddon Papers, Envelope 1001, University of Cambridge.
64. See Sharp, 'Epilogue', in *Stars of Tagai*, especially statements by 'sis' and 'second Meriam man', 251–60.
65. Sharp, *Stars of Tagai*, 58. My thanks to Leah Lui-Chivizhe, whose research makes obvious the importance of recognizing the seasons in which historical actions occurred. Lui-Chivizhe, 'Le op', 10–11.
66. Haddon, 'Journal 1898', 49. Haddon goes on to say that the Ferris wheel made £1,600 in three months.
67. The song 'Oh, You Must Be a Lover of the Lord' was published in 1866 by J.N.S. and Isaac Watts. See Liner notes on New World Records, *Angels' Visits and Other Vocal Gems of Victorian America* (New World Recorded Anthology of American Music, Inc, 1977), http://www.newworldrecords.org/album.cgi?rm=view&album_id=80220 (accessed 26 July 2017).

68. Ibid., 190; Regina Ganter, *The Pearl-Shellers of Torres Strait* (Melbourne: Melbourne University Press, 1994).
69. William Rivers, 'A Genealogical Method of Collecting Social and Vital Statistics', *Journal of the Anthropological Institute of Great Britain and Ireland* 30 (1900), 75–76. For some of the consequences of this, see Nonie Sharp, *No Ordinary Judgement: Mabo, the Murray Islanders' Land Case* (Canberra: Aboriginal Studies Press, 1996).
70. Involvement was measured by a count of the number of times a named individual was referenced in the *Reports*. Philp, 'Resonance', 89–92.
71. Of the adult men tested, about ten are not included here, as their names cannot be identified to a single individual in the *Reports*.
72. Sidney Ray, 'Linguistics', in Haddon, *Reports*, Vol. 3, 228.
73. Ibid., 229.
74. Ibid., 227.
75. Haddon, 'Journal 1888', 79; J.B. Jukes, *Narrative of the Surveying Voyage of H.M.S. Fly, Commanded by Captain F.P. Blackwood, in Torres Strait, New Guinea, and Other Islands of the Eastern Archipelago, during the Years 1842–1846* (London: T. & W. Boone, 1847), Vol. 2, 248; and Philip Parker King, *A Voyage to Torres Straits in Search of the Survivors of the Ship 'Charles Eaton,' which was Wrecked upon the Barrier Reef in the Month of August, 1834, in His Majesty's Colonial Schooner 'Isabella,' C.M. Lewis, Commander. Arranged from the Journal of the Commander by Authority of His Excellency Major-General Sir Richard Bourke, K.C.B., Governor of New South Wales, etc., etc., etc.* (Sydney: E.H. Stratham, 1837), 4.
76. Hart, 'The Place of the 1898 Cambridge Anthropological Expedition'.
77. A.R. Radcliffe-Brown, *The Andaman Islanders* (Cambridge: Cambridge University Press, 1922); Bronisław Malinowski, *Argonauts of the Western Pacific: An Account of Native Enterprise and Adventure in the Archipelagoes of Melanesian New Guinea* (London: Routledge and Kegan Paul, 1922).
78. This conclusion was prompted by conversations with Meriam in the mid 1990s about the *Reports*. My thanks to the Passi, Rice and Day families particularly.
79. Waria, in Haddon, *Reports*, Vol. 3, 192.
80. Ibid., 103; David Moore, *The Torres Strait Collections of A.C. Haddon* (London: British Museum Publications, 1984). Four hundred and fifty-seven objects were definitely from Mer; another one hundred and fifty-four are 'probably' from Mer.
81. Bruce to Haddon, letter dated 26 December 1902, Haddon Papers, Envelope 1004, University of Cambridge.
82. Envelope 1001, Haddon Papers.
83. Herle, 'Objects, Agency and Museums', 231–48.

Bibliography

Barth, Fredrik. 'From the Torres Straits to the Argonauts, 1898–1922', in Fredrik Barth, Andre Gingrich, Robert Parkin and Sydel Silverman (eds), *One Discipline, Four Ways: British, German, French and American Anthropology* (Chicago, IL: University of Chicago Press 2005), 11–21.

Beckett, Jeremy. 'Haddon Attends a Funeral: Fieldwork in Torres Strait, 1888, 1898', in Anita Herle and Sandra Rouse (eds), *Cambridge and the Torres Strait: Centenary Essays on the 1898 Anthropological Expedition* (Cambridge: Cambridge University Press, 1998), 23–49.

———. *Torres Strait Islanders: Custom and Colonialism*. Cambridge: Cambridge University Press, 1987.

Day, Ron. 'Meriam-Le, Anthropologists and the Idea of Logical Understanding'. Unpublished paper for the Sydney Sawyer Seminar *The Impact of the Antipodes on Anthropological Thought: Histories of Human Order*, 27 March 2009.

Edwards, Elizabeth. 'Making Histories: The Torres Strait Expedition of 1898'. *Pacific Studies* 20(4) (1997), 13–34.

———. 'Performing Science: Still Photography and the Torres Strait Expedition', in Anita Herle and Sandra Rouse (eds), *Cambridge and the Torres Strait: Centenary Essays on the 1898 Anthropological Expedition* (Cambridge: Cambridge University Press, 1998), 106–35.

Ganter, Regina. *The Pearl-Shellers of Torres Strait*. Melbourne: Melbourne University Press, 1994.

Goody, Jack. 'The Isnad of the Cambridge Expedition to the Torres Strait 1898'. *The Cambridge Journal of Anthropology* 21(1) (1999), 28–41.

Gruber, Jacob. 'Ethnographic Salvage and the Shaping of Anthropology'. *American Anthropologist* 6 (1970), 1290. http://onlinelibrary.wiley.com/doi/10.1525/aa.1970.72.6.02a00040/epdf (accessed 26 June 2015).

Haddon, Alfred C. 'Ethnography of the Western Tribes of the Torres Straits'. *Journal of the Royal Anthropological Institute of Great Britain and Ireland* 19 (1890), 297–442.

———. *Head-Hunters: Black, White, and Brown*. London: Methuen, 1901.

——— (ed.). *Reports of the Cambridge Anthropological Expedition to Torres Straits*. Cambridge: Cambridge University Press, 1901–35.

———. 'The Saving of Vanishing Data'. *The Popular Science Monthly* 62(13) (1903), 222–29,

———. *The Study of Man*. London: John Murray, 1898.

Hart, Keith. 'The Place of the 1898 Cambridge Anthropological Expedition to the Torres Strait (CAETS) in the History of British Social Anthropology'. Opening session of St John's College, Cambridge centenary conference, August 1998. http://human-nature.com/science-as-culture/hart.html (accessed 27 July 2017).

Herle, Anita. 'The Life Histories of Objects: Collections of the Cambridge Anthropological Expedition to the Torres Strait', in Anita Herle and

Sandra Rouse (eds), *Cambridge and the Torres Strait: Centenary Essays on the 1898 Anthropological Expedition* (Cambridge: Cambridge University Press, 1998), 77–105.

———. 'Objects, Agency and Museums: Continuing Dialogues between the Torres Strait and Cambridge', in Anita Herle et al. (eds). *Pacific Art: Persistence, Change and Meaning* (Hindmarsh, South Australia: Crawford House Publishing, 2002), 231–50.

Herle, Anita, Jude Philp and Jocelyne Dudding. 'Reactivating Visual Histories: Alfred Haddon's Photographs from Mabuyag 1888, 1898', in I.J. McNiven and G. Hitchock (eds). *Goemulgal: Natural and Cultural Histories of the Mabuyag Islands, Zenadth Kes (Torres Strait), Memoirs of the Queensland Museum – Cultural Heritage Series* 8(1) Brisbane: Queensland Museum, 2015, 99–125.

Herle, Anita and Sandra Rouse (eds). *Cambridge and the Torres Strait: Centenary Essays on the 1898 Anthropological Expedition.* Cambridge: Cambridge University Press, 1998.

Jukes, J.B. *Narrative of the Surveying Voyage of H.M.S. Fly, Commanded by Captain F.P. Blackwood, in Torres Strait, New Guinea, and Other Islands of the Eastern Archipelago, during the Years 1842–1846.* London: T. & W. Boone, 1847.

King, P.P. *A Voyage to Torres Straits in Search of the Survivors of the Ship 'Charles Eaton,' which was Wrecked upon the Barrier Reef in the Month of August, 1834, in His Majesty's Colonial Schooner 'Isabella,' C.M. Lewis, Commander. Arranged from the Journal of the Commander by Authority of His Excellency Major-General Sir Richard Bourke, K.C.B., Governor of New South Wales, etc., etc., etc.* Sydney: E.H. Stratham, 1837.

Kuklick, Henrika. 'The Color Blue: From Research in the Torres Strait to an Ecology of Human Behavior', in Roy MacLeod and Philip Rehbock (eds). *Darwin's Laboratory: Evolutionary Theory and Natural History in the Pacific* (Honolulu, HI: University of Hawaii Press, 1994), 339–67.

Lawrence, David. 'Shared Space: Papuan Perspectives of the Torres Strait', in Richard Davis (ed.). *Woven Histories, Dancing Lives* (Canberra: Australian Institute of Aboriginal and Torres Strait Islander Studies, 2004), 190–206.

Lawrie, Margaret. *Myths and Legends of the Torres Strait.* Brisbane: University of Queensland Press, 1970.

Lui-Chivizhe, Leah. 'Le op: An Islander's History of Torres Strait Turtle-Shell Masks'. PhD dissertation. Sydney: University of Sydney, 2017.

Malinowski, Bronisław. *Argonauts of the Western Pacific: An Account of Native Enterprise and Adventure in the Archipelagoes of Melanesian New Guinea.* London: Routledge and Kegan Paul, 1922.

McFarlane, Samuel. *Among the Cannibals of New Guinea.* Philadelphia, PA: Presbyterian Board of Publication, 1888.

Moore, David. *The Torres Strait Collections of A.C. Haddon.* London: British Museum Publications, 1984.

Mullins, Steve. *Torres Strait: A History of Colonial Occupation and Culture Contact, 1864–1897*. Rockhampton: Central Queensland University Press, 1995.
Mullins, Steve, and David Wetherall. 'LMS Teachers and Colonialism in Torres Strait and New Guinea 1871–1915', in D. Munro and A. Thornley (eds). *The Covenant Makers: Islander Missionaries in the Pacific* (Suva, Fiji: Pacific Islands Theological College and the Institute of Pacific Studies at the University of the South Pacific, 1996), 186–207.
Nakata, Martin. *Disciplining the Savages, Savaging the Disciplines*. Canberra: Aboriginal Studies Press, 2007.
Philp, Jude. 'Resonance: Torres Strait Islander Material Culture and History'. PhD dissertation. Cambridge: Darwin College, University of Cambridge, 1999.
Radcliffe-Brown, A.R. *The Andaman Islanders*. Cambridge: Cambridge University Press, 1922.
Ray, Sidney. 'Linguistics', in Alfred C. Haddon (ed.). *Reports of the Cambridge Anthropological Expedition to Torres Straits*, Vol. 3 (Cambridge: Cambridge University Press, 1901–35).
Richards, Graham. *'Race', Racism and Psychology: Towards a Reflexive History*. London: Routledge, 1997.
Rivers, William. 'A Genealogical Method of Collecting Social and Vital Statistics'. *Journal of the Anthropological Institute of Great Britain and Ireland* 30 (1900), 74–82.
———. 'Genealogies', in Alfred C. Haddon (ed.). *Reports of the Cambridge Anthropological Expedition to Torres Straits*, Vol. 6. Cambridge: Cambridge University Press, 1901–35, 64–91.
———. 'Physiology and Psychology', in Alfred C. Haddon (ed.). *Reports of the Cambridge Anthropological Expedition to Torres Straits*, Vol. 2 (Cambridge: Cambridge University Press, 1901–35).
Roldán, Arturo. 'Looking at Anthropology from a Biological Point of View: A.C. Haddon's Metaphors on Anthropology'. *History of the Human Sciences* 5(4) (1992), 21–32.
Schaffer, Simon. 'From Physics to Anthropology and Back Again'. *Prickly Pear Pamphlet No. 3* (Cambridge: Prickly Pear Press, 1994), 1–53.
Sharp, Nonie. *No Ordinary Judgment: Mabo, the Murray Islanders' Land Case*. Canberra: Aboriginal Studies Press, 1996.
———. *Stars of Tagai: The Torres Strait Islanders*. Canberra: Aboriginal Studies Press, 1993.
Shnukal, Anna. *A Dictionary of Torres Strait Creole*. Kuranda, Qld: Rams Skull Press, 2004.
Stocking, George W. 'The Ethnographer's Magic: Fieldwork in British Anthropology from Tylor to Malinowski', in George W. Stocking (ed.), *Observers Observed: Essays on Ethnographic Fieldwork* (Madison, WI: University of Wisconsin Press, 1983), 70–120.

Taussig, Michael. *What Colour Is the Sacred?* Chicago, IL: University of Chicago Press, 2009.

Urry, James. 'Making Sense of Diversity and Complexity: The Ethnological Context and Consequences of the Torres Strait Expedition and the Oceanic Phase in British Anthropology, 1890–1935', in Anita Herle and Sandra Rouse (eds), *Cambridge and the Torres Strait: Centenary Essays on the 1898 Anthropological Expedition*. Cambridge: Cambridge University Press, 1998, 201–33.

———. 'Notes and Queries on Anthropology and the Development of Field Methods in British Anthropology, 1870–1920', *Proceedings of the Royal Anthropological Institute of Great Britain and Ireland* 1 (1972), 45–57.

Chapter 3

DONALD THOMSON'S HYBRID EXPEDITIONS

ANTHROPOLOGY, BIOLOGY AND NARRATIVE IN NORTHERN AUSTRALIA AND ENGLAND

Saskia Beudel

> The days of great exploration in the sense of first discovery are now almost over. But exploration is not extinct. It has only changed its character. In future it will be intensive rather than extensive. What the pioneers accomplished in broad outline the explorers of the future will supplement in detail.
> —Report of the Committee on the Future of the Society, 31 May 1939, Royal Geographical Society

In a tantalizing fragment of a letter written by the Australian anthropologist Donald Thomson to his mentor Alfred Cort Haddon, Thomson writes: 'I wonder whether I mentioned in my previous letter that many of the natives about Thursday Island not only remembered your visits, but were able to tell me quite a lot about you'. Thomson visited the area during his first periods of anthropological fieldwork conducted in northern Australia on the Cape York Peninsula between 1928 and 1933. 'I was greatly interested', he added, 'for of course we grew up with the name of the Cambridge Expedition'.[1] His reference to the 1898 Cambridge Anthropological Expedition to Torres Straits (henceforth 'Cambridge Expedition') is telling, not only for the glimpse it provides of the anthropological observer who is in turn observed, but also for the pervasive allure of the expeditionary form his comment evokes.

By the time of Thomson's Cape York fieldwork, begun during his mid twenties, he had long entertained a 'desire to join a scientific expedition to a remote region'.[2] In 1923 he sought advice on how to secure a position on the Hubert Wilkins Collecting Expedition sponsored by the natural history section of the British Museum to collect mammals in northern Australia in response to fears about imminent indigenous Australian animal extinctions.[3] Wilkins was a romantic adventurer figure, with a history of polar travel and military service, and a background as photographer, cinematographer, geographer, war correspondent, climatologist and aviator. The British Museum also considered him a competent naturalist.[4] Over a two-and-a-half-year period spent mainly in tropical Australia, including Cape York, Wilkins collected plants, birds, insects, fish, minerals, fossils and Aboriginal artefacts in addition to mammals, and published an account of his expedition, *Undiscovered Australia* (1928). When Wilkins was advertising for expedition members, Thomson was in the second year of his biology degree at the University of Melbourne. He turned to the recently retired Sir Baldwin Spencer, who, like his peer Haddon, was a biologist-turned-anthropologist, for 'advice on how to secure a position' on the expedition. Spencer advised Thomson to complete his biology degree first.[5] Six years later, Thomson was accepted briefly onto the Australian and New Zealand Antarctic Expedition as a biologist, until the New Zealand government complained that the expedition party was comprised of too many Australians and not enough New Zealanders.[6] That Thomson applied to join the Antarctic expedition in the year following his first period of anthropological fieldwork demonstrates that the launch of his anthropological career did not foreclose his interest as a biologist in team-based exploration.

In addition to these specific overtures towards joining an expeditionary party, Thomson's biographer notes that during his student years Thomson was inspired by Robert Falcon Scott's Antarctic expeditions, and readied himself for similar undertakings by becoming a proficient photographer to augment his skills as a biologist.[7] He could be said, then, to have been living during this early period in a state of preparedness for exploration. He would later become known for his 'expeditionary zeal'.[8]

Thomson's invocation of the Cambridge Expedition as a significant presence during his youth also suggests useful ways to consider and position his expeditionary efforts in relation to broader histories of exploration and of professional anthropological fieldwork practices. Thomson's expeditions were undertaken as periods of anthropological fieldwork at three main locales across his lifetime: Cape York Peninsula (1928, 1929, 1932–33), Arnhem Land (1935, 1936–37) and Central Australia (1957, 1963, 1965). Although the stated aims of his research focused on anthropological enquiry, his trips involved a serious commitment to simultaneous pursuits including rigorous zoological observation, data collection and interpretation resulting in fieldwork notes and scientific papers and publications; extensive ethnographic documentation through photography, film and sound recordings (technologies the Cambridge Expedition also employed); equally extensive acquisition of natural history specimens, Aboriginal art and artefacts, often gathered in the mode of a nineteenth-century natural history collector; and journalistic reportage on his activities. His voluminous collection of field notes, photographs, art, artefacts and specimens is now housed at Museum Victoria in Melbourne, and Thomson is highly regarded as a master photographer. His pictorial record is sought by descendants of people represented within it for the wealth of cultural information it contains,[9] and Museum Victoria curator Lindy Allen notes that Thomson's images are held in great esteem by Aboriginal people today.[10] However, his 'extra' pursuits put him out of step with influential anthropologists of his time and place, including his teacher A.R. Radcliffe-Brown. Thomson met Radcliffe-Brown when the latter was employed at the University of Sydney as foundation Professor of Anthropology (1925–31) where he established Australia's first university department dedicated to the discipline.[11]

When Thomson embarked on his anthropological career in the late 1920s, fieldwork conducted by a solo university-trained researcher at a particular site for a designated amount of time (often over a year), followed by a period of writing up and eventual publication of results, had become a standard professional practice and 'rite of passage' within the discipline (see Philp, this volume).[12] As historian Henrika Kuklick suggests, large team-based anthropological expeditions, such as the Cambridge Expedition (where each member brought a distinct form of expertise to a joint research project), belong to a late nineteenth-century moment of evolutionist anthropology. This model of team research, led and promoted by Haddon in an effort to elevate the scientific status of anthropology, brought British academics into the field at a time when the formerly clear demarcation between the collector in the field (James Frazer's 'man on the spot') and the interpreting, theorizing and synthesizing armchair scholar of legendary status was being reconfigured.[13] The Cambridge Expedition 'constituted a move toward the professionalization of anthropology' as a formal discipline and was significant for the challenge it mounted to the credibility of armchair scholarship.[14] It was soon superseded, however, by other developments in the field, most particularly anthropology's reliance on the method of participant observation and the concept of the immersed and empathetic solo fieldworker.

Thomson's persistently interdisciplinary approach raises the question of whether his anthropological expeditions can be understood as an extension and modification of practices formed through the Cambridge Expedition, which in turn were likely to have been modelled, according to George Stocking, on large maritime natural history expeditions.[15] The Cambridge Expedition was committed to fostering interdisciplinary knowledge systems that drew upon and integrated aspects of different disciplinary fields – namely anthropology and psychology. This chapter shows that, in Thomson's case, an interdisciplinary approach could be largely undertaken by a lone figure and thinker, rather than through either the kind of scientific teamwork that characterized the Cambridge Expedition, or the collaborative model that became typical in twentieth-century biological sciences.[16] We might think of Thomson as 'interdisciplinary in one mind'.[17]

Thomson's extra-anthropological pursuits also bore many of the hallmarks of earlier exploratory conventions more broadly – of the various practices associated with the field of exploration or the 'production and consumption of voyages and travels' referred to by Felix Driver as 'cultures of exploration'.[18] Firstly, in the early decades of the twentieth century when the notion of adventure was only spuriously associated with principles of rigorous scientific field research,[19] Thomson was unabashed in declaring through his journalism that 'high adventure' had 'given spice' to his 'scientific and exploratory expeditions' through territory 'unknown to the world and virtually unexplored'.[20] Secondly, he sought out and sustained a connection with the Royal Geographical Society (RGS) in London, delivering public lectures there in 1939 and 1952, publishing in the *Geographical Journal* and receiving the society's 'official blessing' for his 1957 and 1963 expeditions.[21] He was also a recipient of the society's Cuthbert Peek Grant in 1948 and a Patron's Medal in 1951. A number of scholars have demonstrated the ways in which the RGS played an instrumental role in shaping 'cultures of exploration' especially during the nineteenth century but also continuing into the early twentieth century, and it is notable that Thomson sought affiliation with this institution.[22] Thirdly, as mentioned above, he amassed collections of artefacts and specimens in a manner akin to earlier expeditionary natural history collecting practices. Fourthly, his activities in the field involved risk-taking and extreme feats of physical endurance and privation, which, as historian Dane Kennedy argues, 'were almost inescapable aspects of exploration'.[23] In Arnhem Land in 1935, to mention a single example, he undertook patrol journeys 'covering a total distance of more than 1000 miles', most of which were covered

Figure 3.1 Photograph published in Donald F. Thomson, 'The Story of Arnhem Land', *Walkabout*, 1 August 1946, 8.

on foot, the rest with 'native canoes', pack horses and mules.[24] On occasion, he survived on seagull flesh, turtle eggs and hermit crabs, and he suffered fevers and dysentery. 'For days I could not walk, so had to crawl, for I had scarcely any skin on the soles of my feet', he wrote in the Australian travel magazine *Walkabout*.[25] He also experienced moments of heightened sensory perception and wellbeing, noting in *National Geographic Magazine* that specific ordeals would be succeeded by a feeling of tirelessness: 'difficulties were made to be laughed at; one could carry the world on one's back. While under the spell one is unconquerable'.[26] Such representations of endurance and physical prowess not only attest to the material conditions of his expeditions, but also emphasize the explorer's body as integral to his (usually his) reputation – either as a 'maker of ways' or as a form of 'scientific instrument' gleaning hard-won knowledge in the field.[27]

Lastly, the multiplicity of endeavours mentioned above is another of the key characteristics of the explorer as defined by recent historians and theorists of exploration. Through these endeavours, Thomson produced knowledge across numerous domains, while also publicizing, narrating and reporting extensively on his activities in the field. Kennedy observes that a number of nineteenth-century explorers struggled under the breadth of their duties in the field – surveying, measuring, observing, recording, collecting and reporting across the nascent fields of geology, astronomy, meteorology, anthropology, botany, zoology and more, while also in many instances producing narrative accounts of their activities for general audiences.[28] Driver suggests that from the eighteenth century onwards, 'the idea of exploration was freighted with multiple and contested meanings, associated variously with science, literature, religion, commerce and empire'. So, too, the 'business of the scientific explorer was not always, or easily, distinguished from that of the literary *flâneur*, the missionary, the trader or the imperial pioneer';[29] or, in an Australian context, from the settler with 'speculative purposes'.[30] Rather than providing 'neat distinctions' between discourses of adventurous travel and scientific exploration, the undertakings of the explorer unsettle the 'frontier between them'.[31]

This chapter proposes that for Thomson the expedition was a flexible form that harked back to recognizable characteristics of 'cultures of exploration' – especially the contested multiplicity so fundamental to the idea of exploration – while also producing knowledge of particular peoples and environments in innovative ways. It allowed him to be always doing more than one thing at once – anthropology, zoology, photography, cinematography, collecting and journalism – which in turn facilitated his operation both within and apart from the conventions of functionalist anthropology dominant during his lifetime. The expedition enabled him to undertake an overarching form of interdisciplinary enquiry that considered people, nature and particular environments as interlinked rather than separate realms of concern, and provided an audience for his activities that reached beyond the strictly academic. In taking up these lines of enquiry, this chapter focuses on Thomson's Arnhem Land expeditions and the different layers of research, reporting and authorship he derived from these experiences. I focus on his formation of distinctive interdisciplinary anthropological fieldwork practices, influenced at least in part by Haddon's example, and on his cultivation of a public audience for his expeditionary activities through his association with the RGS and through his non-academic or journalistic writing.

In the Field

Thomson was among the first small group of students to study under Radcliffe-Brown in Sydney and the first to graduate with a Diploma in Anthropology in 1927. Despite this lineage, Thomson 'liked to speak of himself as a student of Haddon's'.[32] He credited the work of the Cambridge Expedition with showing 'the promise of Cape York Peninsula' as a fieldwork site, and Haddon supervised Thomson's research during the tenure of a Rockefeller Travelling Fellowship at Christ's College in Cambridge from 1938 to 1939.[33] They had already corresponded since at least 1934 and Haddon had assisted with the publication of two of Thomson's papers on Cape York in the *Journal of the Royal Anthropological Institute*.[34] Among his collection Haddon kept copies of, and made extensive notes on, Thomson's anthropological articles. He kept copies of Thomson's official Arnhem Land reports

Figure 3.2 *Herald and Weekly Times*, 'Prof. [Professor] Donald Thomson' with family, 1936 (Herald and Weekly Times Limited portrait collection, State Library of Victoria, Accession no. H38849/4515).

and newspaper articles and sent Thomson his references to North Queensland from the final volume of his *Reports of the Cambridge Anthropological Expedition to Torres Straits* (1935).[35] 'I appreciate your generous and kindly references to my own work in the notes you sent me', Thomson wrote in reply. In 1934, he expressed his hope to Haddon that he would soon 'get to England for further study and training', explaining that his imminent fieldwork in Arnhem Land would delay these plans.[36]

Thomson may have been drawn to Haddon as a supporter and mentor for prosaic reasons of personal connection. His father, Harry Thomson, was a Scottish-born musician who had moved to Australia from London. He knew Haddon and seems to have introduced Donald to him.[37] During Thomson's absence on his first Arnhem Land expedition, Harry Thomson corresponded with Haddon to 'help to keep my son's memory green', as he put it.[38] Both men 'stumbled into' anthropology from biology. When Haddon conducted zoological research in the Torres Strait Islands for almost a year in 1888 (a decade prior to the Cambridge Expedition), he began anthropological work as a sideline but found his attention increasingly drawn away from marine biology to the islands' human inhabitants.[39] Shortly after completing his biology degree, Thomson first applied for fieldwork funds from the anthropological research committee of the newly established Australian National Research Council (ANRC). His biographer suggests that he may have been motivated by his long-standing desire to take part in an expedition. Radcliffe-Brown replied, 'indicating that there was money available ... but that Thomson must first get some training [in anthropology]'.[40] Once in the field as anthropologists, Haddon and Thomson each carried 'schemes' they had learned from biology to their new profession.

Kuklick argues that Haddon employed a biogeographical approach to his anthropology, plotting 'variation along geographical axes, consistently understanding variations in life forms in ecological terms and observing that geographical isolation was an important factor in speciation'. He understood cultural variation as adaptation to environmental conditions.[41] Thomson too employed a biogeographical approach. He used it explicitly in his bird survey *Birds of Cape York Peninsula* (1935), identifying patterns on a landscape scale and delineating five zones made up of associated vegetation communities and faunal areas, along with gradations within the five main zones.[42] During his second expedition to Arnhem Land (1936–37), he collected soil and rock specimens for analysis, each related to 'definite types of country ... characterized by a distinctive type of floral association' with a view to matching these with data obtained from aerial photographs to determine 'the distribution [of] the various types of country'.[43] He explained his methodology in relation to an almost completed article on Arnhem Land for the *Geographical Journal* in 1955 in these terms: 'I have tried to relate the account of ... the people themselves to the geographical background. In particular I am dealing with fishing techniques developed in adaptation to local geographic conditions'.[44] Attention to geography, its associated flora and fauna and other environmental characteristics also underpins his monograph *Economic Structure and the Ceremonial Exchange Cycle in Arnhem Land* (1949).

Thomson's deployment of a biogeographical approach in *Economic Structure* and in a series of articles on Arnhem Land in the *Geographical Journal* differs somewhat from Haddon's. Stocking argues that Haddon drew on his background as a biologist to construct an evolutionary approach concerned with 'the distribution of forms within a single geographical area' rather than with the 'documentation of a universal sequence of development'. Nevertheless, his published works, such as *Evolution in Art* (1895), employed evolutionary metaphors based on assumptions about 'the minds of savages', and also identified the supposed 'racial "tendencies" and cultural "stages"' that were characteristic of late nineteenth-century evolutionist anthropology.[45] Thomson was less concerned with locating a 'speciation' or 'ranking' of discrete customs, groups or material practices, for example in Arnhem Land, than with examining cultural practices grounded in relationship with distinctive material local conditions, often at the level of the micro-environment, and driven by complex networks of kinship, economic and ceremonial exchange obligations – 'intricate patterns of obligatory conduct', to use his words.[46] He was also at pains to portray the people of Arnhem Land as exemplary ecologists in their own right, and rigorously scientific in their environmental knowledge: they 'classify the country into "types" or formations as accurately as any ecologist, and they are able to state without hesitation what food supply, animal and vegetation, each association will yield' across an annual cycle divided into six defined periods of climatic variation.[47] Such statements aimed to underscore the sophistication and highly organized nature of Aboriginal knowledge in order to dispel assumptions about an apparently unstructured or aimless Aboriginal way of life.

It is worth turning here to differences between Thomson's methodologies, which integrated approaches from biology, ecology, biogeography and cultural anthropology, and those expounded by his teacher Radcliffe-Brown. Thomson's troubles with the ANRC have been thoroughly documented and discussed: after receiving one ANRC grant to conduct fieldwork on Cape York, he resigned a second grant in 1929 due to disputes about the handling of funds and the contested ownership of his photographs taken during the first period of fieldwork. He would never apply for ANRC funds again.[48] This severance from a significant source of research funding, which forced a number of other Australian anthropologists who fell out with the ANRC to find alternative means of financial and professional survival,[49] may have compounded Thomson's interest in the expeditionary form. Mounting an expedition offered an alternative research revenue stream, even though it presented its own challenges. Support through a medley of financial backers had to be solicited and gained, and 'expedition work' was, Thomson admitted, 'so costly'.[50] It is not the place of this chapter to retell the story of Thomson's relations with the ANRC, except to examine one thread of its consequences: the exposure of tensions between Radcliffe-Brown's views on properly scientific anthropological fieldwork and Thomson's own. During an exchange of opinions between ANRC Executive Committee members, Radcliffe-Brown accused Thomson of dedicating too much time to 'some extraneous subject', meaning photography, which was not a 'satisfactory use of the funds'. Radcliffe-Brown declared that Thomson was not

> wholeheartedly a scientist ... [he] said when he first came [to Sydney] that his real interest is exploring the bush, what he really wanted [to do] was natural history observation ... I always had the feeling that Thomson is perhaps not so much a scientist as rather a person who is fond of the bush – a good field naturalist, but who looks upon his journey not so much as a scientific expedition as a journalistic expedition.[51]

A.P. Elkin, who succeeded Radcliffe-Brown as Professor of Anthropology at the University of Sydney from 1933 to 1956, and with whom Thomson had conflicted relations, would also write disparagingly of Thomson as 'a medley of zoologist, anthropologist and journalist'.[52]

That Radcliffe-Brown's comments on Thomson's plural activities cordon off photography and journalism from 'wholehearted' scientific enquiry is hardly surprising during a period of anthropology's development when writing for a public audience diminished academic authority and credibility. During the discipline's earlier incarnations, anthropologists had expected to relay their findings and activities to the public.[53] Like most academic disciplines, increasing specialization brought some 'closure' in public communication. As Peter Weingart argues, 'the essence of discipline formation and evolution is self-referential communication' represented by specialized journals, forums, scholarly associations and peer review processes.[54] Thomson's voluminous journalistic output, amounting to over nine hundred articles, most of them generously illustrated with his photographs, was unorthodox, and Radcliffe-Brown seems to have assumed that communication of scientific exploration to the public precluded scientific rigour.

What is perhaps more surprising about Radcliffe-Brown's comments is his suggestion that natural history observation was as 'unscientific' as journalism, love of the bush and photography. In the context of arguments over what kind of anthropology and what kind of scientific fieldwork was worthy of funding, natural history was cast in disparaging terms. Felix Driver, Lynn Nyhart and Robert Kohler have all cautioned against 'summary version[s] of historical shifts in the nature of scientific investigation' that argue that a 'natural history' model of science was superseded by experimental laboratory sciences of the twentieth century.[55] Although natural history's status, dominance, techniques and institutional and disciplinary frameworks shifted markedly, it persisted in various guises in the twentieth century. According to Driver, its key imperatives of mapping, fieldwork and inventory remain 'central to the pursuit of modern science'.[56] Following these lines of argument, Thomson is a clear example of a university-trained scientist who deliberately sustained a 'natural history' mode of enquiry well into the twentieth century.

Thomson was as capable of laboratory science as he was of natural history fieldwork with its methods of survey, reconnaissance and data and specimen collecting. From 1929 he worked on antivenins at the Walter and Eliza Hall Institute of Research in Pathology and Medicine in Melbourne, and in 1932 he became a research fellow in the Department of Anatomy at the University of Melbourne. We can assume that there were good reasons for his commitment to natural history, rather than want of other forms of scientific expertise. Early in his career he argued clearly for the incorporation of 'natural history' enquiry within anthropological research: 'I am of the opinion that, for the ethnographer, especially in Australia where the relation between man and nature is a peculiar and specialized one, an intimate knowledge of the natural history of the area in which he is working is essential to an understanding of the totemic beliefs of the people, and therefore should form a part of the problem presented by a study of the Aboriginal'.[57] He sometimes referred to his zoological research as 'natural history' but seemed to imply, in his use of the term, both a broadly 'ecological' approach that considered interrelationships between life forms and the places they inhabit (one 'concerned with relation, interdependence, and holism' to use Donald Worster's broad definition)[58] and, more particularly, an approach aligned with the concept of biogeography and floral and faunal 'association zones', as discussed earlier. In his journalism, he used the term 'natural history' much in its vernacular sense as the study and description of natural objects, plants and animals of a particular place, conveyed with passion and enthusiasm. Despite Thomson's credentials as a 'hard scientist'[59] (as opposed to a social scientist), his expertise in the fields of biology and natural history and his interdisciplinarity diminished his credibility as an anthropologist in the estimation of Radcliffe-Brown and Elkin.

Functionalist anthropology, within which Radcliffe-Brown was, to use Stocking's term, a 'culminating figure', has been strongly critiqued for creating oversimplified models of supposedly fundamental social processes.[60] As Kuklick has suggested, functionalists assumed that 'they could determine and describe pre-contact conditions ... Virtually abstracted from the vagaries of actual historical experiences, their subjects' pasts were rendered as expressions of the structured possibilities permitted by persistent social systems'.[61] Geography and environment were stripped from these imaginings of sealed-off, pre-colonial social orders to the extent that the field site 'became cultural rather than physical space'. The remedy, Kuklick argues further, to this widely criticized and deficient model has been to pay 'renewed attention to the factors of geography and history that were so important to Haddon' (and to W.H.R. Rivers).[62]

It is not surprising, then, that within the culture of functionalist anthropology that dominated the field from the 1920s, Thomson turned to Haddon as a supporter, even though the latter's influence as a mentor and teacher had waned since its 'zenith' from 1901 to 1925.[63] Thomson did use functionalist frameworks to a certain degree, especially in relation to kinship study, and even turned to Radcliffe-Brown in the late 1940s for advice on these matters.[64] Nevertheless, his shared background in natural sciences and his congenial relations with Haddon must have bolstered his efforts to integrate biological concepts and findings with anthropological conceptual paradigms at a time when it was not easy to do so within the local anthropological establishment. We might understand Thomson as having taken Haddon's commitment to interdisciplinary approaches to anthropological research to heart – as did a number of his other earlier students.[65] Haddon observed that a 'proper anthropologist' required 'wider knowledge and more versatile talents' than lay within any one person's capacities: they should be 'a linguist, artist, musician and have an extensive knowledge of natural and mechanical science', to which list he later added psychology, physiology and sociology.[66]

Recent theorists of interdisciplinarity have observed the profusion of potentially confusing or overlapping terms describing interdisciplinary research and scholarship. In her taxonomy of interdisciplinarity, Julie Thompson Klein suggests that 'integration' of disciplines is a defining characteristic of interdisciplinarity. Klein contrasts this with 'multidisciplinarity' that juxtaposes disciplines while retaining the discrete identity of each, so that 'the existing structure of knowledge is not questioned'.[67] In the field of global environmental change studies (or Global Change Research), an area currently drawing urgent attention to notions of interdisciplinarity, Poul Holm et al. argue that interdisciplinary research 'tends to challenge both the disciplinary boundaries and the dominating paradigms' within particular disciplines. Ideally, traditions and paradigms of any given field are transcended to acquire 'new epistemological frameworks and methodological practices that exceed any one discipline'.[68] I follow these distinctions here: the Cambridge Expedition aimed not only to bring distinct disciplines to a common research project, but to create 'common ground' for the disciplines of anthropology and psychology, 'drawing them closer together and enlarging the comparative dimension of each'.[69] This was expressed by Haddon as a 'long felt' expectation 'that psychological investigations must be undertaken before any real advance could be made in ethnology'.[70]

In contrast to Haddon, whose work is associated with the consolidation of anthropology as a professional discipline, Thomson was operating within an increasingly specialized field, with cultural anthropology now firmly aligned with the social sciences and not the natural sciences (sciences and social sciences being two of the 'three cultures' that structure the modern university, identified by Jerome Kagan since C.P. Snow's renowned 1959 Rede Lecture articulation of the polarized 'two cultures' of the arts and sciences).[71] Thomson's work in Arnhem Land began as an applied anthropology project in the wake of killings of non-Aboriginal people in the area, where he was entrusted with a peacekeeping and mediatory role by the Commonwealth government. He referred to this undertaking explicitly as an 'expedition' and the expeditionary form seems to have given Thomson enough flexibility and independence from the dominant conceptual paradigms of functionalist anthropology for him to maintain unfashionably heterogeneous activities in the field. His interdisciplinary understanding of Aboriginal knowledge systems as an articulation of local biophysical environments and social, material and cultural systems, developed through close 'attune[ment] over time to these environments', can be understood to have anticipated research paradigms within the fields of cultural ecology of the 1950s and ecological anthropology of the 1960s.[72] His work predates Julian Steward's *Theory of Culture Change* (1955), for example, which is commonly associated with the founding of cultural ecology.[73] The area of global environmental change studies recognizes these fields, which fuse findings from the fields of both biology and anthropology, as early responses to the challenge of initiating a sustained interrogation of human–environment interactions – a challenge not taken up until the 1970s in other social sciences.[74] Thomson's work can be viewed as a pioneering effort in this direction.

In the Metropole

Frank Debenham, the first Professor of Geography at Cambridge University and a fellow of the RGS, had been the geologist and cartographer on Scott's last British Antarctic expedition (1910–13). In June 1938, he wrote Thomson a letter of introduction to Arthur Hinks, mapmaker and secretary of the RGS, and editor of the *Geographical Journal*. Debenham, a fellow Australian, hoped that the society might publish some of Thomson's work, and requested Hinks' cartographic assistance with drawing up maps of Arnhem Land.[75] Thomson's own letter explained that very little was known geographically about his field site, where he had 'encountered many unnamed and uncharted rivers'.[76] By this time based in Cambridge on a Rockefeller Travelling Fellowship, he was anxious to know if anything could be done with his sketch maps. 'We should be glad ... to see your map material and oblique [aerial] photographs and discuss how they can be worked up', Hinks replied.[77]

In May the following year, Thomson gave a lecture at the RGS on his 'Journeys in Arnhem Land', accompanied by film footage portraying the 'tree-dwelling Djinba clan' in the Arafura swamps.[78] It would be a decade though, with the war intervening, before the appearance of his lecture material as a three-part series in the *Geographical Journal* (1948–49). On Christmas eve 1947, prior to the first article's publication, Thomson wrote with alarm to G.R. Crone, librarian and map curator at the RGS, expressing his dismay at news of the impending American-Australian Scientific Expedition to Arnhem Land (supported by the National Geographic Society, the Smithsonian

Institution and the Commonwealth of Australia) (see chapters by Thomas and Harris and Harris, this volume). Anxious about his own account of research in this area, he argued the case to 'expedite publication in view of the pending American expedition to this territory'.

> I feel that this is more than necessary because of claims now being made in the Australian press, as part of the advance publicity for the American expedition, that Arnhem Land is still unexplored, whereas I myself spent in all some three and a half years in the Territory ... I am the only Australian who knows this territory and its people well and feel that it would be a pity to wait any longer for additions to the maps before getting the account printed. This is the last large area in Australia that remained unexplored.[79]

Crone replied, reassuring Thomson that the society would publish the paper as soon as they received it. 'You can rest assured that we appreciate the importance of this work and the necessity to forestall any publication by the proposed American expedition'.[80] To these ends, a notice was placed in the *Geographical Journal* outlining the extent of Thomson's 'research mission' in Arnhem Land and crediting him with 'the discovery of the great Arafura swamp, many rivers, and portions of the coastline' for which, along with his 'anthropological discoveries', he had just been awarded the society's Cuthbert Peek Grant.[81] The first of Thomson's articles appeared in the next issue of the journal; his 'An Arnhem Land Adventure' went into print in the *National Geographic Magazine* the same year. A few days after writing to Crone, an article by Thomson appeared in the Brisbane *Courier-Mail* announcing the impending arrival of the 'American expedition', outlining its aims and pointing out the 'many long journeys of exploration' already undertaken in Arnhem Land (his own). 'Why are Australians willing to leave to others the final exploration of the last of their frontiers?' he asked.[82]

Clearly, claims of opening up 'final frontiers' mattered a great deal to Thomson. By way of comparison, the anthropologists Ronald and Catherine Berndt were also concerned about reports of the 'expedition by the National Geographic Society', and published an article titled 'Arnhem Land Is Far from Unknown' in the Adelaide *Advertiser*, debunking myths that 'Arnhem Land is a glamorous, exotic, unexplored and dangerous land'.[83] As students of Elkin, the notion of the expedition was suspect to them, just as it was to their mentor. '[I] took an expedition which I normally severely refrain from doing', Elkin wrote of his own field trip to southern Arnhem Land in 1949.[84] In his newspaper and magazine articles, Thomson placed far more emphasis on a locale 'shunned by the white man' than the Berndts. Throughout

Australia's settlement history, it had been 'a vast untamed No Man's Land', he claimed.[85] As an anthropologist, he was acutely aware, of course, that this supposed wilderness was an intimately known home to the people he hoped to study. As a seasoned journalist, he realized the narrative potential of his expeditions and was able to create his own copy relaying his experiences. Thomson's Arnhem Land expeditions also received the attention of the popular press, which charted the preparations for and launch of his journeys, covered controversies surrounding his selection for the government commission, and made announcements when he was assumed missing. A single example serves here to convey how his activities were represented in the public domain. Ernestine Hill, a high-profile journalist and popular author

Dr. Donald Thomson, the Melbourne University anthropologist and special patrol and research officer for the Federal Government, who returned to Melbourne recently, after having spent 15 months among the aborigines in Arnhem Land.

Figure 3.3 'Portrait of Dr. Donald Thomson', circa 1937. Unknown photographer. By permission of the National Library of Australia (G.M. Mathews Collection of Portraits of Ornithologists, nla.pic-vn3799007).

renowned for her sensationalist promotion of the untapped economic potential of Australia's 'magnificent empty lands', described Thomson as a 'keen, wiry young man in the early 30s, ready to endure any hardships and to face any dangers in his thirst for knowledge'. He would live alone, she wrote, on 'one of the few coasts in the world that have totally missed civilisation'.[86]

Thomson's own articles on his Arnhem Land activities can be broken roughly into two groups: those produced during or shortly after the completion of the two expeditions in 1935 and 1936–37 and published in a wide variety of newspapers including the London *Times*, the Melbourne *Herald* and *Argus*, the *Sydney Morning Herald*, the Adelaide *Advertiser*, the Brisbane *Courier-Mail*, the *Queenslander* and *Sydney Mail*; and those produced in the postwar period including his articles in *Walkabout*, the *Geographical Journal* and the *National Geographic Magazine* mentioned earlier. It is difficult to say for certain why Thomson was drawn to publish so extensively in the popular and non-academic press. It could possibly have been for extra income, although he was employed by the University of Melbourne for most of his career, from 1932 onwards. Or it could be that his style of writing lent itself to a wider readership. Even his official government reports – *Interim General Report of Preliminary Expedition to Arnhem Land, Northern Territory of Australia 1935–36* (1936) and *Report on Expedition to Arnhem Land, 1936–37* (1939) – make for surprisingly vivid and compelling reading. Thomson submitted the reports to the Royal Anthropological Institute of Great Britain and Ireland for the Wellcome Medal for applied anthropology, which he won in 1939. One of the judges commented on the thrilling nature of Thomson's narratives: 'Here you have ... a story, wonderfully told, of adventure. I have seldom read a story which, as this essay does, tells of high courage, fortitude and determination as is related in this extraordinarily interesting, and indeed thrilling, account'.[87]

Thomson drew on the material contained within these reports and in his expedition journals, recycling the 'most remarkable experiences' of his travels across a number of articles, often reusing portions of text verbatim. Here, perhaps, was a way to garner recognition, accolades and support for his intrepid activities on a last frontier; to write, also, of distinctive natural history phenomena in little-known terrain; to draw attention to the plight of a people whose culture he was sure was on the brink of destruction; and to take pleasure in communication through his literary flair.

With the RGS's long history of negotiating the unsettled terrain between discourses of adventurous travel and scientific exploration, it is not surprising that Thomson turned to it as a platform for disseminating accounts of his travels, research findings and adventurous exploits, without one discourse necessarily nullifying the other. Felix Driver argues persuasively that since its inception in 1830, the RGS was, above all, a hybrid and heterogeneous institution – 'part social club, part learned society, part imperial information exchange and part platform for the promotion of sensational feats of exploration'. In the mid Victorian years it endeavoured to perform two roles simultaneously, and often irreconcilably: 'to acquire the status of a scientific society and to provide a public forum for the celebration of a new age of exploration'.[88] The society's history, suggests Driver, can be understood through a sequence of differences over its role and purpose, and about the contested nature of scientific knowledge when coupled with a 'craving for sensation'.[89] Nevertheless, it played a pivotal role during the nineteenth century in supporting and promoting exploration, and in setting parameters for how explorers should perform and behave in the field. Nicola J. Thomas and Jude Hill observe that the RGS maintained its influence at the turn of the century during a perceived crisis surrounding the future of exploration by promoting the challenges of those areas of the globe that were 'still unknown'.[90]

In 1938 the question of the future of exploration was again raised. Thomson contacted the RGS at a time when the society was going through a process of self-examination over its relevance to 'the times'.[91] In a memorandum to the RGS Council, Dudley Stamp wrote: 'Since its inception over one hundred years ago the Society has been concerned especially with Travel and Exploration. So much has been accomplished in the last century that this particular field of geographical work is of necessity one of ever increasing restriction'.[92] His provocations as a professional geographer, then based at the London School of Economics where he held a readership in economic geography, precipitated the appointment of a committee to consider the 'future, organisation, and work of the Society'. The committee's findings acknowledged that the work of exploring the 'still unknown' was now largely complete. However, instead of conceding that the age of exploration might now, finally, be over, the committee responded with the statement quoted at this chapter's head: it envisaged and encouraged a future of intensive rather than extensive exploration, providing practical and modest financial support towards its realization. Thomson's 'discoveries' of particular waterways, swamps and coastal areas are a clear instance of 'intensive exploration'. Rather than traversing large amounts of territory in the form of a linear projection that 'sampled' terrain in a way more typical of nineteenth-century exploration,[93] he gathered detailed local knowledge recursively within a circumscribed area.

Nicolas Peterson and Geoffrey Gray both argue that in the postwar period Thomson became increasingly isolated from the Australian anthropological establishment with its stronghold under Elkin at the University of Sydney, which remained the only Department of Anthropology in Australia until 1950. Thomson was the only anthropologist at the University of Melbourne. In 1948 Thomson wrote: 'it is rather difficult to stand and to work quite alone here – and of course it means no recognition for one's work except overseas – and I have always known that it [is] that that matters anyway'.[94] He was offered a lectureship at Cambridge, which he declined, during this period, and was awarded the Rivers memorial medal of the Royal Anthropological Institute of Great Britain and Ireland in 1952. His connections to the RGS were also important in this regard. As noted, through the society's journal and lecture series, Thomson could integrate film, photography, personal accounts of travel including the joys and challenges of adventurous exploration and of scientific discovery as a matter of course, given the society's long history of fusing these diverse genres, modes of address and media. He could thereby reach a wider audience than that available at home in strictly anthropological circles. Furthermore, as his alarm about competing claims to opening up 'unexplored' territory makes clear, both his journalism and his relationship with the RGS provided a way to shape a reputation as a 'last explorer' and to reap any associated rewards – such as the society's medals and public acclaim. These rewards may have gone some way towards compensating him for the lack of wider recognition.

A Curious Expeditionary

Although there was much that was orthodox about Thomson's evocation of the expeditionary form – the emphasis on romantic adventure and heroic feats of endurance – the expedition also provided a flexible form of scientific travel during a period of twentieth-century disciplinary specialization in the field of anthropology, as this chapter has shown. On the ground in Arnhem Land, Thomson made use of his expeditions to develop idiosyncratic fieldwork methodologies. He drew an important distinction between the coast of Arnhem Land and the inland. In 1935 he undertook lengthy overland journeys on foot as part of a larger strategy to 'demonstrate to the natives that the white man is not helpless away from his boat [and] to impress upon them the fact that he has the strength and resourcefulness necessary to make long journeys through their country, and that he is able to live as they live'.[95] This was a way to win trust and respect, and to ensure he did not transgress strict forms of etiquette to do with entry to particular peoples' land or camps. To these ends, Thomson stripped away 'almost all the white man's usual impedementa [sic]', sometimes carrying only a toothbrush and sheath knife, and sharing in all daily activities as far as possible – disposing even of that legendary locus of retreat, the 'ethnographer's tent'.

Thomson's adoption of a peripatetic Aboriginal lifestyle ups the ante on anthropology's long-held ambition to establish rapport, dating back to Haddon's foundational pronouncement that it is essential to understand 'native actions ... from a native and not from a European point of view'.[96] Thomson undertook an unusually immersed form of fieldwork through his relinquishment of a fixed and sedentary research base, such as that used by his contemporary Lloyd Warner who conducted research in Arnhem Land at the Milingimbi Methodist Mission from 1927 to 1929. The mobility that is so fundamental to the idea of an expedition found a good fit with the culture of nomads. It allowed Thomson to spend time with people who were 'self-supporting' and 'truly independent' from European settlement[97] – one of anthropology's most cherished aims. It also enabled him to place more emphasis on the 'participatory' part of anthropology's defining methodology. Stocking suggests that a simpler rephrasing of the fieldworker's key activities of 'participation, observation, interrogation' might be 'doing, seeing, talking', and argues that even Malinowski ('like most fieldworkers since?'), who is credited with setting the discipline's methodological standard, spent more time in the Trobriands gathering information through seeing and talking than through doing.[98] In contrast, once embarked on an expeditionary journey, Thomson undertook much of the daily hands-on activity of a nomadic lifestyle – sleeping on the ground, sharing a fire and camp, hunting and killing game, attending ceremonial events and travelling vast areas of country. 'I found that once I was on a journey', he wrote, 'I was obliged to live the same life as they lived'.[99]

Thomson's expedition reports reveal a curious enmeshment between himself and the people he had been commissioned to study, 'pacify' and 'control': they are simultaneously members of his expedition, his indispensable assistants, guides, interpreters, mediators and labourers; the purported recipients of his peacekeeping aims; and subjects of anthropological survey and research. Through these entangled methods and encounters in the field, he fell 'under the spell of my black brothers', to use his phrase (always with the proviso that they abided by a culture not yet 'broken down' by colonizing forces). 'I felt that I had more in common with these splendid and virile natives than with my own people', he wrote.[100]

He became wedded to this notion of immersed, mobile and participatory anthropological research through the form of the expedition, and hoped to repeat it on his 1957 trip to the Lake Mackay region in Central Australia, for which he received the RGS's 'official blessing'.[101] He turned to the society again for further support to mount a return expedition to the region, emphasizing that the country 'is still only partly explored' and inhabited by a remnant group of desert-dwelling people adapted to a harsh desert ecology whom he planned to study before it was 'too late'. Again, he expressed anxiety about competing American expeditions he believed would follow in the wake of his own, especially once his photographs had been distributed by the press.[102] In 1962, during a period when the RGS was inundated with requests for support from proposed university and youth expeditions, Thomson was granted £250 (the most generous sum allocated to any of the applicants).[103] For his return expedition, he hoped to find a surveyor, geologist and botanist to accompany him. 'I was trained in botany and zoology as well as in anthropology, but I cannot do all the scientific work single-handed as I tried to do this year', he wrote at the age of fifty-six.[104] Together they would study desert ecology and desert people in tandem. In his near-to-final expedition he had turned full circle back to a scientific team approach, reminiscent of Wilkins or Haddon, and drawing on diverse forms of expertise as a way to continue his commitment to a form of interdisciplinary enquiry that considered people and particular environments as interlinked, rather than separate realms of concern.

Saskia Beudel is Adjunct Associate Professor at the Centre for Creative and Cultural Research, University of Canberra, where she also lectures in writing and literary studies. She was a 2016 Fellow at the Rachel Carson Center for Environment & Society in Munich, Germany. Prior to that she was a Postdoctoral Research Fellow at the University of Sydney (2013–16).

Notes

1. Thomson to Haddon, n.d., Envelope 5425, Haddon Papers, Cambridge University Library [henceforth CUL].

2. Nicolas Peterson, 'A Biographical Sketch of Donald Thomson', in Donald Thomson, *Donald Thomson in Arnhem Land* (Carlton: Miegunyah Press, 2003), 2.
3. Ibid.; Simon Nasht, *The Last Explorer: Hubert Wilkins Australia's Unknown Hero* (Sydney: Hodder, 2005), 120–21; and G.H. Wilkins, *Undiscovered Australia: Being an Account of an Expedition to Tropical Australia to Collect Specimens of the Rarer Native Fauna for the British Museum, 1923–1925* (London: Ernest Benn Limited, 1928), 265–67.
4. Wilkins, *Undiscovered Australia*, 266.
5. Peterson, 'A Biographical Sketch', 2.
6. Ibid., 3–4.
7. Ibid., 2.
8. Allen McEvey quoted in Bruce Rigsby and Nicolas Peterson, 'Introduction', in Bruce Rigsby and Nicolas Peterson (eds), *Donald Thomson: The Man and Scholar* (Canberra: The Academy of Social Sciences in Australia, 2005), 3.
9. Gatjil Djerrkura, 'Foreword', in Thomson, *Donald Thomson in Arnhem Land*, n.p.
10. Lindy Allen, 'A Photographer of Brilliance', in Rigsby and Peterson, *Donald Thomson*, 60.
11. Geoffrey Gray, 'A Deep-Seated Aversion or a Prudish Disapproval: Relations with Elkin', in Rigsby and Peterson, *Donald Thomson*, 83–100; Peterson, 'A Biographical Sketch', 4–5.
12. Henrika Kuklick, 'Personal Equations: Reflections on the History of Fieldwork, with Special Reference to Sociocultural Anthropology', *Isis* 102(1) (2011), 1–33; Henrika Kuklick, *The Savage Within* (Cambridge: Cambridge University Press, 1991), 1–26; James Clifford, *The Predicament of Culture* (Cambridge, MA/London: Harvard University Press, 1988), 21–41; and George W. Stocking, *After Tylor: British Social Anthropology 1888–1951* (London: Athlone, 1995), 98–123.
13. James Frazer, quoted in Clifford, *The Predicament of Culture*, 26; Kuklick, 'Personal Equations', 9, 17.
14. Kuklick, 'Personal Equations', 9.
15. Stocking, *After Tylor*, 114.
16. Warren Burggren, Kent Chapman, Bradley Keller, Michael Monticino and John Torday, 'Biological Sciences', in Robert Frodeman, Julie Thompson Klein and Carl Mitcham (eds), *The Oxford Handbook of Interdisciplinarity* (Oxford: Oxford University Press, 2010), 119.
17. Personal communication with Libby Robin in discussion about interdisciplinary approaches to environmental thought, December 2014.
18. Felix Driver, *Geography Militant: Cultures of Exploration and Empire* (Oxford/Malden, MA: Blackwell, 2001), 8–11.
19. Robert E. Kohler, *All Creatures: Naturalists, Collectors, and Biodiversity, 1850–1950* (Princeton, NJ/Oxford: Princeton University Press, 2006), 14.

20. Donald F. Thomson, 'An Arnhem Land Odyssey: High Adventure in the Back of Beyond', *Courier-Mail*, 30 October 1937, 23; Donald F. Thomson, 'Among the Savages of Arnhem Land: Story of Caledon Bay', *Sydney Morning Herald*, 7 January 1939, 13; Donald F. Thomson, 'An Arnhem Land Adventure', *National Geographic Magazine* 93(3) (1948), 403.
21. Evening Minutes, 8 May 1939 and 19 May 1952, Royal Geographical Society Archives [henceforth RGS Archives].
22. Driver, *Geography Militant*, 24–67; Dane Kennedy, *The Last Blank Spaces: Exploring Africa and Australia* (Cambridge, MA/London: Harvard University Press, 2013), 34–50; Simon Naylor and James R. Ryan, 'Exploration and the Twentieth Century', in Simon Naylor and James R. Ryan (eds), *New Spaces of Exploration: Geographies of Discovery in the Twentieth Century* (London/New York: I.B. Tauris, 2010), 3, 11; and Nicola J. Thomas and Jude Hill, 'Explorations in the Libyan Desert: William J. Harding King', in Naylor and Ryan, *New Spaces of Exploration*, 78–80.
23. Kennedy, *The Last Blank Spaces*, 88–94.
24. Donald F. Thomson, *Interim General Report of Preliminary Expedition to Arnhem Land, Northern Territory of Australia 1935–36* (Canberra: Commonwealth Government Printer, 9 April 1936), 2.
25. Ibid., 6–8; Donald F. Thomson, 'The Story of Arnhem Land', *Walkabout*, 1 August 1946, 15.
26. Thomson, 'An Arnhem Land Adventure', 421.
27. Driver, *Geography Militant*, 69–71; Kuklick, 'Personal Equations', 13–15.
28. Kennedy, *The Last Blank Spaces*, 52–62, 82.
29. Driver, *Geography Militant*, 2.
30. W.A. Horn, quoted in D.J. Mulvaney, '"A Splendid Lot of Fellows": Achievements and Consequences of the Horn Expedition', in S.R. Morton and D.J. Mulvaney (eds), *Exploring Central Australia: Society, the Environment and the 1894 Horn Expedition* (Chipping Norton: Surrey Beatty & Sons, 1996), 4.
31. Driver, *Geography Militant*, 2, 22.
32. Personal communication, Nicolas Peterson, June 2015.
33. Donald F. Thomson, 'The Hero Cult, Initiation and Totemism on Cape York', *Journal of the Anthropological Institute of Great Britain and Ireland* 63 (1933), 454.
34. Thomson to Haddon, 15 September 1934, Envelope 3012, Haddon Papers, CUL.
35. Alfred C. Haddon (ed.), *Reports of the Cambridge Anthropological Expedition to Torres Straits*, Cambridge: Cambridge University Press, 1901–1935.
36. Thomson to Haddon, 15 September 1934, Envelope 3012, Haddon Papers, CUL.

37. H.A. Thomson to Haddon, 25 November 1935, Envelope 1025, Haddon Papers, CUL.
38. H.A. Thomson to Haddon, 6 February 1935, Envelope 5425, Haddon Papers, CUL.
39. Kuklick, 'Personal Equations', 11; Kuklick, 'Islands in the Pacific: Darwinian Biogeography and British Anthropology', *American Ethnologist* 23(3) (1996), 611; and Stocking, *After Tylor*, 100.
40. Peterson, 'A Biographical Sketch', 2–3.
41. Kuklick, 'Personal Equations', 11.
42. Donald F. Thomson, *Birds of Cape York Peninsula* (Melbourne: H.J. Green, Government Printer, 1935).
43. Donald F. Thomson, *Report on Expedition to Arnhem Land, 1936–37* (Canberra: Commonwealth Printer, 1938), 10.
44. Thomson to Kirwan, 8 March 1955, Correspondence 1954–55, Box 434, RGS Archives.
45. Stocking, *After Tylor*, 105, 106; Alfred C. Haddon, *Evolution in Art*, London: W. Scott, 1895.
46. Donald F. Thomson, *Economic Structure and the Ceremonial Exchange Cycle in Arnhem Land* (Melbourne: Macmillan, 1949), 40.
47. Donald F. Thomson, 'Arnhem Land: Explorations among an Unknown People. Part II: The People of Blue Mud Bay', *The Geographical Journal* 113 (1949), 6.
48. Gray, 'A Deep-Seated Aversion', 84–89; and Peterson, 'A Biographical Sketch', 4–5.
49. Saskia Beudel and Margo Daly, 'Gallant Desert Flora: Olive Pink's Australian Arid Regions Flora Reserve', *Historical Records of Australian Science* 25 (2014), 227–52; and Geoffrey Gray, '"Piddington's Indiscretion": Ralph Piddington, the Australian National Research Council and Academic Freedom', *Oceania* 64(3) (1994), 217–45.
50. Thomson to Kirwan, 8 March 1955, Correspondence 1954–55, Box 434, RGS Archives.
51. Radcliffe-Brown, quoted in Gray, 'A Deep-Seated Aversion', 86; see also Peterson, 'A Biographical Sketch', 4.
52. Elkin, quoted in Athol Chase, 'Anthropology through a Biological Lens', in Rigsby and Peterson, *Donald Thomson*, 19.
53. Kuklick, *The Savage Within*, 8–11.
54. Peter Weingart, 'A Short History of Knowledge Formations', in Frodeman et al., *The Oxford Handbook of Interdisciplinarity*, 6, 8.
55. Felix Driver, 'Modern Explorers', in Naylor and Ryan, *New Spaces of Exploration*, 247–48; Lynn K. Nyhart, 'Natural History and the "New" Biology', in N. Jardine, J.A. Secord and E.C. Spary (eds), *Cultures of Natural History* (Cambridge: Cambridge University Press, 2000), 426–43; and Kohler, *All Creatures*, xi.
56. Driver, 'Modern Explorers', 248.
57. Thomson, *Birds of Cape York Peninsula*, 7.

58. Donald Worster, *Nature's Economy: A History of Ecological Ideas*, 2nd edition (Cambridge: Cambridge University Press, 1995), 58.
59. Thomson completed a Doctorate of Science in 1934. C.G. Seligman, another former member of the Cambridge Expedition, was one of his examiners.
60. Stocking, *After Tylor*, xvii.
61. Kuklick, 'Islands in the Pacific', 625.
62. Ibid., 625–26.
63. Sandra Rouse, 'Expedition and Institution: A.C. Haddon and Anthropology at Cambridge', in Anita Herle and Sandra Rouse (eds), *Cambridge and the Torres Strait: Centenary Essays on the 1898 Anthropological Expedition* (Cambridge: Cambridge University Press, 1998), 71.
64. Nicolas Peterson, '"I Can't Follow You on This Horde-Clan Business At All": Donald Thomson, Radcliffe-Brown and a Final Note on the Horde', *Oceania* 76(1) (2006), 16–26.
65. Stocking, *After Tylor*, 114.
66. Haddon, quoted in Stocking, ibid.
67. Julie Thompson Klein, 'A Taxonomy of Interdisciplinarity', in Frodeman et al., *The Oxford Handbook of Interdisciplinarity*, 17.
68. Poul Holm et al., 'Collaboration between the Natural, Social and Human Sciences in Global Change Research', *Environmental Science and Policy* 28 (2013), 25, 28–29.
69. Kuklick, *The Savage Within*, 137.
70. Haddon, quoted in Kuklick, ibid.
71. Jerome Kagan, *The Three Cultures* (Cambridge: Cambridge University Press, 2009); and C.P. Snow, *The Two Cultures and the Scientific Revolution* (Cambridge: Cambridge University Press, 1959).
72. Chase, 'Anthropology through a Biological Lens', 21.
73. Ibid. Julian Steward, *Theory of Culture Change*, Urbana, IL: University of Illinois Press, 1955.
74. Gisli Palsson et al., 'Reconceptualizing the "Anthropos" in the Anthropocene: Integrating the Social Sciences and Humanities in Global Environmental Change Research', *Environmental Science and Policy* 28 (2013), 5.
75. Debenham to Hinks, 8 June 1938, Dr Donald Thomson 1931–40, CB 10, RGS Archives.
76. Thomson to Hinks, 10 June 1938, Dr Donald Thomson 1931–40, CB 10, RGS Archives.
77. Hinks to Thomson, 13 June 1938, Dr Donald Thomson 1931–40, CB 10, RGS Archives.
78. Anon., 'Dr. Donald Thomson's Work in Arnhem Land', *The Geographical Journal* 112(1/3) (1948), 124.
79. Thomson to Crone, 24 December 1947, Thomson, Donald F., CB 11, RGS Archives.

80. Crone to Thomson, 6 January 1948, Thomson, Donald F., CB 11, RGS Archives.
81. Anon., 'Dr. Donald Thomson's Work in Arnhem Land', 124.
82. Donald F. Thomson, 'What Secrets Are in Our Far North?', *Courier-Mail*, 5 January 1948, 2.
83. R.M. and C.H. Berndt, 'Arnhem Land Is Far from Unknown', *The Advertiser*, 28 February 1948, 6.
84. Elkin, quoted in Martin Thomas, 'Expedition as Time Capsule', in Martin Thomas and Margo Neale (eds), *Exploring the Legacy of the 1948 Arnhem Land Expedition* (Canberra: ANU E Press, 2011), 9.
85. Donald Thomson, 'Arnhem Land: Explorations among an Unknown People. Part I: The Journey to Bennett Bay', *The Geographical Journal* 112(4/6) (1948), 146.
86. Ernestine Hill, 'To Live among Natives: Young Anthropologist's Mission for Government', *The Advertiser*, 7 August 1934, 14.
87. Henry Galway to K.M. Martindell, The Wellcome Medal for Research in Anthropology, 22 March 1939, A88/1/128, Royal Anthropological Institute Archives.
88. Driver, *Geography Militant*, 24–25.
89. Ibid., 46–48.
90. Thomas and Hill, 'Explorations in the Libyan Desert', 78–79.
91. Francis Younghusband et al., Report of the Committee on the Future of the Society, 31 May 1939, Council Minutes, March 1939–March 1947, RGS Archives.
92. L. Dudley Stamp, Memorandum on Certain Aspects of Policy of the Royal Geographical Society, 12 December 1938, Council Minutes, January 1936–February 1939, RGS Archives.
93. Kohler, *All Creatures*, 13.
94. Thomson, quoted in Peterson, '"I Can't Follow You"', 23.
95. Thomson, *Interim General Report*, 22.
96. Haddon, quoted in Kuklick, 'Personal Equations', 15.
97. Peterson, '"I Can't Follow You"', 20.
98. Stocking, *After Tylor*, 260.
99. Thomson, *Interim General Report*, 22.
100. Thomson, 'An Arnhem Land Odyssey', 23; Thomson, 'The Story of Arnhem Land', 22.
101. Donald F. Thomson, *Bindibu Country* (Melbourne: Nelson, 1975), 10.
102. Thomson to Rennell, 6 November 1957, Donald Thomson Correspondence 1957–58, Box 476, RGS Archives.
103. Recommendations of the Expeditions Committee, 12 March 1962, Council Minutes, 10 January 1956–24 June 1963, RGS Archives.
104. Thomson to Rennell, 6 November 1957, Donald Thomson Correspondence 1957–58, Box 476, RGS Archives.

Bibliography

Allen, Lindy. 'A Photographer of Brilliance', in Bruce Rigsby and Nicolas Peterson (eds), *Donald Thomson: The Man and Scholar* (Canberra: The Academy of Social Sciences in Australia, 2005), 45–62.

Anon. 'Dr. Donald Thomson's Work in Arnhem Land'. *The Geographical Journal* 112(1/3) (1948), 124.

Berndt, R.M., and C.H. Berndt. 'Arnhem Land Is Far from Unknown'. *The Advertiser*, 28 February 1948, 6.

Beudel, Saskia, and Margo Daly. 'Gallant Desert Flora: Olive Pink's Australian Arid Regions Flora Reserve'. *Historical Records of Australian Science* 25 (2014), 227–52.

Burggren, Warren, Kent Chapman, Bradley Keller, Michael Monticino and John Torday. 'Biological Sciences', in Robert Frodeman, Julie Thompson Klein and Carl Mitcham (eds), *The Oxford Handbook of Interdisciplinarity* (Oxford: Oxford University Press, 2010), 119–32.

Chase, Athol. 'Anthropology through a Biological Lens', in Bruce Rigsby and Nicolas Peterson (eds), *Donald Thomson: The Man and Scholar* (Canberra: The Academy of Social Sciences in Australia, 2005), 17–28.

Clifford, James. *The Predicament of Culture*. Cambridge, MA/London: Harvard University Press, 1988.

Djerrkura, Gatjil. 'Foreword', in Donald Thomson, *Donald Thomson in Arnhem Land* (Carlton: Miegunyah Press, 2003), n.p.

Driver, Felix. *Geography Militant: Cultures of Exploration and Empire*. Oxford/Malden, MA: Blackwell, 2001.

———. 'Modern Explorers', in Simon Naylor and James R. Ryan (eds), *New Spaces of Exploration: Geographies of Discovery in the Twentieth Century* (London/New York: I.B. Tauris, 2010), 241–49.

Gray, Geoffrey. 'A Deep-Seated Aversion or a Prudish Disapproval: Relations with Elkin', in Bruce Rigsby and Nicolas Peterson (eds), *Donald Thomson: The Man and Scholar* (Canberra: The Academy of Social Sciences in Australia, 2005), 83–100.

———. '"Piddington's Indiscretion": Ralph Piddington, the Australian National Research Council and Academic Freedom'. *Oceania* 64(3) (1994), 217–45.

Haddon, Alfred C. *Evolution in Art*. London: W. Scott, 1895.

———. *Reports of the Cambridge Anthropological Expedition to Torres Straits*, Cambridge: Cambridge University Press, 1901–1935.

Hill, Ernestine. 'To Live among Natives: Young Anthropologist's Mission for Government'. *The Advertiser*, 7 August 1934, 14.

Holm, Poul, et al. 'Collaboration between the Natural, Social and Human Sciences in Global Change Research'. *Environmental Science and Policy* 28 (2013), 25–35.

Kagan, Jerome. *The Three Cultures*. Cambridge: Cambridge University Press, 2009.

Kennedy, Dane. *The Last Blank Spaces: Exploring Africa and Australia*. Cambridge, MA/London: Harvard University Press, 2013.

Klein, Julie Thompson. 'A Taxonomy of Interdisciplinarity', in Robert Frodeman, Julie Thompson Klein and Carl Mitcham (eds), *The Oxford Handbook of Interdisciplinarity* (Oxford: Oxford University Press, 2010), 15–30.

Kohler, Robert E. *All Creatures: Naturalists, Collectors, and Biodiversity, 1850–1950*. Princeton, NJ/Oxford: Princeton University Press, 2006.

Kuklick, Henrika. 'Islands in the Pacific: Darwinian Biogeography and British Anthropology'. *American Ethnologist* 23(3) (1996), 611–38.

———. 'Personal Equations: Reflections on the History of Fieldwork, with Special Reference to Sociocultural Anthropology'. *Isis* 102(1) (2011), 1–33.

———. *The Savage Within*. Cambridge: Cambridge University Press, 1991.

Mulvaney, D.J. '"A Splendid Lot of Fellows": Achievements and Consequences of the Horn Expedition', in S.R. Morton and D.J. Mulvaney (eds), *Exploring Central Australia: Society, the Environment and the 1894 Horn Expedition* (Chipping Norton: Surrey Beatty & Sons, 1996), 3–12.

Nasht, Simon. *The Last Explorer: Hubert Wilkins Australia's Unknown Hero*. Sydney: Hodder, 2005.

Naylor, Simon, and James R. Ryan. 'Exploration and the Twentieth Century', in Simon Naylor and James R. Ryan (eds), *New Spaces of Exploration: Geographies of Discovery in the Twentieth Century* (London/New York: I.B. Tauris, 2010), 1–22.

Nyhart, Lynn K. 'Natural History and the "New" Biology', in N. Jardine, J.A. Secord and E.C. Spary (eds), *Cultures of Natural History* (Cambridge: Cambridge University Press, 2000), 426–43.

Palsson, Gisli, et al. 'Reconceptualizing the "Anthropos" in the Anthropocene: Integrating the Social Sciences and Humanities in Global Environmental Change Research'. *Environmental Science and Policy* 28 (2013), 3–13.

Peterson, Nicolas. 'A Biographical Sketch of Donald Thomson', in Donald Thomson, *Donald Thomson in Arnhem Land* (Carlton: Miegunyah Press, 2003), 1–21.

———. '"I Can't Follow You on This Horde-Clan Business At All": Donald Thomson, Radcliffe-Brown and a Final Note on the Horde'. *Oceania* 76(1) (2006), 16–26.

Rigsby, Bruce, and Nicolas Peterson. 'Introduction', in Bruce Rigsby and Nicolas Peterson (eds), *Donald Thomson: The Man and Scholar* (Canberra: The Academy of Social Sciences in Australia, 2005), 1–16.

Rouse, Sandra. 'Expedition and Institution: A.C. Haddon and Anthropology at Cambridge', in Anita Herle and Sandra Rouse (eds), *Cambridge and the Torres Strait: Centenary Essays on the 1898 Anthropological Expedition* (Cambridge: Cambridge University Press, 1998), 50–76.

Snow, C.P. *The Two Cultures and the Scientific Revolution*. Cambridge: Cambridge University Press, 1959.

Steward, Julian. *Theory of Culture Change*. Urbana, IL: University of Illinois Press, 1955.
Stocking, George W. *After Tylor: British Social Anthropology 1888–1951*. London: Athlone, 1995.
Thomas, Martin. 'Expedition as Time Capsule', in Martin Thomas and Margo Neale (eds), *Exploring the Legacy of the 1948 Arnhem Land Expedition* (Canberra: ANU E Press, 2011), 1–30.
Thomas, Nicola J., and Jude Hill. 'Explorations in the Libyan Desert: William J. Harding King', in Simon Naylor and James R. Ryan (eds), *New Spaces of Exploration: Geographies of Discovery in the Twentieth Century* (London/New York: I.B. Tauris, 2010), 78–104.
Thomson, Donald F. 'Among the Savages of Arnhem Land: Story of Caledon Bay'. *Sydney Morning Herald*, 7 January 1939, 13.
———. 'Arnhem Land: Explorations among an Unknown People. Part I: The Journey to Bennett Bay'. *The Geographical Journal* 112(4/6) (1948), 146–64.
———. 'Arnhem Land: Explorations among an Unknown People. Part II: The People of Blue Mud Bay'. *The Geographical Journal* 113 (1949), 1–8.
———. 'An Arnhem Land Adventure'. *National Geographic Magazine* 93(3) (1948), 403–30.
———. 'An Arnhem Land Odyssey: High Adventure in the Back of Beyond'. *Courier-Mail*, 30 October 1937, 23.
———. *Bindibu Country*. Melbourne: Nelson, 1975.
———. *Birds of Cape York Peninsula*. Melbourne: H.J. Green, Government Printer, 1935.
———. *Economic Structure and the Ceremonial Exchange Cycle in Arnhem Land*. Melbourne: Macmillan, 1949.
———. 'The Hero Cult, Initiation and Totemism on Cape York'. *Journal of the Anthropological Institute of Great Britain and Ireland* 63 (1933), 453–537.
———. *Interim General Report of Preliminary Expedition to Arnhem Land, Northern Territory of Australia 1935–36*. Canberra: Commonwealth Government Printer, 9 April 1936.
———. *Report on Expedition to Arnhem Land, 1936–37*. Canberra: Commonwealth Printer, 1938.
———. 'The Story of Arnhem Land'. *Walkabout*, 1 August 1946, 5–22.
———. 'What Secrets Are in Our Far North?' *Courier-Mail*, 5 January 1948, 2.
Weingart, Peter. 'A Short History of Knowledge Formations', in Robert Frodeman, Julie Thompson Klein and Carl Mitcham (eds), *The Oxford Handbook of Interdisciplinarity* (Oxford: Oxford University Press, 2010), 3–14.
Wilkins, G.H. *Undiscovered Australia: Being an Account of an Expedition to Tropical Australia to Collect Specimens of the Rarer Native Fauna for the British Museum, 1923–1925*. London: Ernest Benn Limited, 1928.
Worster, Donald. *Nature's Economy: A History of Ecological Ideas*. 2nd edition. Cambridge: Cambridge University Press, 1995.

PART II

Exploration, Archaeology, Race and Emergent Anthropology

Chapter 4

LOOKING AT CULTURE THROUGH AN ARTIST'S EYES

WILLIAM HENRY HOLMES AND THE EXPLORATION OF NATIVE AMERICAN ARCHAEOLOGY

Pamela M. Henson

Introduction

During the second half of the nineteenth century, the United States government commissioned a series of exploring expeditions to the western region of North America. The goals of the expeditions were primarily to map the remainder of the continent, to document the natural resources, to report on Native Americans and to search for the best routes to lay railroad lines to the west coast. The early explorers were military, primarily trained as topographers, interested in the physical environment and focused on drawing maps for later use. In the late 1840s and 1850s, topographical surveys led by military officers such as Major Howard Stansbury, Lieutenant John W. Gunnison and Lieutenant Gouverneur Kemble Warren, provided a basic understanding of the lands west of the Mississippi. The military surveyors did record some linguistic and ethnographic observations on Native Americans, but their interest was limited. In addition to settlement, interest in the West was stimulated by the discovery of gold in 1848 at Sutter's Mill in California and silver in the Comstock Lode in Nevada in 1859. Exploration was deferred during the American Civil War from 1861 to 1865. The late 1860s and 1870s saw a series of civilian expeditions, the Geological and Geographical Surveys by Dr Ferdinand Vandeveer Hayden, Clarence King, Major John Wesley Powell and Lieutenant George M. Wheeler. These scientific surveys documented nature resources and began to study sites of ancient Native American settlement, as well as current Indian communities. The expeditions facilitated the completion of the transcontinental railroad in the 1860s and the settlement of the West.[1]

These expeditions created the popular image of the American West. Painters such as Thomas Moran and photographers such as William Henry Jackson, Jack Hillers and Timothy O'Sullivan sent back images of the region that were disseminated in magazines and exhibited in major cities. Moran's work, such as *The Grand Canyon of the Yellowstone* (1872), was valued for its beauty and drama rather than the accuracy of its scientific detail. Photographs likewise reflected the individual beliefs of their creators, rather than being objective scientific records. These images reveal a belief in catastrophism rather than uniformitarianism. Dramatic angles, highlighting the power of natural forces, were usually favoured.[2]

The civilian explorers also became quite interested in the remains of vanished civilizations that they encountered, such as burial mounds in the Mississippi Valley and cliff dwellings in the Southwest. They began to collect and study the artefacts left behind in these uninhabited regions. Pottery, weavings, stone implements and ornaments were collected and sent back to the United States National Museum (USNM) for analysis and preservation. The collectors thought these artefacts were from people who had vanished long ago, with no relationship to living Native Americans. With no cultural information concerning their creators, the objects were analysed in terms of design and technology.[3]

William Henry Holmes (1846–1933)

One window onto these expeditions is provided by William Henry Holmes, an artist who joined the Hayden expedition in 1872 and subsequently moved from artist to geologist to archaeologist to museum director. He worked at the Smithsonian from 1871 to 1932, a sixty-year career that spanned the most important developments in the field of anthropology in the United States. Holmes grew up on a farm in Ohio but left in 1871 to pursue his love of art. He studied in Washington, DC, with the noted artist Theodore Kauffman. He was encouraged to visit the Smithsonian Institution, founded in 1846 for 'the increase and diffusion of knowledge', which served as the young nation's National Museum. Intrigued by the natural history specimens on display, he took out his sketchbook and began to draw. Museum curators were taken with the quality of his work, especially his accuracy, and he was hired to illustrate specimens. The following year, in 1872, he was invited to join the US Geological and Geographical Survey of the Territories directed by Ferdinand Vandeveer Hayden. On 1 March 1872, President Ulysses S. Grant had signed a law creating Yellowstone National Park. The goal of the 1872 expedition was to document the geology and topography of the Yellowstone area, particularly the Snake River and the Missouri. The Hayden Survey employed the pioneering photographers William Henry Jackson, Jack Hillers and Timothy O'Sullivan, but Hayden also hired artists who could capture the three-dimensional aspect of the landscape and biological specimens. The noted artist Thomas Moran accompanied them to produce his majestic landscapes of the American West that informed American images of the region for decades. Moran wrote, 'I place no value upon literal transcripts from Nature. My general scope is not realistic; all my tendencies are toward idealization'. In contrast, Holmes' panoramic drawings of the American West reflected his scientific training. Detailed and accurate, rather than dramatically artistic, they captured depth as well as length and width, providing a three-dimensional view of the majestic Rockies that two-dimensional photography could not reproduce.[4]

From 1872 to 1878, Holmes participated in further Geological and Geographical Surveys of the Territories directed by Hayden. These were the first non-military expeditions to the American West and they began a shift in emphasis in the exploration of the region. Hayden had participated in earlier military surveys and the civilian surveys had military escorts, but the imperative of the new surveys was the increase of knowledge rather than territorial conquest. This knowledge could assist in later domination of Native Americans, but its primary goal was scientific. Hayden assembled a team of naturalists specializing in botany, palaeontology, mammalogy, geology and mineralogy, as well as cartographers, artists and photographers. Holmes fitted in well with the expedition party. There were sixty men on the 1872 trip, including Hayden, a veteran explorer, and his assistant James Stevenson who was also experienced. Hayden's team also included such noted naturalists as Cyrus Thomas, C. Hart Merriam and John M. Coulter.[5]

In addition to seeing natural history fieldwork first-hand, Holmes was introduced to the concepts of geographic distribution and adaptation to specific environments. Holmes had been introduced to geographic imagery through the work of photographers including Jackson and the paintings of Moran and others. But Holmes developed his own unique technique of illustration, combining art and scientific

Figure 4.1 Sketch of participants in the Hayden Survey (United States Geological and Geographical Survey of the Territories, 1871–77). From left, William H. Holmes, George B. Chittenden, Dr Ferdinand V. Hayden, Story B. Ladd and William H. Jackson pose in front of a tent in Colorado, 1874. Drawing by William H. Holmes. By permission of Smithsonian Institution Archives.

accuracy to produce breathtaking views that captured stratigraphy and earth movement, as they developed over eons. In these early days, the skills he learned as a scientific illustrator could be applied to geology and the new field of anthropology, especially archaeology.

By the end of the first year of fieldwork, he was assigned the role of geologist because of his growing knowledge and understanding of the physical world they studied. Indeed, he co-discovered a geological phenomenon called the laccolithic theory.[6]

Hayden was quite satisfied with Holmes' work as an artist, saying that as an artist, he rendered 'most important services in all departments of the survey. His sections and sketches have proved useful not only for the geological reports, but have been of great value to the topographers in preparing their maps'. The 'admirable sketches of Mr. Holmes' were further praised for making 'the relations of the strata clear to the general reader as well as the professional geologist'. Holmes relished the experience of working in the field and spending evenings listening to Hayden or Merriam analyse their finds. Talented, eager and easy-going, Holmes soon became a valued member of the expedition. At the end of the summer, he returned to Washington to deliver his specimens to the USNM, finish his illustrations and write up his observations and reports.[7]

On the 1874 survey, Holmes got his chance to prove his new skills as a naturalist when a topographer named Shanks fell ill. Holmes and a small party spent two weeks surveying the northwestern portion of the Elk Range in Colorado Territory. Holmes' account of the journey was published in Hayden's *Annual Report* – a fully professional piece of scientific work, showing no sign of the author's usual artistic

Figure 4.2 'Panorama from Point Sublime', from Clarence E. Dutton, *Atlas to Accompany the Monograph on the Tertiary History of the Grand Cañon District*, 1882. Illustration by William H. Holmes. By permission of Smithsonian Institution Archives.

sensibility. He had made a rapid transition to scientist and learned his craft well.[8] Holmes' growing interests can be seen in this and other publications from the Hayden Surveys. From the 1876 trip, he prepared 'Report of William H. Holmes, on the Geology of the Sierra Abajo and West San Miguel Mountains'. But by the 1875 and 1876 surveys, he also turned to archaeology, writing 'Report of William H. Holmes on the Ancient Ruins of Southwestern Colorado, Examined during the Summers of 1875 and 1876'.[9]

By the summer of 1875, his fourth year in the field, Holmes was placed in charge of a field party sent to survey the San Juan Valley of Arizona and New Mexico. It was there that Holmes saw, for the first time, the ruins of the Anasazi people and became drawn into the new science of archaeology for the remainder of his career. The following year, he did the primary triangulation of the mountains of the Colorado region, climbing over thirty summits, some in excess of 4,000 metres. This encounter led to a carefully documented archaeology publication with drawings of artefacts, site plans, architecture and rock art. His drawings for his archaeological work display the same eye for visual beauty with exacting details as we find in his panoramas of the mountains. Holmes and the photographer Jackson together recreated the Puebloan cliff houses for the Centennial Exposition in Philadelphia the following year. For the remainder of the Hayden Survey, Holmes divided his energies between scientific illustration, geology and archaeology.[10]

When not in the field, Holmes worked in the red-stone towers of the Castle, as the original headquarters of the Smithsonian are known, finalizing drawings, writing up his observations and soaking up new knowledge. In working closely with naturalists, Holmes learned their scientific methodology and their form of visual observation and analysis. With his visual talents, he was able to identify subtle differences between various specimens and artefacts, and trace changing patterns. He also gained theoretical grounding in the classification of organisms by comparing and contrasting morphological changes of important characteristics. This zoological training had a major impact on all of his subsequent work. Darwin's *On the Origin of Species* had been published in the US only a decade before, but the National Museum's naturalists had immediately adopted its thesis, looking for sequences of adaptive changes. Holmes' illustrations carefully and clearly show subtle changes in adaptive characteristics over time.[11]

Holmes returned to the field in 1878 to survey the Wind River Mountains and Snake River to Yellowstone Park. That season included a total eclipse, which Holmes captured in colour drawings. Perhaps most importantly, he spent two months studying the geology of Yellowstone, including Obsidian Canyon where he noticed artefacts of human manufacture. The site was littered with arrow points and other stone implements – all defective, however – and Holmes speculated that many different tribes had come to the site to make obsidian implements, leaving behind those that broke or were not made correctly. This focus on manufacturing technique and identification of defective materials left behind would soon play an important role in his archaeological work. But his research was still primarily geological. Each winter he would draw, map and write up his work from the previous field season. In recognition of his contribution to science, mountains, peaks and fossil shells from across the region were named in his honour.[12]

These surveys of the West allowed a young man like Holmes to create a career he could not have conceived of before he entered the Smithsonian Castle. There were limits in what Holmes called twenty-five-mile-a-day fieldwork. The survey parties never stayed very long in one place, so the depth of research was limited. But fieldwork offered freedom that work in a university or museum could not, as well as sudden opportunities to step in when a colleague fell ill or help was needed on a project. He could collect specimens for the museum and publish reports on his work. Once trained in geology and natural history fieldwork, Holmes accepted concepts of evolution and looked for progressions of improvement in mammal adaptation and southwestern pottery. He used his knowledge of geological stratigraphy to develop a methodology for archaeological digs that documented the geological period from which objects originated. Thus, Holmes transferred his field skills and methods of analysis from geology and natural history to archaeology. The field of archaeology was so new that anyone with Holmes' interests and talents could enter the field and make a name. Holmes spent the 1879 season in Europe, enhancing his skills and learning from European collections and museum practices. Meanwhile, geological fieldwork in the United States underwent a major reorganization.[13]

Institutions Replace Expeditions

By 1879, the age of exploration of the American West had entered a new phase. The temporary expeditions were replaced by the US Geological Survey (USGS), a government agency established to direct and carry out geological studies across the continent. Also, by 1879 the Native American population had diminished dramatically as they were forced onto small reservations where resources were lacking and the bison on which they depended approached extinction. Thus, the Bureau of American Ethnology (BAE) was established as a unit of the Smithsonian to document the vanishing Native Americans, whom most people in the US thought would be extinct within the next two decades.[14]

Many people believed that the living Native Americans were not descendants of the advanced civilizations who had created massive burial mounds and hillside cities in the Southwest. It was up to the new field of archaeology to study and determine the relationships between ancient civilizations and the Native Americans now scratching out a living in remote and unproductive lands.[15]

The USGS was created because geological fieldwork was deemed very important to the economic growth of the republic. A permanent bureau of the government, the USGS mandate was to carry out geological research across the nation – not only exploration of the West but also replacing the many state surveys in the eastern states. The new USGS was headed by Clarence King, a Yale-educated civilian. The focus of geological fieldwork in the American West had moved from short-term military mapmaking to long-term civilian scientific study of the continent and its natural resources.[16]

The Bureau of American Ethnology was placed under Smithsonian aegis to document the archaeology and ethnology of Native Americans, with an emphasis on the living groups that were likely to be extinct by the turn of the century. Famed explorer Major John Wesley Powell was placed in charge of the BAE as he had become progressively more interested in the relics of ancient cities and living Native Americans than the geology of the West. Fieldwork among Native American communities and archaeological investigations provided material for a steady stream of publications by BAE researchers. All the artefacts they collected were transferred to, and cared for by, the curators in the USNM's Department of Anthropology. After King's resignation in 1881, Powell was also placed in charge of the USGS, keeping the ties between the three organizations close.[17]

By 1879, Holmes was at a crossroads in his career. He returned from Europe to the USGS as head of the Division of Illustration, where he put forth the guiding principles of scientific illustration for all USGS work: illustrators were to report, in visual form, scientific facts and concepts, not create artistic visions. But Holmes was drawn to non-natural features he found in the western lands – evidence of past occupation of majestic cliffs, such as dwellings, pottery and inscriptions on walls. His interest can be seen in the detailed report in 1875 on the Cliff Dweller ruins, and over the next several decades he spent more and more time on studies of southwestern archaeology. He became a major player in the emerging field of anthropology, especially archaeology and the analysis of material culture. Accepting the notion that Native Americans were heading to extinction, Holmes' colleagues dedicated themselves to documenting that culture before it vanished. But Holmes himself had little interest in living Native Americans, whom he regarded as untrustworthy savages. Eventually Holmes became a leader in the emerging field of archaeology, but did little ethnological work with living Native American communities.[18]

Holmes continued to pursue his interest in archaeology while at the USGS, transferring his specimens to the Smithsonian's National Museum. He continued to publish substantial analyses of these artefacts,[19] and in 1882 he was named an honorary curator of aboriginal pottery at the USNM. In 1884, he surveyed geology and archaeology in Mexico with photographer William Henry Jackson.[20] His first field trip solely devoted to archaeology was in 1887, when he joined a party studying the Indian tribes and ancient ruins of Arizona and New Mexico, although work was cut short by a climbing injury. In 1889, Holmes left the USGS and was appointed archaeologist at the BAE, while he continued as a USNM curator. Holmes was charged with addressing the question of the American Palaeolithic and began excavations at nearby sites, such as the Piney Branch site in Washington, DC. He left Washington briefly in the 1890s for Chicago, where he worked on the BAE exhibits for the World's Columbian Exposition of 1893. He then accepted a position at the Chicago Field Museum, but returned to Washington in 1897 to serve as head curator of the museum's Department of Anthropology, focusing on local field studies and sharing his knowledge through exhibits.[21]

Holmes' interest in function – how objects were made and used – led to him being embroiled in the controversy of the American Palaeolithic. Many archaeologists who examined these roughly flaked stones, found across the continent from the eastern seaboard to the Midwest and West, believed that they were similar to the palaeoliths of the Old World. They were regarded as primitive tools used by the first groups to fashion objects out of stone – a view that Holmes rejected summarily. He published a comprehensive overview of the 'Natural History of Flaked Stone Implements', in which he used the extensive collections amassed by the Bureau of American Ethnology for the

National Museum to debunk those claims. He set out a methodology for analysing these objects: separating natural objects from ones fashioned by human hands, outlining the techniques for production, identifying artefacts typical of certain cultural groups and demonstrating how they were used. The influence of the biological theory of evolution can be seen in this writing, as is apparent in a section titled 'Evolution of Species'.

> That nothing springs into being without cause and that no highly-developed form comes into existence without predecessors and ancestry, may be as safely maintained of art as of nature. The existence of a highly-specialized group of implements implies a long line of antecedent groups reaching back to an original primal form having no such phenomena as variation or specialization.

This evolution of artefacts 'is a progress accompanied by specialization and differentiation'. He visually demonstrated how even advanced societies began work on each implement by simple actions to create the basic shape – some were then completed, others were discarded as defective. He pointed out that these apparently crude palaeoliths were very much like the discards he found in contemporary Indian workshops. They were not products of earlier, more primitive civilizations; rather, they were the by-products of the tool manufacture by recent Indians. Stones that could not be used because of defects were tossed aside. The so-called primitive palaeoliths were actually modern. Holmes' argument was soon accepted and the American Palaeolithic concept was abandoned. Over time, however, Holmes had to modify his stance. For example, after the discovery of Folsom materials in 1926, he did accept that Native Americans had been in North America earlier than he had previously claimed.[22]

Holmes' study of cultural history took a museum approach, in which objects were collected, carefully documented and described, without Native American input. Properties of the object were analysed, including materials, tools and techniques used to make the object, decorations and wear patterns and so on. These features were compared in relation to their geographic distribution, rather than through time. Holmes brought a 'uniformitarian' perspective from geology, rather than a 'catastrophic' one. He believed cultural changes were evolutionary, that is, they came about through many imperceptible small changes over long periods of time, rather than due to sudden major changes. And this change was progressive, from primitive to complex. From his museum training, he insisted that every object had to be carefully documented as to where, when, how, by whom and in relation to what the object was found or excavated. Holmes shared this object-based approach with the USNM ethnology curator Otis T. Mason. Mason wrote that past civilizations could be best understood through the products of their hands. He focused on human technology and changes over time, creating exhibits that were 'synoptic series', showing the development of a technology, such as weaving or boat making, across time. The Mason exhibits were displayed at the National Museum and many of the late nineteenth-century expositions and world fairs, reaching a very broad audience. Mason's series were progressive, starting with 'primitive' cultures and moving forward over time to that pinnacle of human evolution, the modern American man.[23]

Holmes brought his artist's eye and systematic training to his anthropological research and writing. He collected artefacts across the Potomac tidewater, Mississippi Valley, Southwest and Mexico, and began to study the development of pottery decoration over time. His artistic talents can be seen in his analysis of pattern and his interest in technique and material. He drew conclusions about fabrics from their use to press patterns into pottery. He even studied how shells were carved into ornamental objects. This careful analysis also made him aware of the existence of spurious antiquities, and he wrote about them in journals such as *Science* to try to halt their trade.[24] His analyses were accompanied by his exquisite drawings that highlighted similarities and differences between pieces. Works in the *Fourth Annual*

Figure 4.3 Topographic sketch of the Mayan city at Copan, Honduras, 1916. Drawing by William H. Holmes. By permission of Smithsonian Institution Archives.

Report of the Bureau of American Ethnology in 1886 reveal the range and impact of his work, with articles like 'Pottery of the Ancient Pueblos', 'Ancient Pottery of the Mississippi Valley' and 'Origin and Development of Form and Ornament in Ceramic Art'. He began with detailed studies of materials, technique, form and function, but then moved to broad comparative syntheses from his focused studies. These were major contributions to the study of culture and cultural history through objects, written from an archaeological perspective that did not bring living cultures to bear on the work. His research reached a broad audience at the many expositions held in the late nineteenth and early twentieth centuries.[25]

Holmes saw humans as part of the natural environment, which allowed him to apply the theory of evolution to his work. He held a progressive view of the various stages of man and even argued for a pre-human stage and a pre-savage stage. Evolution of technology was gradual but progressively more complex and rational. Although a proponent of gradual evolution of culture, Holmes did not rely on the concept of Darwinian natural selection when it came to human society. Human culture evolved as the product of progressive human intelligence rather than strictly environmental factors.[26]

Holmes had also become embroiled in the American 'early man' controversy over how far back human occupation of the Americas went. George F. Becker, for instance, had argued that human remains were found in the Tuolumne Mountain in California in association with extinct animal remains from the glacial period. He presented this as evidence of human occupation since the Pleistocene. Holmes travelled to California, relying on his geological as much as his anthropological training, and concluded that the gravels discussed by Becker were from the Miocene and even perhaps the Eocene, rather than Becker's claimed Pleistocene. Other advocates of the presence of early man in America argued that contemporary Native Americans were too primitive to be the descendants of the advanced civilization that had built the burial mounds in the Mississippi Valley and the pueblos in the Southwest. Although Holmes initially accepted this theory, his detailed research on the development of art styles and technologies led him to conclude that contemporary Native Americans were indeed descendants of these earlier societies. He rejected the notion that present-day Zunis or Seminoles were inferior to the earlier peoples. He established a Division of Physical Anthropology at the museum in 1903, led by Dr Aleš Hrdlička. Holmes and Hrdlička resoundingly rejected the antiquity of humans on the continent. Over time, Hrdlička's claims became less and less tenable and his methodology of measuring cranial size to determine human progress on an evolutionary scale was rejected by the rest of the field. Clovis and Folsom sites established human occupation of the Americas at circa 12,000 BC; evidence of travel across the Bering Sea land bridge was accepted. Holmes later admitted he might have been too adamant in his early man pronouncements but maintained his views on the North American Palaeolithic.[27]

After the death of John Wesley Powell in 1902, Holmes reluctantly accepted an appointment as director of the BAE, but he also continued as head curator of anthropology at the museum. Serving simultaneously as head of the BAE and head curator of the National Museum's Department of Anthropology, Holmes was now one of the most influential anthropologists in the United States. However, his colleague John Swanton wrote of him that Holmes 'had singularly few contacts with the living Indians in spite of his seven years' service as Chief of the Bureau of American Ethnology'. In 1906, he helped write the United States Antiquity Act, which required that permits be secured from the Smithsonian for all archaeological fieldwork on public lands. He had the authority to approve fieldwork, dispense funds, hire budding anthropologists and select research for publication.[28]

A New Field Anthropology

Holmes' talents and training were in observation, visual analysis and drawing – skills useful in geology and archaeology, but not ethnology. Other expedition colleagues, such as John Wesley Powell and James Stevenson, turned to the study of contemporary Native American life and culture and encouraged others to pursue it as well. Thus, by the end of the nineteenth century, Holmes' work had begun to diverge from that of many of the BAE and USNM anthropologists he supervised. His colleagues' methods now involved living among contemporary tribes, developing relationships and studying their language, kinship, music, religion, ceremonial practices, economy and values. They were less concerned with objects, being primarily interested in human behaviours. A new generation of researchers was focused on the Native Americans who had survived European settlement of the continent. Short-term and twenty-five-mile-a-day expeditions were replaced by extended fieldwork within Native American communities.[29]

The new ethnologists spent years among those people, documenting every aspect of their lives from speech and music to religion, family and child rearing. They still collected material culture and used it as supplementary information in their analyses, but the artefacts were then sent to the curators at the National Museum for more detailed study, preservation and display. Some of these ethnologists, such as former journalist James Mooney, also became advocates for these displaced people, in the courts and in public opinion. Alice Cunningham Fletcher focused on the music of the Omaha, collecting recordings and information for the BAE for several decades. Even J. Walter Fewkes, who also came from a museum zoology and object background, took up work that included analyses of folklore.[30]

Powell had hired Frank Hamilton Cushing to accompany James Stevenson to the Zuni pueblo in 1879. Cushing lived with the community for six years from 1879 to 1884, 'going native'. He was accepted as a member of the Zuni community, inducted into secret societies and given a Zuni name, 'Tenatsali'. He studied creation stories and folk tales, as well as the practices of everyday life. He was, in fact, the first ethnologist to engage in the participant/observer method that would later become standard in anthropology. He also brought Zuni family members to tour the East and learn about his culture – a practice now known as reflexive anthropology. He produced numerous writings from his stay at Zuni, although involvement in politics prevented him from continuing his fieldwork. Unlike Holmes, he was deeply engaged in the lives of the people he studied and he had no interest in the 'objective' approach Holmes had learned when he entered science.[31]

The fundamental principles of analysis were also changing. Franz Boas had become a major figure in American ethnology and rejected the evolutionary sequences from primitive to complex modern society that mimicked classification of organisms. Boas wrote of anthropology, 'I believe it will not become fruitful until we renounce the vain endeavor to construct a uniform systematic history of the evolution of culture'.[32] Boas criticized the progressive series proposed by Otis Mason and Holmes in their writing and exhibits. Boas's students developed this approach into 'cultural relativism', rejecting a progression of cultures from savage to civilized. His students also immersed themselves in the cultures, living in Native American communities and studying their social structure, kinship relationships and ritual practices. They found complexity in cultural practices and relationships, not simple progressions. As the field changed, so did Holmes' interests.[33]

Holmes served as director of the Bureau of American Ethnology until he resigned in 1909. He was always a reluctant administrator and the growing divide between his own anthropological interests and those of the newer field ethnologists made it even more of a chore.

He then chaired the Department of Anthropology in the National Museum, where he hired Neil Merton Judd as curator of archaeology. Judd's work in the Southwest was far more object-based and traditional than that of the new BAE anthropologists. Completing his career as a Renaissance man, Holmes took responsibility to develop an art museum, the National Gallery of Art, for the Smithsonian. The donation of an art collection had provoked a lawsuit, resulting in a judgement that the Smithsonian's holdings of visual art constituted the 'National Gallery of Art' – something that had not previously existed in the United States. A formal museum structure was needed immediately. So Holmes returned to his first love – art – and focused on building the art gallery until he retired in 1932. He also devoted his energies to editing a journal, *Art and Archaeology*, which reflected his broad interests. He continued to produce exhibits in the National Museum, notably the 'life groups', which were a radical departure from the traditional cases of artefacts lined up in a progression. The design of the cultural life groups borrowed from the museum's animal life displays. The exhibit consisted of a small group of humans from a specific culture, posed to carry out everyday tasks. Holmes used data from physical anthropology to ensure that the body size and shape were typical of that group and ensured the accuracy of all soil, plant life and other features. Holmes' life groups were very popular and remained on display until the 1960s.[34]

Conclusion

Expeditionary anthropology in the United States arose as a side effect of the military-topographical and civilian-geological exploration of the American West. Early explorers of archaeological sites were military officers with good training in observation and scientific method, but their relationships with living tribes were, for the most part, hostile and colonial. As exploration of the West became the province of civilian scientists, more interest was paid to the magnificent cliff dwellings and decorated pottery encountered along the way. But both types of expedition travelled relatively rapidly across the landscape, leaving no time for in-depth studies of remains of ancient cities or deep relationships with living Native Americans.

The Hayden expeditions not only mapped the geology and geography of the American West, they also surveyed the communities of ancient inhabitants and current Native Americans. They amassed a collection of Native American artefacts for the National Museum and commissioned art works that created public images of Native Americans. This second generation of geological explorers, notably John Wesley Powell and William Henry Holmes, were able to establish themselves as major scholars of anthropology in the American West. The field of anthropology was new and open to all comers, and their position as first on the scene afforded them distinguished reputations as experts on Native American archaeology. The new field of research had few set theories and even fewer rules for practice. An energetic and intelligent young man could make a career out of anthropological research.

Trained as scientists, they believed they brought an 'objective' viewpoint to work that argued for processes of biological and cultural evolution. Holmes used his artistic eye to develop detailed analyses of the changes in lithic implements and decorated pottery, arguing for progressive evolution from the simple to the complex. He was not confused, however, by simple discards from modern work and he rejected the concept of a North American Palaeolithic. Both Powell and Holmes were trained to carefully document their fieldwork and the specimens and artefacts they collected, which were then deposited in the United States National Museum. Holmes developed stratigraphic and other techniques that later became standard in archaeology. Their writings reflect their training in the natural sciences and the theories in vogue in their era.

Field anthropology began to change when the BAE was established in 1879 as part of the Smithsonian. Although archaeology continued, the mandate to study contemporary Native American societies meant that fieldworkers would spend extended periods of time living in Native American communities and in some cases even adopting their lifestyles. This new generation of ethnologists was not trained in the traditional taxonomic methods of geology and biology. Their backgrounds ranged from journalism to music and their mandate was to work with the remnants of Native American communities. They were far more likely to be influenced by Franz Boas's ethnology and view of cultures, arguing that Native Americans were not primitive savages or inferior to Caucasians of European descent. Both their mode of fieldwork and their research worldview were radically different from those of the early military explorers and the pioneer anthropologists of the Powell/Holmes generation.

William Henry Holmes played a major role in the development of expeditionary anthropology in the United States, pushing the transition from military-topographic and civilian-geological exploration of the American West to anthropological studies of ancient cities.

He applied careful scientific methods and standards to his own work and the work he supervised, influenced by geology and biology, especially the theory of evolution as progressive change. By the end of his long career, expeditionary anthropology had changed again to focus on extended stays in the society being studied and implementation of the participant/observer methodology. While Holmes himself did not make that shift, his fieldwork established the study of Native Americans as a respectable area of scholarship. His administrative duties allowed the field to mature into a more interactive approach based on cultural studies, as the BAE focus turned to contemporary Native American communities by the turn of the twentieth century.

Pamela M. Henson is Institutional Historian at the Smithsonian Institution Archives, where she is responsible for research on the history of the Institution and the Oral History Program. She is also Historian in Residence at the American University. She received her PhD in the history and philosophy of science from the University of Maryland. Her research interests concentrate on the history of tropical biology, natural history and museums, the use of visual information in historical research, and the role of women in science. Recent publications include contributions to *Environmental History* and *Science Museums in Transition: Cultures of Display in Ninteteenth-Century Britain and America* (University of Pittsburgh Press, 2017).

Notes

1. Don Fowler, *A Laboratory for Anthropology: Science and Romanticism in the American Southwest, 1846–1930* (Albuquerque, NM: University of New Mexico Press, 2000), 38–49, 71–78, 79–87; William H. Goetzmann, *Exploration and Empire: The Explorer and the Scientist in the Winning of the American West* (New York: Knopf, 1966), 265–331.
2. Joni L. Kinsey, *Thomas Moran's West: Chromolithography, High Art, and Popular Taste* (Lawrence, KS: University of Kansas Press, 2006); Rick Dingus, *The Photographic Artifacts of Timothy O'Sullivan* (Albuquerque, NM: University of New Mexico Press, 1982), discusses the influence of Clarence King on expedition photography.
3. Fowler, *Laboratory for Anthropology*, 80–87; and Chip Colwell-Chanthaphonh, *Living Histories: Native Americans and Southwestern Archaeology* (Lanham, MD: AltaMira Press, 2010), 9.
4. Kevin J. Fernlund, *William Henry Holmes and the Rediscovery of the American West* (Albuquerque, NM: University of New Mexico Press, 2000), 1,

7–17, 22–23, Moran quote from p. 22; John R. Swanton, 'Biographical Memoir of William Henry Holmes, 1846–1933'. *Biographical Memoirs of the National Academy of Sciences* 17 (1935), 224–25; William H. Goetzmann, 'Limner of Grandeur: William Henry Holmes', *The American West: The Magazine of Western History* 15(3) (May–June 1978), 20–21, 61–63; Clifford M. Nelson, 'William Henry Holmes: Beginning a Career in Art and Science', *Records of the Columbia Historical Society* 50 (1980), 252–58.

5. F.V. Hayden, *Sixth Annual Report of the United States Survey of the Territories* (Washington, DC: US Government Printing Office, 1873), 5.
6. A laccolith is a large mass of igneous rock that pushes through sedimentary rock beds but does not actually reach the surface, producing a rounded bulge in the sedimentary layers above. Nelson, 'William Henry Holmes', 264–76; Swanton, 'Biographical Memoir of Holmes', 224–25.
7. Hayden, *Sixth Annual Report*, 6, 58.
8. William Henry Holmes, 'Report on the Geology of the North-Western Portion of the Elk Range', in F.V. Hayden, *Annual Report of the United States Geological and Geographical Survey of the Territories: Embracing Colorado and Parts of Adjacent Territories, for the Year 1874* (Washington, DC: US Government Printing Office, 1876), 59–71.
9. Hayden, *Sixth Annual Report*; William Henry Holmes, 'Report of William H. Holmes, on the Geology of the Sierra Abajo and West San Miguel Mountains', in F.V. Hayden, *Ninth Annual Report of the United States Geological and Geographical Survey of the Territories* (Washington, DC: US Government Printing Office, 1877), 237–76; William Henry Holmes, 'Report of William H. Holmes on the Ancient Ruins of Southwestern Colorado, Examined during the summers of 1875 and 1876', in F.V. Hayden, *Tenth Annual Report of the United States Geological and Geographical Survey of the Territories* (Washington, DC: US Government Printing Office, 1878), 381–408.
10. Swanton, 'Biographical Memoir of Holmes', 225; Wallace Stegner, *Beyond the Hundredth Meridian: John Wesley Powell and the Second Opening of the West* (Boston, MA: Houghton Mifflin, 1954), 187–91; David J. Meltzer and Robert C. Dunnell (eds), 'Introduction', in *The Archaeology of William Henry Holmes* (Washington, DC: Smithsonian Institution, 1992), xii–xiii; William Henry Holmes, 'A Notice of the Ancient Ruins of Southwestern Colorado, Examined during the Summer of 1875', in *Bulletin of the US Geological and Geographical Survey of the Territories*, Vol. II (Washington, DC: US Government Printing Office, 1876), 3–24.
11. Nelson, 'William Henry Holmes', 258–60.
12. Meltzer and Dunnell, *Archaeology of Holmes*, xiii; Anon. 'The Closing Report of Hayden's Survey', *Science* 3(51) (25 January 1884), 103–7.
13. Fernlund, *Holmes and the Rediscovery*, 99–101.
14. Ibid., 145–64; Goetzmann, *Exploration and Empire*, 591–95.

15. Daniel Goldstein, '"Yours for Science": The Smithsonian Institution's Correspondents and the Shape of Scientific Community in Nineteenth Century America', *Isis* 85(4) (1984), 573–99.
16. Samuel Franklin Emmons. 'Biographical Memoir of Clarence King'. *Biographical Memoirs of the National Academy of Sciences* 6 (1909), 44–45.
17. Donald Worster, *A River Running West: The Life of John Wesley Powell* (New York: Oxford University Press, 2001), 394–95, 419–20; Goetzmann, *Exploration and Empire*, 590–97.
18. Holmes, 'Notice of Ancient Ruins'; and Fernlund, *Holmes and the Rediscovery*, 170.
19. William Henry Holmes, 'Art in Shell of the Ancient Americans', in J.W. Powell, *Bureau of American Ethnology, 1880–1881, Second Annual Report* (Washington, DC: US Government Printing Office, 1883), 179–305.
20. William Henry Holmes, 'Monoliths of San Juan Teotihuacan, Mexico', *American Journal of Archaeology* I (1885), 361–71.
21. Swanton, 'Biographical Memoir of Holmes', 232–33; and Curtis M. Hinsley, *The Smithsonian and the American Indian: Making a Moral Anthropology in Victorian America* (Washington, DC: Smithsonian Institution Press, 1981), 100–9, 271.
22. William Henry Holmes, *Natural History of Flaked Stone Implements* (Chicago, IL: Schulte Publishing Co., 1894), 120–39, quotes from pp. 136 and 137; Meltzer and Dunnell, *Archaeology of Holmes*, xxxii–xxxv; David J. Meltzer, 'Why Don't We Know When the First People Came to North America?', *American Antiquity* (1989), 471–90.
23. Meltzer and Dunnell, *Archaeology of Holmes*, vii; Kevin J. Fernlund, 'Ode on an Anasazi Jar: William Henry Holmes and the Archaeology of the American Southwest', *New Mexico Historical Review* 76(3) (2001), 239–40; Pamela M. Henson, '"Objects of Curious Research": The History of Science and Technology at the Smithsonian', *Isis* 90 (1999), S249–69.
24. William Henry Holmes, 'The Trade in Spurious Mexican Antiquities', *Science* VII (1886), 170–72, 264; Meltzer and Dunnell, *Archaeology of Holmes*, xxxv–xxxviii.
25. William Henry Holmes, *Fourth Annual Report of the Bureau of American Ethnology* (Washington, DC: US Government Printing Office, 1886), 257–465. See, for example, William Henry Holmes, 'Anthropological Exhibit of the US National Museum at the Omaha Exposition', *Science* VII (1898), 37–40; Meltzer and Dunnell, *Archaeology of Holmes*, xxxviii; Fernlund, 'Ode on an Anasazi Jar', 247–49.
26. Meltzer and Dunnell, *Archaeology of Holmes*, xxix–xxx; David J. Meltzer, 'The Antiquity of Man and the Development of American Archaeology', *Advances in Archaeological Method and Theory* (1983), 1–51; Kevin R. Hart, 'Government Geologists and the Early Man Controversy: The Problem of "Official" Science in America, 1879–1907', PhD dissertation (Manhattan, KS: Kansas State University, 1976), 144–69.

27. Fernlund, 'Ode on an Anasazi Jar', 247–50.
28. Fernlund, *Holmes and the Rediscovery*, 205; Swanton, 'Biographical Memoir of Holmes', 231, 236; and William Henry Holmes, 'Random Records of a Lifetime in Art and Science, 1846–1931', Vol. 9, p. 71, unpublished manuscript, Record Unit 311, Smithsonian Institution Archives.
29. Worster, *A River Running West*, 286–91.
30. William M. Colby, *Routes to Rainy Mountain: Biography of James Moony, Ethnologist* (Madison, WI: University of Wisconsin Press, 1977); Dorothy Sara Lee and Maria La Vigna (eds), *Omaha Indian Music: Historical Recordings from the Fletcher/La Flesche Collection* (Washington, DC: Library of Congress, 1985); Nancy J. Parezo, 'Cushing as Part of the Team: The Collecting Activities of the Smithsonian Institution', *American Ethnologist* 12(4)(1985), 763–74; J. Walter Fewkes, 'Contribution to Passamaquoddy Folk-Lore', *Journal of American Folk-Lore* III(11) (October–December 1890), 257–80; David R. Wilcox and Don D. Fowler, 'The Beginnings of Anthropological Archaeology in the North American Southwest: From Thomas Jefferson to the Pecos Conference', *Journal of the Southwest* 44(2) (2002), 121–234; James Mooney, *The Ghost-Dance Religion and the Sioux Outbreak of 1890*, (Omaha, NE: University of Nebraska Press, 1896); and Matilda Coxe Stevenson, 'The Zuni Indians', in *Bureau of American Ethnology Annual Report*, Vol. 23 (Washington, DC: US Government Printing Office, 1904).
31. W.J. McGee et al., 'In Memoriam: Frank Hamilton Cushing', *American Anthropologist* 2(2) (1900), 354–80; Fowler, *Laboratory for Anthropology*, 119–27; Gwyneira Issac, 'Anthropology and Its Embodiments: 19th Century Museum Ethnography and the Re-enactment of Indigenous Knowledge', *Etnofoor* 22(1) (2010), 15–18.
32. Franz Boas, 'The Limitations of the Comparative Method of Anthropology', *Science* 4(103) (December 18, 1896), 908
33. Curtis M. Hinsley and Bill Holm, 'A Cannibal in the National Museum: The Early Career of Franz Boas in America', *American Anthropologist* 78(2) (1976), 306–16; Fowler, *Laboratory for Anthropology*, 240–41.
34. Meltzer and Dunnell, *Archaeology of Holmes*, xxii–xxv; Isaac, 'Anthropology and Its Embodiments', 20–21.

Bibliography

Anon. 'The Closing Report of Hayden's Survey'. *Science* 3(51) (25 January 1884), 103–7.

Boas, Franz. 'The Limitations of the Comparative Method of Anthropology'. *Science* 4(103) (18 December 1896), 901–908.

Colby, William M. *Routes to Rainy Mountain: Biography of James Moony, Ethnologist*. Madison, WI: University of Wisconsin Press, 1977.

Colwell-Chanthaphonh, Chip. *Living Histories: Native Americans and Southwestern Archaeology*. Lanham, MD: AltaMira Press, 2010.

Dingus, Rick. *The Photographic Artifacts of Timothy O'Sullivan*. Albuquerque, NM: University of New Mexico Press, 1982.

Emmons, Samuel Franklin. 'Biographical Memoir of Clarence King'. *Biographical Memoirs of the National Academy of Sciences* 6 (1909), 25–55.

Fernlund, Kevin J. 'Ode on an Anasazi Jar: William Henry Holmes and the Archaeology of the American Southwest'. *New Mexico Historical Review* 76(3) (2001), 231–54.

———. *William Henry Holmes and the Rediscovery of the American West*. Albuquerque, NM: University of New Mexico Press, 2000.

Fewkes, J. Walter. 'Contribution to Passamaquoddy Folk-Lore'. *Journal of American Folk-Lore* III(11) (October–December 1890), 257–80.

Fowler, Don. *A Laboratory for Anthropology: Science and Romanticism in the American Southwest, 1846–1930*. Albuquerque, NM: University of New Mexico Press, 2000.

Goetzmann, William H. *Exploration and Empire: The Explorer and the Scientist in the Winning of the American West*. New York: Knopf, 1966.

———. 'Limner of Grandeur: William Henry Holmes'. *The American West: The Magazine of Western History* 15(3) (May–June 1978), 20–21, 61–63.

Goldstein, Daniel. '"Yours for Science": The Smithsonian Institution's Correspondents and the Shape of Scientific Community in Nineteenth Century America'. *Isis* 85(4) (1984), 573–99.

Hart, Kevin R. 'Government Geologists and the Early Man Controversy: The Problem of "Official" Science in America, 1879–1907'. PhD dissertation. Manhattan, KS: Kansas State University, 1976.

Hayden, F.V. *Sixth Annual Report of the United States Survey of the Territories*. Washington, DC: US Government Printing Office, 1873.

Henson, Pamela M. '"Objects of Curious Research": The History of Science and Technology at the Smithsonian'. *Isis* 90 (1999), S249–69.

Hinsley, Curtis M. *The Smithsonian and the American Indian: Making a Moral Anthropology in Victorian America*. Washington, DC: Smithsonian Institution Press, 1981.

Hinsley, Curtis M., and Bill Holm. 'A Cannibal in the National Museum: The Early Career of Franz Boas in America'. *American Anthropologist* 78(2) (1976), 306–16.

Holmes, William Henry. 'Anthropological Exhibit of the US National Museum at the Omaha Exposition'. *Science* VII (1898), 37–40.

———. 'Art in Shell of the Ancient Americans', in J.W. Powell, *Bureau of American Ethnology, 1880–1881, Second Annual Report* (Washington, DC: US Government Printing Office, 1883), 179–305.

———. *Fourth Annual Report of the Bureau of American Ethnology*. Washington, DC: US Government Printing Office, 1886.

———. 'Monoliths of San Juan Teotihuacan, Mexico'. *American Journal of Archaeology* I (1885), 361–71.

———. *Natural History of Flaked Stone Implements*. Chicago, IL: Schulte Publishing Co., 1894.

———. 'A Notice of the Ancient Ruins of Southwestern Colorado, Examined during the Summer of 1875', in *Bulletin of the US Geological and Geographical Survey of the Territories*, Vol. II (Washington, DC: US Government Printing Office, 1876), 3–24.

———. 'Report on the Geology of the North-Western Portion of the Elk Range', in F.V. Hayden, *Annual Report of the United States Geological and Geographical Survey of the Territories: Embracing Colorado and Parts of Adjacent Territories, for the Year 1874* (Washington, DC: US Government Printing Office, 1876), 59–71.

———. 'Report of William H. Holmes, on the Geology of the Sierra Abajo and West San Miguel Mountains', in F.V. Hayden, *Ninth Annual Report of the United States Geological and Geographical Survey of the Territories* (Washington, DC: US Government Printing Office, 1877), 237–76.

———. 'Report of William H. Holmes on the Ancient Ruins of Southwestern Colorado, Examined during the summers of 1875 and 1876', in F.V. Hayden, *Tenth Annual Report of the United States Geological and Geographical Survey of the Territories* (Washington, DC: US Government Printing Office, 1878), 381–408.

———. 'The Trade in Spurious Mexican Antiquities'. *Science* VII (1886), 170–72, 264.

Issac, Gwyneira. 'Anthropology and Its Embodiments: 19th Century Museum Ethnography and the Re-enactment of Indigenous Knowledge'. *Etnofoor* 22(1) (2010), 15–18.

Kinsey, Joni L. *Thomas Moran's West: Chromolithography, High Art, and Popular Taste*. Lawrence, KS: University of Kansas Press, 2006.

Lee, Dorothy Sara, and Maria La Vigna (eds). *Omaha Indian Music: Historical Recordings from the Fletcher/La Flesche Collection*. Washington, DC: Library of Congress, 1985.

McGee, W.J., et al. 'In Memoriam: Frank Hamilton Cushing'. *American Anthropologist* 2(2) (1900), 354–80.

Meltzer, David J. 'The Antiquity of Man and the Development of American Archaeology'. *Advances in Archaeological Method and Theory* 6 (1983), 1–51.

———. 'Why Don't We Know When the First People Came to North America?' *American Antiquity* 54(3) (1989), 471–90.

Meltzer, David J., and Robert C. Dunnell (eds). *The Archaeology of William Henry Holmes*. Washington, DC: Smithsonian Institution, 1992.

Mooney, James. *The Ghost-Dance Religion and the Sioux Outbreak of 1890*. Omaha, NE: University of Nebraska Press, 1896.

Nelson, Clifford M. 'William Henry Holmes: Beginning a Career in Art and Science'. *Records of the Columbia Historical Society* 50 (1980), 252–78.

Parezo, Nancy J. 'Cushing as Part of the Team: The Collecting Activities of the Smithsonian Institution'. *American Ethnologist* 12(4) (1985), 763–74.

Stegner, Wallace. *Beyond the Hundredth Meridian: John Wesley Powell and the Second Opening of the West*. Boston, MA: Houghton Mifflin, 1954.

Stevenson, Matilda Coxe. 'The Zuni Indians', in *Bureau of American Ethnology Annual Report*, Vol. 23 (Washington, DC: US Government Printing Office, 1904), 13–608.

Swanton, John R. 'Biographical Memoir of William Henry Holmes, 1846–1933'. *Biographical Memoirs of the National Academy of Sciences* 17 (1935), 223–252.

Wilcox, David R., and Don D. Fowler. 'The Beginnings of Anthropological Archaeology in the North American Southwest: From Thomas Jefferson to the Pecos Conference'. *Journal of the Southwest* 44(2) (2002), 121–234.

Worster, Donald. *A River Running West: The Life of John Wesley Powell*. New York: Oxford University Press, 2001.

Chapter 5

THE ANOMALOUS BLONDS OF THE MAGHREB

CARLETON COON INVENTS THE AFRICAN NORDICS

Warwick Anderson

'The public is still largely ignorant of what actually happens on scientific expeditions', lamented American anthropologist Carleton Stevens Coon in 1935. 'Most truly scientific ones receive no popular write-ups.'[1] Coon had spent many of the previous ten years in northern Africa, especially in the Rif Mountains along the Mediterranean coast of Morocco, measuring bodies, snapping photographs, taking blood, looting graves and inquiring into local culture. He was eager to tell his story. 'It is my habit to corral, by some form of persuasion, as many as possible of the adult males of the district, for women, in the countries in which we work, are difficult or impossible to measure'. His daily grind could be tedious and painstaking, even if in the eyes of local inhabitants 'the handling of the instruments back and forth becomes a lavish ritual, full of sweeps and flourishes, for it is part of a showmanship calculated to stimulate the interest of the idle'. Often the locals seemed to regard him as 'a magician, slapstick comedian, and father-confessor rolled into one'. Some thought he was 'a sorcerer bent on imprisoning their souls within the uncomfortable confines of a camera, or on altering their spiritual faces by contact with calipers'.[2] A mercurial personality and extravagant conversationalist, Coon was proud of his ability to persuade these reluctant subjects 'against their will, principle, and better judgment that they should submit their bodies to measurement and to peerings, pryings, and mouth openings which go with our non-metrical observations'. Imagining himself an adventurer and explorer, the Harvard anthropologist disparaged any Europeanized natives or mixed-race degenerates who got in his way. In northern Morocco and in Ethiopia, Coon instead was seeking a 'racial *terra incognita*'. He longed 'to weep with the primitive and oppressed' and to lead noble and savage races in the struggle to overthrow degrading Mediterranean colonialism.[3] He fancied himself, in a jejune daydream that almost came true, as T.E. Lawrence – Coon of the Rif, perhaps – inciting anti-colonial revolt across northern Africa.[4]

Coon always enjoyed the sense of power that the tools of physical anthropology conferred on him. The battle-hardened men he measured 'did not understand what I was doing and the shiny calipers looked to them like instruments of torture'. Moreover, his 'droning out of the numbers and observations ... sounded like ritual, and since they could not recognize it, some new and elaborate form of magic'. Coon noted with pleasure that 'many of the men, their faces expressing the last extremes of terror, sweated profusely and jumped every time I touched them'.[5] Such masculine tournaments and contests, with their whiff of brutality, torture and black magic, would have been all too familiar to the Moroccans whom Coon measured in the 1920s. Indeed, it was the reputation of Arabs and Berbers (or Amazighs) in the Maghreb for violence and conflict and blood feuds that had attracted the neophyte anthropologist to the region. Like so many of the lost generation after the First World War, Coon – a chubby, sickly man – was fascinated by aggression and self-assertion.[6]

As a Harvard undergraduate anthropology major, Coon had read avidly journalist Walter Harris's tales of the sultanate and protectorate of Morocco – 'a closed house, tenanted by suspicion, fanaticism, and distrust'.[7] Having in his youth perused Richard F. Burton's narratives, Coon yearned to visit the blue city of mystery, Chefchaouen, a Moslem spiritual centre in the Jibala, adjacent to the Rif Mountains, closed to Christians until 1920.[8] He lapped up British explorer Rosita Forbes's account of Berber leader and brigand Mulai Ahmed el Raisuni (or Raisuli) – ruthless, handsome and charming – and his rebellions in the early twentieth century against declining Moroccan sultans and Spanish authorities in the Rif and around Tangier. 'Cruelty, like morality', Forbes wrote, 'is a matter of latitude'.[9] Coon also followed closely news in the 1920s of Muhammad ibn Abd al-Karim's Berber uprising in the Rif and his slaughter of the Spanish army – the beginning of the Moslem revival across Arab lands that is still being played out today (and which I later came to experience for myself, as I recount here).[10] Before long, Coon would, in effect, be tagging after

American journalist Vincent Sheean among the 'savage, primitive, warlike' Berbers of the Rif, both of the adventurers intrigued by el Raisuni and Abd al-Karim and the Rifis they led – blond and blue-eyed and 'indubitably white men'.[11] As Harris once observed, the democratic Berber 'mentality is [northern] European and not African'.[12] These, then, were a people that no fledgling race scientist armed with callipers could ignore or disavow. Thus, 'their sanguinary sociology, blue eyes, blond hair, and scorn for [colonizing southern] Europeans fired the imagination of at least one young anthropologist looking for kindred spirits among the wilder whites'.[13] For Carleton Coon, Morocco became a place – like Spain for W.H. Auden – where 'our thoughts have bodies; the menacing shapes of our fever/ are precise and alive'.[14]

From 1912, the French and Spanish protectorates etched more deeply the divisions between supposedly slothful and corrupt Arabs on the plains and the spirited and warlike Berbers in their mountain fastness.[15] The Fez mutiny in 1911 against Mulai Abdelhafid had led to the establishment of a French protectorate, with Hubert Lyautey as resident-general, which covered most of Morocco; and to Spanish sub-protectorates in the north enclosing the Rif Mountains and in the far south, desert country. Lyautey gave the Berbers in the Atlas Mountains considerable autonomy, enriching and empowering the major clans, such as the Glaoui of Telouet, while the Spanish, huddling around Tétouan (or Tetuán), mostly tried to leave the Berbers in the Rif alone. Meanwhile, el Raisuni continued to foment trouble against the effete Iberian power. Combative and xenophobic Berbers, so it seemed, were offering an increasingly sharp contrast to pliant and mercantile Arabs. In 1919, a Spanish force chased el Raisuni into the rugged mountains of the Rif, and the following year it occupied nearby Chefchaouen for the first time. But within a few months, a coalition of Rifi Berber tribes, under the brilliant leadership of Abd al-Karim, fought back and defeated the Spanish at Annual, killing more than fifteen thousand soldiers. Abd al-Karim brutally took control of the mountains, declaring himself the Amir of the Rif. By 1925, however, the coordinated Spanish and French armies, including in their leadership Francisco Franco and Philippe Pétain, attacked from the north and the south, smashing the Rifi bands. In May 1926, Abd al-Karim surrendered, going into permanent exile in the French colony of Réunion. Scattered fighting continued for a few more years.[16] It was a curious time for Coon to contemplate anthropological research on Berbers in Morocco.

Between the wars, Earnest A. Hooton, the leading Harvard anthropologist, sent off most of his graduate students to study race mixing, a topic he regarded as the most pressing in physical anthropology. As mixed populations became more salient in settler societies like the United States and in the colonized world, their civic capacities and potential for incorporation into modern economies seemed to posit problems worth investigating. Did these groups show some sort of hybrid vigour, or did they represent degrading mismatches?[17] Many of the Harvard graduate students – the Peabody boys, as they called themselves, after the anthropology museum there – went to the Pacific and Australasia, where they had a smashing time and returned with praise for the 'half-castes' they had encountered and measured. Often their field experiences made them sceptical of facile racial typologies, prompting them to invent in the late 1920s a new evolutionary style of anthropological inquiry, named 'human biology' to distinguish it from the old Mendelian race science. After the Second World War, many of these Peabody boys, including Harry L. Shapiro and Joseph B. Birdsell, joined other activists in the explicit and public critique of racial typology in physical anthropology.[18] Not so, Coon. In contrast, Coon had persuaded his PhD advisor to let him study the anomalous blonds of the Maghreb – likely, Hooton thought, to be another mixed population. Disingenuously, the graduate student went along with this notion, though race mixing never really interested him. Coon's field experiences would reinforce his racism, which caused him in postwar years to become one of the leading advocates of racial typologies in physical anthropology.[19]

As historians, we are inclined to reframe expeditionary anthropology so as to foreground affective bonds, sentimental ties and intimate attachments between investigators and their subjects – to highlight the reappraisal and discrediting of racial difference and distance, often obscured in conventional publications.[20] But Coon's engagement with the anomalous blonds of the Maghreb tells another story. It demonstrates how a certain mode of romantic racialism, a race conceit, in the twentieth century could be set in opposition to capitalist development and European globalization or modernization. Thus, Coon's radical racism, confirmed in the Rif, inspired his anti-colonial vision and gave sustenance to his rancorous and antagonistic personality.

Descended from an old New England family, Coon grew up in a largely white, Protestant community in Wakefield, Massachusetts. Having a father who boasted of business connections with Egypt made Coon, while a pupil at Andover, vulnerable to the Egyptology craze of the

Figure 5.1 Presumably Carleton S. Coon (on left) with others in Morocco, late 1920s. C.S. Coon Papers, by permission of National Anthropological Archives, Smithsonian Institution.

early twentieth century.[21] At Harvard, he learned more about Moslem North Africa in anthropology classes. Eager for adventure, the twenty-year-old undergraduate seized the opportunity to visit Morocco in 1924 with Gordon Browne, a recent Harvard graduate about to embark on a lifetime of gunrunning and espionage in Tangier. 'Athletic in build, with an aquiline nose and a shock of stiff blond hair that stood erect on his scalp', Browne made an attractive travelling companion.[22] Stepping ashore from a Bordeaux packet at Casablanca, they recoiled at first from the baking heat and the glare. A few days later, they became disoriented in the spice markets of the souk in Fez.

Taking the bus to Taza, in the narrow corridor between the Rif and the Middle Atlas Mountains, they constantly feared Berber attack. Along the way, Coon looked for skeletons in caves, hoping to propitiate Hooton, but he found nothing. At the end of summer, the young adventurer resumed studies at Harvard, full of stories and glowing with enthusiasm for the Maghreb.

On his return to Morocco the following summer, with fellow undergraduate Thomas A.B. Scudder – 'a huge amateur boxer' and would-be painter – Coon made sure he was better prepared.[23] As the Rif rebellion collapsed, Coon and Scudder began to dig out a Palaeolithic site, Tit Mellil, on the outskirts of Casablanca, collecting bones, axes and other artefacts. But preparation proved futile. Before long, Coon came down with dysentery and sunstroke. 'I went out of my head, raving', he recalled. The young men then moved on to Marrakesh, where Coon 'started to make anthropometric measurements of country people'.[24] 'Yesterday measured my first man', he wrote to Hooton. 'These are shy people but are beginning to warm up now. The measuring game in this country is a ticklish business and I can't promise any more.'[25] He still felt weak and soon gave up. Instead, the two undergraduates sat every day at a cafe at the edge of Jamaa el Fna, the vast square in the medina, eating liver kebabs and watching 'Shluh dancing boys, water vendors, jugglers, native healers bleeding and cupping their patients, and other diverting spectacles'.[26] From 'various loafers around the cafés ... Americans and other bums', he heard the 'wildest tales' about atrocities in the Rif.[27] Eventually, Coon contracted malaria, and as he was recovering, he ran his Model-T Ford off the road outside Marrakesh. He stepped ashore at Bordeaux a few weeks afterwards, blind in one eye and walking with a cane – most likely hysterical reactions to his traumatic experiences in the Maghreb. Scudder died a few years later, shot in Chicago.[28]

Since Coon was an inveterate fabulist, it is hard to know how much of this is true. When Anne Roe assessed him psychologically some twenty-five years later, she did not believe most of his stories. His mother had attempted to suppress her son's aggression, Roe surmised, giving rise to a 'pattern of violent, and physically expressed, revolt against authority of any sort'. Something had gone very wrong in his childhood. Coon's Rorschach testing, Roe noted, was 'fantastic, looks at first like a violently aggressive psychopath and winds up very good humoredly'. She found the anthropologist unusually paranoid and distrustful. He was garrulous, unreliable and prone to violence. Coon's 'professional history is one of digs in wild places, of rows with colleagues, of being put upon in one way or another and blowing up,

Figure 5.2 Warrior on horseback. Photograph by Carleton S. Coon, late 1920s. C.S. Coon Papers, by permission of National Anthropological Archives, Smithsonian Institution.

and so on'. He lived 'on a diet of bloodshed and adventure'.[29] In other words, Coon was perfectly suited to fieldwork in the Rif Mountains during the 1920s.

The ferry that took Coon, his new wife Mary (a 'Wellesley girl') and a Great Dane called Marduk to Tangier in June 1926 was full of returning Rifi refugees. 'I saw blond men who might have been Harvard football backs walking around in yellow turbans and brown jellabas', recalled Coon, who was about to begin his PhD fieldwork.[30] Clearly, they were his kind of people.

Tangier was teeming with Riffians and Soussis, as Coon called the Berbers from the Atlas. French and Spanish military also crowded into the town, adding to the sense of chaos, of being perched at the edge of a war. 'The blondness of the [Berber] country folk who came to town' stood out among the Mediterranean swarthiness.[31] Coon began to lure them into his quarters for measurement. They particularly enjoyed the trials of strength with his dynamometer. 'Our laboratory', he wrote to Hooton, 'has become more of a club and less of a workshop'.[32] All the same, the physical anthropologist longed to lose himself in the Rif. But when he ventured out to Tétouan, the Spanish officers stole his passport and beat him up. The Spanish, he told Hooton, were 'without question the most stupid and utterly fecal people in existence'.[33] It was very hot away from the coast and his vision was blurring. His 'usual misfortunes' were happening again, he feared. His dog became rabid and had to be shot, while he and Mary, who had been bitten, received a series of painful anti-rabies inoculations into their abdomens. Coon did not know what to do. 'To camp out in the Rif without a dog is impossible.' They were running out of money. The French authorities temporarily purloined his callipers and other measuring instruments, 'saying that any attempt at anthropometry in the bled would be suicide'.[34]

With suicidal persistence and sheer bloody mindedness, Coon defied obstructive colonial authorities. He and Mary moved to labyrinthine, ancient Fez in July 1927 and proceeded to arrange an expedition, including two Rifi retainers (a muleteer and a cook), guns, foodstuffs, two riding mules and two pack mules. Mohammed Amar, the cook, was tall and lean and incredibly resourceful; Hamid, the muleteer, was short, barrel-chested, with a florid complexion and watery blue eyes, and perpetually agitated and apprehensive. They started out from Taza, following tracks across barren country in incinerating heat, heading into the mountains towards the vale of Iherrushen. At each police post, they sought permission to venture further into the Rif. When they reached Tiddest, the village leaders offered warm hospitality. 'I soon found myself feeling more at home here than I had felt even in Europe', Coon recalled. 'My new friends expressed surprise and pleasure that I laughed at the right times and entered into their jests. They were as different from the Arabs as night is from day.'[35] Mary set up a small clinic to treat and dress cuts, ulcers and sores, but otherwise mostly conversed in seclusion with the women. Since the French authorities had confiscated his callipers, Coon concentrated on recording pedigrees and observing social life. His Arabic and French language skills proved adequate, but he struggled with Berber and Spanish. At Tiddest, Coon conveniently met a young man called Mohammed Limnibhy who could translate from Berber into French. Limnibhy attached himself to Coon and became an essential intermediary in all of the anthropologist's subsequent fieldwork among Berbers, and a close friend, even accompanying him back to Cambridge, Massachusetts. It was Limnibhy who advised Coon to convince his hosts that he was neither Spanish nor French, in order to assure them he was not spying on them. But Coon may have been too persuasive: the nearby French commandant suspected he was actually an American spy and expelled the expedition, sending them to Marrakesh for interrogation.[36]

Coon and his party returned to the Rif later in 1927, when the weather was cooler and the people less given to hostilities. 'I mounted and oiled my precious instruments', Coon wrote, 'and unpacked three sets of five-by-eight blanks – for individual measurement, village data, and census-like facts and figures of the personnel and possessions of individual heads of households, starting with Tiddest'.[37] He measured more than four hundred Berbers in Tiddest, a scattered town with a meagre market. They then headed up the vale of Iherrushen to the headwaters at Telmest, 'filling out dossiers and measuring men all the way'. In the tribal territory of Beni Amart – which had submitted to the Spanish a few weeks earlier – Coon observed 'the blondest people of the Rif, and reputedly the most ferocious'. Yet most cooperated with the anthropologist; some even confused him with the journalist Sheean, whom they had liked. It proved harder in more urban Adjir:

> Measured fourteen, of which three refused to give blood. Most are unwilling to submit to measurement here. There were plenty looking on, but when I asked a man to let me measure him he almost invariably fled. None but the cowards are left.[38]

Through December they went among the recently subdued Rifis, 'measuring, measuring, measuring' – when they could.[39] But just as he gained momentum, Coon had to interrupt his fieldwork to take Mary to Paris for the birth of their first child.[40]

In his reports, Coon frequently felt obliged to contrast Spanish colonial excrement with the Nordic cleanliness of Berbers. 'We went ... to that hideous place, the Spanish camp', the anthropologist noted in his description of the December trip to the Rif. 'The outskirts of it, the path, and the wed [stream bed], are covered with a black coating of human excrement; the aroma of twenty or more dead mules arises from the wed, which is their water supply.' Later that day he described 'coming from the vile to the beautiful. Up beyond the camp to the north is a fine mosque, and a white marabout [shrine of a holy man] with a green tile roof. How clean and good to look at after the camp'.[41] The injustice of making blond Nordics subject to swarthy Mediterranean masters led Coon to despair. 'The Rifi always bury their mules, and are decent about their stooling. Truly the conquistadores are the embodiment of the defecation with which they befoul the springs and watercourses.'[42]

When Coon came back to Morocco in 1928, along with wife and young child, he resided in Marrakesh. There, he recalled, 'no one stopped me from measuring men, and subjects were plentiful'. This time, Coon flourished in Marrakesh, away from the loathed Spanish. He was able to measure hundreds of Berbers from the Middle Atlas Mountains, and even a few Soussis from the High Atlas. He photographed his subjects and took blood for grouping, while Mary made sociological observations and recorded all the data on individual cards for filing and collating. The paperwork was trying and daunting, but essential to the project, necessary for the eventual conjuring up of racial types.[43] As Coon told Hooton:

> Measuring here is a funny proposition. I send ex-measurees up to the Jamaa el Fna to herd their compatriots who are watching the snake charmers and dancing boys, having just got in from the mountains. These come down in great flocks, from which I weed out those too young, those who have already been measured, and Arabs. Then we bring them into the courtyard and I take the most confident looking one first, meanwhile letting the others play with the dynamometer. There are always some who get panicky and need reassuring. Some think that we are shanghaiing them to work at Bordeaux. They run about the house trying to escape, and explain tearfully that their sons are already in the army and they don't want to go too. Several have fled when I pointed the camera at them.[44]

Additionally, pimps would direct the Berber clients of their prostitutes to him, so 'the visitors who squandered their money on women could earn a little more to take home'.[45]

The souks in the main towns and markets in the hills generally offered Coon the most effective access to male bodies. But it was never easy. At each new souk, they needed first to present their papers at the police bureau, ask for permission to take measurements, and then wait hours while their credentials were checked:

> Then we are given a place to work and a mokhazni [an Arab member of the auxiliary forces] with a big stick to round up subjects. Generally a sheikh or some other big traitor condescendingly submits. All refuse to disrobe even to the extent of taking their turbans off, which we do surreptitiously, not giving them back to them until after their pictures are taken.... Persuasion will not induce these people to be measured, for they see no material profit in it to themselves. I cannot spend too much soft speech through Limnibhy, due to the presence of Spanish stool pigeons mixed in the crowd.[46]

It was a frustrating business, requiring a certain degree of forcefulness. Since they rarely received permission for their studies until 11 a.m. and the souks closed around 2 p.m., the pressure of time was severe. Coon warned Hooton that his measurements often were unreliable:

> My measurements of the bi-iliac, chest depth, and chest breadth are not accurate. I cannot make them take off any of their clothes, which ... are copious. So I allow, in each measurement, a certain number of millimeters depending on each individual layout. The other measurements are as accurate as I can make them.[47]

In the circumstances, any sociological inquiry was perfunctory at best. Coon worried, too, about the accuracy of his sampling technique. Many of his subjects were traumatized by war; some were starving. 'The men we get represent the socially lowest stratum of whatever tribes they belong to', he told Hooton, 'or they wouldn't be loafing about'.[48] All the same, his Berber numbers grew steadily until they reached above a thousand.

As the days passed slowly in Marrakesh, Coon began to chafe against urban civilization. He was sick of city people and wanted to get back to the mountains – this time to the High Atlas. He decided to visit the Glaoui in the kasbah at Telouet, two days by mule along a rough and steep track across the Tizi-n-Tishka pass. The party struggled with their mules 'through the snow over bandit-infested country'.[49] As usual, Coon was tired, dirty and hungry. 'Proper foodstuffs do not exist in the bled', he wrote to Hooton. 'Owing to the nature of the country, we cannot overload the mules with canned goods. We take a bottle of bouillon and a bag of rice, and practically on that we live for two weeks.'[50] They laboured on, over the backbone of the High Atlas, happy to reach fabled Telouet. The huge fortress stood at the head of a rich agricultural valley, its fields tended by hundreds of slaves from south of the Sahara.[51] The Khalifa gave them two black slaves and found them a house there, from which Coon could interview the local Berbers. But the French officer at the local post forbade any measurement, and again Coon's instruments were confiscated. Moreover, the sociological inquiries proved disappointing: the local Berbers were 'a close-lipped lot and will give absolutely no information', he told Hooton.[52] It was terribly frustrating, but at least Coon could say he had been there.

All of the field notes, even those from the Rif, convey the impression that Coon kept a distance from the Berbers he examined and appraised. The records present little evidence of social entanglement or sentimental attachment. Rather, his relations with research subjects seem unusually instrumental and abstract – that is, remote and objective. Thus, he could write:

> The few Riffians having even a trace of Negroid blood are engaged in ironworking trade, and the men ... holding offices ... are apt to be of the Nordic-Alpine type ... and the men noted for bravery but not for political ability, are more apt to be purer Nordic. The Mediterranean exists throughout either as a substratum or as a later invading or infiltrating type.[53]

Coon showed no real sympathy for a people ravaged by war and famine. His narcissistic investment in their superior Nordic qualities allowed for no intimations of affection, or concern for mundane suffering.

'Searching beneath the Berber and Arab blankets, beneath the Negroid seepings and the European scaldings', Coon wrote in *Tribes of the Rif* (1931), 'it is still possible to discern the relics of a bygone age, a time when northern Morocco was closer to Europe culturally, and a still dimmer time when the races of North Africa and [northern] Europe were the same'. The physical anthropologist had determined that the harsh mountains of the Rif constituted the 'asylum' of the 'African Nordics'.[54] Thus, the blonds of the Maghreb were probably the last vestiges of originary Nordics, and not, as commonly assumed, the descendants of Vandal invaders. As he later put it, 'both the Riffians and the Scandinavians are partly Nordic; both probably derive their somatic similarities from a single source'.[55] In general, Coon found the Rifis intelligent, cooperative and generous – unlike their southern European colonial masters. He admired particularly their 'virile spirit of independence'.[56] Although 'primitive', the Rif, Coon asserted, was 'wholesome and vigorous', not depraved and 'sodomitic' like the surrounding Arab cultures.[57] Over a three-year period, the anthropologist had measured and taken observations on 1,292 individuals, all except five of them male. Almost half were Rifis, and the rest represented a mixture of Soussi Berbers and Arabs. Comparing his data, so laboriously accumulated yet so makeshift and unreliable, with studies of the bodies of Spaniards, West Africans and European-Americans seemed to confirm that the Berbers made up a mostly Nordic salient in a field of inferior Mediterranean types. Fortunately, their isolation and xenophobia had kept most of them blond. But how much longer could they stay pristine? 'The world is full of small remnants of brave and worthwhile peoples', Coon wrote, 'who have been ground into oblivion by the drab conquest of modern civilization'. But he remained hopeful. The Rifis, he concluded, were 'white men and can take over white men's ways without too much anguish'.[58]

In 1928, Coon, with his increasingly disaffected wife and their child, and Limnibhy, had tried to settle in Cambridge, Massachusetts. But Mary soon abandoned him, running away to Michigan for a few months. Coon and Limnibhy moved in with Gordon T. Bowles, a physical anthropologist focusing on Asia, Patrick T.L. Putnam, who became obsessed with the Pygmies (Mbuti) of the Belgian Congo, and an unruly chimpanzee, with a tendency to chase children and policemen.[59] The household did not last long. Mary returned to a troubled,

Figure 5.3 Hunting in the Rif. Photograph by Carleton S. Coon, late 1920s. C.S. Coon Papers, by permission of the National Anthropological Archives, Smithsonian Institution.

restless marriage that somehow held together another decade or more. Limnibhy went back to Morocco, but shortly afterwards, according to Coon, 'the French got him and poisoned him'.[60] During the 1930s, Coon lingered at Harvard, holding down jobs as lecturer and assistant professor in anthropology, depressingly exploitative positions in his opinion. Specializing in what may be called 'aftermath anthropology', he ventured from time to time into Albania and Ethiopia as they recovered from conflict and colonial aggression, where he could flirt with bandits and brigands. 'I did all sorts of desperate things', Coon recalled. 'It was after that they [Harvard] told me I was too irresponsible and they wouldn't keep me any longer at the university and I got discouraged and I looked for jobs at filling stations and I didn't know what I wanted to do.' In the early 1940s, Coon was 'always trying to get into the war'.[61] He was delighted when William J. 'Wild Bill' Donovan, a family friend, recruited him in 1942 to the new Office of Strategic Services (OSS), the precursor of the Central Intelligence Agency, and sent him back to Tangier. 'I had the Riffians all organized', Coon later told Anne Roe, 'so I was going to parachute in to take over Spanish Morocco'.[62] But since fascist Spain refused to enter the war formally on Hitler's side, the rebellion was called off, leaving Coon distraught. 'I suppose he has been doing a Lawrence of the Riff', Hooton mused cynically.[63] Coon also claimed to have trained the French resistance in Morocco and led a column of British commandos. 'During that time I got my head injury and went to pieces', he recalled. 'I couldn't speak and so on.' His old problems recurred. 'I began to get a pain in the back of the neck ... and then down my spine and hands would go to sleep and my eyes would go out of focus and then I went into spastic contractions.' His superiors put him in hospital and 'operated' on him. 'It was a very humiliating business', he told Roe. He wanted to 'kill' all his psychiatrists. 'I mean it', he kept repeating. Eventually Coon was discharged with 'extreme anxiety and hysteria', and his wife divorced him.[64] In the postwar years, Coon would remarry and settle down, becoming a disgruntled and irritable professor of anthropology at the University of Pennsylvania, and briefly president of the American Association of Physical Anthropologists. Through the 1950s he continued to stir up trouble in expeditions across the Middle East.

While clinging to the margins of Harvard anthropology before the war, Coon had managed to write *The Races of Europe* (1939), a sympathetic revision of American economist William Z. Ripley's influential fin-de-siècle tract, which charted the destinies of Teutons (later Nordics), Alpines and Mediterraneans in Europe.[65] In his elaborate 'reconstruction of the racial biology of the white race', Coon emphasized mingling and competition between Nordics and Mediterraneans, ascribing to the latter a Middle Eastern origin, and more positive characteristics than those he previously had discerned in the field.[66] The anthropologist suggested that different forces of selection and environmental adaptation had shaped geographically isolated human races and sub-races, even if later mixing and amalgamation greatly confused any typological classification. He regarded a race as a 'group of people who possess the majority of their physical characteristics in common', though obviously the category must be 'elastic'.[67] Toward the end of this tome, Coon observed, with considerable self-deprecation, that 'for many years physical anthropologists have found it more amusing to travel to distant lands and to measure small remnants of little known or romantic people than to tackle the drudgery of a systematic study of their own compatriots'. Therefore, he called for intensive study of white Americans like him, subject to new 'race-building forces' in the New World.[68]

The Races of Europe was well received – but the critical response to Coon's postwar studies of race would prove far less enthusiastic. The intellectual milieu was changing through the 1950s and into the 1960s, rendering racial theories less creditable and acceptable.[69] Finding the emerging anti-racist sentiment overstated and repugnant, Coon reacted by hardening his views. His consorting with a distant cousin, Carleton Putnam, a staunch segregationist and anti-Semite, annoyed many of his more liberal colleagues.[70] Friendship with R. Ruggles Gates, a notoriously racist biologist, also raised hackles. Coon's *The Origin of Races* (1962) might have passed without controversy before the war, but many of his fellow anthropologists now deplored what they interpreted as implied support for racial prejudice and discrimination.[71] Coon responded that he simply was hoping that 'the role of adaptation versus the role of tight genetic inheritance can be worked out cleanly'.[72] While he continued to protest that his theory of separate evolutionary (and hence endocrine) pathways for each race did not necessarily mean one was superior to another, he did not discourage racists who used his analysis to support continuing disparagement and segregation. Coon's typically fierce and unyielding attacks on friends and foes alike never helped his cause. In 1951, he described his own work as 'too broad to be scholarly, too intelligible. It shatters the five-cent mystery of the pundits, breaks their little shell and exposes their clammy white flesh'.[73] Coon came to appear a racist remnant, trying to hold back the new physical, or biological, anthropology – a rebel to the bitter end.

Coon's measurements and observations in Morocco in the 1920s served to sharpen colonial distinctions between Arabs and Berbers, adding a white somatic component to the romantic stereotype of the Berber, which had been primarily a cultural composite. The anthropologist chose to ignore or trivialize – to whitewash, in effect – the mixed ancestry, or heterogeneity, of most Berbers, positing them as a Nordic salient among degraded Mediterraneans, whether Arabs or colonizers. Coon of the Rif thus embraced modern Nordicism, distinguishing his enthusiasm from Lawrence of Arabia's orientalism. By identifying racially with the colonized and rebellious Nordics rather than the Spanish or French colonizers, Coon gave the conventional colonial categorical distinction a peculiar personal twist. At the same time as he was objectifying the Berbers, he was projecting himself into the Rif as their similarly rebellious, similarly white leader, imagining himself at the head of the movement for Nordic supremacy in North Africa. For him, the scientific expedition was prologue to insurrection; the essentialism and epistemic violence of its scientific procedure seemed to rationalize anti-colonial political resistance and aggression. Coon's physical anthropology, his classificatory enterprise, thus made

Berbers visible as figures unrecognizable to themselves and in forms inimical to the colonial state. In effect, Coon was holding up a distorting mirror to himself.

'My restless and scientifically cloaked wanderings brought me to this mountain village in Morocco', wrote American cultural anthropologist Paul Rabinow in 1977, reflecting on a research trip to the Middle Atlas in the late 1960s. 'That I would journey to Morocco to confront Otherness and myself was typical of my culture.'[74] Rabinow evoked the attachment and distance created through the dialectics of encounters in the field. He hung out longer and deeper than Coon ever did. He seems to have cared for his 'informants' in ways that Coon's techniques and inclinations precluded. 'Different webs of signification separated us', Rabinow concluded, 'but these webs were now at least partially intertwined'.[75] The tone and style of interaction may have differed, but both anthropologists sought, in Paul Ricoeur's formulation, according to Rabinow, 'the comprehension of the self by the detour of comprehension of the other'.[76] For both anthropologists, it was probably a hopeless quest.

When hiking through the Rif in February 2011, I came to appreciate the endurance of Carleton and Mary Coon, as I trod the same paths. The previous week I spent in Tangier and Tétouan, waiting hours to meet people who might help me get into the mountains, often just staring at the endless traffic or watching girls dance to Madonna tunes in the cafes. Eventually, I set off from Chefchaouen with Mohammed, guide and muleteer, and his glum, uncooperative pack mule. Still recovering from a serious illness – or rather, a severe treatment – I found the walk tiring and demanding. As we made our way laboriously along rocky trails, we often stopped and shook hands with passing Berbers, many of them blond with blue eyes, and chatted in poor French. It was too cold for tourists to come to the mountains. At one point an old man grabbed me by the shoulder and began ranting, telling me, according to Mohammed, that it was refreshing to see youngsters doing real work, old-fashioned work, transporting hashish, and not just catering to foreign travellers. He told us to beware of gendarmes and pretended to fire a rifle. I was tanned and dressed in local fashion, but could pass as a youthful Berber only to a near blind, half-deaf old man. Over dinner that night in Mohammed's village, I caused some irritation and concern when I asked naively what sort of work the men did in the mountains. Later, I used a French word that was new to them – after all, it had been the Spanish zone – and made them think I was referring to them as the sons of terrorists. It was an awkward, even threatening, moment. This was the Arab Spring, of course, with rebellion breaking out even in Morocco, so everyone assumed I must be a spy, probably for the Americans. When I told them I am a historian of science, they laughed, and asked what that could mean – and if such a person did exist, why should he be asking questions in the Rif during winter? They insisted I tell them which agency was paying me. They seemed to mistake me for Carleton Coon.

From wandering in the Rif in an unsettled period, I learned some things about Coon and his expedition and the assumptions people make. Soon it became clear that Coon had not ventured as deeply into the mountains as I imagined, or as he implied. Mostly, he walked in for a few days from the major Spanish garrisons at Tétouan, Taza and Mellila – still, a remarkable achievement at the time. Like me, he relied on intermediaries such as Mohammed to find informants and research subjects. I learned, too, that no one was ever sure who anyone really was. Everything, and everyone, was mistaken and confused. The key question was always *who* is an expedition, not *what* is an expedition. Coon had managed to make his expeditions all about him – just as I was trying, and failing, to make mine about me. I also began to share his distrust and paranoia, his sense of vulnerability and obtuseness. After a few weeks, I retreated to a cafe on Jamaa el Fna in Marrakesh, perhaps the cafe where he had sat, and there I ate liver kebabs, observing the storytellers, the dancing boys, the strong men and the snake charmers. We heard reports of protests and demonstrations, usually in Casablanca and Rabat, but sometimes in Marrakesh too. One night there was a curfew. Gradually I came to understand Coon's excitement and fascination with impending violence. A month or so after I left, a bomb destroyed my cafe, killing seventeen people and leaving more than twenty-five injured. The government blamed Al Qaeda in the Islamic Maghreb, but experts said it was not their particular mode of terrorism. At Jamaa el Fna I had been reading Rosita Forbes' stirring account of el Raisuni, in which she reports her response to his parting questions:

> 'Well, was your visit good? Are you satisfied?' I nodded, remembering, rather wistfully, those days spent in a strange world, wondering how much or how little I had learned in them.[77]

Warwick Anderson is an Australian Research Council Laureate Fellow and Professor in the Department of History and the Centre for Values, Ethics and the Law in Medicine at the University of Sydney. His books include *The Cultivation of Whiteness: Science, Health and Racial Destiny in Australia* (Duke University Press, 2006); *Colonial Pathologies:*

American Tropical Medicine, Race, and Hygiene in the Philippines (Duke University Press, 2006); and *The Collectors of Lost Souls: Turning Kuru Scientists into Whitemen* (Johns Hopkins University Press, 2008). His most recent book, written with Ian R. Mackay, is *Intolerant Bodies: A Short History of Autoimmunity* (Johns Hopkins University Press, 2014).

Notes

I would like to thank Martin Thomas for suggesting I write this chapter, and for his comments. Sebastián Gil-Riaño, Emma Kowal, Richard Pennell, Hans Pols and Charles Rosenberg also offered helpful advice; Charles Griefenstein assisted me at the American Philosophical Society; and James Dunk provided research assistance. Abdeslam Moudden got me into the Rif, where Mohammed was my patient muleteer and guide. Grants from the US National Science Foundation (NSF 0720951) and the Australian Research Council (DP 0881067 and FL 110100243) supported this research.

1. Carleton S. Coon, *Measuring Ethiopia and Flight into Arabia* (Boston, MA: Little, Brown and Co., 1935), viii.
2. Ibid., 3–4, 4–5, 5.
3. Ibid., 5–6, 6, 10. Coon was one of the few anthropologist members of the New York Explorers Club. On later Harvard anthropology in Ethiopia, see Thomas Zitelman, 'Anthropology and Empire in Post-Italian Ethiopia: Makannen Desta and the Imagination of an Ethiopian "We-Race"', *Paideuma* 47 (2001), 161–79.
4. Along with four million others, Coon had watched Lowell J. Thomas's *With Allenby in Palestine and Lawrence in Arabia* (1919), and read his book, *With Lawrence in Arabia* (New York: The Century Co., 1924). Coon also reviewed T.E. Lawrence's *The Seven Pillars of Wisdom* (New York: G.H. Doran, 1926).
5. Coon, *Measuring Ethiopia*, 247.
6. While in Morocco, Coon read Ernest Hemingway, *The Sun Also Rises* (New York: Scribner, 1926).
7. Walter Harris, *Morocco That Was* (Edinburgh: William Blackwood and Sons, 1921), 293. The London *Times* correspondent in Tangier, Morocco, Harris had been captured by el Raisuni in 1903. He remembered the brigand as 'tall, remarkably handsome, with the whitest of skins, a short dark beard and moustache, and black eyes, with profile Greek rather than Semitic' (p. 181).
8. Coon recalled that Burton and Charles M. Doughty were his 'heroes': see Coon, *Adventures and Discoveries: The Autobiography of Carleton S. Coon* (Englewood Cliffs, NJ: Prentice-Hall, 1981). See also Richard F. Burton, *Personal Narrative of a Pilgrimage to El-Medinah and Meccah*, 3 Vols

(London: Longman, Brown, Green, Longmans, 1855); and Charles M. Doughty, *Travels in Arabia Deserta*, introduction by T.E. Lawrence, 2 Vols (London: P.L. Warner, [1888] 1921).

9. Rosita Forbes, *El Raisuni: The Sultan of the Mountains* (London: Thornton Butterworth, 1924), 15. Always stylishly dressed, and a friend of Noël Coward, Benito Mussolini and Adolf Hitler, Forbes was the first European woman to reach the Kufara Oasis in the Libyan desert. Her later encounter with el Raisuni was fictionalized (in part) in John Milius's film *The Wind and the Lion* (1975), with Candice Bergen speaking her dialogue. Tangier was an international zone until the First World War and after 1928.

10. David S. Woolman, *Rebels in the Rif: Abd el Krim and the Rif Rebellion* (Stanford, CA: Stanford University Press, 1968); C.R. Pennell, *A Country with a Government and a Flag: The Rif War in Morocco, 1921–1926* (Wisbech: Menas Press, 1986); and C.R. Pennell, 'The Rif War: Link or Cul-de-Sac? Nationalism in the Cities and Resistance in the Mountains', *Journal of North African Studies* 1(3) (1996), 234–47.

11. Vincent Sheean, *An American among the Riffi* (New York: Century Co., 1926), ix, xii. A drinking buddy of Hemingway, Sheean was the model for Alfred Hitchcock's *Foreign Correspondent* (1940).

12. Harris, *Morocco That Was*, 305. Coon also was familiar with the work on sexuality and culture of the Finnish anthropologist Edvard A. Westermarck, who spent much of the 1920s in Tangier. Westermarck spoke Berber but never visited the Rif. See Westermarck, *Marriage Ceremonies in Morocco* (London: Macmillan, 1914), and *Ritual and Belief in Morocco*, 2 Vols (London: Macmillan, 1926). Most likely he also read Auguste Mouliéras, *Le Maroc inconnu: étude géographique et sociologique. Exploration du Rif* (Paris: Augustin Challamel, 1899), the best account of the tribes of the Rif.

13. Earnest Hooton, 'Foreword', in Carleton Stevens Coon, *Flesh of the Wild Ox: A Riffian Chronicle of High Valleys and Long Rifles* (New York: William Morrow, 1932), ix–xi. See also Hooton, 'An Untamed Anthropologist among the Wilder Whites', *Harvard Alumni Bulletin* 33 (1930), 34–45.

14. W.H. Auden, *Spain* (London: Faber and Faber, 1937).

15. Edmund Burke III, 'The Image of the French Colonial State in Ethnological Literature: A New Look at Lyautey's Berber Policy', in Ernest Gellner and Charles Micaud (eds), *Arabs and Berbers: From Tribe to Nation in North Africa* (London: Duckworth, 1972), 175–99; C.R. Pennell, *Morocco since 1830: A History* (New York: New York University Press, 2000); and Susan Miller and Katherine Hoffman (eds), *Berbers and Others: Beyond Tribe and Nation in the Maghrib* (Bloomington, IN: Indiana University Press, 2010).

16. Pennell, *Country with a Government and a Flag*.

17. Earnest A. Hooton, 'Progress in the Study of Race Mixtures with Special Reference to Work Carried on at Harvard University', *Proceedings of the American Philosophical Society* 65 (1926), 312–25. See also his 'Race

Mixture in the United States', *Pacific Review* 2 (1921), 116–27; and *Up from the Ape* (London: Allen and Unwin, 1931). Hooton, to a degree and actually ambivalently, was following the lead of Franz Boas: see Boas, *The Mind of Primitive Man* (New York: Macmillan, 1911).

18. On Shapiro, see Warwick Anderson, 'Hybridity, Race, and Science: The Voyage of the *Zaca*, 1934–35', *Isis* 103(2) (2012), 229–53, and 'Racial Anthropology and Human Biology in the Island Laboratories of the United States', *Current Anthropology* 53(S5) (2012), S95–107. On Birdsell, see Warwick Anderson, *The Cultivation of Whiteness: Science, Health and Racial Destiny in Australia* (Durham, NC: Duke University Press, 2006), ch. 8.
19. Alan H. Goodman and Evelynn Hammonds, 'Reconciling Race and Human Adaptability: Carleton Coon and the Persistence of Race in Scientific Discourse', *Kroeber Anthropological Society Papers* 84 (2000), 28–44; John P. Jackson Jr., '"In Ways Unacademical": The Reception of Carleton S. Coon's *The Origin of Races*', *Journal of the History of Biology* 34(2) (2001), 247–85; and Peter Sachs Collopy, 'Race Relationships: Collegiality and Demarcation in Physical Anthropology', *Journal of the History of the Behavioral Sciences* 51(3) (2015), 237–60.
20. See, for example, Martin Thomas (ed.), *Expedition into Empire: Exploratory Journeys and the Making of the Modern World* (New York: Routledge, 2015).
21. Coon was in the same year at Andover as (paediatrician) Benjamin Spock and (artist) Joseph Cornell.
22. Coon, *Adventures and Discoveries*, 27.
23. Ibid., 30. Coon later claimed he had wanted to join Abd al-Karim's army but arrived too late.
24. Ibid., 31, 32.
25. Coon to Hooton, 15 August 1925, Riffian trip correspondence file, box 17, C.S. Coon papers, National Anthropological Archives, Smithsonian Institution, Suitland, MD [hereafter Coon papers].
26. Coon, *Adventures and Discoveries*, 32. Shluh is a term for the Berber people of the Atlas Mountains.
27. Coon to Hooton, 30 August 1925, Riffian trip correspondence file, box 17, Coon papers.
28. Coon, *Adventures and Discoveries*.
29. Anne Roe, Summary [typescript], March 1952, Carleton Stevens Coon file, Anne Roe papers, Mss.B.R621, American Philosophical Society, Philadelphia, PA [hereafter Roe papers]. Roe, a clinical psychologist and wife of palaeontologist George Gaylord Simpson, was conducting a study of the making of successful scientists.
30. Coon, *Adventures and Discoveries*, 35.
31. Coon to Hooton, 26 June 1926, Riffian trip correspondence file, box 17, Coon papers.
32. Coon to Hooton, 5 July 1926, Riffian trip correspondence file, box 17, Coon papers.

33. Coon to Hooton, 14 July 1926, Riffian trip correspondence file, box 17, Coon papers.
34. Coon to Hooton, 20 August 1926, Riffian trip correspondence file, box 17, Coon papers. Coon's use of 'the bled' refers to rural Morocco.
35. Coon, *Adventures and Discoveries*, 42. See also Carleton Coon, Notes on Trip in Riff [typescript], box 43, Coon papers.
36. Coon, *Adventures and Discoveries*.
37. Ibid., 50.
38. Carleton Coon, Report on December Riff Trip [typescript], box 43, Coon papers, 21.
39. Coon, *Adventures and Discoveries*, 51, 51, 54.
40. The son, Carleton S. Coon, Jr., served as a US diplomat, spending a few years in Morocco during the Cold War.
41. Carleton Coon, Report on December Riff Trip [typescript], box 43, Coon papers, 14, 15.
42. Ibid., 15. This is a reversal of the more common trope of the excremental colonized: see Warwick Anderson, 'Excremental Colonialism: Public Health and the Poetics of Pollution', *Critical Inquiry* 21(3) (1995), 640–69.
43. Warwick Anderson, 'Following Racial Paper Trails', in Alexandra Widmer and Veronika Lipphardt (eds), *Health and Difference: Rendering Human Variation in Colonial Engagements* (New York: Berghahn Books, 2016), 224–31.
44. Coon to Hooton, 8 November 1928, Riffian trip correspondence file, box 17, Coon papers. (The date seems to be misidentified as 1926.)
45. Coon, *Adventures and Discoveries*, 56.
46. Coon to Hooton, 24 January 1927, Riffian trip correspondence file, box 17, Coon papers.
47. Ibid.
48. Coon to Hooton, 19 January 1927, Riffian trip correspondence file, box 17, Coon papers.
49. Coon, *Adventures and Discoveries*, 57. See also Carleton Coon, Notes on Telwet Trip [typescript], box 43, Coon papers.
50. Coon to Hooton, 8 November 1928, Riffian trip correspondence file, box 17, Coon papers.
51. Gavin Maxwell, *Lords of the Atlas: The Rise and Fall of the House of Glaoua, 1893–1956* (London: Pan Books, 1970).
52. Coon to Hooton, 8 November 1928, Riffian trip correspondence file, box 17, Coon papers.
53. Coon to Hooton, 1 April 1927, Riffian trip correspondence file, box 17, Coon papers.
54. Carleton S. Coon, *Tribes of the Rif*, Harvard African Studies IX (Cambridge, MA: Peabody Museum, 1931), 410. This book is essentially his 1928 Harvard PhD dissertation.
55. Carleton S. Coon, 'The People of the Rif', *Natural History* 35 (1935), 92–106, here 102.

56. Coon, *Tribes of the Rif*, viii.
57. Ibid., 111.
58. Coon, 'The People of the Rif', 106.
59. Pat Putnam lived for more than twenty-five years among the Mbuti at 'Camp Putnam': see Joan T. Mark, *The King of the World in the Land of the Pygmies* (Ann Arbor, MI: University of Michigan Press, 1995). Gordon Browne also stayed in the Cambridge household when visiting from Tangier.
60. Coon interview [typescript, c. 1952], p. 6, Carleton Stevens Coon file, Roe papers.
61. Ibid., 7.
62. Ibid., 8.
63. Hooton to George W. Harley, 13 April 1943, box 6, E.H. Hooton papers, 995-1, Peabody Museum Archives, Harvard University, Cambridge, Massachusetts [hereafter Hooton papers].
64. Coon interview [typescript, c. 1952], pp. 8–9, Carleton Stevens Coon file, Roe papers.
65. William Z. Ripley, *The Races of Europe: A Sociological Study* (New York: D. Appleton and Co., 1899). Ripley became professor of economics at Harvard soon after his book's publication.
66. Carleton S. Coon, *The Races of Europe* (New York: Macmillan, 1939), 650.
67. Ibid., 11, 5.
68. Ibid., 649, 652.
69. Elazar Barkan, *The Retreat of Scientific Racism: Changing Concepts of Race in Britain and the United States between the Wars* (New York: Cambridge University Press, 1993); and Michelle Brattain, 'Race, Racism, and Antiracism: UNESCO and the Politics of Presenting Science to the Postwar Public', *American Historical Review* 112(5) (2007), 1386–413.
70. Carleton Putnam, *Race and Reason: A Yankee View* (Washington, DC: Public Affairs Press, 1961). On the relations between Putnam and Coon, see Jackson, '"In Ways Unacademical"'.
71. Carleton S. Coon, *The Origin of Races* (New York: Alfred A. Knopf, 1962). Coon also wrote a transitional text in which he tried to reconcile racial distinctions and evolutionary theory, with the assistance of Stanley Garn and Joseph B. Birdsell (who later regretted his involvement): *Races: A Study in the Problems of Race Formation in Man* (Springfield, IL: C.C. Thomas, 1950). On Coon's use of race as 'shorthand for biological variation' (p. 29), see Goodman and Hammonds, 'Reconciling Race and Human Adaptability'. Coon found a few defenders: Julian Huxley took Ashley Montagu to task for his criticisms, claiming 'Coon's exaggerations are in part a reaction against the equally unwarranted exaggerations of what I may call the anti-racist school, who want to deny there are or can be any "racial" differences' (17 January 1963, folder 1455, box 22, Ashley Montagu papers, MS 109, American Philosophical Society, Philadelphia PA).

72. Coon to Hooton, 23 February 1953, box 6, Hooton papers.
73. Coon to Froelich Rainey, 23 August 1951, in Folder: Iran Correspondence 1949–51, box 1, C.S. Coon papers, University of Pennsylvania Museum Archives.
74. Paul Rabinow, *Reflections on Fieldwork in Morocco* (Berkeley, CA: University of California Press, 1977), 161, 161–62.
75. Ibid., 162. Interestingly, even at the height of the Cold War Rabinow was more often mistaken for a Christian missionary than a spy.
76. Paul Ricoeur's essay 'Existence et herméneutique', published in *Le Conflit des interprétations* (Paris: Editions du Seuil, 1969), is quoted by Rabinow in *Reflections on Fieldwork*, 5.
77. Forbes, *El Raisuni*, 317

Bibliography

Anderson, Warwick. *The Cultivation of Whiteness: Science, Health and Racial Destiny in Australia*. Durham, NC: Duke University Press, 2006.
———. 'Excremental Colonialism: Public Health and the Poetics of Pollution'. *Critical Inquiry* 21(3) (1995), 640–69.
———. 'Following Racial Paper Trails', in Alexandra Widmer and Veronika Lipphardt (eds), *Health and Difference: Rendering Human Variation in Colonial Engagements* (New York: Berghahn Books, 2016), 224–31.
———. 'Hybridity, Race, and Science: The Voyage of the *Zaca*, 1934–35', *Isis* 103(2) (2012), 229–53.
———. 'Racial Anthropology and Human Biology in the Island Laboratories of the United States'. *Current Anthropology* 53(S5) (2012), S95–107.
Auden, W.H. *Spain*. London: Faber and Faber, 1937.
Barkan, Elazar. *The Retreat of Scientific Racism: Changing Concepts of Race in Britain and the United States between the Wars*. New York: Cambridge University Press, 1993.
Boas, Franz. *The Mind of Primitive Man*. New York: Macmillan, 1911.
Brattain, Michelle. 'Race, Racism, and Antiracism: UNESCO and the Politics of Presenting Science to the Postwar Public'. *American Historical Review* 112(5) (2007), 1386–413.
Burke, III, Edmund. 'The Image of the French Colonial State in Ethnological Literature: A New Look at Lyautey's Berber Policy', in Ernest Gellner and Charles Micaud (eds), *Arabs and Berbers: From Tribe to Nation in North Africa* (London: Duckworth, 1972), 175–99.
Burton, Richard F. *Personal Narrative of a Pilgrimage to El-Medinah and Meccah*. 3 Vols. London: Longman, Brown, Green, Longmans, 1855.
Collopy, Peter Sachs. 'Race Relationships: Collegiality and Demarcation in Physical Anthropology'. *Journal of the History of the Behavioral Sciences* 51(3) (2015), 237–60.

Coon, Carleton S. *Adventures and Discoveries: The Autobiography of Carleton S. Coon*. Englewood Cliffs, NJ: Prentice-Hall, 1981.

———. *Measuring Ethiopia and Flight into Arabia*. Boston, MA: Little, Brown and Co., 1935.

———. *The Origin of Races*. New York: Alfred A. Knopf, 1962.

———. 'The People of the Rif'. *Natural History* 35 (1935), 92–106.

———. *Races: A Study in the Problems of Race Formation in Man*. Springfield, IL: C.C. Thomas, 1950.

———. *The Races of Europe*. New York: Macmillan, 1939.

———. *Tribes of the Rif*. Harvard African Studies IX. Cambridge, MA: Peabody Museum, 1931.

Doughty, Charles M. *Travels in Arabia Deserta*. Introduction by T.E. Lawrence. 2 Vols. London: P.L. Warner, [1888] 1921.

Forbes, Rosita. *El Raisuni: The Sultan of the Mountains*. London: Thornton Butterworth, 1924.

Goodman, Alan H., and Evelynn Hammonds. 'Reconciling Race and Human Adaptability: Carleton Coon and the Persistence of Race in Scientific Discourse'. *Kroeber Anthropological Society Papers* 84 (2000), 28–44.

Harris, Walter. *Morocco That Was*. Edinburgh: William Blackwood and Sons, 1921.

Hemingway, Ernest. *The Sun Also Rises*. New York: Scribner, 1926.

Hooton, Earnest. 'Foreword', in Carleton Stevens Coon, *Flesh of the Wild Ox: A Riffian Chronicle of High Valleys and Long Rifles* (New York: William Morrow, 1932), ix–xi.

———. 'Progress in the Study of Race Mixtures with Special Reference to Work Carried on at Harvard University'. *Proceedings of the American Philosophical Society* 65 (1926), 312–25.

———. 'Race Mixture in the United States'. *Pacific Review* 2 (1921), 116–27.

———. 'An Untamed Anthropologist among the Wilder Whites'. *Harvard Alumni Bulletin* 33 (1930), 34–45.

———. *Up from the Ape*. London: Allen and Unwin, 1931.

Jackson Jr., John P. '"In Ways Unacademical": The Reception of Carleton S. Coon's *The Origin of Races*'. *Journal of the History of Biology* 34(2) (2001), 247–85.

Lawrence, T.E. *The Seven Pillars of Wisdom*. New York: G.H. Doran, 1926.

Mark, Joan T. *The King of the World in the Land of the Pygmies*. Ann Arbor, MI: University of Michigan Press, 1995.

Maxwell, Gavin. *Lords of the Atlas: The Rise and Fall of the House of Glaoua, 1893–1956*. London: Pan Books, 1970.

Miller, Susan, and Katherine Hoffman (eds). *Berbers and Others: Beyond Tribe and Nation in the Maghrib*. Bloomington, IN: Indiana University Press, 2010.

Mouliéras, Auguste. *Le Maroc inconnu: étude géographique et sociologique. Exploration du Rif*. Paris: Augustin Challamel, 1899.

Pennell, C.R. *A Country with a Government and a Flag: The Rif War in Morocco, 1921–1926*. Wisbech: Menas Press, 1986.

———. *Morocco since 1830: A History*. New York: New York University Press, 2000.

———. 'The Rif War: Link or Cul-de-Sac? Nationalism in the Cities and Resistance in the Mountains'. *Journal of North African Studies* 1(3) (1996), 234–47.

Putnam, Carleton. *Race and Reason: A Yankee View*. Washington, DC: Public Affairs Press, 1961.

Rabinow, Paul. *Reflections on Fieldwork in Morocco*. Berkeley, CA: University of California Press, 1977.

Ricoeur, Paul. 'Existence and Hermeneutics [trans. Kathleen McLaughlin]', in Don Ihde (ed.) *The Conflict of Interpretations: Essays in Hermeneutics* (Evanston,IL: Northwestern University Press, 1974), 3–24.

Ripley, William Z. *The Races of Europe: A Sociological Study*. New York: D. Appleton and Co., 1899.

Sheean, Vincent. *An American among the Riffi*. New York: Century Co., 1926.

Thomas, Lowell J. *With Lawrence in Arabia*. New York: The Century Co., 1924.

Thomas, Martin (ed.). *Expedition into Empire: Exploratory Journeys and the Making of the Modern World*. New York: Routledge, 2015.

Westermarck, Edvard A. *Marriage Ceremonies in Morocco*. London: Macmillan, 1914.

———. *Ritual and Belief in Morocco*. 2 Vols. London: Macmillan, 1926.

Woolman, David S. *Rebels in the Rif: Abd el Krim and the Rif Rebellion*. Stanford, CA: Stanford University Press, 1968.

Zitelman, Thomas. 'Anthropology and Empire in Post-Italian Ethiopia: Makannen Desta and the Imagination of an Ethiopian "We-Race"'. *Paideuma* 47 (2001), 161–79.

Chapter 6

MEDIUM, GENRE, INDIGENOUS PRESENCE

SPANISH EXPEDITIONARY ENCOUNTERS IN THE MAR DEL SUR, 1606

Bronwen Douglas

This chapter combines narrative and historiographic enquiries into the Spanish voyages of Pedro Fernández de Quirós and Luis Váez de Torres across the Mar del Sur (South Sea) in 1606. I aim to elucidate the 'anthropological' significance of maritime expeditions in the first, Iberian phase of the 'expansion of Europe' between 1400 and 1900 – the process often conceived teleologically as the wellspring of modernity.[1] A narrative of episodes occurring during these linked voyages – in Espiritu Santo (now in Vanuatu), the southern New Guinea coast (now in Papua New Guinea and Indonesian West Papua) and the Torres Strait Islands (now mostly in Queensland, Australia) – enables critical reflection on the production and historical value of empirical knowledge about exotic people and places, expressed in graphic and written mediums. Manuscript drawings and maps, with prominent legends, are juxtaposed with diverse written genres. Each medium or genre throws light on the others in a twofold investigation: into the significance of expeditionary encounters in the genesis of early voyagers' representations; and into the import of such representations for an ethnohistory of encounters and a history of the science of man or anthropology, focusing on emergent European ideas about human difference.

Reading Indigenous Presence

My theory of knowledge production, elaborated elsewhere,[2] positions local inhabitants as crucial, if usually unintentional, contributors to representations of people and places produced by foreigners in the wake of encounters on the ground. The varied meanings attributed to these meetings were often opposed and generally ambiguous but they provided stimuli for acting, including the action of representation. Foreigners' representations are thus partly products of encounters because their understandings were stimulated by local behaviours. The powerful emotional impact of exotic experience imbues representations with obvious and covert traces of indigenous presence, actions and agency, filtered through observers' preconceptions, prejudices, feelings and perceptions and expressed in the language, content, iconography and tone of what they wrote or drew.

I differentiate these traces into consciously processed, if often misconstrued signs, and inadvertent counterparts, or complements, that I call 'countersigns'. Indigenous countersigns are discernible in choice of words, names and motifs; in tense, mood and voice; in tone, style, presence, emphasis, ambiguity and absence. Generated in the uncertainties and seesawing emotions of encounters, countersigns cluster in expressions of doubt, frustration or fear.

Voyages and Settings

The Spanish noun *expedición* had multiple meanings and shifting emphases in the two hundred years after 1600. In the early seventeenth century, it usually meant 'dispatch', 'expediting', 'facilitating'.[3] A century later, the new *Diccionario de autoridades* foregrounded military connotations, defining *expedición* as an 'enterprise of war ... in a distant foreign country'. Yet the third edition of 1791 reinstates 'facility, ease, promptness and speed' as the primary meaning, while the military application is labelled metaphoric.[4] By the late eighteenth century, the non-martial extended sense of 'voyage' or 'enterprise' was a key signified of 'expedition' in English and in Romance languages and it became the main general definition in the twentieth century. The term *expedición* scarcely appears in the texts considered in this chapter but participants in the voyages applied two other concrete nouns to their undertakings. The most usual is *jornada*, defined as 'the march that can regularly be done in a day' with the further, military meaning of 'expedition undertaken by the army'.[5] A cognate of English 'journey', *jornada* in these texts denotes a journey by sea, a voyage. The less common noun is *viaje* (voyage). In my usage, 'expedition' signifies an undertaking by a fleet and 'voyage' the journey of a single ship.

From the early fifteenth century, Portuguese maritime enterprise and trade steadily expanded with advances in naval technology and navigational expertise. Having explored the Atlantic islands and the African west coast, they reached the Indian Ocean by 1490. Within two years, Spain riposted by sailing westwards to seek Asian trade. This venture was portentously interrupted by encounters with unknown lands offering novel possibilities for colonial exploitation, settlement and Christian conversion of 'heathens'. Spanish overseas expeditions materialized a pragmatic marriage of royal ambition (to outface rivals and advance the interests of Catholic Spain) with the geographic, economic and religious visions of individual mariners (many not of Spanish origin). The sixteenth-century era of Hispanic exploration in the Mar del Sur paralleled Spain's movement from colonial conquest to the heyday of empire to incipient exhaustion. After the pioneer crossing of the *mar pacífico* (Pacific Sea) by Portuguese-born Ferdinand Magellan in 1521,[6] most Spanish voyages departed from the frontier colonies of New Spain (Mexico) and Peru. From 1565 to 1815, Spanish trading vessels plied regular return passages across the north Pacific along the fixed galleon routes linking Acapulco (New Spain) and Manila (Philippines). However, Quirós' expedition from Peru in December 1605 was Spain's last major exploratory undertaking before the late eighteenth century.

Quirós, also Portuguese-born, had been chief pilot on Alvaro de Mendaña y Neira's troubled voyage of 1595 in search of the Solomon Islands, visited by Mendaña nearly thirty years before. This experience authorized Quirós' subsequent argument that 'many islands or a continent', filled with untold wealth and myriad souls needing conversion, must cover 'a quarter of the whole globe' in Europe's 'antipodes'.[7] The new expedition left Callao aboard two galleons and a small launch, led overall by Quirós on the *capitana* (flagship), with Torres in charge of the *almiranta* (second ship). They crossed the Mar del Sur in a third and final chapter of the Spanish quest 'to discover' Terra Australis Incognita, the great southern continent deduced by sixteenth-century cosmography and graphically materialized in contemporary world maps.[8]

After briefly visiting several islands in modern French Polynesia, Cook Islands, the eastern Solomons and north Vanuatu, Quirós found his 'unknown southern region' in Vanuatu's largest island and named it La Austrialia del Espiritu Santo. He planned to establish a 'town' called New Jerusalem and claimed for God and king 'all the islands and lands that I have newly discovered and shall discover as far as the [south] pole'. But there was no sign of the gold, silver and pearls he had promised his unhappy crew. The inhabitants obdurately opposed the incomers and were clearly unreceptive to the prospect of salvation.[9] The settlement lasted little more than a month. Separated from the other ships by bad weather, Quirós headed for Acapulco on the *capitana*, content to have 'discovered so many fine peoples and lands, knowing not where they ended'.[10] Torres took the remaining vessels far enough around Espiritu Santo to prove it was not a continent but an island 'about thirty leagues in circumference'.[11] He then made his way to Manila via the uncharted south coast of New Guinea, passing unaware through the strait later named in his honour.

In Spanish imperial ontology, the Mar del Sur, its littorals and islands comprised the 'western' portion of *las Indias* (the Indies), the newly encountered geographical entity dominated by 'northern' and 'southern' divisions in the Americas. Spain's twin preoccupations with American colonization and Asian trade rendered the island Pacific largely irrelevant and reduced the great ocean to a maritime highway between the Philippines and its metropole in New Spain.[12] Obsessive official secrecy, recently documented by Rainer Buschmann, ensured that few maps or travelogues were published at the time. Most empirical products of Spanish voyaging – including all graphic and written materials considered here – remained buried in archives until burgeoning imperial rivalry in the eighteenth and nineteenth centuries impelled publication to establish the priority of Spanish Pacific claims.[13]

Published ethnographic description of Islanders colonized by Spain was largely a preserve of missionaries who had lived among them in the Philippines and Guam (Mariana Islands). Unusually, Quirós' 'eighth memorial' to the king of 1609–10 – a fervid account of his 'discovery' of the southern continent – was published in Spain and widely disseminated in translations.[14] This crucial text validated the reality of Terra Australis and the striking physical diversity of its inhabitants for cartographers, geographers, travellers and anthropologists until the late eighteenth century.[15] Yet dozens of subsequent memorials sent by Quirós seeking support to colonize the *tierras Australes* (Austral lands) were ignored or suppressed by a state now too impoverished to attempt further imperial conquests, but still determined to conceal information about 'new discoveries' from Spain's 'enemies'.[16]

Representations

I preface my discussion of the voyages of Quirós and Torres by considering a drawing and a short text produced in Manila in about 1590 but unknown until the mid-twentieth century.[17] Fallout from a transitory encounter between Spaniards and Pacific Islanders, these materials encapsulate key elements of my dual enquiry. The drawing, probably by a Chinese artist, depicts exchanges in progress off the island of Guam in May 1590 between canoe-borne indigenous Chamorro and the crew and passengers of a Spanish galleon (see Figure 6.1). It is inserted in the 'Boxer Codex', a richly illustrated manuscript prepared for a Spanish governor of the Philippines. The sketch illuminates a four-page 'Relación' (account) of the islands of the Ladrones (Thieves).[18] The name memorialized the agency of the Chamorro who infuriated Magellan in 1521 by coming to the ships in canoes and seizing everything they could, including a small boat. The Spanish retaliated with a bloody, destructive shore raid, completely out of all proportion to the insult but a telling countersign of their plight: they were in extremis from scurvy and deprivation after more than three months on a vast, empty ocean.[19] Claimed by Spain in 1565, Guam became a regular stopping point on the Manila galleon route.

There is no depth or context in these cursory representations of a fleeting encounter but, read together, sketch and description are more evocative than either the written or the visual medium alone. The protagonists are embodied in the drawing which the prose explicates to produce a vivid scene of ships, persons and objects flowing between them. The galleon is surrounded by 'light' canoes, manoeuvrable like 'very tame and disciplined horses', some tethered to the ship. A local man, 'like fish in water', is diving to retrieve something before it sinks. The Chamorro are bringing local produce and fresh water to

Figure 6.1 Anon., [Spanish–Chamorro encounter, Guam], [c. 1590]. Chinese ink and paint on rice paper. By permission of the Lilly Library, Indiana University, Bloomington, IN, USA (LMC 2444).

exchange for 'iron because it is their gold', greatly valued for its utility and power. Sketch and words combine to convey a contemporary European sense of collective human difference, not between separate races but between *gente* (people) positioned at opposite poles of a universalized continuum between civility and barbarity.[20] Overdressed, light-skinned Spaniards cluster demurely aboard the vessel, encircled by a disorderly crowd of 'very brown' men of massive stature and great 'strength', with 'wide, flat' faces, 'very long' hair and – shocking to the Spanish – all unclothed, 'men and women alike', just 'as they were born'.

A few years later, a series of maps and four ink-and-gouache drawings illustrated places and people seen by the Spanish in Espiritu Santo and during Torres' passage to Manila. The four extant landscape maps, probably done in situ, are signed by Diego de Prado y Tovar, the expedition's aristocratic *capitán-entretenido* (second or supernumerary captain) who initially sailed under Quirós on the *capitana*.[21] Prado, who despised Quirós' origin and background (a 'Portuguese storekeeper') and claimed that his crew was plotting mutiny, joined Torres on the *almiranta* several months into the voyage.[22] The unsigned, spirited but rather clumsy drawings are usually attributed to Prado but might have been produced by an artist in Manila.[23] They are among the earliest surviving visual representations of Pacific Islanders, showing their varied appearance, weapons, body decoration and dress.

These graphic genres are complemented by words: titles, names and legends condense information of imperial interest such as the inhabitants' skin colour, build, clothing, arms and foodstuffs as well as the contours and quality of land or ports. With respect to Espiritu Santo, the map and the drawing supplement diverse writings produced during the voyage, notably Quirós' narrative and the journals of the pilot Gaspar Gonçalez de Leza and the chaplain Martin de Munilla.[24] In contrast, the visual materials and their inscribed words are crucial resources for historians with respect to Torres' subsequent voyage to Manila, since extant written texts are either exiguous or retrospective. Torres wrote two brief letter-reports while in Manila in July 1607, one to the king to which he evidently annexed Prado's maps and the four drawings, and one to Quirós who very selectively summarized it in a memorial printed in 1610.[25] Prado's narrative, worked and reworked over the following decade, bears imprints of reconsidered memory and perhaps forgetting.[26] My own narrative, compiled from these materials, shows how encounters contributed to their content and enunciation. Signs and countersigns of the powerful emotional valency of encounters permeate the written genres and more subtly inflect the maps and drawings.

Encounter to Representation

The pious Spanish desire to find the unknown South Land is patent in Leza's recounting of the little fleet's slow approach towards 'a great land, with high mountains, that promised to be no less than a continent' – 'if God so wants'. On 3 May 1606, the ships anchored off the north coast of Espiritu Santo in a vast inlet that Quirós named St Philip and St James, since it was the two saints' commemorative day. Now Big Bay, it was 'populated by many people' and is depicted in Prado's map (Figure 6.2).[27]

The Spanish accounts vary instructively. Quirós framed his narrative as the compassionate tale of a fledgling Christian colony ruined from the first days because Spanish 'maltreatment' – wanton killings and ruthless plunder of houses, gardens and pigs – provoked 'the *indios*' (Indians) of the bay to 'war'. His archetypal early clash involved an 'encounter' with a well-armed but jittery shore party led by Torres, ordered 'to bring some Indians' to the ship 'to affirm peace and friendship' through Spanish 'good works'. An old, clearly respected man drew a line in the sand, gestured to the strangers not to cross and seemingly proposed that both parties lay down their arms. Munilla inverted the agency involved: some of 'the *yndios*' feigned peace while 'many archers' lay in ambush to attack the landing party, which aimed to build a defensive stockade. Leza represented agency shared: the Spanish party of 'forty arquebusiers and thirty shield-bearers' was confronted by 'many people', 'all excited and armed' but, disastrously for them, with 'no knowledge of arquebuses'. Torres 'told them to move back', since the Spanish 'were coming en masse, and all armed', but their 'impudence and audacity' stung him into ordering shots 'in the air'. All accounts agree that one soldier fired low and killed a man. Perhaps, as in Quirós' story of an incident in the Marquesas in 1595, he did so 'in order not to lose his reputation as a good arquebusier'. The corpse was mutilated and hung by the foot from a tree – 'as the means for the so-called peace', said Quirós sardonically. After further skirmishes, the aforementioned old man was killed in an ambush and 'peace became war', foundering Quirós' hopes for unhindered exploration of 'the glory of the land'.[28]

Quirós' lament for peace aborted from the outset by mutual lack of understanding and arrogant soldiers contrasts with Munilla's

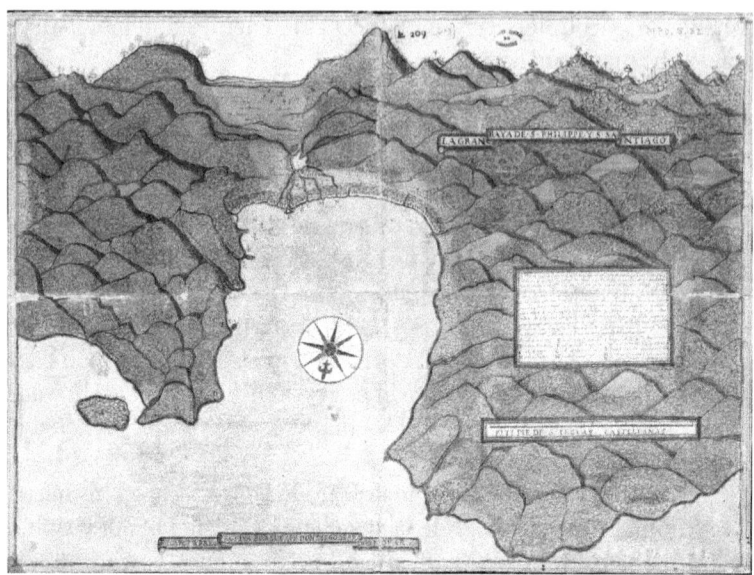

Figure 6.2 Diego de Prado y Tovar, *La gran baya d. S. Philippe y S. Santiago*, [1606]. Ink and gouache on paper. By permission of the Ministerio de Educación, Cultura y Deporte, Archivo General de Simancas, Spain (MPD, 08, 082).

representation of the visit's first week as a period of 'good peace and friendship with the *yndios*', using *indios* in its general contemporary sense as a preferred synonym for *naturales* (natives). But, added the chaplain in retrospect, the goodwill of these 'brutish barbarians' was afterwards proven to have been 'false and feigned'. As fighting became more intense, Munilla's language changes markedly. The Islanders, thus far *yndios*, are henceforth usually *negros* (blacks), even within a particular sentence: 'some *yndios* emerged from ambush and shot darts and arrows at our people who ... fired arquebuses at them and the *negros* withdrew'. In the final days of the visit, he denounced the 'malice and cunning' of 'vile', 'despicable people'.[29] This lexical trajectory hints at another, restricted contemporary usage of *indio* to mean 'like a native of the Indies', sometimes in implied contrast to *negro*, which as a noun acquired steadily more negative connotations during the sixteenth century. Leza's rhetoric shifts even more dramatically in response to local actions during bitter fighting. In a single page, the people are successively *naturales*, *bárbaros* (barbarians) and the *enemigo* (enemy).[30]

Such derogatory words do not merely express embedded Christian distaste and Spanish contempt for heathen barbarians. Rather, the

Figure 6.3 [Diego de Prado y Tovar], *Esta xente es d'esta baia st felipe y st tiago*..., [1607]. Ink and gouache on paper. By permission of the Ministerio de Educación, Cultura y Deporte, Archivo General de Simancas, Spain (MPD, 18, 081).

words, their changing usages and their textual placement are also countersigns of disquieting, volatile indigenous behaviour. Torres blamed the inhabitants for the violence: 'they never wanted peace with us though we often spoke to them and I gave them gifts; I never set foot on shore with their agreement they [were] always wanting to forbid it and always fighting'.[31] All four drawings depict men bearing arms described in the legends – variously darts, spears, clubs, bows and arrows and shields. However, only the sketch of the 'people' of Big Bay lacks a representative woman and child (Figure 6.3). Their omission is a further countersign of how male belligerence here impinged on Spanish experience and emotions.

Torres waited a fortnight after the *capitana*'s disappearance before opening his sealed royal orders. Obeying their injunction to 'make every effort to get to twenty degrees south latitude and see if there is any land in that region', he sailed the *almiranta* and the launch southwest to slightly beyond the twentieth parallel. Finding no 'sign of land', he headed northwest or north until, on 14 July 1606, the ships reached what Torres took to be the south coast of New Guinea.[32] The north coast of the great island, which had been seen by a few Iberian voyagers since 1526, was named by a Spaniard in 1545 and appeared on maps in the 1550s.[33] Torres' landfall was actually the

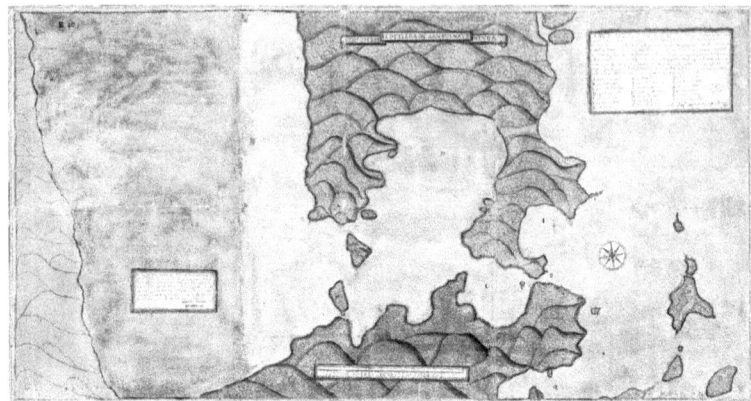

Figure 6.4 Diego de Prado y Tovar, *Puertos i bayas de Tiera de San Buenaventura*, [1606]. Ink and gouache on paper. By permission of the Ministerio de Educación, Cultura y Deporte, Archivo General de Simancas, Spain (MPD, 12, 034).

most easterly of the Louisiade Archipelago, southeast of the main island, and named by Louis-Antoine de Bougainville in 1768.[34] After sailing for five days along the reefs south of the Archipelago, Torres anchored in Sukuri Bay on Sideia Island, close to the southeastern tip of the New Guinea mainland, the locality marked 'A' on Prado's map (Figure 6.4). During a two-week sojourn, the Spaniards examined nearby bays and islands, reaching as far as modern Milne Bay. In encounters with local people, portrayed in a drawing (Figure 6.5), the Spanish killed 'some' men with their arquebuses and seized garden produce, pigs and two canoes. In this and other 'ports' along the New Guinea coast, Torres and/or Prado 'took possession of all the land' in the name of the king.[35]

Torres next spent nearly three weeks in what is now Orangerie Bay, about a hundred kilometres further west. Prado's map (Figure 6.6) graphically anticipates the 'densely populated and cultivated' district mentioned in his narrative while its legend lauds 'the best land and most fertile to settle of that discovered'.[36] In an initial encounter, the Spanish 'captured some *indios* in a canoe who were ransomed for a splendid large pig'. Prado's narrative describes friendly exchanges with the inhabitants of a 'large village' in Mullins Harbour or Puro, at the eastern end of the bay. Here, sleight of hand with arquebuses enabled the soldiers to kill and bear off two 'very large pigs'. During a subsequent landing, a large body of *indios* fled from an African slave belonging to Torres' pilot.[37] This incident cast a long textual shadow.

Figure 6.5 [Diego de Prado y Tovar], *Esta xente es desta baya de san millan* ..., [1607]. Ink and gouache on paper. By permission of the Ministerio de Educación, Cultura y Deporte, Archivo General de Simancas, Spain (MPD, 18, 082).

West of Orangerie Bay, at Mailu Island, a bloody clash took place on 24 August 1606 following the failed ambush of a Spanish landing party. According to Prado, 'some' warriors died in an initial 'skirmish'. Others were killed as they fled, discarding their weapons, and still more died while 'escaping' to the mainland in canoes. In the meantime, the women, children and old men had taken refuge in a cliff-top stronghold, defended only by the terrain. When two Spaniards armed with swords and shields tried to reach them, they were 'so stoned with pebbles' that they retreated. But twenty disciplined Spanish 'marksmen', protected by shieldbearers, 'wreaked slaughter' with their arquebuses and 'sacked' the stronghold. Many women and children were killed and wounded. Of the surviving children, Prado kidnapped fourteen, who were eventually baptized in Manila, and freed 'the rest'.[38] On the four hundredth anniversary of the battle in 2006, the people of Mailu held a 'reconciliation event', attended by one or two Spanish citizens, in order to 'cleanse the land' and achieve closure – a striking instance of the present reality of past events for indigenous communities.[39]

Abduction was a routine stratagem for Spanish voyagers. Before leaving Peru, Quirós received ecclesiastical sanction to seize 'some natives' in order to save their souls. Yet he admitted pragmatically that the 'manifest risk' to ships and crews in small islands – local agency

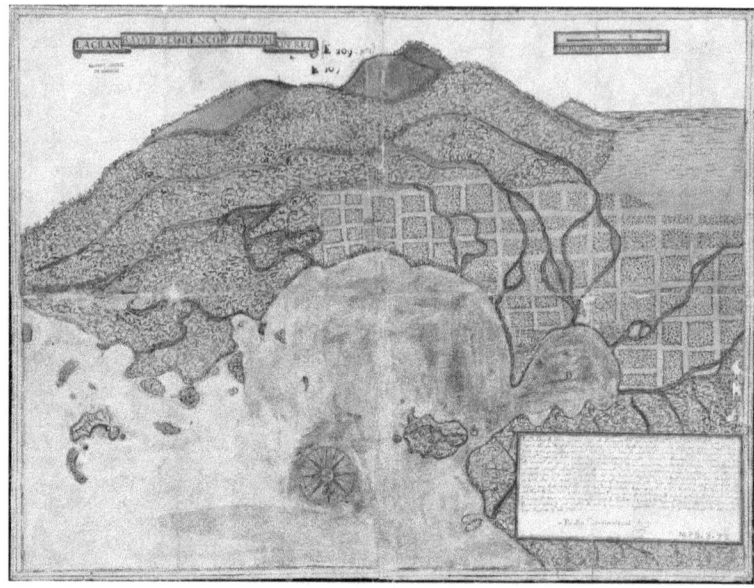

Figure 6.6 Diego de Prado y Tovar, *La gran baya d. S. Lorenço y puerto d. Monterei*, [1606]. Ink and gouache on paper. By permission of the Ministerio de Educación, Cultura y Deporte, Archivo General de Simancas, Spain (MPD, 08, 083).

– made kidnap a 'necessity' to obtain vital supplies of water and wood. He regularly abducted local people as interpreters, guides, informants and hostages but justified his action as promising 'greater good' than the 'sight and community of heathen parents and friends'.[40] Torres reported that he 'seized' twenty persons 'of different nations' in New Guinea in order to make a 'better account' to the king. His captives provided 'much news on other peoples', despite communication difficulties.[41] Such information left shadowy countersigns in Spanish representations. Thus, the young *indios* taken from Mailu informed their captors that the area was regularly raided by '*negros* who eat human flesh' and that the African who inspired the large group of warriors to flee at Puro was thought to be one of them.[42]

The third drawing (Figure 6.7) depicts 'burly' people seen at an island 'in the area south of New Guinea', now Torres Strait. There is no extant map but Prado recorded landings at islands identified as Zagai and Yam by the master mariner-historian Brett Hilder.[43] At the first, a 'very well-built' man who was 'guarding' a group of women left his bow and arrows on the ground, climbed a tall tree and refused to come down. When the soldiers fired at him with his own bow, he caught the arrows – a 'bizarre thing', said Prado. Finally, they shot him with an arquebus and he fell, 'lifeless'. Three of the 'youngest' women were taken aboard 'for the service' of the crew. One was pregnant. Observation of her parturition and conversation 'after she learned to speak' (Spanish!) gave Prado the ethnographic opportunity 'to tell how women give birth in this country'. The child later died in the Philippines. The 'gigantic men' seen at the second island were armed with massive clubs and bows too 'strong' for the Spaniards to bend. Here, the Spanish killed a very tall young man without compunction. They later justified the killing by assuming that human skulls and bones found in a village were relics of men who had been 'eaten'. Presumably resonant with the Mailu children's story about '*negros* who eat human flesh', this discovery prompted Prado to name Yam the 'island of very tall *caribes* [cannibals]'.[44] The toponym is doubly a countersign: of the intimidating physical presence of these people, their weapons and their presumed human trophies; and of the convoluted narrative agency of the Spaniards' young indigenous interlocutors.

Torres probably transited the shoal- and reef-strewn waters between New Guinea and modern Australia via the southern passage that James Cook called Endeavour Strait in 1770. However, the low land to the south, Cook's 'York Cape', seemed to Torres to be only 'very

Figure 6.7 [Diego de Prado y Tovar], *Esta xente delas yslas questan alaparte del sur de la Nueva Guinea*..., [1607]. Ink and gouache on paper. By permission of the Ministerio de Educación, Cultura y Deporte, Archivo General de Simancas, Spain (MPD, 18, 083).

large islands'.⁴⁵ The Spanish did not land again until they reached 'the land of those called *papuas* [Papuans]' (West Papua) in October 1606.⁴⁶ Having briefly stopped at Lakahia Island, where people lived in houses atop high trees, Torres anchored for nine days in Iris Strait, near Triton Bay. Both names commemorate nineteenth-century Dutch expeditionary vessels. The legend on Prado's map (Figure 6.8) describes a population numerically 'few' thanks to the 'rugged' terrain. By implication, they were less barbarous than people seen previously because they used large, full-body wooden shields, 'very well worked in half relief', and made 'small things in iron' such as 'fishhooks' and 'harpoons', using 'bellows of cane with clay nozzles'. Torres, too, remarked on the 'very large shields' seen all along this coast. One is depicted in the drawing of the inhabitants of 'the end of New Guinea' (Figure 6.9). Their weapons also included darts, spears, cane bows with bone-tipped arrows, and 'cane tubes' filled with quicklime that they blew into their enemies' eyes at close quarters to try to blind them. Prado noted a 'good village with plank houses' near the anchorage. There, a large party of *gente de guerra* (warriors) approached the ships in 'eight large canoes', bearing banners, arrows

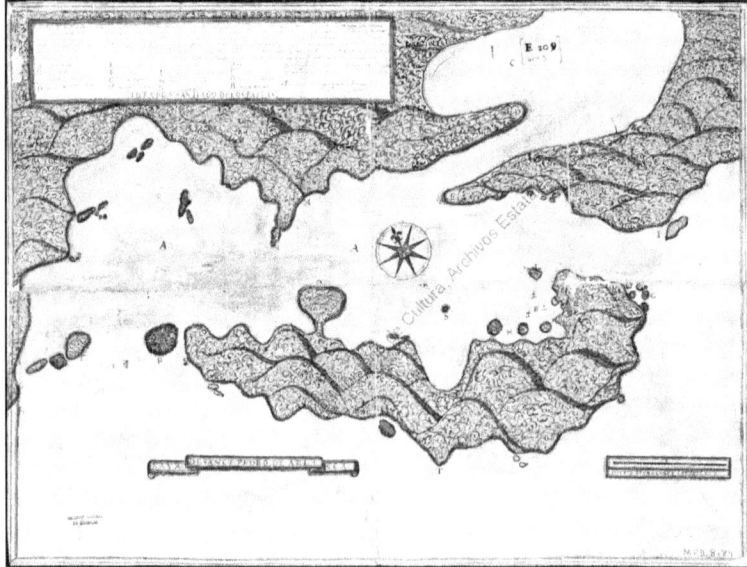

Figure 6.8 Diego de Prado y Tovar, *Baya de Sanct Pedro de Arlança, Tiera de S. Santiago de los Papuas*, [1606]. Ink and gouache on paper. By permission of the Ministerio de Educación, Cultura y Deporte, Archivo General de Simancas, Spain (MPD, 18, 084).

Figure 6.9 [Diego de Prado y Tovar], *Esta xente es del rremate dela nueva guinea ...*, [1607]. Ink and gouache on paper. By permission of the Ministerio de Educación, Cultura y Deporte, Archivo General de Simancas, Spain (MPD, 18, 084).

and spears. After a single arquebus volley, they leapt into the water and dragged their canoes out of range before retreating.[47]

From Iris Strait, the vessels proceeded along the southwest coast of New Guinea and its offshore islands. In several places 'at the end of this land', signs of the residents' use of iron and possession of 'a few small things' attributed to 'China' showed the relieved Spaniards that 'we were not lost, as we thought', but were near Maluku, 'where the Chinese trade'. In the Yef Fam group, a Portuguese-speaking man told them 'where we were' and directed them to Ternate, recently captured by Spanish forces from Manila. Prado 'gave much thanks to god' for 'such good news'. They had, he said, given themselves up 'for lost' because 'modern maps' represented New Guinea 'as the mainland of the crown of the antarctic pole' – the northern extremity of Terra Australis. This they had believed until local knowledge, doubtless confirming their own experience, proved conclusively otherwise.[48]

Thinking Ethnohistory

At this point, I illustrate the ethnohistorical potential of these travellers' representations by highlighting two key themes. The first speaks to a long-standing debate about violence and weaponry in early Pacific encounters, drawing on Dorothy Shineberg's seminal insistence that these interactions were far more complex than allowed by the complacent stereotype of the gun's 'invincible power'.[49] Before the late nineteenth century, European firearms conveyed ambiguous benefits over indigenous projectile weapons, especially the bow and arrow, while 'circumstances' and 'the specific situation' were pivotal. The Spaniards' arquebuses were inferior to bows and arrows in speed, reliability, range and accuracy but their superior discipline as 'trained soldiers', often marksmen, gave them 'an advantage' over both Islanders and later Europeans with improved firearms. Moreover, Spanish defensive use of shields – as occurred during the lethal clash in Mailu – could neutralize the impact of arrows, spears and slingstones. By the eighteenth century, shields had vanished from European arsenals.[50]

A key military variable was European 'purpose'. These encounters confirm Shineberg's contention that firearms were far more effective when 'destruction' was intended, rather than colonization or local trade. While Islanders struggled to defeat Spaniards 'in pitched battle', their continual harassment of the foreigners and refusal or inability to supply food prevented interior exploration or permanent settlement.[51] In Espiritu Santo, where Quirós hoped to found a colony, local people soon grasped the arquebus' lethal potential – but also its limitations, especially when fired 'humanely' in the air. The offensive weaknesses of indigenous weapons are apparent in Leza's account of an inland patrol by 'thirty men' on 17 May. After inflicting great 'damage' on the inhabitants during a sudden attack, the Spaniards captured three boys and some 'very good, fat pigs' – crucial to men's status and much prized. Presumably incensed by their losses, the warriors continually attacked the detachment with arrows and darts as it 'retired' to the ships but could neither hurt the soldiers nor make them abandon the captives.[52] Nonetheless, the failure of firepower to guarantee supplies or safeguard settlement triggered Quirós' conviction that, 'since the natives of this bay were at war, and we had no chance', the only viable option was to leave Big Bay and explore 'the lands to windward'.[53] However, in southeastern New Guinea, Zagai and Yam, Torres and his men were transient, free of Quirós' scruples and happy to pillage people whom they had no need to entice or placate. Accordingly, they shot quickly when faced by insult or threat during fleeting contacts with groups who were ignorant of firearms and terrified by their 'surprise factor': 'noise, flash and smoke'.[54] In Iris Strait, the canoe-borne warriors were evidently familiar with the weapons since they withdrew in reasonable order at the first shots.

The second important ethnohistorical theme illuminated by these early representations is the well-established cosmopolitan movement of people, goods and faith between Maluku, far western New Guinea and intervening islands. At Sabuda Island, near the mouth of Berau (McCluer) Gulf, the Spanish 'found' an 'iron harpoon', fishhooks and fishing lines supposedly 'from China', 'two onions like ours' and fragments of porcelain.[55] A century later, the English mariner William Dampier reported these Islanders' great enthusiasm for 'Knives and other Toys'. They went to nearby New Guinea in 'large Boats' for 'Slaves, fine Parrots, &c.', which they exchanged in Ceram (Seram, Maluku) for cotton cloth. They seemed not to be Mohammedans because they drank brandy 'out of the same Cup with us without any Scruple'.[56] At 'the end' of New Guinea, Torres saw '*moros* [Moors, Mohammedans]', 'clothed', with artillery, arquebuses and metal-bladed weapons. They raided 'the *papuas*' and preached 'the sect of Mahomet', Islam having reached Maluku by the late fifteenth century.[57] In the Yef Fam Islands, the Spanish met a resident *moro* who spoke good Italian and reported New Guinea's untapped riches. Captured as a boy during a Spanish expedition in North Africa, he had been a slave in Spain and the Philippines but escaped and eventually joined the retinue of the local 'governor'.[58]

These passing testimonies chime with an earlier account by Miguel Roxo de Brito, transcribed in the 'Boxer Codex' and summarized second-hand in Quirós' memorial of 1610. Roxo de Brito, a Portuguese trader in search of gold, travelled widely in 1581–82 between south Maluku, northwest New Guinea and nearby islands.[59] Sailing mostly with Malay crews, often in alliance with the 'king' of Waigeo (Raja Ampat Islands), he noted that New Guineans exchanged medicinal *Massoia* bark, slaves and gold for 'iron', 'swords' and 'gongs'. Such trading initiatives were by no means exclusively Malukan, since the 'black' inhabitants of a 'kingdom' on the south of Berau Gulf were 'all merchants' who bought slaves locally and sold them in Ceram Laut. Other New Guineans were said to raid Gebe (Maluku) for captives to exchange for gongs. They valued iron over gold for its far greater utility and they cultivated 'fields of rice'.[60]

Seeing Human Difference

I turn now to the specifically anthropological significance of these Spanish voyage materials. In content and emphasis, they consistently evince the importance travellers themselves attributed to what I call 'seaborne ethnography' – empirical description of people encountered, their behaviour, homelands, crops, material culture and milieus.[61] However, apart from Quirós' eighth memorial and brief published excerpts paraphrased from his narrative,[62] their contemporaneous ethnographic potential was stifled by long elision. Torres' letter-report to the king was unknown until published in English translation in 1806. The surviving maps, Quirós' narrative and Leza's journal were unpublished until 1876–80, the drawings until 1907, and Munilla's journal until 1963. Prado's narrative, published in 1930, was only discovered a decade earlier.

Brought to light during the nineteenth century, these materials have since provided empirical ballast for opposed agendas: on the one hand, for unthinking historicization of racial presumptions dominant in anthropology until after the Second World War; on the other hand, for historical critique of such imposition of present concepts and values onto the past. Sharpening European concepts of human difference were triggered from the fifteenth century by novel Iberian encounters with non-Europeans in Africa, the Americas, Asia and the 'fifth part of the world' – the East Indies, New Guinea and the elusive Austral lands. Voyagers reported wide diversity in the skin colour and appearance of populations seen during sixteenth- and seventeenth-century expeditions to the Mar del Sur. Contemporary Europeans were not insensitive to human physical variations but regarded them as momentary products of the effects of climate, lifestyle, station and bodily humours on individuals of a single human race. The modern idea that permanent, discrete, hypostasized races are materialized in indelible somatic markers was unknown before the 1770s. Dogmatic religiosity dovetailed with highly ethnocentric notions of relative civility or barbarity as primary criteria for evaluating unfamiliar people. Neither mapped neatly onto skin colour, though they converged in the growing identification of 'heathen', 'barbarous', 'black' African 'Negroes' with chattel slavery.[63] Spatialized racial categories for the fifth part of the world – Oceanic Negro, Melanesian, Polynesian, Micronesian and Aborigine – were unknown before the nineteenth century.[64] But retrospective application of these terms and of the modern concept of 'a race' is commonplace in subsequent scholarship.

Spanish terminology for the Islanders of Espiritu Santo varies significantly between authors, genres and even during the course of the visit, but descriptive recourse to skin colour is standard. The shipboard texts are more discriminating. Munilla's alteration of his wording from *yndios* to *negros* when confronted by indigenous violence has been mentioned. Quirós described them as 'neither quite black nor mulatto', with 'frizzled' hair and 'good eyes'. Leza saw 'many extremely beautiful women'. Conversely, in retrospect Torres collapsed them as 'all black naked people' while Prado qualified 'the *indios*' adjectivally as '*negros* and very ugly'.[65] The drawing (Figure 6.3) depicts men with very dark skin and its legend substantivizes them as '*negros* with coarse bodies'. The legend to the map (Figure 6.2) populates the bay with *gente negra* (black people). Prado's English translators, Clements Markham and George Barwick, anachronistically projected the reified modern idea of race onto earlier Spanish usage by rendering *gente negra* as 'a black race'. Similarly, Markham imposed the now conventional term 'natives' on both Leza's aggregate noun *gente* and Quirós' plural noun *indios*.[66]

In New Guinea, Torres and Prado encountered ancestors of people whom later racial typologies would negatively homogenize as primitive blacks: Papuans, Oceanic Negroes or Melanesians.[67] Without an a priori spatial and conceptual grid for already racialized populations, the early observers reported very varied skin colour and were coyly prudish about nudity as a key sign of relative barbarity. Denying the materiality of discrete races, I see subtle chromatic uncertainty in the drawings normally attributed to Prado. However, in the 1970s, when the ontological reality of races was still widely assumed, Hilder implied that the drawings could not have been Prado's work because they failed to register 'the racial variations which would have been noticeable'.[68] The degree of barbarity attributed to particular people depended at least as much on their perceived mode of life, demeanour and dress or its absence as on their skin colour. According to Roxo de Brito, the 'traders' who supplied *esclavos negros* (black slaves) to the *yndios* of Ceram Laut were *negros* from the shores of Berau Gulf. A host of 'uncouth', 'naked' *negros* attacked the Waigeo fleet 'in crescent formation with thirty-five vessels on each cusp and all the rest disposed not like barbarians but like skilled and rational people'. They fled in disarray only when terrified by Roxo de Brito's unfamiliar firearms.[69]

The legend on Prado's map of Sukuri Bay (Figure 6.4) calls the inhabitants *gente blanca* (white people). Again, Markham and Barwick, echoed by Hilder, anachronized *gente* as 'a race'.[70] The drawing (Figure 6.5) makes its subjects noticeably lighter in hue than those of the other sketches but its legend describes 'slightly white *yndios*'. Torres said that New Guineans generally were 'not very white *yndios*'. The contemporary paradox of clothed nudity is patent in Prado's map legend: the people at Sukuri Bay were 'naked and cover their shame [genitals] with mats of coconut palm leaves'. Torres generalized New

Guinean dress similarly: they were 'naked, though with their shame well covered by bark resembling highly painted cloth'.[71]

At Orangerie Bay, Prado described an amicable meeting with 'exceptionally tall', 'white' *gente*. The connotations of whiteness are again ambiguous as the map legend (Figure 6.6) represents the *naturales* of this area as having 'the colour of mulattos'. By implication, they were less barbarous than people seen previously, since the men wore mats and the women 'petticoats to the knees'.[72] The uncertainty in early modern European perceptions of skin colour across the spectrum is striking with respect to the 'very burly', 'naked' *jente negra* (black people) described by Torres at Zagai and Yam. Prado initially assumed they were 'the *negros* that we were told the *indios* were fleeing from when they saw our [African] *negro*'. When 'the experience' of examining the slain man's corpse showed 'they are not *negros*', Prado further deduced that 'they blacken themselves to appear more fierce'. Not all *negros* (blacks), then, were Negroes (Africans or African-like).[73] Yet three centuries later, the French ethnologist Ernest-Théodore Hamy had not 'the least doubt', on a priori racial grounds, that Torres' *jente negra* inhabited Muralag Island, adjacent to Cape York and well south of Yam. Rigid ideas about skin colour alone drove Hamy's reasoning: the 'judicious' Scottish naturalist John MacGillivray had classified the population of Muralag as 'a Papuanized colony of Australians', at the 'junction' of the 'nearly black' 'Australian race' and the 'yellowish brown' 'Papuan or frizzled-haired race'. By contemporary racial logic, the '*black* tint' written and drawn by the Spanish in 1606 both confirmed Hamy's geographical identification and signified that the *papouanïsation* process 'was not well advanced'.[74]

Far to the northwest at Triton Bay, the legend to Prado's map (Figure 6.8) notes a small population of *gente negra* who included some 'brown, well-built, robust' people. Torres described the inhabitants of the 'many places' where the Spanish landed along New Guinea's southeast coast as 'black people different from all the rest' and 'much more adorned'. Prado variously reported seeing *indios bien negros* (very black *indios*) and 'black people with long hair and beards'. Yet the legend on the drawing (Figure 6.9) describes the inhabitants of 'the end of New Guinea' as *bermexa* (*bermeja*, reddish) and they are sketched with lighter skin colouring than the people at Big Bay and Yam (Figures 6.3 and 6.7).[75] This empirical kaleidoscope was anticipated by Roxo de Brito. Around Berau Gulf, he successively saw or heard about '*negros* like those of Guinea [west Africa]'; 'some black people and among them mulatto'; 'white people with red hair and freckles [Albinos]'; and 'uncouth *negros* like those of Guinea but blacker'.[76] In striking contrast, when anchored at Triton Bay in April 1839, the French navigator-naturalist Jules Dumont d'Urville was in no doubt as to the materiality of races. He reported that the tiny population was *noir* (black) in colour and 'small' in stature, with bodily forms close to 'the Australian type', but 'frizzy hair'. Some, of 'a quite light colour approaching that of the Malays', were evidently 'of mixed blood'.[77]

Conclusion

Anthropologically, the varied inscription of these expeditionary encounters shows both the instability of the term *negro* in early modern European lexicons and its growing negative associations. The most common words for indigenous people are the all-inclusive aggregate noun *gente* and the general but more specific plural *indios* – often adjectivally *negros*, as in Prado's phrase *indios bien negros*. Munilla in Espiritu Santo and Prado in Zagai and Yam used *indios* in its restricted sense, opposed to the noun *negros*. But substantive usage of *negro* was reserved for particular people whose actions or demeanour provoked or intimidated the visitors. It is as much a countersign of disapproved indigenous behaviour as a sign of conspicuous skin colour.

The great human diversity reported in Spanish representations suggests chaotic variety, crosscutting and subverting modern regional anthropological stereotypes. But recurrent emphasis on skin colour and hair texture can be interpreted racially by a later eye sensitized to such categories. To examples already cited in this chapter, I add the confident statement of Roberto Ferrando Pérez, Quirós' latest editor, that the 'people' described in Espiritu Santo 'belong to the Melanesian family, fruit of the mixture of the Papuan Negroes and the Polynesians and Malays', though 'here the Negro and the Papuan predominate'.[78] Anachronistic readings unwittingly transpose present discourses, terminologies and categories to the past. Yet these travellers neither suggested nor anticipated a racial cartography or typology – they made no categorical correlation of skin colour and other supposedly innate characters with geography or group differentiation, as was the norm from the nineteenth century. Assumed identity of their representations with later scientific racial categories is proleptic and unsustainable.

I conclude with a methodological reflection. The legends on maps and drawings are not simply abbreviated prose genres, analogous to journals, reports and narratives. Rather, they are a hybrid medium, decontextualized, lacking formal structure and reliant for meaning on intimate association with their visual vehicles of expression. The art historian Bernard Smith pointed out: 'taken in combination with the extant written records, the contemporary visual documentation of events provides us with the best evidence we possess not only of *what* happened but *how* it happened'.[79] He cautioned: 'the linguistic and the visual coding of information possess a different syntax and differing conventions'. This different visual syntax or structure is primarily spatial rather than temporal. The syntax of hybrid mediums, sharing both qualities, underwrites their historical significance, elaborating and interpreting graphic genres, mediating between them and conventional written texts. The sum of their ethnohistorical value markedly outstrips that of any individual item, medium or genre.

Bronwen Douglas is Honorary Professor in the College of Arts & Social Sciences at the Australian National University. She is a Pacific historian and historian of science who works on the interplay of race, geography and encounters in representations of Indigenous people and places in Oceania. She is the author of *Across the Great Divide: Journeys in History and Anthropology* (Harwood Academic Publishers, 1998) and *Science, Voyages, and Encounters in Oceania 1511–1850* (Palgrave Macmillan, 2014) and is currently editor of the *Journal of Pacific History*.

Notes

1. The linkage of modernity with the 'expansion of Europe' remains common currency. One of its earliest usages is Wilbur Cortez Abbott, *The Expansion of Europe: A History of the Foundations of the Modern World*, 2 Vols (New York: Henry Holt, 1918).
2. See Bronwen Douglas, *Science, Voyages, and Encounters in Oceania 1511–1850* (Basingstoke: Palgrave Macmillan, 2014), 18–26.
3. Real Academia Española [henceforth RAE], *Nuevo Tesoro Lexicográfico de la Lengua Española* (2015), http://buscon.rae.es/ntlle/SrvltGUILoginNtlle (accessed 1 July 2015). All translations are my own.
4. RAE, *Diccionario de la lengua castellana* ... 6 Vols (Madrid: Francisco del Hierro, 1732), Vol. 3, 686; 3rd edition (Madrid: Joaquín Ibarra, 1791), 415.
5. RAE, *Diccionario*, Vol. 4 (1734), 320–21.

6. Antonio Pigafetta, *Magellan's Voyage around the World*..., translated and edited by James Alexander Robertson, 3 Vols (Cleveland, OH: Arthur H. Clark, 1906), Vol. 1, 68.
7. Pedro Fernandéz de Quirós, *Memoriales de las Indias Australes*, edited by Oscar Pinochet (Madrid: Historia 16, 1990), 35–41.
8. Bronwen Douglas, 'Terra Australis to Oceania: Racial Geography in the "Fifth Part of the World"', *Journal of Pacific History* 45(2) (2010), 179–94.
9. Pedro Fernández de Quirós, *Descubrimiento de las regiones austriales*, edited by Roberto Ferrando Pérez (Madrid: Dastin, 2000), 198, 248–80; Diego de Prado y Tovar, 'Relación sumaria ...', in George F. Barwick (trans.), Henry N. Stevens (ed.), *New Light on the Discovery of Australia: As Revealed by the Journal of Captain Don Diego de Prado y Tovar* (London: Hakluyt Society, 1930), 100, 124–26.
10. Quirós, *Descubrimiento*, 281–85.
11. Prado, 'Relación sumaria', 132.
12. Antonio de Herrera y Tordesillas, *Descripción de las Indias Ocidentales* (Madrid: Emplenta. Real, 1601), 1–2, 72–79, plates 1, 14; [Juan López de Velasco], 'Demarcacíon y division de las Indias', in Anon. (ed.), *Colleccion de documentos inéditos, relativos al descubrimiento, conquista y organizacion de las antiguas posesiones Españolas de América y Oceanía* ... (Madrid: Imprenta de José María Perez, 1871), Vol. 15, 409–10, 528–32. See also John M. Headley, 'Spain's Asian Presence, 1565–1590: Structures and Aspirations', *Hispanic American Historical Review* 75(4) (1995), 628–33.
13. Rainer F. Buschmann, *Iberian Visions of the Pacific Ocean, 1507–1899* (Basingstoke: Palgrave Macmillan, 2014).
14. Carlos Sanz, *Australia su descubrimiento y denominación: con la reproducción facsimil del memorial número 8 de Quirós en español original, y en las diversas traducciones contemporáneas* (Madrid: Ministerio de Asuntos Exteriores, 1973), 37–44.
15. Bronwen Douglas, 'Naming Places: Voyagers, Toponyms, and Local Presence in the Fifth Part of the World, 1500–1700', *Journal of Historical Geography* 45 (2014), 16–17; Douglas, *Science*, 39–41, 89–90.
16. Consejo de Estado, [Consulta], 25 September 1608, in Barwick and Stevens, *New Light*, 210–12; Quirós, *Memoriales*, 133–441.
17. Marjorie G. Driver, 'An Account of the Islands of the Ladrones', *Journal of Pacific History* 26(1) (1991), 103–6.
18. Anon., [Sino-Spanish (Boxer) Codex], [c. 1590], LMC 2444, Lilly Library, Indiana University, Bloomington, http://purl.dlib.indiana.edu/iudl/general/VAB8326 (accessed 1 July 2015), 1r–4v. See also C.R. Boxer, 'A Late Sixteenth Century Manila MS', *Journal of the Royal Asiatic Society of Great Britain and Ireland* (1/2) (April 1950), 37–38, 45–48.
19. Pigafetta, *Magellan's Voyage*, Vol. 1, 90–94.
20. Douglas, *Science*, 39–68.

21. See Brett Hilder, *The Voyage of Torres: The Discovery of the Southern Coastline of New Guinea and Torres Strait by Captain Luis Baéz de Torres in 1606* (St Lucia: University of Queensland Press, 1980).
22. Prado, 'Relación sumaria', 112–14, 194–96.
23. Ernest-Théodore Hamy, 'Luis Vaës de Torres et Diego de Prado y Tovar, explorateurs de la Nouvelle-Guinée 1606–1607: étude géographique et ethnographique', *Bulletin de géographie historique et descriptive* 1 (1907), 50; and Roberto Ferrando Pérez, 'Zeichnungen von Südsee-Eingeborenen aus dem frühen 17. Jahrhundert', *Zeitschrift für Ethnologie* 79(1) (1954), 75; cf. Hilder, *Voyage of Torres*, 162–63.
24. Quirós, *Descubrimiento*, 248–80; Gaspar Gonçalez de Leza, 'Relaçion verdadera del viaje y suçesso que hizo el capitan Pedro Fernandez de Quirós, por órden de S.M., á la tierra Austral é incógnita ... Año 1605', in Justo Zaragoza (ed.), *Historia del descubrimiento de las regiones Austriales hecho por el general Pedro Fernandez de Quirós* (Madrid: Manuel G. Hernandez, 1880), Vol. 2, 142–73; Martin de Munilla, 'Relaçion del descubrim[ien]to de la parte Austral y incognita del Sur y de n[uest]ros frayles', in Celsus Kelly (ed.), *Austrialia franciscana* (Madrid: Franciscan Historical Studies and Archivo Ibero-Americano, 1963), Vol. 1, 61–83.
25. Quirós, *Memoriales*, 290–92; Luis Váez de Torres, [Carta á Don Felipe III], Manila, 12 July 1607, in Justo Zaragoza, 'Descubrimientos de los Españoles en el Mar del Sur y en las costas de la Nueva-Guinea', *Boletín de la Sociedad Geográfica de Madrid* 4(1) (1878), 20–27. See also Hilder, *Voyage of Torres*, 165–70.
26. Prado, 'Relación sumaria', 132–92. See also Hilder, *Voyage of Torres*, 170–71.
27. Leza, 'Relaçion', 136–37, 141–44; Quirós, *Descubrimiento*, 269.
28. Leza, 'Relaçion', 148–49; Munilla, 'Relaçion', 65–66; Quirós, *Descubrimiento*, 75, 250–51, 262–64, 268, 278.
29. Munilla, 'Relaçion', 61–82.
30. Leza, 'Relaçion', 161–62.
31. Torres, [Carta á Don Felipe III], 19.
32. Prado, 'Relación sumaria', 132–34; Torres, [Carta á Don Felipe III], 20.
33. Douglas, 'Naming Places', 14–16.
34. Louis-Antoine de Bougainville, *Voyage autour du monde ... en 1766, 1767, 1768 & 1769* (Paris: Saillant & Nyon, 1771), 255; Hilder, *Voyage of Torres*, 22–24.
35. Prado, 'Relación sumaria', 134–42, 154; Torres, [Carta á Don Felipe III], 21–22.
36. Prado, 'Relación sumaria', 148.
37. Ibid., 144–50.
38. Ibid., 150–54.
39. Rowland Croucher et al., 'Papua New Guinea Seeks to Heal the Past', *International News 21st August 2006*, John Mark Ministries

(2000–15), http://jmm.aaa.net.au/articles/17945.htm (accessed 17 June 2015).
40. Pedro Fernández de Quirós and Jeronimo de Valera, 'Memorial de Quirós al Arzobispo de Lima: con el parecer de Fray Jeronimo de Valera, O.F.M., sobre las dudas propuestas por Quirós', Lima, 8 November, 14 December 1605, in Kelly, *Austrialia franciscana*, Vol. 1, 12–16; Quirós, *Descubrimiento*, 223–29, 241–43, 276–78.
41. Torres, [Carta á Don Felipe III], 21.
42. Prado, 'Relación sumaria', 150.
43. Hilder, *Voyage of Torres*, 72, 76.
44. Prado, 'Relación sumaria', 158–60, 168–70.
45. James Cook, *The Journals of Captain James Cook on His Voyages of Discovery*, edited by J.C. Beaglehole, 4 Vols (Cambridge: Hakluyt Society, 1955–74), Vol. 1, 385, 391; Hilder, *Voyage of Torres*, 82–97; Torres, [Carta á Don Felipe III], 21.
46. Prado, 'Relación sumaria', 170. The Portuguese adopted the term *Papua* from Malukans to designate the *Ilhas das Papuas* ('Papuan Islands'), east of Maluku, their inhabitants *os Papuas* ('the Papuans'), and ultimately New Guinea and its people. See J.H.F. Sollewijn Gelpke, 'On the Origin of the Name Papua', *Bijdragen tot de Taal-, Land- en Volkenkunde* 149(2) (1993), 318–32.
47. Prado, 'Relación sumaria', 168–72; Torres, [Carta á Don Felipe III], 21.
48. Prado, 'Relación sumaria', 170–78; Torres, [Carta á Don Felipe III], 21–22; Figure 6.9, legend.
49. Dorothy Shineberg, 'Guns and Men in Melanesia', *Journal of Pacific History* 6 (1971), 61–82; Shineberg, *They Came for Sandalwood: A Study of the Sandalwood Trade in the South-West Pacific 1830–1865* (Carlton, Vic.: Melbourne University Press, 1967), 169–75.
50. Shineberg, 'Guns and Men', 62, 65–69, 77.
51. Ibid., 62, 73–74.
52. Leza, 'Relaçion', 161–62.
53. Quirós, *Descubrimiento*, 168, 178.
54. Shineberg, 'Guns and Men', 68.
55. Prado, 'Relación sumaria', 170–72; Torres, [Carta á Don Felipe III], 21–22; Figure 6.9, legend.
56. William Dampier, *A Continuation of a Voyage to New-Holland, &c. in the Year 1699* (London: James Knapton, 1709), 97, 101.
57. Torres, [Carta á Don Felipe III], 22. Magellan's chronicler Antonio Pigafetta learned in 1521 that 'these *mori* [Moors] have lived in Malucho [Maluku] for about fifty years' (Pigafetta, *Magellan's Voyage*, Vol. 2, 112).
58. Prado, 'Relación sumaria', 176–78.
59. Miguel Roxo de Brito, 'Relación que Migel Rojo de Brito da de la Nueva Guinea', in Anon., [Sino-Spanish (Boxer) Codex], fol. 139r–149v; Quirós, *Memoriales*, 289–90. See also C.R. Boxer and P.-Y. Manguin,

'Miguel Roxo de Brito's Narrative of His Voyage to the Raja Empat, May 1581–November 1582', *Archipel* 18 (1979), 177–94; J.H.F. Sollewijn Gelpke, 'The Report of Miguel Roxo de Brito of His Voyage in 1581–1582 to the Raja Ampat, the MacCluer Gulf and Seram', *Bijdragen tot de Taal-, Land- en Volkenkunde* 150(1) (1994), 123–45.
60. Roxo de Brito, 'Relación', 140r, 141v, 142v, 143r, 144v; Gelpke, 'The Report', 137n54.
61. Bronwen Douglas, 'Seaborne Ethnography and the Natural History of Man', *Journal of Pacific History* 38(1) (2003), 3–27.
62. Sanz, *Australia*; Juan de Torquemada, *Los veynte y un libros rituales y monarchia Yndiana con el origen y guerras de los Yndios Occidentales: de sus poblaçones descubrimiento conquista conversion y otras cosas maravillosas de la mesma tierra* ..., 3 Vols (Seville: Matthias Clauiso, 1615), Vol. 1, 809–29.
63. Douglas, *Science*, 39–73.
64. Bronwen Douglas, 'Geography, Raciology, and the Naming of Oceania, 1750–1900', *Globe* 69 (2011), 1–28.
65. Leza, 'Relaçion', 161; Munilla, 'Relaçion', 61; Quirós, *Descubrimiento*, 270; Prado, 'Relación sumaria', 120; Torres, [Carta á Don Felipe III], 19.
66. George Barwick (trans.), 'The Legends on the Four Prado Maps, Translated from the Copies in the British Museum', in Barwick and Stevens, *New Light*, 243; and Clements Markham (trans. and ed.), *The Voyages of Pedro Fernandez de Quiros, 1595 to 1606*, 2 Vols (London: Hakluyt Society, 1904), Vol. 1, 240–78; Vol. 2, 370–77, 470–71.
67. Bronwen Douglas, '"*Novus orbis Australis*": Oceania in the Science of Race, 1750–1850', and Chris Ballard, '"Oceanic Negroes": British Anthropology of Papuans, 1820–1869', in Bronwen Douglas and Chris Ballard (eds), *Foreign Bodies: Oceania and the Science of Race 1750–1940* (Canberra: ANU E Press, 2008), 99–201.
68. Hilder, *Voyage of Torres*, 163.
69. Roxo de Brito, 'Relación', 139r, 142v, 143v, 144r, 144v.
70. Barwick, 'Legends', 243; Hilder, *Voyage of Torres*, 36; Markham, *Voyages*, Vol. 2, 470–71.
71. Torres, [Carta á Don Felipe III], 20.
72. Prado, 'Relación sumaria', 144.
73. Ibid., 160; Torres, [Carta á Don Felipe III], 21.
74. Hamy, 'Luis Vaës de Torres et Diego de Prado y Tovar', 64–65, original emphasis; John MacGillivray, *Narrative of the Voyage of H.M.S. Rattlesnake ... during the Years 1846–1850, Including Discoveries and Surveys in New Guinea, the Louisiade Archipelago, etc.....*, 2 Vols (London: T. & W. Boone, 1852), Vol. 1, 125; Vol. 2, 3.
75. Prado, 'Relación sumaria', 170–72; Torres, [Carta á Don Felipe III], 21–22.
76. Roxo de Brito, 'Relación', 142v–144v.

77. Jules Dumont d'Urville, *Voyage au pôle sud et dans l'Océanie sur les corvettes l'Astrolabe et la Zélée ... pendant les années 1837-1838-1839-1840 ... Histoire du voyage*, 10 Vols (Paris: Gide, 1841–1846), Vol. 6, 111–12.
78. Quirós, *Descubrimiento*, 270n210.
79. Bernard Smith, *Imagining the Pacific: In the Wake of the Cook Voyages* (Carlton, Vic.: Miegunyah Press, 1992), 33, my emphasis.

Bibliography

Abbott, Wilbur Cortez. *The Expansion of Europe: A History of the Foundations of the Modern World*. 2 Vols. New York: Henry Holt, 1918.

Anon. [Sino-Spanish (Boxer) Codex], [c. 1590], LMC 2444, Lilly Library, Indiana University, Bloomington. http://purl.dlib.indiana.edu/iudl/general/VAB8326.

Barwick, George (trans.). 'The Legends on the Four Prado Maps, Translated from the Copies in the British Museum', in George F. Barwick (trans.), Henry N. Stevens (ed.), *New Light on the Discovery of Australia: As Revealed by the Journal of Captain Don Diego de Prado y Tovar* (London: Hakluyt Society, 1930), 242–45.

Bougainville, Louis-Antoine de. *Voyage autour du monde ... en 1766, 1767, 1768 & 1769*. Paris: Saillant & Nyon, 1771.

Boxer, C.R. 'A Late Sixteenth Century Manila MS'. *Journal of the Royal Asiatic Society of Great Britain and Ireland* (1/2) (April 1950), 37–49.

Boxer, C.R., and P.-Y. Manguin. 'Miguel Roxo de Brito's Narrative of His Voyage to the Raja Empat, May 1581–November 1582'. *Archipel* 18 (1979), 177–94.

Buschmann, Rainer F. *Iberian Visions of the Pacific Ocean, 1507–1899*. Basingstoke: Palgrave Macmillan, 2014.

Consejo de Estado. [Consulta], 25 September 1608, in George F. Barwick (trans.), Henry N. Stevens (ed.), *New Light on the Discovery of Australia: As Revealed by the Journal of Captain Don Diego de Prado y Tovar* (London: Hakluyt Society, 1930), 210–12.

Cook, James. *The Journals of Captain James Cook on His Voyages of Discovery*. Edited by J.C. Beaglehole. 4 Vols. Cambridge: Hakluyt Society, 1955–74.

Croucher, Rowland, et al. 'Papua New Guinea Seeks to Heal the Past'. *International News 21st August 2006*, John Mark Ministries (2000–15). http://jmm.aaa.net.au/articles/17945.htm.

Dampier, William. *A Continuation of a Voyage to New-Holland, &c. in the Year 1699*. London: James Knapton, 1709.

Douglas, Bronwen. 'Geography, Raciology, and the Naming of Oceania, 1750–1900'. *Globe* 69 (2011), 1–28.

———. 'Naming Places: Voyagers, Toponyms, and Local Presence in the Fifth Part of the World, 1500–1700'. *Journal of Historical Geography* 45 (2014), 12–24.

———. *Science, Voyages, and Encounters in Oceania 1511–1850*. Basingstoke: Palgrave Macmillan, 2014.
———. 'Seaborne Ethnography and the Natural History of Man'. *Journal of Pacific History* 38(1) (2003), 3–27.
———. 'Terra Australis to Oceania: Racial Geography in the "Fifth Part of the World"'. *Journal of Pacific History* 45(2) (2010), 179–210.
Douglas, Bronwen, and Chris Ballard (eds). *Foreign Bodies: Oceania and the Science of Race 1750–1940*. Canberra: ANU E Press, 2008.
Driver, Marjorie G. 'An Account of the Islands of the Ladrones'. *Journal of Pacific History* 26(1) (1991), 103–6.
Dumont d'Urville, Jules. *Voyage au pôle sud et dans l'Océanie sur les corvettes l'Astrolabe et la Zélée ... pendant les années 1837-1838-1839-1840 ... Histoire du voyage*. 10 Vols. Paris: Gide, 1841–1846.
Ferrando Pérez, Roberto. 'Zeichnungen von Südsee-Eingeborenen aus dem frühen 17. Jahrhundert'. *Zeitschrift für Ethnologie* 79(1) (1954), 75–81.
Gelpke, J.H.F. Sollewijn. 'On the Origin of the Name Papua'. *Bijdragen tot de Taal-, Land- en Volkenkunde* 149(2) (1993), 318–32.
———. 'The Report of Miguel Roxo de Brito of His Voyage in 1581–1582 to the Raja Ampat, the MacCluer Gulf and Seram'. *Bijdragen tot de Taal-, Land- en Volkenkunde* 150(1) (1994), 123–45.
Hamy, Ernest-Théodore. 'Luis Vaës de Torres et Diego de Prado y Tovar, explorateurs de la Nouvelle-Guinée 1606–1607: étude géographique et ethnographique'. *Bulletin de géographie historique et descriptive* 1 (1907), 47–72.
Headley, John M. 'Spain's Asian Presence, 1565–1590: Structures and Aspirations'. *Hispanic American Historical Review* 75(4) (1995), 623–46.
Herrera y Tordesillas, Antonio de. *Descripcion de las Indias Ocidentales*. Madrid: Emplenta. Real, 1601.
Hilder, Brett. *The Voyage of Torres: The Discovery of the Southern Coastline of New Guinea and Torres Strait by Captain Luis Baéz de Torres in 1606*. St Lucia: University of Queensland Press, 1980.
Leza, Gaspar Gonçalez de. 'Relaçion verdadera del viaje y suçesso que hizo el capitan Pedro Fernandez de Quirós, por órden de S.M., á la tierra Austral é incógnita ... Año 1605', in Justo Zaragoza (ed.), *Historia del descubrimiento de las regiones Australes hecho por el general Pedro Fernandez de Quirós* (Madrid: Manuel G. Hernandez, 1880), Vol. 2, 77–185.
[López de Velasco, Juan]. 'Demarcacíon y division de las Indias', in Anon. (ed.), *Colleccion de documentos inéditos, relativos al descubrimiento, conquista y organizacion de las antiguas posesiones Españolas de América y Oceanía ...* (Madrid: Imprenta de José María Perez, 1871), Vol. 15, 409–539.
MacGillivray, John. *Narrative of the Voyage of H.M.S. Rattlesnake ... during the Years 1846–1850, Including Discoveries and Surveys in New Guinea, the Louisiade Archipelago, etc. ...* 2 Vols. London: T. & W. Boone, 1852.

Markham, Clements (trans. and ed.). *The Voyages of Pedro Fernandez de Quiros, 1595 to 1606*. 2 Vols. London: Hakluyt Society, 1904.
Munilla, Martin de. 'Relaçion del descubrim[ien]to de la parte Austral y incognita del Sur y de n[uest]ros frayles', in Celsus Kelly (ed.), *Austrialia franciscana* (Madrid: Franciscan Historical Studies and Archivo Ibero-Americano, 1963), Vol. 1, 21–94.
Pigafetta, Antonio. *Magellan's Voyage around the World....* Translated and edited by James Alexander Robertson. 3 Vols. Cleveland, OH: Arthur H. Clark, 1906.
Prado y Tovar, Diego de. 'Relación sumaria ...', in George F. Barwick (trans.), Henry N. Stevens (ed.), *New Light on the Discovery of Australia: As Revealed by the Journal of Captain Don Diego de Prado y Tovar* (London: Hakluyt Society, 1930), 83–205.
Quirós, Pedro Fernández de. *Descubrimiento de las regiones austriales*. Edited by Roberto Ferrando Pérez. Madrid: Dastin, 2000.
———. *Memoriales de las Indias Australes*. Edited by Oscar Pinochet. Madrid: Historia 16, 1990.
Quirós, Pedro Fernández de, and Jeronimo de Valera. 'Memorial de Quirós al Arzobispo de Lima: con el parecer de Fray Jeronimo de Valera, O.F.M., sobre las dudas propuestas por Quirós', Lima, 8 November, 14 December 1605, in Celsus Kelly (ed.), *Austrialia franciscana*. Madrid: Franciscan Historical Studies and Archivo Ibero-Americano, 1963, Vol. 1, 12–16.
Real Academia Española. *Diccionario de la lengua castellana ...* 6 Vols. Madrid: Francisco del Hierro, 1726–39.
———. *Diccionario de la lengua castellana ...* 3rd edition. Madrid: Joaquin Ibarra, 1791.
———. *Nuevo Tesoro Lexicográfico de la Lengua Española*. 2015. http://buscon.rae.es/ntlle/SrvltGUILoginNtlle.
Roxo de Brito, Miguel. 'Relación que Migel Rojo de Brito da de la Nueva Guinea', in Anon., [Sino-Spanish (Boxer) Codex], [c. 1590], LMC 2444, Indiana University Library, Bloomington, fol. 139r–149v. http://purl.dlib.indiana.edu/iudl/general/VAB8326.
Sanz, Carlos. *Australia su descubrimiento y denominación: con la reproducción facsimil del memorial número 8 de Quirós en español original, y en las diversas traducciones contemporáneas*. Madrid: Ministerio de Asuntos Exteriores, 1973.
Shineberg, Dorothy. 'Guns and Men in Melanesia'. *Journal of Pacific History* 6 (1971), 61–82.
———. *They Came for Sandalwood: A Study of the Sandalwood Trade in the South-West Pacific 1830–1865*. Carlton, Vic.: Melbourne University Press, 1967.
Smith, Bernard. *Imagining the Pacific: In the Wake of the Cook Voyages*. Carlton, Vic.: Miegunyah Press, 1992.
Torquemada, Juan de. *Los veynte y un libros rituales y monarchia Yndiana con el origen y guerras de los Yndios Occidentales: de sus poblaçones descubrimiento*

conquista conversion y otras cosas maravillosas de la mesma tierra ... 3 Vols. Seville: Matthias Clauiso, 1615.

Torres, Luis Váez de. [Carta á Don Felipe III], Manila, 12 July 1607, in Justo Zaragoza, 'Descubrimientos de los Españoles en el Mar del Sur y en las costas de la Nueva-Guinea', *Boletín de la Sociedad Geográfica de Madrid* 4(1) (1878), 12–27.

Chapter 7

ETHNOGRAPHIC INQUIRY ON PHILLIP PARKER KING'S HYDROGRAPHIC SURVEY

Tiffany Shellam[1]

In its Oceania collection the British Museum has an Aboriginal spearhead made of grey stone, very neatly chipped to a serrated edge and covered with red ochre. This spearhead was made by a Worora man from Hanover Bay on the northwest coast of Australia and, as museum provenance tells us, is connected to Phillip Parker King's hydrographic survey of the Australian coasts – four voyages undertaken between December 1817 and April 1822 – jointly funded and directed by the Admiralty and the Colonial Office. In her history of Captain Cook's meeting with the Gweagal at Botany Bay in 1770, Maria Nugent describes a bark shield obtained during the meeting that is now displayed in the Enlightenment Gallery in the British Museum. She writes that the 'dents and scratches preserved on its surface are clues to its biography, in the same way that scars on skin recall scraps and skirmishes'. The shield, she observes, is 'unique among [other objects in the gallery] for having a *known* story attached to it. And so it's an object with a place in a particular history'.[1]

This chapter focuses on the encounter that took place at Hanover Bay in early August 1821 between the crew of King's expedition and some Worora people. The textual representations of this encounter by King and his crew, the subsequent history of the Aboriginal material culture that was seized during it and the circulation of both texts and material culture through ethnographic and antiquarian networks in England are important reminders that ethnographic collection and study were key goals of Royal Navy expeditions in the early nineteenth century. While encounters with Aboriginal people were frequently considered *secondary* to the principal goal of charting the coastline, I argue here that, in the event of voyaging, encounters became pragmatically central aspects of King's expedition. The expedition's encounters and dealings with Aboriginal people and the involvement of the Aboriginal intermediaries on board indicate motivations for collecting Aboriginal material that combined individual curiosity with the Admiralty and Colonial Office's broader directives and, in the event of Hanover Bay, pillaging fuelled by a desire to punish the Worora for 'treacherous' conduct.

Centrality of Human Encounters

John Croker, Secretary to the Admiralty, who was directing the expedition from England, stated in his instructions to Phillip Parker King that the 'principle object' of King's expedition was 'to examine the hitherto unexplored coast of New South Wales from Arnheem [sic] Bay ... Westward & Southward as far as the North West Cape including the ... deep Bay called Van Diemens Bay and the cluster of Islands called Rosemary Islands'. The chief motive was to ascertain whether there was 'any river' that might 'lead to an interior navigation of the continent'.[2] King had a second boss, the Secretary of State for the Colonies, Earl Bathurst, who also issued him instructions. He was to actively seek out Aboriginal people to discover what minerals or materials they valued for trade, to describe and note the 'characteristic difference of the several tribes ... on the Coast ... The state of their arts or Manufactures and their comparative perfection in different tribes ... [and to collect] a vocabulary of the language spoken by every tribe with which' he might meet.[3] The Colonial Office and Admiralty directives highlight the role of these agents in the production of scientific, geographic and ethnographic knowledge in this period. They attempted to coordinate the collection of knowledge of the New World in centralized, uniform ways. As Felix Driver has argued, this could be understood as an assertion of imperial and scientific ways of seeing, observing and collecting.[4] For King's team, how and what they saw was brokered through a combination of naval discipline and Enlightenment ideas about science, human difference and knowledge collection.[5] However, exploration was a 'collective effort', and King's team included a variety of people from across social divisions, including Port Jackson Aboriginal mediators. Expeditions involved cultures coming together, sometimes for a sustained time, at others only briefly, in various kinds of relationships and interactions, which affected the ways in which the crew observed and collected information and material.[6]

The centrality of human encounters to this expedition is evidenced in the way they are inscribed in the expeditions' texts. Philip Jones has noted how expeditions prepared for human encounters before they travelled, evident in their provision lists which included 'metal axes and knives, mirrors, cloth and tobacco', signalling that '"encounters with the natives" were envisaged and accepted as integral to the expedition's key aims'.[7] British *and* Aboriginal objects played a critical, mediating role in the volatile space of encounter.

Encounters with King's expedition were commemorated in situ in the naming of places where encounters with Aboriginal people occurred around the coast: *Retaliation Point* where the crew met with hostile Aboriginal people; *Bottle Rocks* where they left a note in a bottle to warn future voyagers about the Aboriginal hostility at Retaliation Point; and *Encounter Cove* at Vansittart Bay, named after another dangerous and hostile encounter. *Interview Island* and the *Intercourse Islands* in Dampier's Archipelago reflect a more amicable meeting that the crew had with the Yaburara people in February 1818. As Bronwen Douglas has shown in her history of the mapping and naming of Oceania (c. 1500–1700), some early European voyage accounts reveal a 'subtle countersign of indigenous conduct', reflected in the choice of toponyms traced to encounters with, and physical descriptions of, indigenous people.[8]

During King's survey, naming occasionally honoured material culture rather than the inhabitants themselves. For example, at Port Essington in April 1818, midshipman Frederick Bedwell found a spear

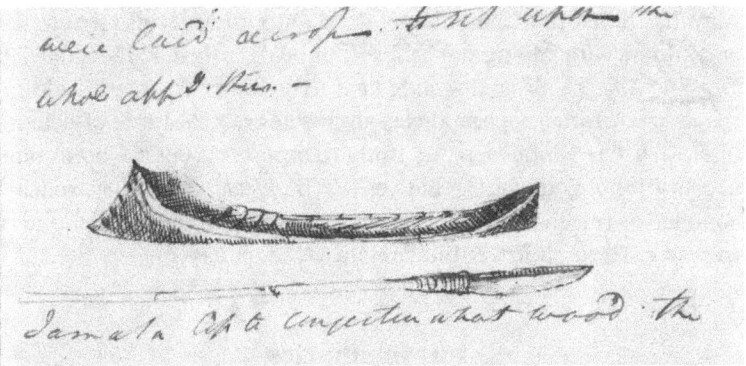

Figure 7.1 Sketch of the spear in Phillip Parker King's Remark Book, April 1818. By permission of Mitchell Library (King, Remark Book, April 1818, MLMSS 5277, CY reel 2565, items 1–3, SLNSW).

and a canoe on the beach. King was very taken by the unusual looking spear. It had a piece of pointed quartz, 'shaped like a knife blade at its head, with a jagged edge'. He wrote, 'the spear was brought on board but the canoe left on the beach... From which I call this Spear Point'.[9]

An ethnographic approach is also revealed in the crew's enthusiasm to clarify and enhance imperial understanding of Aboriginal people for non-travellers, their authority augmented by prolonged and intimate interactions and observations in 'the field'. Throughout the course of their four-year expedition, King, the botanist Allan Cunningham and midshipman John Septimus Roe developed an ethnographic method of inquiry, which included accruing knowledge by attempting comparative vocabulary lists, measuring and closely observing Aboriginal people where possible, learning from the brokering techniques of their intermediaries, as well as obtaining a large cache of material culture.

There was a strong hunger for tales of encounters with 'treacherous savages' from the English readers of published voyage accounts. King was keenly aware of this as he wrote up his journal for publication. Roe also crafted the stories he related to his family in letters home, rarely offering details of friendly meetings with Aboriginal people, focusing instead on examples of hostility and moments of crisis. King's published *Narrative* was generally poorly received in England, critically reviewed in arts, literary and scientific journals as being long and boring.[10] The publisher, John Murray, had urged King to consider the desire of his readers for adventure stories when finalizing his manuscript, sending him a copy of Denham, Clapperton and Oudney's *Narrative of Travels and Discoveries in Northern and Central Africa: In the Years 1822, 1823 and 1824* as a model.[11] Several reviews of King's *Narrative* noted that the only points of interest for readers were the encounters with Aboriginal people that he described. For example, in *The New Monthly Magazine and Literary Journal* it was remarked that the detail of King's 'operations is almost entirely destitute of general interest. There is not even any thing to amuse, except the occasional appearance of some of the natives'.[12] The *London Magazine* explicitly confined its review to 'the anecdotes of popular interest to be found in the work. These almost entirely relate to the natives'.[13]

Intermediaries

In recent years, scholars studying the exploration and colonization of Africa and the Americas have highlighted the role of the go-between in facilitating knowledge collection by European newcomers and providing valuable local information. Alida Metcalf focuses on the lasting effect of go-betweens, from first encounters to possession and colonial settlement in her book *Go-Betweens and the Colonization of Brazil: 1500–1600*. She argues that 'go-betweens clearly took centre stage, for they were the means of communication in the middle grounds of encounters'.[14] She stresses that go-betweens were not neutral figures, but had 'complex and shifting loyalties that are difficult for modern historians to reconstruct'.[15] David Turnbull also highlights the slippery loyalty of go-betweens, who could 'both dissolve and create boundaries in the process of linking people, practices, and places in networks'.[16] Intermediaries – the guides, translators, hosts, porters and labourers – who became involved in expeditions have received recent attention by historians seeking to recover 'hidden histories' of exploration, to use the terms of Felix Driver and Lowri Jones. Driver and Jones have recast intermediaries as central figures in exploration enterprises, writing their histories into the narrative of exploration and empire.[17] A 'focus on intermediaries in the history of exploration', they argue, 'not only unsettles the myth of the lone explorer but it also draws attention to the ways in which exploration was a form of labour requiring a locally-sourced workforce'.[18] In exploration archives, intermediaries are only partially visible. As Driver suggests, in the archive we might ask questions such as 'when and how ... were these individuals actually named? In what way was their work and its relationship to the project of exploration presented?'[19]

The centrality of ethnographic inquiry to the culture of King's expedition is most explicit in the crew's reliance on the Port Jackson Aboriginal intermediaries who accompanied the first and fourth voyages. A 'native aid', Bungaree, called Boongaree by the crew, joined the expedition for the first voyage from 22 December 1817 to 29 July 1818, on board the brig *Mermaid*. The second and third voyages did not include an intermediary, but on the fourth and final voyage, from 26 May 1821 to 24 April 1822, Bundle replaced Boongaree in this role and on their replacement brig, the *Bathurst*.

Boongaree, an iconic yet elusive go-between in the history of Port Jackson, was a crucial figure and central protagonist in the crew's encounters with Aboriginal people along the northwest coast.[20] King praised Boongaree, whom he believed to have had a vital role in communicating with Aboriginal people in Dampier's Archipelago: 'Boongaree was made very much of' by the local Yaburara, who 'appeared quite delighted to find his shoulders scarified like their own he always spoke to them in Broken English - - He however, is of great use to us ... the appearance of a Black man being with us [has] given them a confidence what it could be difficult otherwise to instil'.[21]

Crew members noted how Boongaree's body was an effective conduit to communication with Aboriginal people on shore. Roe also hoped that Boongaree's successor, Bundle, while not sharing the language of the Aboriginal people on the 'opposite coast', might 'nevertheless inspire with a quarter share of confidence those natives who have never before seen Europeans, and who may in consequence be induced to risk an interview with us, whereas they might otherwise have fled on our first approach'.[22] Dane Kennedy has observed in his history of the exploration of Africa and Australia that 'the very presence of these guides in the company of the pale strangers eased anxieties'.[23] But how did people like Boongaree and Bundle converse with strangers? What skills or techniques did they draw on? Were they directed *how* to mediate by the crew, or were they free to broker in their own ways? Their bodies were crucial vehicles in such exchanges.

Exploration archives indicate that European explorers were well aware of the ways in which the presence of a 'native aid' or 'intermediary' altered the dynamic of encounters. They stress, for instance, their unfamiliarity with new environments, the limits of their languages, and the misunderstandings that arose between them and the Aboriginal people they encountered. Cunningham differentiated between the expedition's intermediaries, Boongaree and Bundle, and Aboriginal people met along the way by referring to the latter as 'Stranger-Aborigines'. Despite this cultural distance, the Admiralty saw the value in the presence of local people and the inclusion of an intermediary was listed in Admiralty instructions to explorers. In planning for the *Beagle*'s third voyage and Australian survey, for example, the Admiralty encouraged the new commander and captain, John Wickham, to 'hire, at a low rate, some person acquainted with the dialects of the natives, which you are subsequently to visit, and with whom it will be essential to be on friendly terms'.[24] Lieutenant John Lort Stokes, assistant surveyor on the *Beagle* and chronicler of the voyage, wrote that:

> Among the many useful hints, for which we were indebted to Mr Roe, was that of taking a native with us to the northward; and accordingly, after some trouble, we shipped an intelligent young man, named Miago; he proved in some respects, exceedingly useful, and made an excellent gun-room waiter.[25]

Like Boongaree on King's earlier hydrographic survey, Miago's Aboriginal body would also become the object of much observation on the *Beagle*'s voyage, by crew and Aboriginal strangers alike.[26] Miago did not enjoy this close scrutiny when he mediated between the Worora at Hanover Bay and the crew of the *Beagle* in 1837: a group of Worora men very closely examined Miago's body, while Miago, Stokes wrote,

> submitted to be handled by them with a very rueful countenance, and afterwards construed the way in which one of them had gently stroked his beard, into an attempt to take him by the throat and strangle him! An injury and indignity which, when safe on board, he resented by repeated threats, uttered in a sort of wild chant, of spearing their thighs, backs, loins, and indeed, each individual portion of the frame.[27]

Opening up communication was only one function, though a crucial one, of a maritime intermediary. The botanist, Cunningham, benefited from Boongaree's presence and protection throughout the first voyage, writing at the end of a day botanizing on Bathurst Island in May 1818: 'During the whole of this day's excursion I was accompanied by our worthy native chief, Bongaree [sic] armed with a musket of whose little attentions to me and others when on these excursions I have been perhaps too remiss in making mention, to the enhancement of the character of this enterprising Australian'.[28] Indeed, this expeditionary team – in particular Cunningham and the midshipman, John Septimus Roe – were the first Europeans to use the term *Australians* for Aboriginal people, and specifically for Boongaree throughout the first voyage.[29] This suggests the real and significant effect of Boongaree's presence on the voyagers' ideas about human difference.[30]

At the end of the first voyage in July 1818, Boongaree's usefulness was questioned by Roe, who viewed Boongaree's retirement from the expedition as a step backwards. At the same time, he was pleased that Boongaree had left the expedition as he did not think of him as part of the *team* of survey work, writing: 'Boongaree, the native chief of the Broken Bay Tribe, does not now go with us, having been found of comparatively little use, and not so advantageous to the expedition as an able seaman that might be carried in his room'.[31] Retirement from physically demanding expeditions was a frequent occurrence (both by seamen and intermediaries). However, the departure of intermediaries was viewed by explorers as *desertion* and is one reason why those intermediaries who stayed for the duration were deemed 'loyal' and 'brave'.[32] Bundle replaced Boongaree on the fourth and final voyage, and Roe expressed his approval of Bundle, whom he described as a seaman *and* an intermediary:

> We have got a Port Jackson black on board, accompanying us on our voyage, to facilitate our intercourse with any natives we may fall in

with at different parts of the country – his name is Bundle; he is a more useful man than any Australian Black I have seen – having sailed onboard several whalers & other vessels on this coast and although one of his eyes has been knocked out or in with a spear – his sight is excellent, like all other Australians. – Boongaree, the chief of the Broken Bay Tribe was the man who accompanied us on our first voyage and was to have sail'd with us both on our present & *last* voyage: but his resolution forsook him when the time of embarkation arrived & we were by no means disappointed when we found that he had secreted himself in the woods; Bundle is preferable to him, is about 40 years of age, 5 feet 9 or 10 inches high, & now being rigged out with a red cap, red shirt & pair of old trowsers [sic] is a perfect dandy.[33]

Bundle had a long history of sea voyaging by the time he joined King's expedition. In 1791, as a young boy, he sailed aboard His Majesty's brig *Supply* to Norfolk Island, making him the first recorded Aboriginal person to go to sea in an English ship.[34] He was an orphan from Dharawal country, a region stretching from Botany Bay south to the Shoalhaven River and inland to Camden.[35] In 1811, David Dickenson Mann singled out Bundle as a notable Aboriginal sailor in the colony, who made himself 'extremely useful on board colonial vessels employed in the fishing and sealing trades', for which he was 'in regular receipt of wages'.[36] In this nearly one-year-long voyage attached to King's expedition, Bundle was represented as part of the expeditionary team. Like other lower-ranked able seamen, he rarely appeared in the expedition archive and his experience was represented anonymously alongside other team members. The only exception to this was during encounters on shore, when his role as an intermediary pulled him from the margins and thrust him to the centre of expedition accounts.

Techniques of Encounter: Hanover Bay, 1821

On the morning of 7 August 1821, the expedition's ship, *Bathurst*, was anchored in Hanover Bay, and as the crew were washing the decks they heard 'sounds seeming to be the cries of Natives'.[37] They had heard similar calls the day before, which Bundle had returned with a call of his own, but the tide had not let the eager crew go ashore. On this morning Bundle led the encounter, again returning the Worora's call, and at eleven o'clock a boat was sent to communicate with them.[38] King, with the two midshipmen Frederick Bedwell and Percival Baskerville, and the surgeon Dr Montgomery, rowed towards the shore, while Bundle 'who generally accompanied us on these occasions divested of his clothes, stood in the bow of the boat'.[39] As they approached the shore, Bundle 'made signs of friendship, which the natives returned'.[40] Such gestures of friendship included Bundle stretching his arms up and out, keeping his hands open, then occasionally touching his breast with the palms of his hands. This was one of his techniques for mediation that the crew also adopted, assuming it was a universal Aboriginal sign after witnessing a similar gesture by the Guugu Yimithirr people in July 1820 at Endeavour River. The Guugu Yimithirr had made 'signs of friendship by laying their hands upon their hearts' and repeating the word '*itchew*' (friend).[41] Two months prior to the expedition's visit to Hanover Bay, during an encounter on Lizard Island, King recorded that 'the appearance of Bundle, who on these occasions always took his clothes off, perhaps gave the [Guugu Yimithirr] greater confidence' in meeting the strangers.[42] According to Cunningham, at Lizard Island the Guugu Yimithirr 'vociferously manifested their surprise on seeing our native friend Bundle (who we had ship'd from Port Jackson) among us, especially as he had strip'd off his shirt *and exhibited a scarified body, nearly a Counterpart of their own*'.[43] This was a ready phrase of Cunningham's, who had used the exact same description during Boongaree's meeting with the Yaburara in Dampier's Archipelago in February 1818.[44] Cunningham recorded the effect that Bundle's nudity and presence had on the Worora at Hanover Bay: 'Seeing Bundle perfectly naked, they were encouraged to stand till our party had reached them, at the same time, they dropped their spears; but it was not without show of fear or distrust they allowed Mr King' to approach.[45]

At first, only King and Bundle climbed up the rocks on which the two Worora men were standing, the other three staying close to the boat. The explorers were, by now, well versed in the necessity of bringing gifts when meeting with Aboriginal strangers, knowing that the Worora would be expecting to receive something. As Philip Jones has written, 'when visitors arrived [on Aboriginal country], it was assumed that they came for social reasons; even if trade was the apparent or superficial goal, its transactions were socially derived and expressed, tangled closely with obligation and the governing principle of reciprocity'.[46] At Hanover Bay, King inferred the importance of English objects in volatile encounters: 'when we joined them their spears were ready to throw', and so he offered some biscuit to the taller of the two men, who instantly reciprocated, giving King a 'waddie' in return. Roe later examined this gift closely, describing it as 'about 2 feet in length, an inch and ¼ in diam. and sharply pointed at both ends to answer either as a club or a double dagger for close quarters; and at such times, in the hands of a man so quick in his motions as an Australian this would be a formidable weapon'.[47] To keep the transaction moving, King immediately offered the same man a clasp knife, while Bundle received a belt made of opossum fur from the other Worora man, which he tied around his head in the same manner as the man who gifted it to him.[48]

From the ship, Roe and Cunningham viewed the encounter through their glasses. Roe was still recovering from an epic eighty-foot fall from the masthead and was not cleared to go ashore.[49] After about half an hour, they watched as Dr Montgomery and Bedwell approached the men. Montgomery threw some fish that the crew had caught the day before towards the Worora men. Either the act of throwing the fish, or the growing numbers of strangers on their beach, unsettled the Worora; they picked up their spears and began talking to each other. King, in an attempt to keep the encounter light, took the clasp knife back from the Worora man he had given it to, hoping to awe him by showing him how to open and close it. This attempt to redirect the encounter was a technique that the crew used on their first visit to Endeavour River in June 1819. When twelve Guugu Yimithirr came to the explorers' camp one morning, one seaman pulled out his clasp knife, showing the group collected around him how he could fold it back into its handle; 'the Aborigines recoiled in horror'.[50] At Hanover Bay, King recorded that this tactic 'instead of pacifying, only served to increase their anger, the knife was thrown at the Worora man's feet, which he instantly picked up, and then both retired a few paces in a very suspicious manner'.[51] The accrual of mediating techniques involved much trial and error. The crew then waved goodbye, and as they turned to go to their boat the Worora men each threw a heavy spear. One spear hit a rock and broke in half and the other speared Montgomery in the back.

Montgomery yelled out, 'Good god, I'm speared!' He reached for his pistol, firing off a shot; King and Bedwell picked up rocks and threw them, to no effect; Bundle instantly grabbed the broken spear and ran after the Worora men but could not catch them. The wounded surgeon was helped back on board the brig.[52] Never to miss an opportunity for collecting Aboriginal weapons and other material, Roe (who had gone to shore as soon as the spears were thrown to assist Montgomery) recorded that the two spears were brought on board. They measured 'about 12 or 14 feet in length without barbs' and were described as 'rather heavily made – they were thrown by the hand nor had the natives any of the throwing sticks that are in such general use for discharging these weapons in nearly every part of this country'.[53]

This statement proved, however, to be incorrect; the 'double dagger' or 'waddie' that Roe examined, which had been gifted to King, was in fact a spear thrower.

The following morning, two men, a woman and a child were seen on two catamarans paddling themselves to a little sandy bay. The two men then walked to the rocks where the encounter occurred the day before. Desperate to retaliate, two expedition boats went ashore, the crew firing their muskets as soon as they were close enough to the men. Bundle fired a musket too, his shot, according to King, hitting one of the men on the shoulder. This man, Roe wrote, 'fell 8 or 10 feet down the perpendicular wall upon which they were seated, and the other not being touched sprang upon his feet in an instant and had retreated out of sight before the pernicious running fire with muskets and pistols touched him'.[54]

The wounded man was recognised as the same man who had speared Montgomery the previous day and the crew described their feelings of vindication in discovering this. He awkwardly scrambled up the rocks while under further fire from the crew, and limped away. The crew returned to the boats and hoped to find the man near to where the catamarans had been hauled up in the sandy bay. King, Roe, Bedwell, Baskerville and Bundle, armed with muskets, walked overland in the hope of finding the wounded man to end their payback. Roe wrote:

> The traces of blood upon the stones were observed as we walked along and we followed them smartly for about a mile and a half, until they disappeared at the edge of a swampy muddy morass, where the feet marks of 2 men in the mud plainly indicated the route they had taken ... the severity of the injury he had received was sufficiently conspicuous from the quantity of blood that he had lost and which was streaming down the rocks.[55]

Collecting Culture

The expeditionary team's ethnographic interest is evident in their desire for Aboriginal material culture for their own collections as well as the Colonial Office. In Roe's private letters to his family, he described the 'collection of curiosities', obtained during his voyages, for the museum that he hoped to open with his brother William and their father, Reverend James Roe.[56] He wrote about shells and animals he collected, and occasionally the Aboriginal weapons that he obtained, such as 'a long case of spears'.[57] At Port Jackson, before the second expedition departed in December 1818, he collected a 'very fine diamond snake', which he was going to 'stuff for William's museum' and which 'would have been a valuable addition to my small collection of curiosities'.[58] He wrote:

> During our short walks for recreation on shore ... our time is not thrown away, for both Mr Bedwell and myself (the Botanist likewise of course) are making a collection of insects; and mine amounts to about 300 different species, carefully preserved in boxes scented with camphire [sic] to guard against invasion from ants, or other destructive vermin. I hope that the few which I took home from my China voyage are not destroyed & that Wm. will take care of every thing he can collect to put in our museum.[59]

At Port Essington, during the April 1818 visit in which King named Spear Point, Roe and Cunningham came across human remains. Cunningham wrote in his journal that under a tree he found 'the bones of a Native. The skull and jaw bones were partly perfect, but wanted some teeth, those that remained in the jaws were ... in good condition. – Leg bones and one of the Ribs were also discovered. – All of which were carefully taken on board and delivered to Mr King'.[60] In his *Narrative*, King wrote that these remains 'were too imperfect to be worth preserving'.[61] Cunningham's interest in human remains developed further in subsequent expeditions. In his 1828 expedition to Moreton Bay with Patrick Logan and Charles Fraser, he took the 'skin of one of the female aborigines, which was procured by Private Platt of the 57th Regiment, from the hut of a native on the Brisbane River'.[62]

At Hanover Bay, the crew returned to the beach where the catamarans were and, to their delight, found a large cache of Aboriginal belongings; Cunningham described it as an Aboriginal 'depôt'. Roe recorded his excitement: 'Here we found 2 catamarans hauled upon the beach, with 15 or 16 spears upon each; and a little higher up among a grove of Pandanus trees we had the good luck to fall in with what appeared to constitute a whole of these people's treasure, and which it will cost them a considerable length of time and great trouble to replace'.[63] The crew collected the two catamarans, thirty-five spears and many stone hatchets and tools.

Cunningham described the objects in detail and he was probably assisted by Bundle in his interpretation of the use and meaning of some of the items – another advantage of including an intermediary. He studied the following:

> several strong stone hatchets – several rude waddies two feet long. Bundles of dried sticks to attain fire by friction. Six most curious spearheads of the following figure made of stone ... jagged with great care

on the Edge & formed to a very sharp point. These spear heads were perfectly new & were carefully pack'd in hair to prevent their delicate ... Points or Edges from being injured. A spear was also found, pointed with a stonehead of this description, the wound such weapons would affect, when thrown with a wammerah, must be dreadful ... Bundles of the soft down of the kangaroo were found among the spoil, which they form into a wasted, which is then manufactured into a kind of fillet for their hair, in Girdles for their locks.

Bundle had received one of these girdles in the encounter of the previous day. Cunningham also found 'red pigment in order to colour their ladies, and lumps of gum were carefully tied up for use'.[64]

Roe and Cunningham made sketches of items that intrigued or awed them. Cunningham was particularly taken by a basket 'made of Eucalyptian [sic] bark, & rendered watertight by large Coats of the gum of the same tree that had been previously heated in the fire'. But what Cunningham found so interesting about this basket was that 'a sharp instrument was made by these people of a piece of ironhoop, placed up the end of a stick for a handle'. Cunningham later added an asterisk to this statement, noting that the ironhoop handle 'appears only accountable, by supposing an Ironhoop was left onshore at Careening Bay, when we were encamped, during the progress of the Repairs of the Mermaid in Sept. 1820'.[65] Roe and King also thought this most likely.

Figure 7.2 Sketch of the basket with ironhoop handles, by Allan Cunningham. By permission of Archives Office of New South Wales (Allan Cunningham, Journal, Colonial Secretary's Papers, 1788–1825, GM47 reel 6034).

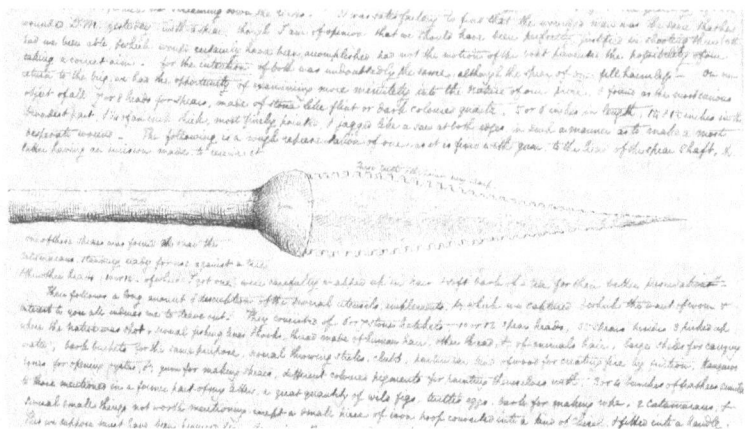

Figure 7.3 Sketch of a spearhead by John Septimus Roe, September 1821. By permission of Mitchell Library (Roe, letter to his father, 28 September 1821, item 162, MLMSS 7964/vol. 5, safe 1/368, SLNSW).

Once back on board, Roe examined 'more minutely into the nature of our prize'. In a long letter to his father written six weeks after the encounter, Roe recounted his story of Hanover Bay, copying large excerpts from his private journal into the letter. The spearhead he collected was next to him on the table as he wrote, and a large sketch of it interrupts the story in his letter. These spearheads, he wrote, were 'the most callous' objects of all.

> 7 or 8 heads for spears, made of stone like flint or dark coloured quartz, 5 or 8 inches in length, 1 ¼ and 1 ½ inches in the broadest part, and ¼ of an inch thick, most finely pointed, and jagged like a saw at both edges in such a manner as to make a most desperate wound – the following is a rough representation of one, as it is fixed with gum, to the head of the spear shaft, the latter having an incision made to receive it.

Along the pointed edge of the sketched spearhead, Roe wrote, 'these teeth and the point [are] very sharp'. One of these spears 'was found near the catamarans, standing ready for use against a tree and the other heads (10 or 12 *of which I got one*) were carefully wrapped up in hair and soft bark of a tree for their better preservation'.[66]

A spearhead of the same style and shape to the one Roe sketched was also drawn for Volume 2 of King's published *Narrative*. The plate depicts a drawing of several weapons made by Francis Chantrey Esq, a well-known sculptor and artist in England and member of the Royal Society.[67] This drawing was titled 'Weapons & c. of the Natives

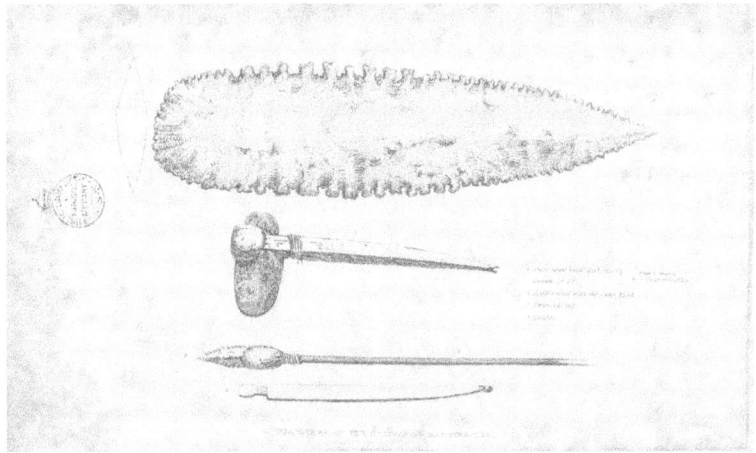

Figure 7.4 'Weapons & c. of the Natives of Hanover Bay'. Drawing by Francis Chantrey, published in Phillip Parker King, *Narrative of a Survey of the Intertropical and Western Coasts of Australia, Performed between the Years 1818 and 1822* (London: John Murray, 1826), Vol. 2. By permission of the State Library of New South Wales.

of Hanover Bay' and featured a large representation and a sectional sketch of a stone spearhead. Chantrey's drawing of the spearhead, as Felix Driver and Luciana Martins have observed, 'sits somewhat abstractly, alongside other artefacts, isolated from the text and identified by a key'.[68] The plate also includes a drawing of a spear armed with a stone spearhead, a throwing stick and a hatchet. In Roe's letter, his sketch of the spearhead, as Driver and Martins observe, 'pierces the text of a personal letter, interrupting its flow and giving a much more immediate sense of co-presence'.[69] While the crew found interest in the other material collected – the basket with an ironhoop handle that Cunningham sketched, for example – it was the 'most callous object', the spearhead, that shaped the event at Hanover Bay, as the crew began turning this encounter into story.[70]

The repeated recycling of images and written representations of Aboriginal people from expeditionary encounters occurred throughout the empire for various purposes, creating hardened tropes of Aboriginal characteristics.[71] King was a keen observer and collector of Aboriginal watercraft and he made two sketches of the Worora rafts that the crew brought on board. A woodcut of a woman sitting on the raft, holding a basket and several spears while a man propels the raft along with a further spear appears on the title page of Volume 2 of his published *Narrative*.

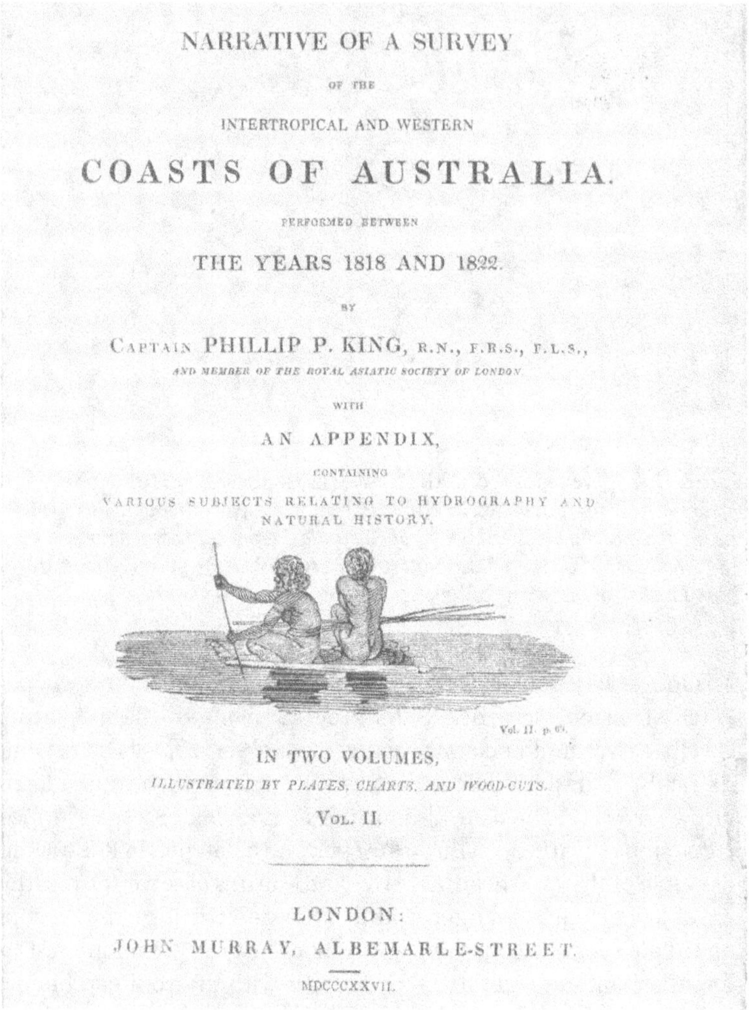

> NARRATIVE OF A SURVEY
>
> OF THE
>
> INTERTROPICAL AND WESTERN
>
> # COASTS OF AUSTRALIA.
>
> PERFORMED BETWEEN
>
> ## THE YEARS 1818 AND 1822.
>
> BY
>
> CAPTAIN PHILLIP P. KING, R.N., F.R.S., F.L.S.,
> AND MEMBER OF THE ROYAL ASIATIC SOCIETY OF LONDON
>
> WITH
>
> AN APPENDIX,
>
> CONTAINING
>
> VARIOUS SUBJECTS RELATING TO HYDROGRAPHY AND NATURAL HISTORY.
>
> Vol. II. p. 6.
>
> IN TWO VOLUMES,
>
> ILLUSTRATED BY PLATES, CHARTS, AND WOOD-CUTS.
>
> VOL. II.
>
> LONDON:
> JOHN MURRAY, ALBEMARLE-STREET.
>
> MDCCCXXVII.

Figure 7.5 Title page of Phillip Parker King, *Narrative of a Survey of the Intertropical and Western Coasts of Australia, Performed between the Years 1818 and 1822* (London: John Murray, 1826), Vol. 2. By permission of the State Library of New South Wales.

This illustration was altered and printed in the *Missionary Register* in September 1834, under the heading 'Scenery and Natives of New Holland'. In this reprocessing of the image for missionary propaganda, the woman's basket was removed and the scene vastly enhanced with an imagined landscape; it is also devoid of the violent context within which the illustration was created, suggesting instead a peaceful scene of Aborigines in a state of nature, before contact with Europeans. The article accompanying this image also recycled the statements about Worora material culture made by King, expanding his observations about Hanover Bay and the Worora people into a statement about the 'natives of New Holland' more broadly:

> The accompanying Engraving represents two of the Natives of New Holland, among whom the Church Missionary Society has lately established a Mission. They appear on a float, consisting of *five mangrove stems, lashed together, and fastened to a frame. On these floats the Natives cross their rivers: they are buoyant enough to carry two persons with their baskets and spears.*[72]

The mission was Wellington Valley, in Wiradjuri country, central New South Wales.[73] Many years later, in 1905, when the nascent discipline of anthropology was developing, King's statements and sketches of the rafts of Hanover Bay were included in Northcote Whitridge Thomas's discussion on 'Australian Canoes and Rafts' published in *The Journal of the Anthropological Institute of Great Britain and Ireland*. Thomas, an expeditionary anthropologist who was involved in Alfred Cort Haddon's 1898 Anthropological Expedition to Torres Strait, and later worked as a government anthropologist in Nigeria, included King's 'field work' ethnography on the Worora in debates about Aboriginal watercraft and the origins of the human settlement of Australia.[74]

After the return of King's expedition in 1823, some of the Worora weapons that were seized in 1821 began their own stories of circulation. The history of this material remains hard to trace, but from the known collections at the British Museum identified as having links to this encounter, and research into antiquarian networks in England, it is clear that King, Cunningham and the Roe family were connected to a community in England interested in obtaining ethnographic collections from Royal Navy expeditions. The collection and reception of Aboriginal material by King's expedition may also have been prompted by the popularity of the ethnographic displays collected by earlier, famed navigators Captain James Cook and Captain George Vancouver.[75]

Gaye Sculthorpe, curator of Oceania collections at the British Museum, has traced links between King and George Annesley, the second Earl of Mountnorris, owner of Arley Castle in Staffordshire and a traveller-collector himself. A spear thrower, catalogued as 'Oc982 Hanover Bay' in the British Museum's Oceania collection, was auctioned at Arley Castle in 1852 after the earl's death, and is most likely the one illustrated in Chantrey's drawing for King's *Narrative*, and possibly the waddie that was gifted to him during the encounter.[76] The spearhead of grey stone, covered in ochre, also in Chantrey's drawing and similar to the one sketched by Roe, was donated to the museum by Augustus Wollaston Franks. Franks was also one of the trustees of the Christy collection and associated Christy Fund, which from the late 1860s made major contributions to the development of the British Museum's ethnographic and archaeological collections.

Roe's family museum of curiosities, referred to by Roe as 'Roevial' in his letters, was established in Newbury and operated by his father, Reverend James Roe, Rector of the Parish in Newbury. In *Pigot and Co.'s Pocket Atlas* (1838), it was recorded that '[a] private museum here, the property of the Rev James Roe, is well worth the inspection of the privileged visitor; it has been pronounced the finest collection in the country, unequalled alike by the rarity and variety of the subjects and their admirable arrangement'.[77] It is also likely that some of the Australian Hydrographic Survey's Aboriginal collections and specimens of natural history were presented to the museum at Haslar Hospital. Haslar Hospital was established by the Admiralty at Portsmouth Harbour for injured or sick seamen and its museum was opened in 1827. The museum was described by one visitor in 1854 as

> a well-arranged and tolerably extensive collection of skeletons of human beings, mammalia, birds, fishes, reptiles, serpents, and other species ... some strange-looking weapons – axes, knives, etc. – from various savage tribes ... Although the museum is an interesting collection; it has been formed principally by donations from naval officers and others, who 'go down unto the sea in ships' and bring from foreign climes their varied curiosities.[78]

The museum was also a sort of shrine, honouring past Lords of the Admiralty and famous navigators within the collection.[79] As Natasha McKinney has noted, Augustus Wollaston Franks had overseen a 'mixed collection from the Haslar Naval Hospital in 1853' to the British Museum's collection.[80] A sketch of Haslar Hospital appears in Roe's sketchbook, dated October 1823, coinciding with his return to England at the end of the expedition. The Haslar Hospital museum's visitor book for 31 May 1833 records that Reverend James Roe visited the museum with James Everard Home, a senior naval officer in the Royal Navy and member of the Royal Society who was engaged in human and animal anatomy.[81] This visit reveals the existence of a wider museum network focused on Australia at this time, as well as the possibility that James Roe donated his son's Aboriginal collections to Haslar.[82]

Conclusion

This tale of object transactions in the exploration era brings me back to Maria Nugent's focus on the bark shield obtained by the crew during Cook's landing at Botany Bay in 1770. Nugent shifts our understanding of Aboriginal motivations during that foundational encounter, concluding that it was 'courage, not cowardice' that created 'the clearing that made the landing possible'. The Gweagal man who opposed Cook's landing left the beach to retrieve a shield from his 'house', and that shield is most likely the shield housed in the British Museum's Enlightenment Gallery.

Some of the material collected during King's four-year expedition was obtained in a transactional way, and undertaken largely to follow Earl Bathurst's instructions about gaining an understanding of 'the state of [the Aborigines'] arts or manufactures and their comparative perfection in different tribes'. Following this encounter at Hanover Bay, in December 1821, the expedition made a prolonged visit to King George Sound, where the crew engaged with the local Noongar people in intense trading exchanges each day. Over the course of two weeks, the crew had collected 'one hundred spears, thirty throwing-sticks, forty hammers, one hundred and fifty knives and a few hand-clubs', costing them 'one eighth of a biscuit for each piece'.[83] King was aware that these weapons were 'not perfect artefacts', but made specifically for sale. Cunningham viewed the transactions as a tourist trade, noting how quickly the Noongar had sold 'their entire stock of [ready] weapons' and had to manufacture more to 'secure themselves of continued meals of bread'.[84] Cunningham likened them to 'Jew's Hatchets', stating that they were 'so hastily finish'd off and so badly were the handles cemented with Gum [of the] Xanthorrhoea' that they were made 'simply for sale'.[85]

By contrast, the collection at Hanover Bay was a retaliatory theft for the spearing of Dr Montgomery, not a consensual exchange. The expedition texts refer to the collection variously as 'riches', a 'prize', 'treasure' or 'spoil', noting their pleasure in 'capturing' an Aboriginal 'depôt'. Individual crew members obtained their own collections too, for personal benefit and, as Roe suggested in his letter, for gratification: 'We were greatly rejoiced at having been afforded an opportunity of punishing conduct so revolting to human nature as that we had experienced from these natives, and we do not think they will again be in any great hurry to communicate with strangers; for next day we saw 6 or 7 of them on the top of a hill near the same spot, very busily engaged making spears to replace those we had taken'.[86]

Intermediaries played a significant part in exploration ethnography, and specifically in the collection of material culture. Mediating meetings and exchanges with strangers, they received gifts themselves and assisted with the crew's interpretations of the items collected. Intermediaries were sometimes collectors themselves, and this is occasionally inferred from Australian exploration archives. For example, Manyat, a Noongar man from King George Sound who guided Alexander Collie in the early 1830s, assembled his own collection of specimens of foreign trees to take back home with him.[87] Boongaree also established his own collection during his role as mediator: 'He brought away a small hand basket, made of some kind of leaf, capable of containing five or six pints of water'.[88]

The cultural assessments by intermediaries included suggestions to the crew about the process of making weapons, their practical and ritual use. At Spear Point in Port Essington, Boongaree helped King make sense of the construction of the spear which had a piece of sharp, serrated quartz stuck to the head: attached to its shaft 'was a ligature of grass, plaited and waxed over'. King wrote that Boongaree called the wax honey – leading him to believe it was beeswax.[89] Bundle was also able to assist the crew in this way. His authority on Aboriginal protocols and the culture of strangers is subtle, but evident at Hanover Bay; as soon as he was gifted the possum skin girdle, he knew its purpose, wrapping it around his forehead.

In linking the Worora weapons in the British Museum to the encounter from which they were obtained, and the subsequent textual representations of them and their original owners, this chapter has attempted not only to trace the biography of these objects, but to explore the context in which they were seized, the motivations for their theft and the centrality of Bundle to the encounter. Bundle's presence shaped the encounter at Hanover Bay – he was sought out by the Worora, played a part in the exchange of gifts and went back to the brig with some Worora material culture. He was also a key player in the retributive attack, wielding a spear in the first meeting. The following day, King suggested that it was Bundle's musket shot that ended the encounter. Focusing on the centrality of encounters to this expedition allows us to explore the crucial role played by Aboriginal intermediaries. As members of the expeditionary team, their very presence influenced the expedition's ethnographic inquiry and had the power to direct the crew's assumptions about Aboriginal Australians.

Tiffany Shellam is Senior Lecturer in History at Deakin University. Her research focuses on the development of relationships between Aboriginal Australians and newcomers in the nineteenth century, particularly during exploration expeditions. She is co-editor of *Indigenous Intermediaries: New Perspectives on Exploration Archives* (ANU Press and Aboriginal History, 2015) and author of *Shaking Hands on the Fringe: Negotiating the Aboriginal World at King George's Sound* (UWA Publishing, 2009).

Notes

1. Maria Nugent, *Captain Cook Was Here* (Cambridge/Port Melbourne: Cambridge University Press, 2009), 41.
2. J.W. Croker to King, 4 February 1817, Instructions from Admiralty, Admiralty Office, transcribed by NSW archivist, in Phillip Parker King letter book relating to survey voyages around New South Wales, 1817–23, MLMSS 4429, State Library of NSW (SLNSW).
3. Memorandum accompanying letter from Earl Bathurst, Downing Street, 8 February 1817, in Phillip Parker King letter book relating to survey voyages around New South Wales, 1817–23, MLMSS 4429, SLNSW.
4. Felix Driver, *Geography Militant: Cultures of Exploration and Empire* (Oxford/Malden, MA: Blackwell Publishers, 2001), 49.
5. Ibid., 58.
6. Shino Konishi, Maria Nugent, Tiffany Shellam and Allison Cadzow, 'Introduction', in Shino Konishi, Maria Nugent, Tiffany Shellam and Allison Cadzow (eds), *Brokers and Boundaries: Colonial Exploration in Indigenous Territory* (Canberra: ANU Press and Aboriginal History, 2016), 1–13.
7. Philip Jones, 'The Theatre of Contact: Aborigines and Exploring Expeditions', in Martin Thomas (ed.), *Expedition into Empire: Exploratory Journeys and the Making of the Modern World* (New York: Routledge, 2015), 92.
8. Bronwen Douglas, 'Naming Places: Voyagers, Toponyms, and Local Presence in the Fifth Part of the World, 1500–1700', *Journal of Historical Geography* 45 (2014), 17–18.
9. King, Remark Book, April 1818, MLMSS 5277, CY reel 2565, items 1–3, SLNSW. The name Spear Point remains today. Francis Beaufort, later hydrographer of the navy, instructed navy captains on naming practices: 'in really new discoveries it would be really more beneficial to make the name convey some idea of the sense of the place, or some allusion to the inhabitants, or still better to adopt the native appellation, than to exhaust the catalogue of public characters and private friends', quoted in Marsdern Hordern, *King of the Australian Coast: The Voyages of Phillip Parker King in the Mermaid and the Bathurst* (Carlton, Vic: Melbourne

University Press, 1997), 110. The British Museum has early objects from Port Essington which are most likely linked to King. Personal communication, Gaye Sculthorpe, 4 March 2014.
10. Phillip Parker King, *Narrative of a Survey of the Intertropical and Western Coasts of Australia, Performed between the Years 1818 and 1822* (London: John Murray, 1826).
11. Letter from King to John Murray, 1 April 1826, MS 40650, John Murray Archive, Edinburgh; F.R.S. Denham, *Narrative of Travels and Discoveries in Northern and Central Africa: In the Years 1822, 1823 and 1824, by Major Denham FRS, Captain Clapperton and the Late Dr Oudney, Extending across the Great Desert to the Tenth Degree of Northern Latitude, and from Kouka in Bornou to Sackatoo, the Capital of the Felatah Empire*, 2 Vols (London: John Murray, 1826).
12. *The New Monthly Magazine and Literary Journal*, 'Critical Notices', 1827, Part III, Vol. 21, 327.
13. *London Magazine*, March 1827, Vol. 7, 380.
14. Alida Metcalf, *Go-Betweens and the Colonization of Brazil: 1500–1600* (Austin, TX: The University of Texas Press, 2005), 8.
15. Ibid., 10.
16. David Turnbull, 'Boundary-Crossings, Cultural Encounters and Knowledge Spaces in Early Australia', in Simon Schaffer, Lissa Roberts, Kapil Raj and James Delbourgo (eds), *The Brokered World: Go-Betweens and Global Intelligence, 1770–1820* (Sagmore Beach: Science History Publications USA, 2009), 396.
17. Felix Driver and Lowri Jones (eds), *Hidden Histories of Exploration: Researching the RGS-IBG Collections* (London: Royal Holloway, University of London, in association with the Royal Geographical Society, 2009).
18. Ibid.
19. Felix Driver, 'Intermediaries and the Archive of Exploration', in Shino Konishi, Maria Nugent and Tiffany Shellam (eds), *Indigenous Intermediaries: New Perspectives on Exploration Archives* (Canberra: ANU Press and Aboriginal History, 2015), 19, http://press.anu.edu.au/titles/aboriginal-history-monographs/indigenous-intermediaries.
20. For a discussion on Boongaree's centrality to encounters during the circumnavigation of Australia with Matthew Flinders, see Bronwen Douglas, 'The Lure of Texts and the Discipline of Praxis: Cross-Cultural History in a Post-Empirical World', *Humanities Research* XIV(1) (2007), 11–30.
21. King, Remark Book, 26 February 1818, MLMSS 5277, CY reel 2565, items 1–3, SLNSW. For a history of this encounter in detail, see Tiffany Shellam, 'Mediating Encounters through Bodies and Talk', in Konishi, Nugent and Shellam, *Indigenous Intermediaries*, 85–102.
22. Roe to his brother William, written off Cape Capricorn, 6 June 1821, item 160, no. 04, MLMSS 7964/vol. 51, safe 1/468, SLNSW.

23. Dane Kennedy, *Last Blank Spaces: The Exploration of Africa and Australia* (Cambridge, MA/London: Harvard University Press, 2013), 181.
24. F. Beaufort, 8 June 1837, Hydrographer's Instructions to Wickham, printed in John Lort Stokes, *Discoveries with an Account of the Coasts and Rivers Explored and Surveyed during the Voyage of H.M.S. Beagle, in the Years 1837–38–39–40–41–42–43*, Project Gutenberg online, http://www.gutenberg.org/ebooks/12115 (accessed 2 June 2015). Captain James Cook's 1770 voyage had set a precedent for indigenous aides to be attached to maritime expeditions.
25. Stokes, *Discoveries*, ch. 1.3.
26. Shellam, 'Mediating Encounters'.
27. Stokes, *Discoveries*, ch. 3.
28. Allan Cunningham, Journal, 28 May 1818, Bathurst Island, Colonial Secretary's Papers, 1788–1825, GM47 reel 6034, State Library of Victoria (SLV).
29. This term has been used recently by indigenous artists in postcolonial repartee. An exhibition of indigenous art works reflecting on the life and experiences of Bungaree, curated by Djon Mundine for Mosman Art Gallery in 2012, was titled *Bungaree: The First Australian*, a witty reference to Cunningham and Roe's conferral of this term on their shipboard intermediary. See Tiffany Shellam, 'Bungaree: The First Australian', *Australian Historical Studies* 44(2) (June 2013), 280–87.
30. Bronwen Douglas, *Science, Voyages and Encounters in Oceania: 1511–1850* (Basingstoke: Palgrave Macmillan, 2014), 120–21.
31. Letter from Roe to his father, 19 April 1819, Port Jackson, written on the eve of his departure on the second voyage, MLMSS 7964/vol. 4, safe 1/467, SLNSW.
32. Kennedy, *Last Blank Spaces*, ch. 6 passim.
33. Roe to his brother William, written off Cape Capricorn, 6 June 1821, item 160, no. 04, MLMSS 7964/vol. 51, safe 1/468, SLNSW.
34. Keith V. Smith, *Mari Nawi: Aboriginal Odysseys* (Dural, NSW: Rosenberg Publishing, 2010), 20.
35. Carol Liston, 'The Dharawal and Gandangara in Colonial Campbelltown, New South Wales, 1788–1830', *Aboriginal History* 12(1) (1988), 49.
36. David Dickinson Mann, *Present Picture of NSW 1811* (London: John Booth, 1811) [Sydney: John Ferguson, in association with the Royal Australian Historical Society, 1979], 47.
37. Cunningham, Journal, 7 August 1821, SLV.
38. King, *Narrative*, 7 August 1821.
39. Ibid.
40. Ibid.
41. Cunningham, Journal, 30 July 1820, SLV; King, *Narrative*, 30 July 1820.
42. King, *Narrative*, 7 August 1821.
43. My italics. Cunningham, Journal, 20 June 1821, Lizard Island, SLV.
44. Shellam, 'Mediating Encounters', 90.

45. Cunningham, Journal, 7 August 1821, SLV.
46. Jones, 'The Theatre of Contact', 89.
47. Roe, letter to his father, 28 September 1821, item 162, MLMSS 7964/vol. 5, safe 1/368, SLNSW.
48. Ibid.
49. His head was 'still green'. Ibid.
50. Hordern, *King of the Australian Coast*, 175.
51. King, *Narrative*, 7 August 1821.
52. Roe, letter to his father, 28 September 1821, item 162, MLMSS 7964/vol. 5, safe 1/368, SLNSW.
53. Ibid.
54. Ibid.
55. Ibid.
56. Mentioned in several letters: John Septimus Roe letters, series 04 MLMSS 7964/vol. 4, safe 1/467; and series 05 MLMSS 7964/vol. 5, safe 1/468, SLNSW.
57. Roe to his father, 23 June 1823, series 06 MLMSS 7964/vol. 6, safe 1/469, SLNSW.
58. Roe to his father, 7 December 1818, series 04 MLMSS 7964/vol. 4, safe 1/467, SLNSW.
59. Roe to his father, 22 March 1819, series 04 MLMSS 7964/vol. 4, safe 1/467, SLNSW.
60. Cunningham, Journal, 21 April 1818, SLV.
61. King, *Narrative*, 22 April 1818. Hordern writes that this skeleton was 'dropped over the side' of the boat by Cunningham. However, I have found no suggestion anywhere in the expedition archive that this occurred. Hordern, *King of the Australian Coast*, 112.
62. Quoted in Phillip A. Clarke, *Aboriginal Plant Collectors: Botanists and Australian Aboriginal People in the Nineteenth Century* (Dural, NSW: Rosenberg Publishing, 2008), 75.
63. Roe, letter to his father, 28 September 1821, item 162, MLMSS 7964/vol. 5, safe 1/368, SLNSW.
64. Cunningham, Journal, 8 August 1821, SLV.
65. Ibid.
66. My italics. Roe, letter to his father, 28 September 1821, item 162, MLMSS 7964/vol. 5, safe 1/368, SLNSW.
67. Chantrey's work was connected to the Admiralty. He sculpted busts of the Admirals Duncan, Howe, Vincent and Nelson for Greenwich Hospital, and constructed a statue of Joseph Banks for the British Museum. See George Jones, *Sir Francis Chantrey, R.A., Recollections of His Life, Practice and Opinions* (London: E. Moxon, 1849).
68. Felix Driver and Luciana Martins, 'Visual Histories: John Septimus Roe and the Art of Navigation, c. 1815–1830', *History Workshop Journal* 54(1) (Autumn 2002), 153.
69. Ibid.

70. In the *London Reader* in 1867, an article titled 'Australian Weapons' re-documented the material obtained by King's crew at Hanover Bay. The basket was mentioned here, but only because of what it contained: 'a small bundle of bark, tied up with more than unusual care ... several spearheads'. 11 May 1867, vol. 9, no. 209, p. 47.
71. Elisabeth Findlay, 'Peddling Prejudice: A Series of Twelve Profile Portraits of Aborigines of New South Wales', *Postcolonial Studies* 16(1) (2013), 2–27.
72. My italics show which phrases are directly from King's *Narrative*. Miscellanies, 'Scenery and Natives of New Holland', *Missionary Register*, September 1834, L. & G. Seeley, London, p. 424.
73. The recycling of such images has meant it can be difficult to trace them back to their original incarnation. Jessie Mitchell used this image of the Worora assuming it related to Wellington Valley for the cover of her book *In Good Faith? Governing Indigenous Australians through God, Charity and Empire, 1825–1855*, Aboriginal History Monograph 23 (Canberra: ANU E Press, 2011).
74. Northcote W. Thomas, 'Australian Canoes and Rafts', *The Journal of the Anthropological Institute of Great Britain and Ireland* 35 (January–June 1905), 55–79.
75. Natasha McKinney, *The Marquesan Collection at the British Museum, London: Genesis, Growth and Stasis*, MA thesis in museum studies (Palmerston North, New Zealand: Massey University, 2012), 46.
76. Personal communication, Gaye Sculthorpe, 4 March 2014. See also Arley Castle, Staffordshire, *Catalogue of the Valuable Contents of the Castle ... the Property of the Late Earl Mountnorris and Viscount Valentia, Deceased: Which Will Be Sold at Auction by Messrs. Fairbrother, Clark and Lye at the Castle, on Monday the 6th December, 1852, and Twelve Days Following* (London: J. Davy & Son, 1852).
77. James Pigot, *Pigot and Co.'s Pocket Atlas, Topography and Gazetteer of England* (London and Manchester: J. Pigot and Co., 1838), 26.
78. 'A Visit to Haslar Hospital, Near Portsmouth, England', *The Illustrated Magazine of Art* 4(24) (1854), 330.
79. 'Inauguration of the Bust of the Right Hon Sir John Pakington, in the Museum of Haslar Hospital', *Lancet*, 16 June 1860, 607–8.
80. McKinney, *The Marquesan Collection*, 46. See also David Wilson, *The British Museum: A History* (London: British Museum Press, 2002).
81. Haslar Hospital Museum visitor book, 31 May 1833, Institute of Naval Medicine, Gosport.
82. There are spearheads listed in the museum that could match Roe's collection from Hanover Bay. I am grateful to Daniel Simpson for sharing the information about Rev. Roe and Haslar Hospital with me.
83. Tiffany Shellam, *Shaking Hands on the Fringe: Negotiating the Aboriginal World at King George's Sound* (Crawley, WA: UWA Publishing, 2009), 183.
84. Ibid., 184.

85. Ibid.
86. Roe to his father, 28 September 1821, item 162, MLMSS 7964/vol. 5, safe 1/368, SLNSW.
87. Tiffany Shellam, '"Manyat's Sole Delight": Travelling Knowledge in Western Australia's Southwest, 1830s', in Desley Deacon, Penny Russell and Angela Woollacott (eds), *Transnational Lives: Biographies of Global Modernity, 1700–Present* (London: Palgrave Macmillan, 2010), 121–32.
88. Keith V. Smith, *King Bungaree: A Sydney Aborigine Meets the Great South Pacific Explorers, 1799–1830* (Kenthurst, NSW: Kangaroo Press, 1992), 30.
89. King, Remark Book, MLMSS 5277, CY reel 2565, items 1–3, SLNSW.

Bibliography

Arley Castle, Staffordshire. *Catalogue of the Valuable Contents of the Castle ... the Property of the Late Earl Mountnorris and Viscount Valentia, Deceased: Which Will Be Sold at Auction by Messrs. Fairbrother, Clark and Lye at the Castle, on Monday the 6th December, 1852, and Twelve Days Following.* London: J. Davy & Son, 1852.

Clarke, Phillip A. *Aboriginal Plant Collectors: Botanists and Australian Aboriginal People in the Nineteenth Century.* Dural, NSW: Rosenberg Publishing, 2008.

Denham, F.R.S. *Narrative of Travels and Discoveries in Northern and Central Africa: In the Years 1822, 1823 and 1824, by Major Denham FRS, Captain Clapperton and the Late Dr Oudney, Extending across the Great Desert to the Tenth Degree of Northern Latitude, and from Kouka in Bornou to Sackatoo, the Capital of the Felatah Empire.* 2 Vols. London: John Murray, 1826.

Douglas, Bronwen. 'The Lure of Texts and the Discipline of Praxis: Cross-Cultural History in a Post-Empirical World'. *Humanities Research* XIV(1) (2007), 11–30.

———. 'Naming Places: Voyagers, Toponyms, and Local Presence in the Fifth Part of the World, 1500–1700'. *Journal of Historical Geography* 45 (2014), 12–24.

———. *Science, Voyages and Encounters in Oceania: 1511–1850.* Basingstoke: Palgrave Macmillan, 2014.

Driver, Felix. *Geography Militant: Cultures of Exploration and Empire.* Oxford/Malden, MA: Blackwell Publishers, 2001.

———. 'Intermediaries and the Archive of Exploration', in Shino Konishi, Maria Nugent and Tiffany Shellam (eds), *Indigenous Intermediaries: New Perspectives on Exploration Archives* (Canberra: ANU Press and Aboriginal History, 2015), 11–29. http://press.anu.edu.au/titles/aboriginal-history-monographs/indigenous-intermediaries.

Driver, Felix, and Lowri Jones (eds). *Hidden Histories of Exploration: Researching the RGS-IBG Collections*. London: Royal Holloway, University of London, in association with the Royal Geographical Society, 2009.

Driver, Felix, and Luciana Martins. 'Visual Histories: John Septimus Roe and the Art of Navigation, c. 1815–1830'. *History Workshop Journal* 54(1) (Autumn 2002), 144–61.

Findlay, Elisabeth. 'Peddling Prejudice: A Series of Twelve Profile Portraits of Aborigines of New South Wales'. *Postcolonial Studies* 16(1) (2013), 2–27.

Hordern, Marsdern. *King of the Australian Coast: The Voyages of Phillip Parker King in the Mermaid and the Bathurst*. Carlton, Vic: Melbourne University Press, 1997.

Jones, George. *Sir Francis Chantrey, R.A., Recollections of His Life, Practice and Opinions*. London: E. Moxon, 1849.

Jones, Philip. 'The Theatre of Contact: Aborigines and Exploring Expeditions', in Martin Thomas (ed.), *Expedition into Empire: Exploratory Journeys and the Making of the Modern World* (New York: Routledge, 2015), 88–107.

Kennedy, Dane. *Last Blank Spaces: The Exploration of Africa and Australia*. Cambridge, MA/London: Harvard University Press, 2013.

King, Phillip Parker. *Narrative of a Survey of the Intertropical and Western Coasts of Australia, Performed between the Years 1818 and 1822*. London: John Murray, 1826.

Konishi, Shino, Maria Nugent, Tiffany Shellam and Allison Cadzow. 'Introduction', in Shino Konishi, Maria Nugent, Tiffany Shellam and Allison Cadzow (eds), *Brokers and Boundaries: Colonial Exploration in Indigenous Territory* (Canberra: ANU Press and Aboriginal History, 2016), 1–13.

Liston, Carol. 'The Dharawal and Gandangara in Colonial Campbelltown, New South Wales, 1788–1830'. *Aboriginal History* 12(1) (1988), 49–92.

Mann, David Dickinson. *Present Picture of NSW 1811*. London: John Booth, 1811 [Sydney: John Ferguson, in association with the Royal Australian Historical Society, 1979].

McKinney, Natasha. *The Marquesan Collection at the British Museum, London: Genesis, Growth and Stasis*. MA thesis in museum studies. Palmerston North, New Zealand: Massey University, 2012.

Metcalf, Alida. *Go-Betweens and the Colonization of Brazil: 1500–1600*. Austin, TX: The University of Texas Press, 2005.

Mitchell, Jessie. *In Good Faith? Governing Indigenous Australians through God, Charity and Empire, 1825–1855*. Aboriginal History Monograph 23. Canberra: ANU E Press, 2011.

Nugent, Maria. *Captain Cook Was Here*. Cambridge/Port Melbourne: Cambridge University Press, 2009.

Pigot, James. *Pigot and Co.'s Pocket Atlas, Topography and Gazetteer of England*. London and Manchester: J. Pigot and Co., 1838.

Shellam, Tiffany. 'Bungaree: The First Australian', *Australian Historical Studies* 44(2) (June 2013), 280–87.

———. '"Manyat's Sole Delight": Travelling Knowledge in Western Australia's Southwest, 1830s', in Desley Deacon, Penny Russell and Angela Woollacott (eds), *Transnational Lives: Biographies of Global Modernity, 1700–Present* (London: Palgrave Macmillan, 2010), 121–32.

———. 'Mediating Encounters through Bodies and Talk', in Shino Konishi, Maria Nugent and Tiffany Shellam (eds), *Indigenous Intermediaries: New Perspectives on Exploration Archives* (Canberra: ANU Press and Aboriginal History, 2015), 85–102. http://press.anu.edu.au/titles/aboriginal-history-monographs/indigenous-intermediaries.

———. *Shaking Hands on the Fringe: Negotiating the Aboriginal World at King George's Sound*. Crawley, WA: UWA Publishing, 2009.

Smith, Keith V. *King Bungaree: A Sydney Aborigine Meets the Great South Pacific Explorers, 1799–1830*. Kenthurst, NSW: Kangaroo Press, 1992.

———. *Mari Nawi: Aboriginal Odysseys*. Dural, NSW: Rosenberg Publishing, 2010.

Stokes, John Lort. *Discoveries with an Account of the Coasts and Rivers Explored and Surveyed during the Voyage of H.M.S. Beagle, in the Years 1837–38–39–40–41–42–43*. Project Gutenberg online. http://www.gutenberg.org/ebooks/12115 (accessed 2 June 2015).

Thomas, Northcote W. 'Australian Canoes and Rafts'. *The Journal of the Anthropological Institute of Great Britain and Ireland* 35 (January–June 1905), 55–79.

Turnbull, David. 'Boundary-Crossings, Cultural Encounters and Knowledge Spaces in Early Australia', in Simon Schaffer, Lissa Roberts, Kapil Raj and James Delbourgo (eds), *The Brokered World: Go-Betweens and Global Intelligence 1770–1820* (Sagmore Beach: Science History Publications USA, 2009), 387–428.

Wilson, David. *The British Museum: A History*. London: British Museum Press, 2002.

PART III

The Question of Gender

Chapter 8

GENDER AND THE EXPEDITION

FEMINIST ANTHROPOLOGIST ELSIE CLEWS PARSONS AND THE POLITICS OF FIELDWORK IN THE AMERICAS IN THE 1920s AND 1930s

Desley Deacon

'Kidder is off on another Expedition', the feminist anthropologist Elsie Clews Parsons wrote scornfully to a colleague in 1923.[1] With a sure sense of the modern, Parsons saw the Expedition with a capital 'E' as an outmoded and gendered form of science, part of the nineteenth-century culture she had spent most of her forty-nine years consigning to the dustbin.[2]

This chapter will explore the difference Parsons perceived between 'the Expedition' and the more personal, experimental, cooperative and gender-neutral fieldwork she practised, encouraged and funded among Franz Boas' students at Columbia University, New York, during the 1920s and 1930s. Parsons, who became the first female president of the American Anthropology Association in 1941, carried out fieldwork in the American Southwest, Mexico and Ecuador from 1912 to 1941, and her books, *Mitla: Town of Souls* (1936), *Pueblo American Religion* (1939) and *Peguche: A Study of Andean Indians* (1945), among many other studies, were the results of her innovative way of working and living – what she called 'getting life at first-hand'. At Columbia she supported, with her Southwest Society, the work of Ruth Benedict, Gladys Reichard, Ruth Bunzel, Leslie Spier, Leslie White, Melville and Frances Herskovits and Ralph Beals. Fieldwork was an important part of her feminist project, personally and for women professionals in general, encouraging the inclusion of women in fieldwork schools and urging men and women to view each other as colleagues who could go to the field together without embarrassment or censure.

Parsons was always critical of the 'expedition attitude' exemplified during the first half of the twentieth century by large East Coast institutions such as the American Museum of Natural History (AMNH), New York, under the presidency of Henry Fairfield Osborn, the Robert S. Peabody Museum of Archaeology at the Phillips Academy, Andover and the Carnegie Institution of Washington under John C. Merriam. Supported by wealthy WASP patrons, these institutions promoted eye-catching expeditions by rugged, manly (and Nordic) 'adventurer-scientists' such as Roy Chapman Andrews at the American Museum and Alfred Kidder at the Peabody and the Carnegie. With her own Southwest Society, she demonstrated how the dispersal of funds through a small, focused organization could be more efficient and allow greater experimentation, while at the same time promoting more modern gender relations.

Elsie Clews Parsons was born in 1874, the daughter of a wealthy New York banker and his socialite wife. From an early age, she resisted her mother's attempts to induct her into the mysteries and restrictions of upper-class social life and gendered behaviour. Instead of 'Coming Out', she entered Barnard College in 1892, graduating in 1896 and receiving a Master's degree the following year. She completed a PhD

Figure 8.1 Elsie Clews Parsons in the Southwest, 1920. By permission of the Rye Historical Society, Rye, New York.

in Education in 1899 and spent a year in the Sociology Department of Columbia University supervising students' fieldwork in New York's tenements. After much hesitation, she married lawyer and politician Herbert Parsons in 1900, in what she considered an 'experimental' marriage, and continued her teaching, writing and settlement house work through six pregnancies that resulted in four living children. During this period, she gained considerable notoriety as the author of a number of scathing feminist books on the sociology of the family and of gender, and on the ideological sources of inequality and violence.

After a trip to the American Southwest in 1910, Parsons gradually moved into anthropology and became an anomalous part of the circle of 'queer foreigners or half-foreigners' at Columbia University who had gathered around the charismatic Franz Boas, with whom she established a long and affectionate friendship.[3] During the teens and early twenties she did extensive fieldwork in the Southwest, also making major collections of African-American folklore, which she extended into the Caribbean in the twenties. In the late twenties she moved on to Mexico, where she spent long periods immersing herself in the daily life of Mitla, Oaxaca; her final fieldwork was in Ecuador in the late thirties and early forties. She was president of the American Folklore Society in 1919 and of the American Anthropology Association at her death in 1941.

The 'Expedition Attitude' and the American Museum of Natural History

The scientific world that Parsons encountered when she entered anthropology was dominated by the American Museum of Natural History. Founded in 1869 by a group of wealthy New Yorkers, its original Victorian Gothic building expanded along West 77th Street and Central Park West through the 1930s, when the New York State Memorial to the museum's patron saint, Theodore Roosevelt, was added to the Central Park West entrance. Much of the material in its spectacular display halls was collected during the museum's 'Golden Age', beginning in 1888, when its president Morris K. Jesup began to send out scientific and collecting expeditions, and ending in 1933, when his successor Henry Fairfield Osborn retired.

Jesup was a self-made, enormously wealthy banker, typical of the amateur science enthusiasts who made up the original trustees of the museum, ready to spend their own fortunes to support scientific research that interested them. Osborn, the son of a railroad tycoon, was, on the other hand, a scientist who rose from curator of vertebrate palaeontology and professor of zoology at Columbia University to president of the museum in 1908. Well connected and autocratic, Osborn had the ability to tap the interests and sentiments of the public and of the wealthy patrons who continued to support the museum's expeditions. He also had a genius for publicity. A headline in the *New York Times* soon after he became president announced, 'AMERICAN MUSEUM'S FIELD BROADENING: President Osborn's Report Shows Institution Has Made Searches That Are Worldwide. GREAT PUBLIC BEQUESTS'.[4] Morris Jesup had left the museum $1m, and Jesup's widow left a further $5m when she died in 1916. These bequests, and those of other trustees and benefactors, paid for the museum's enormously expensive expeditions during Osborn's presidency. Each year Osborn boasted in his Annual Reports of the number of expeditions the museum had sent out and he ensured that their exploits were closely followed by newspapers and magazines and disseminated in radio talks, public lectures and after-dinner speeches. During the 1920s the museum mounted over a hundred expeditions, and visitors to the museum could follow their progress on a wall map showing the locations of the exploring parties.[5]

The expeditions to 'Darkest China' led by Roy Chapman Andrews from 1916 to 1933 demonstrate vividly the characteristics of museum expeditions of the period. The first two Asiatic Expeditions, in 1916–17 and 1918–19, to search for and collect 'rare forms of animal life' in areas of China and Mongolia that 'had never been opened for exploration by white men', established the ingredients of an Osborn-Chapman expedition: a gruelling journey to an area that was difficult to access; use of the latest technology; complex organization of men and animals; high-level political negotiations for access; physical danger from men, animals, insects and illness; huge financial cost; and constant publicity, much of it supplied by Chapman's engaging and fluent pen in popular magazines.[6]

The success of Chapman's first two Asian expeditions whetted popular and scientific appetite for a succession of Central Asiatic Expeditions during the affluent 1920s, the first of which was undertaken from 1921 to 1923 in association with the magazine *Asia*. Writing from his camp near Ulissutai, Mongolia, where the climate is 'eleven months Winter and one month late Fall', he described a staff of six Americans, one Swede, one Duriat, nine Chinese and nine Mongols – 'to say nothing of seventy-five camels, one Siberian hunting dog, four pet red-billed crows and three young eagles'. Accompanied this time by geologists, the expedition carried out 'the longest continued topographical and structural geological survey which has ever been made in the same time'. The zoologists kept three Chinese taxidermists busy with large and small mammal specimens, and an artist and a photographer made records of the expedition and the collection.[7]

A series of exciting finds began in September 1922, when a cable from Andrews announced: 'Mongolia expedition discovers vast fossil fields, rich cretaceous, tertiary deposits. Skull baluchithorium. Complete skeletons small dinosaurs. Skulls rhinocerous. Twenty thousand feet film. Two thousand mammals'.[8] A year later, the discovery for the first time of dinosaur eggs excited much public and scientific interest.[9]

These Central Asian Expeditions were of particular interest to palaeontologist Osborn, who believed that 'the most important task before the age' was 'the discovery of the principles and modes of evolution' and that the department of vertebrate palaeontology was where these discoveries were likely to be made.[10] They were also central to his commitment, and that of his trustees, to the museum as a great educational institution. Sensational displays provided by heroic adventurer-scientists attracted visitors; they also attracted generous donations from the trustees and members of the public; and they impressed city politicians, who were persuaded, during Osborn's presidency, to pay for new buildings and the museum's maintenance costs.[11]

Believing that science demonstrated the evolution of the white race as the peak of civilization, Osborn and his fellow trustee Madison Grant established the Galton Society for the Study of the Origins and Evolution of Man at the museum in 1918. The society would further the study of eugenics and apply its findings to the American population, which, they believed, was being corroded by the huge influx of immigrants from Eastern Europe.[12] In his Annual Report for 1919, Osborn made the museum's link with eugenics clear. 'The question of the hour in everyone's mind is Americanization', he wrote, 'and the wisest people are those who see that Americanization is to be accomplished only through the spiritual, moral, mental and physical training of our youth according to American ideals'. 'Education is a great deal more than the three R's', he went on. 'So far as we are concerned, it is inspiration as well as information; it is instruction in local history, in geography and geology, in travel, in climatic laws, in simple economics, in all that concerns health of mind and body, in all branches of natural history, in all that living nature has to tell our youth.'[13] The following year, the Galton Laboratory was set up in the museum's Department of Anthropology under the direction of physical anthropologist Louis R. Sullivan.[14] (One of the society's proposed

Figure 8.2 Professor Henry Fairfield Osborn shares his package of 'Pirates' cigarettes with man on camel, Mongolia, 1923. Photograph by Roy Chapman Andrews. American Museum of Natural History Library Image # 251751. Reproduced with permission.

projects was 'a five-year field study of the Australian aborigines from the medical, biological and anthropological viewpoints'.[15])

In 1921 the museum hosted the Second International Congress of Eugenics. The *New York Times* report of its proceedings summarizes its main topics admirably: 'EUGENISTS DREAD TAINTED ALIENS: Believe Immigration Restriction Essential to Prevent Deterioration of Race Here. MELTING POT FALSE THEORY. Racial Mixture Liable to Lower the Quality of the Stock. Prof. Osborn's Views. THE LESSON OF EVOLUTION. Minute Scrutiny of Family History of Prospective Immigrants Is Advocated. Stricter Immigration Guard'.[16] In his opening address, Osborn rallied his audience to 'a serious struggle to maintain our historic republican institutions through barring the entrance of those who are unfit to share the duties and responsibilities of our well-founded government'. Those now judged unfit would be unfit forever, he warned: it was a matter of scientific fact 'that education and environment do not fundamentally alter racial values'.[17] Four years later, he attributed the passing of legislation 'stopping the flood of undesirable emigrants from every country in Europe' to 'the American Museum's efforts in organizing the International Congress of Eugenics and its collaboration with several of the great eugenists of this country'.[18]

The success of Andrews' Third Asiatic Expedition led Osborn to hope that Mongolia might yield up fossils of early man that would confirm his belief that this was what he called 'the cradle of Man' (or as a more romantic leader writer put it, 'the Garden of Eden').[19] As they began their campaign for funding for a more extensive expedition, the museum publicity machine emphasized this theme: 'BEGINNINGS OF MAN SOUGHT IN MONGOLIA: Andrews Is Returning to New York to Prepare for New Expeditions', reported the *New York Times* in November 1923.[20] Osborn, who had visited the expedition earlier that year, wrote in the Annual Report for 1924 that 'after personal examination of the ancient geologic and zoologic conditions in Mongolia', he was convinced that 'this is one of the most likely places in the world to find the ancestors of man, and determined efforts will be made to discover and describe remains of this most rare and elusive member of the Order of Primates'.[21] When it set out from Peking in 1925, it was the largest land expedition that had ever gone into the field. The company numbered forty men – Americans, British, Mongol and Chinese – representing the disciplines of palaeontology, geology, zoology, palaeobotany, botany, archaeology, topography and photography, and a caravan of 150 camels preceding five specially built touring cars and two trucks. They travelled more than 5,000 miles in the Gobi Desert, 2,200 of which were in new territory along the northern and southern bases of the Altai Mountains.[22] Chaotic conditions in China and Mongolia, however, sent them home within a few months.[23] The following year was one of even greater disappointment as Andrews and his expeditionary force 'spent month after month in doubt and anxiety and finally in despair because a strong hostile army extending across northeast China completely barred the entrance into Mongolia'.[24] Despite these setbacks, Andrews sought more funds for a further expedition in 1928 and 1929, an endeavour that was much aided by the 1926 publication of his book, *On the Trail of Ancient Man: A Narrative of the Fieldwork of the Central Asiatic Expeditions*.[25] They were able to return to the field in 1928, where they had to brave 'bandit bands'. In 1929, however, they were forced to abandon their plans because of increasing difficulties with the Chinese authorities in taking their finds from the country.[26]

'The great age of scientific exploration is just beginning', Osborn wrote to a potential donor in 1929,[27] and in his Annual Report for the following year he was sure that 'the spirit of adventure and exploration is rapidly spreading in this country, and young men and women in increasing numbers are volunteering either to accompany or to partly or wholly finance the invasion of hitherto unexplored regions'.²⁸ Andrews embarked on one more expedition in May 1930, still seeking 'Man's Cradle'.²⁹ The following year, however, the Chinese Commission for the Preservation of Antiquities refused permission for them to continue investigations in China and Inner Mongolia, alleging duplicity and arrogance on Andrews' part.³⁰ Although he continued to hope he would mount a further expedition for the museum based in Manchuria, this never eventuated.³¹ He became director of the museum, married again and settled into a New York penthouse surrounded by priceless reminders of his days as an explorer.³²

The 'Expedition Attitude' and Gender

Donna Haraway, in discussing the habitat groups supplied by the hunter-explorer Carl Akeley in the 1920s and 1930s for the museum's African Hall, argues that the exhibits of the period, drawn from the museum's expeditions, sacralized Manhood, along with Nature, Youth and the State.³³ This almost religious coupling of nature and youth in achieving manhood was emphasized by Henry Fairfield Osborn. 'Says Our Boys Need Cave-Man Training', the *New York Times* reported of Osborn in 1925.³⁴ Their *Sunday Magazine* a month later published a long article on 'Bringing Cave Life to the Modern Boy', illustrated by a cartoon of dinosaurs invading the streets of Manhattan. The article expressed admiration for Osborn's gift for publicity while gently satirizing his enthusiasm for such Cro-Magnon training.³⁵ Even if boys and young men were unable to return to earlier times, they could benefit from the stories and skills of museum adventurers. When the United States joined the war in 1917, the museum prepared motion pictures and illustrated recreational lectures for 'the boys in training and those at the front'. 'The expeditions sent by The American Museum of Natural History to the remote parts of the earth not only have brought together wonderful natural history collections, but are filled with adventures that stir the blood', Osborn wrote in his 1917 Annual Report. 'We believe that the tales of these experiences will appeal to the soldiers and sailors, since the successful explorer must possess in marked degree the qualities which make good fighting men.'³⁶ Following the war, the museum helped train scoutmasters in woodcraft and Indian lore.³⁷

During the 1920s, hundreds of boys wrote to the museum, asking how they could get a job there.³⁸ Young women, too, had responded to Roy Chapman Andrews' announcement of his latest expedition to the Gobi Desert. However, he told a Barnard College class, women had no place in exploration, because they were not suited to its physical strains.[39] When challenged on this by the Society of Women Geographers, he suggested that the problem actually lay elsewhere:

> in a big expedition where the staff included a half dozen or more men I considered women to be a great detriment; they could not do a technical job in most cases any better than a man, and their sex alone made for complications. A leader has enough difficulties in running a big expedition without saddling himself with any that can be avoided.

'If a man and his wife wished to explore alone', Andrews went on, 'or a woman wanted to organize her own expedition, there was no reason why such arrangements should not give excellent results ... I think, however, that you will agree with me that one or two women would not fit to advantage in a large party of men'.[40]

The American Museum of Natural History and Anthropology

The work of the American Museum of Natural History under Henry Fairfield Osborn stood for everything that Franz Boas and his circle opposed. Boas had been the recipient of the museum's largesse early in his career, when president Jesup had financed, from his own fortune, the wide-ranging Jesup Expedition, which Boas directed from 1897 to 1903. The strong-willed Boas did not enjoy being beholden to even such a generous patron as Jesup, and his angry resignation from the museum in 1905 left his relationship with the institution cool and suspicious. Over the next twenty years, as Osborn and many of the museum's trustees promoted their anti-immigrant stance, Boas became their outspoken opponent. Even though the museum's anthropology department was staffed to a large extent by his former students or their students, he did not trust his successor, Clark Wissler, to carry out the detailed, many-sided studies of cultures he considered necessary. Wissler, in turn, had to contend with Osborn's faint regard for anthropology ('merely opinion, or the gossip of the natives ... many years away from being a science' was, famously, his opinion).[41] Most of the administration's time and money went towards the development of the departments of birds, mammals and vertebrate palaeontology, Wissler remembered bitterly many years later.[42] In 1913, he managed to complete a twelve-year survey of the cultures and ceremonials of the Indians of the Northern Plains with the help of Robert Lowie and Alanson Skinner.[43]

Wissler intended a subsequent survey of the Southwestern pueblos to coordinate archaeological excavations with studies of the current indigenous cultures of the region. Begun in 1909 and funded by trustee Archer M. Huntington, it turned out to focus much more from 1912 onwards on the archaeological work of Nels Nelson, to which President Osborn and his publicity machine paid particular attention.[44] In an attempt to carry out the other half of his plan, Wissler assigned the study of the culture of the current inhabitants of the pueblos to H.J. Spinden. In 1915 and 1916 he commissioned Alfred Kroeber, Boas' former student, now at the University of California, to study the family and clan system at Zuni; and he moved Lowie temporarily from his work on the Southern Paiute of southwestern Utah and Nevada to spend a few weeks doing the same among the Hopi.[45] Kroeber's study was published in 1919, but Spinden, who was more interested in his work on Mayan art, never wrote up his findings, and Lowie, who moved to the University of California in 1921, did not publish his notes until 1929. By 1921, when the museum was launching its great Asiatic Expeditions, Wissler's department had halved its capacity, and his attention was redirected to the new areas that were attracting funding: Hawaii and the Pacific and the 'hot' topic of race mixing.[46] When in 1926 he published *The Relation of Nature to Man in Aboriginal America*, a popular version of his 1923 *Man and Culture*, which had generalized the results of the museum's two surveys, Boas dismissed it as 'conceited and slovenly'.[47]

Elsie Clews Parsons and the Southwest Society

In 1918, when Alfred Kroeber spent another year at the museum and consolidated his long friendship with Parsons, the two decided that something needed to be done to ensure that the cultures of the Southwestern pueblos were studied more thoroughly. Drawing up a list of the scattered (and mostly unpublished) recent work on the region, Kroeber despaired of Wissler ever 'bully[ing] his people into coming through'.[48] With Kroeber's encouragement, Parsons decided to set up a means of completing this task, an organization they called the Southwest Society. Launched at the annual meetings of the American Anthropological Association in December 1918, the Southwest Society was Parsons' personal rebellion against the 'manly' – and to her mind inefficient – 'Expeditions' of the AMNH and similar institutions. Writing to her husband, she described the society as 'a syndicalist experiment in research workers running their own machinery & controlling their own funds'.[49] Though everyone knew that the Southwest Society was a cover for Parsons' generosity, they went along with the fiction of cooperative funding, and friends and colleagues happily paid their one-dollar annual subscription and, where they were not members of the profession, joked about their participation.[50]

The financial resources of the Southwest Society were miniscule compared to those of the great institutions. Although Parsons came from a wealthy family, she did not, as she explained to one supplicant, have personal access to her father's or her husband's money.[51] When her father died in 1923 and her husband the following year, she was, indeed, wealthy in her own right and the generosity of the society was able to increase accordingly; but its assistance was always carefully calibrated to achieve a particular result.

Over the twenty-three years until Parsons' death, the Southwest Society funded the fieldwork of numerous scholars in cultural anthropology and folklore, mostly in the American Southwest, Mexico and the Caribbean. It also paid for secretarial and research assistance for Boas, financed the publication of the results of field trips, underwrote the *Journal of American Folklore* and gathered together, edited and published the diaries, field notes and papers of previous scholars and observers. An important outcome of the society's funding was to encourage and support the fieldwork of female students and early researchers, but it also helped many male students whose research did not fit the current interests of the large funding bodies. It rescued Melville Herskovits, for instance, from measuring African-American heads in New York under the auspices of the National Research Council, allowing him and his wife Frances to launch their work on African New World acculturation with extensive fieldwork in Surinam, Haiti and West Africa. Parsons also set Leslie White on his career path when she funded his fieldwork in the still under-studied Southwestern pueblos of Acoma, San Felipe, Santo Domingo and Zia. Perhaps most importantly, she persuaded Boas to return to the field and interest himself in the languages of the Southwest, bringing about an intellectual and physical rejuvenation that invigorated the Columbia department during the 1920s.[52]

It was in the encouragement of female scholars, however, that Parsons and the Southwest Society made its unique impact. In 1926, filling her in on the department's students, Boas wrote to Parsons:

> Ruth Bunzel is doing remarkably well ... Ruth Benedict is going to Europe this summer & intends to attend the Americanist Congress ... We do not know yet if Gladys [Reichard] is to receive her fellowship

... She has nearly finished her Navajo organization... Margaret Mead sends us many reports. I believe she is getting a good deal that will clinch the position that fundamental individual reactions depend upon cultural setting more than upon hereditary or innate characteristics.[53]

Ruth Bunzel, Ruth Benedict, Gladys Reichard and Margaret Mead were part of a close-knit group of graduate students who gathered around Boas during the 1920s, referring to him affectionately as 'Papa Franz' – a far cry from the forbidding and distant figure remembered by his earlier students. His reputation as a mentor of brilliant women was due, to a large extent, to Parsons' generosity and determination. From 1919 Parsons paid for a secretary for Boas. Esther Schiff and Ruth Bunzel, the first two to fill this position, were encouraged to move into graduate work with fieldwork paid for by Parsons. She also supported the brilliant Ruth Benedict with a research fellowship and fieldwork funding during the years after her graduation when she was unable to find a university position or research funding.

Writing to Parsons in 1923, Kroeber chided her affectionately: 'It looks as if the Southwest Society had the secondary aim of helping to liberate individuals'. He was referring to the gossip that had reached him that the society had funded the joint field trip of the married Pliny Goddard and the unmarried Gladys Reichard.[54] He was correct. From the time she began her fieldwork in the Southwest and made her place in the Columbia anthropological community, Parsons had quietly inaugurated a campaign against the sexual taboos that prevented men and women going to the field together. As she worked at the Southwestern pueblos and collected African-American folklore between 1915 and 1922, she was often accompanied on her field trips, without publicity, by her lover Grant LaFarge, who helped her as photographer and artist. In 1918, she and Alfred Kroeber had gone to Zuni together in what she hoped would be the beginning of a professional partnership (and which the widowed Kroeber hoped would be a romantic one as well). In 1919, she persuaded the sixty-one-year-old Boas, who had not been into the field for many years, to accompany her on a working trip to Laguna, and he went with her again the following year. Over the next three years, Parsons, Boas and his secretary (and later graduate student) Esther Schiff surveyed the Southwestern pueblos, Boas concentrating on language and the collection of texts, myths and folk tales, and Schiff and Parsons investigating ceremony, social organization, acculturation and pueblo psychology.

These field trips were deliberate attempts to break down the sexual and social barriers, so pervasive in the expedition attitude that prevented men and women from becoming unselfconscious colleagues.

She had insisted, in her feminist writing, that friendship was a crucial relationship between men and women because it was relatively free of convention. In the same way, she insisted that professional relationships should be free of artificial conventions that helped exclude women. In setting her own example, she made it clear that the nature of her relationships with her fieldwork companions was nobody else's business. Her trips with Kroeber and Boas, and her casual introduction of LaFarge from time to time, established the principle of privacy and reticence for men and women going to the field, helping, she hoped, to destroy a major stumbling block for women's careers.

Following Parsons' example (and supported by funds from the Southwest Society), Gladys Reichard was able to work with her lover, Pliny Goddard, on the Navajo between 1923 and 1928, completing investigations that the less imaginative Goddard would never have done, and advancing her career. And again following Parsons' example, Margaret Mead was able to go to the field in 1925 *without* her husband or any protector, despite the opposition of her mentor, Boas, and her lover, Edward Sapir.

Parsons' campaign attracted vituperative comments and determined obstruction from some of her male colleagues. 'She needs psychoanalysis', Edward Sapir wrote to his graduate student Leslie White in 1926, as White was leaving for fieldwork funded by Parsons. 'You might solve her difficulties by having intercourse with her. Her interest in "science" is some kind of erotic mechanism'.[55] (As Diane Losche points out [this volume], Sapir also widely slandered Mead as a 'bitch'.)

Parsons encountered particular, though more gentlemanly, obduracy from the Harvard 'half-breeds' Alfred Tozzer and Alfred Kidder, whose impeccable WASP credentials sat uncomfortably with their friendship with, and support of, Boas. Alfred Kidder, who led the Phillips Academy's Southwestern Expedition that excavated Pecos pueblo from 1915 to 1929, held the same firm belief as Roy Chapman Andrews that expeditions were masculine affairs and that the presence of women would cause sexual complications. After over thirty years in charge of archaeological digs in the American Southwest, Mexico and Central America, he noted, somewhat tongue in cheek, that 'in popular belief, and unfortunately to some extent in fact, there are two sorts of archaeologists, the hairy-chested and the hairy-chinned'. The hairy-chested archaeologist, he observed, is:

> a strong-jawed young man in a tropical helmet, pistol on hip, hacking his way through the jungle in search of lost cities and buried treasure. His boots, always highly polished, reach to his knees, presumably for

protection against black mambas and other sorts of deadly serpents. The only concession he makes to the difficulties and dangers of his calling is to have his shirt enough unbuttoned to reveal the manliness of his bosom.

'The hairy-chinned archaeologist', he continued, 'is old':

> He is benevolently absent-minded. His only weapon is a magnifying glass, with which he scrutinizes inscriptions in forgotten languages. Usually his triumphant decipherment coincides, in the last chapter, with the daughter's rescue from savages by the handsome young assistant.[56]

These caricatures provide reasonable self-portraits of Kidder in his various roles during a long career, although he went through his hairy-chinned phase as a young man. Newly graduated from Harvard, but with several years of archaeological work behind him, Kidder was appointed in 1915 to lead the Southwestern Expedition, sponsored by the Peabody Museum at Phillips Academy.[57] Every summer from 1915 to 1929, except during the war, he excavated, with the help of his wife Madeleine, professional colleagues and students and local labourers, an abandoned pueblo near Pecos, New Mexico, in what was at that time the largest excavation north of Mexico.[58] This was not an 'Expedition' in the sense that Andrews' expeditions were for the museum: it was hard outdoor work in the heat of the summer, but it did not require the organization of personnel, vehicles and supplies, nor the negotiations with foreign powers, that characterized the typical museum expedition. But Kidder had what his biographer called 'the expedition attitude' and continued to use the term throughout his career.[59]

Elsie Clews Parsons first met Kidder in 1920, when Kroeber had nominated her in his place to carry out a study of Jemez, the pueblo to which the surviving inhabitants of Pecos had migrated. The meeting had not gone well, possibly because she was accompanied by her lover Grant LaFarge. 'You are in the face of something difficult when you try for contacts with people like Kidder and Tozzer [Kidder's former Harvard teacher, who had also been visiting]', Kroeber warned Parsons when she wrote describing their meeting. 'Tozzer ... does want to be medieval until he's assured that the modernism which is facing him hasn't marked his code for attack.'[60] Nevertheless, Kidder did commission Parsons to carry out the Jemez study, but relations between them remained cool. 'It's very amusing, your hate of New England and New England's terror of you', Kroeber wrote to Parsons in 1922 when she felt her work was being ignored by Kidder:

Figure 8.3 Alfred Kidder (right) in his hairy-chinned period in 1912. Photograph by Jesse Nusbaum. Courtesy of Palace of the Governors Photo Archives (NMHM/DCA) Image # 060648.

Don't you realize that Kidder is afraid of you, Tozzer is afraid of you ... ? They put a good face on you, as well-bred drawing-room people put it on an enfant terrible; but they are wary all the time. You are a lady, so must be treated as one; but ladies don't talk of sex, and they would be ever so much more comfortable if you were a bit off-color and they could cut you. Indifference indeed! You may or may not know it, but you are getting a legitimate sadistic satisfaction out of making them wriggle. And I ... get my fun out of watching you do it.

Parsons, who had talked about sex all her adult life, had recently contributed the entry on 'Sex' in a volume on *Civilization in the United States*.[61]

Although Kidder did publish her monograph on Jemez pueblo in his Southwestern series, he still did not count her among the 'real' anthropologists. In 1927, when he called a historic meeting of Southwest scholars to organize the Laboratory of Anthropology at Santa Fe, he wrote to Boas that he 'could not manage to include Mrs Parsons'.[62] The summer field trips sponsored by the laboratory were to be an important part of graduate student socialization and professional bonding, and Parsons was determined, despite this snub, that female students were not to be excluded. When she heard that women were being left out of the first summer school in 1929, which was to be led by Kroeber and Kidder, she wrote to her old friend sharply, 'I am wondering why you have become so anti-feminist ... We understand it in Kidder who was subject to the boy boarding school influence at Cambridge, which you were free from'.[63] Coming to Kroeber's and Kidder's defence, Edward Sapir wrote to Parsons:

> There are, of course, difficulties about a mixed party in the field ... The type of woman who really means business scientifically, like Gladys Reichard or Eva Horner or Ruth Bunzel, is welcomed by all, but I'm afraid there are some – and they may be among the best intellectually – who create highly disturbing and embarrassing problems which are only beginning to be estimated at their true seriousness. It seems to me we have all been refraining, to a dangerous extent, from psychological honesty in these matters.[64]

Kidder himself defended his policy in a long letter to Parsons. 'There are two aspects to this situation', he wrote. 'The first is that it is very difficult, under certain conditions, to attach women to field parties, particularly where the group must break up into small units for scattered investigations. I have stated the position of the committee in an announcement of the award of fellowships ... as clearly as possible', he continued:

> The field work of the training course will be so arranged so that any properly qualified woman can be taken care of at some time during her graduate career. This year it was obviously not feasible to attach women to Kroeber's party. He could only take five people at the outside, and if any women were to go there would have to be at least two. The male applicants, as it happened, for ethnology, were, with one exception, all much better qualified than the women. You have been misinformed, I fear, in regard to Kroeber's attitude. He made no objection whatever, as far as I know, to women as such, but merely stated that it would be difficult for him to take them on for his proposed work on the Wallapai.

'I don't think I should be considered as a persecutor of the sex', Kidder concluded, 'as three out of my five students at Pecos will be women'.

Kidder's second point was less elaborated, but more telling. 'Much fewer professional positions (as field workers) are open to women', he wrote. 'The ratio being, as nearly as I can figure it, after consultation with Tozzer and others, about one to four or five. Hence, it would seem unsound policy to select for training (in field work) women much in excess of that ratio.'[65]

The bottom line was, of course, that Boas was the only male anthropologist who attempted to find funding and positions for his female students on anywhere near the same basis as his male students. Parsons no doubt pointed that out to Kidder, as he elaborated his position in a further letter on the 'perplexing' business of women in the discipline. It is obvious, he wrote, that anthropology should draw on the qualified women who come out of the universities. It should also have the benefit of 'the special abilities' of women for 'typological analysis, and certain branches of sociological investigation'. The trouble is, he went on, that it is hard to find professional positions for them. 'An anthropologist can make his living in one of two ways: as a teacher or a staff member of a museum or research institution.' 'Anthropology is taught at so few women's colleges that there are very few professional jobs open', he continued, voicing the current wisdom that women could (or should) not teach male students, 'and in the institutional field, women are handicapped by the fact that, whether justly or not, the heads of institutions feel that men are better qualified physically and temperamentally to head most institutions expeditions'. 'Another handicap', he added to this mother of four, 'and a very real one from the administrator's point of view, is that a young woman, because of the likelihood of her marriage, is an unreliable element to build into the foundation of a staff structure'.[66]

Kroeber was even less willing to concede the argument to Parsons. 'As to the summer', he wrote:

> does anyone see me wanting to lead a little harem around an Arizona railroad town for two months? I do not know much about the student body in the various institutions, but I did know many of the men at Chicago and Harvard had gone in for archeology and that nearly all women who were studying were ethnologists. I don't think I have changed in views, but if ever Anthropology gets to be prevailingly a feminine science I expect to switch into something else. So, I think, will you![67]

Reporting on the summer, Parsons' protégée Gladys Reichard felt they had won a partial victory. She had led an (all female) field party, one of whom spoke Navajo, she gloated: 'I have had my revenge! Personal, if not scientific'. Not only were they beautiful, she wrote of her students, but they could take care of themselves. Kidder's idea of a 'good' person was one who travelled with a bedroll. Her students had arrived with all living arrangements complete, while Sapir's eight male students did not have as much as a blanket among them. Kidder had two parties, she reported, one all men and one all women. 'The main contention of them all is that the girls are all right, entertaining, etc. But no good in science because you can't do anything with them. Kroeber ends all remarks with "Boas will place her".' 'It never seems to occur to any of them that if he can others might be able to were they sufficiently interested', she went on. 'All the men needed plenty of defense against my two girls', she ended triumphantly. 'But that condition will probably be nothing in favor of their being taken on another year.' 'Kroeber's answer to your message', she added: 'Tell Elsie I never was a feminist, & I'm not an anti-feminist now, appearances to the contrary notwithstanding'.[68]

Parsons came up against a virulent case of Kidder's obduracy in his dealings with Ruth Bunzel, Boas' former secretary and one of his most brilliant students. In 1929 Kidder had extended his reach to Mexican and Central American research when he became chairman of the division of historical research at the Carnegie Institution. Bunzel made an exploratory visit to Mexico that year in anticipation of applying for a Guggenheim award. After extensive conversations with Kidder, she was persuaded to take up her Guggenheim in Guatemala, where the Carnegie planned to begin research. Her understanding was that her work would be a general introduction and orientation to a large interdisciplinary study of the Guatemalan Highlands. After three extensive seasons in a ceremonial and market town, where she boarded with the German priest, she found herself passed over as Carnegie Fellow for a raw graduate with no experience or background of the area.

Responding to Parsons' sympathetic inquiry, Bunzel poured out her distress in a long letter that summed up the non-academic issues that weakened large institutional projects and kept women out of 'expeditions'. 'Kidder, I think, was quite without guile in all this', she wrote to Parsons:

> He is naive to the point of fatuousness in his dealings with people ... So he allowed himself to be led around by the nose by a pair of social climbers and two half-baked boys who were defending their interests in a racket. To please them he pulled the keystone out of a carefully thought out plan and permitted the lazy, the incompetent and the venal to run the Guatemala project to their own advantage. He is right, of

course. If it is to be run as a college on wheels (or wings?) with a lot of Best People running around looking at everyone else not working, I don't belong in it.

'What Tozzer had to do with this dirty business I can't make out', Bunzel continued,

> especially since he has no official connection with the Carnegie Institution. But his interest may, perhaps, be inferred from a conversation I had with him about a year ago ... We were discussing the job situation in general and he remarked quite suddenly that of course I was in a very difficult position; but I was Boas' student and Boas would have to take care of me. He had his hands full with his own students, although the Carnegie Institution was a Godsend to Harvard, since he could place most of his students there. As for me, he knew I was not destitute, he knew I had a family and they lived in a certain way, quite decently, and served good meals (sic!) and presumably they could take care of me. He felt no responsibility; if Boas thought I needed a job he would have to find it for me. This was said quite bluntly as it is written here – you know Tozzer. I remarked that he was quite misinformed if he thought that my family could or would 'take care' of me; and anyway it was not for that that I had fitted myself for a career in anthropology.

Particularly distressing to Bunzel was what she perceived as the lengths Kidder and Tozzer felt they had to go to in order to justify their actions. They were concerned that she had become the object of sexual innuendo – 'that I was Padre Rossbach's mistress; that we had indulged in wild orgies at the Convent (our innocent whisky and soda!)'. Worse still for this skilful and sensitive fieldworker, rumours circulated that she had 'serious trouble with the natives' – a tale, as she pointed out to Parsons, 'made up by someone out of whole cloth'. 'This has turned into quite a document', she concluded.

> Please don't let it go out of your hands ... When I urged you not to press this matter with Kidder or Tozzer I was thinking of my own interests ... It might improve the quality of work in Central America to have these scandals aired, but I don't want to offer my neck for martyrdom. Or do you think it's already in the noose? It looks so, doesn't it? Yours for science Ruth L. Bunzel.[69]

She was right. She never again received research funding and never obtained the tenured position the quality of her work warranted. Her brilliant work on Guatemala, *Chichicastenango*, was not published until the 1950s, by which time the whistle had been blown on Kidder's Central American operation by one of the Harvard gang's own, the young maverick professor Clyde Kluckhohn.[70]

Conclusion

Elsie Clews Parsons' campaign against the sexual and social conventions of 'the Expedition' could be seen as a David and Goliath battle. But though she did not win the battle for Bunzel and her kind against the forces of the giant Carnegie Institution, her side was at that same time winning the war. In 1932, the American Museum of Natural History was forced to suspend their 'great exploration program'.[71] The Chinese Commission for the Preservation of Antiquities refused to permit further work by the Central Asiatic Expeditions, and Roy Chapman Andrews returned from Peiping in October 1931 after a summer spent in fruitless efforts to arrange for a further expedition. As Clark Wissler wrote in a critical report in 1942, the museum 'no longer had anything to sell its wealthy admirers', and they 'consequently dropped away'.[72]

Osborn's retirement from the museum in 1933, at the age of seventy-five, and his death two years later, marked the end of the golden age of the expedition.[73] Ironically, Roy Chapman Andrews, the quintessential expedition leader, presided over the museum's 'drift' as director from 1935 until 1941, when he was forced out in a sweeping review and replaced by a young director who believed that evolution was 'a finished issue' and that evolutionary studies 'would contribute little further knowledge of any importance to the world'. The Department of Paleontology was abolished and the goal of making worldwide collections in every field was abandoned.[74]

Meanwhile, an elderly Boas appeared on the cover of *Time* magazine in May 1936, lauded for his heroic role in combating racial thinking.[75] On his eighty-first birthday in 1939 he was hailed by President Roosevelt and leading public officials, scientists, writers and educators for 'his leadership in organized efforts to make science serve humanity'.[76] He died three years later in the middle of a speech on racism.

The Carnegie's programme in Central America under Kidder's directorship began its 'long goodbye' in the late 1930s, finally winding up in 1958. Vannevar Bush, who replaced Kidder's friend, John C. Merriam, as head of the Carnegie Institution in 1938, was sceptical of the usefulness of Kidder's programme.[77] It suffered a mortal blow in 1940, when the Young Turk, Clyde Kluckhohn, compared current Mayan researchers with a scholar who 'devoted his life to writing a history of the three-pronged fork'. The final death knell was struck in 1946, when Kluckhohn's student, Walter W. Taylor, analysed the programme's aims and accomplishments in critical detail.

Kidder retired, crushed, in 1950. Recent commentators have argued for the value of the programme in establishing a foundation for later more modern and sophisticated research; but for many years it was criticized as methodologically and theoretically naive and without scientific achievement.[78]

Elsie Clews Parsons was no doubt pleased when she was elected the first female president of the American Anthropological Association for 1941, a year ahead of Alfred Kidder. By that time, Margaret Mead was the most famous anthropologist in the world, part of a new generation of women who went where they chose, with whomever they chose, dealing with the sexual entanglements of the field as part of modern life.[79] Gladys Reichard, alone after the sudden death of Pliny Goddard in 1928, had pioneered a new sort of anthropology when she went to live with the family of Red-Point, a well-known Navajo singer, in order to learn how to weave a blanket. And Parsons herself wrote a classic of this new genre based on the three seasons she spent living in the Mexican town of Mitla, Oaxaca.[80] 'The Expedition' had not disappeared, though its heyday was over; it continued to be the bastion of Kidder's hairy-chested adventurers and Osborn's boy explorers and their patrons.[81] But other, more personal forms of fieldwork had gained favour, such as those pioneered in America by Reichard and Parsons, and it was there that women flourished. This is intriguingly demonstrated in a review of the second volume of the report of the 1948 American-Australian Scientific Expedition to Arnhem.[82] Joseph B. Birdsell, Professor of Anthropology at the University of California, Los Angeles, considered it an important publication, despite its fragmented descriptive approach. Its importance lay, in his opinion, in the two papers by Margaret McArthur, one on food consumption by Aborigines living on naturally occurring foods and a second (with F.D. McCarthy) comparing the food procuring activities of coastal and inland groups. (McArthur's difficulties with the expedition are detailed in Harris, this volume.) But what made her research valuable for Birdsell was the fact that she had interpreted her data with a clear understanding of 'the real web of relationships' in gathering and sharing the food.[83]

In picking out McArthur's work as having promise for the future, Birdsell was in effect saying that her work was modern, while the expedition in which her work was embedded was outdated. In other words, the manliness of Roy Chapman Andrews at the American Museum of Natural History and Alfred Kidder at the Peabody Museum and the Carnegie Institution of Washington was no longer necessary for 'real' science.

Desley Deacon is Professor Emerita of History at the Australian National University and former director of Women's Studies at the University of Texas at Austin. She is the author of *Elsie Clews Parsons: Inventing Modern Life* (University of Chicago Press, 1997), editor of Elsie Clews Parsons, *Fear and Conventionality* (University of Chicago Press, 1997), and co-editor of *Transnational Ties: Australian Lives in the World* (ANU Press, 2008) and *Transnational Lives: Biographies of Global Modernity, 1700–Present* (Palgrave Macmillan, 2010). She recently completed a biography of the Australian-born actress Judith Anderson.

Notes

1. Elsie Clews Parsons [henceforth ECP] to Alfred Kroeber [henceforth ALK], [June] 1923, ALK Papers, Bancroft Library, University of California, Berkeley. Archaeologist Alfred Kidder had completed his excavation of Pecos pueblo in the American Southwest in 1922. He spent the 1923 summer 'cruising all over the Southwest' preparatory to writing up his conclusions on the seven-year project. See Alfred Vincent Kidder, 'An Introduction to the Study of Archaeology; with a Preliminary Account of the Excavations at Pecos', Papers of the Southwestern Expedition 1 (published for the Department of Archaeology, Phillips Academy, Andover, MA [New Haven, CT: Yale University Press, 1924]); and Douglas R. Givens, *Alfred Vincent Kidder and the Development of Americanist Archaeology* (Albuquerque, NM: University of New Mexico Press, 1992), 147.
2. I have written extensively about Parsons as a feminist and an anthropologist in Desley Deacon, *Elsie Clews Parsons: Inventing Modern Life* (Chicago, IL: University of Chicago Press, 1997).
3. See ALK to ECP, 14 July 1923, Elsie Clews Parsons Papers, American Philosophical Society [henceforth APS].
4. *New York Times* [henceforth NYT], 17 May 1908, 6.
5. NYT, 30 July 1922, 35.
6. E.g. Roy Chapman Andrews' series in *Harper's Monthly*, including: 'Traveling toward Tibet', 1 December 1917, 617; 'Camps in China's Tropics', 1 June 1918, 124; 'Across Mongolia by Motor-Car', 1 June 1919, 1; 'The Lure of the Mongolian Plains', 1 September 1920, 430; NYT, 20 March 1916, 6; 23 November 1919, E1; 1 August 1920, 80.
7. NYT, 21 August 1922, 19.
8. NYT, 28 September 1922, 9; 1 October 1922, 38; 11 January 1923, 3; 5 February 1923, 2; 29 July 1923, 5.
9. NYT, 26 September 1923, 1; 27 September 1923, 6; 28 September 1923, 6; 7 October 1923, XX1; 2 November 1923, 14; 7 November 1923, 17;

Observer [London], 4 November 1923, 9; *Sydney Morning Herald* [henceforth SMH], 25 December 1923, 5.
10. H.F. Osborn to Hermon C. Bumpus, 17 July 1908; to W.B. Scott, 18 March 1908, quoted in John Michael Kennedy, *Philanthropy and Science in New York City: The American Museum of Natural History, 1868–1968* (Yale University, ProQuest, UMI Dissertations Publishing, 1968), 162, 172.
11. Ibid., 256–59, 184.
12. Claudia Roth Pierpont, 'The Measure of America', *New Yorker*, 8 March 2004, 48–63.
13. AMNH Annual Report 1919, 19, online, Research Library, American Museum of Natural History, New York, NY http://lbry-web-003.amnh.org/museum/annual_reports.
14. AMNH Annual Report 1920, 28.
15. AMNH Annual Report 1924, 103.
16. NYT, 25 September 1921, 25.
17. Pierpont, 'The Measure of America', 57.
18. AMNH Annual Report 1925, 10.
19. NYT, 7 October 1923, XX1.
20. NYT, 7 November 1923, 17.
21. AMNH Annual Report 1924, 10–11. See H.F. Osborn, 'Where Did Man Originate? The Fitness of the Central Asian Plateau for Such a Terrestrial Animal as Fossil Man', *Asia* 24 (June 1924), 427–31, 489, 499; *Manchester Guardian*, 16 September 1924, 10; AMNH Annual Report 1926, 90.
22. AMNH Annual Report 1925, 73; NYT, 4 February 1925, 7; 2 March 1925, 19; 1 April 1925, 4; 19 April 1925, E2; 20 April 1925, 2; 21 May 1925, 3; 24 June 1925, 6; 17 August 1925, 16.
23. NYT, 21 August 1925, 12; 23 August 1925, SM7; 28 August 1925, 7.
24. AMNH Annual Report 1926, 20; SMH, 24 September 1926, 11; NYT, 28 October 1926, 17.
25. NYT, 30 November 1926, 3; 2 December 1926, 8; AMNH Annual Report 1927, 85–87; Roy Chapman Andrews, *On the Trail of Ancient Man: A Narrative of the Fieldwork of the Central Asiatic Expeditions* (New York: Putnam, 1926).
26. AMNH Annual Report 1928, 33; NYT, 15 April 1928, 15; SMH, 1 May 1928, 7; 20 May 1928, 45; 19 July 1928, 22; 20 August 1928, 11; 31 August 1928, 6; 21 October 1928, 35; 30 November 1928, 22; 13 June 1929, 18; 16 July 1929, 5; 28 September 1929, 3.
27. H.F. Osborn to James H. Perkins, 10 September 1929, quoted in Kennedy, *Philanthropy and Science in New York City*, 219.
28. AMNH Annual Report 1930, 21.
29. NYT, 3 May 1930, 10; 26 May 1930, 7; 27 May 1930, 11; 1 June 1930, E7; 10 August 1930, X11; 7 January 1931, 29; 8 January 1931, 18; 18 January 1931, 34.

30. NYT, 3 July 1931, 7; 4 July 1931, 10; 5 October 1931, 8; AMNH Annual Report 1932, 19.
31. NYT, 27 January 1932, 23; 26 August 1932, 19; 2 October 1932, 35; 20 December 1932, 4; 20 July 1936, 4.
32. NYT, 8 January 1935, 23; 15 February 1935, 16; 29 November 1936, RPA3. For Andrews' career, see Charles Gallenkamp, *Dragon Hunter: Roy Chapman Andrews and the Central Asiatic Expeditions* (New York: Viking, 2001).
33. Donna Haraway, 'Teddy Bear Patriarchy: Taxidermy in the Garden of Eden, New York City, 1908–1936', *Social Text* 11 (Winter 1984–85), 20–64, esp. 22.
34. NYT, 23 March 1925, 6.
35. NYT, 12 April 1925, SM9.
36. AMNH Annual Report 1917, 52.
37. AMNH Annual Report 1919, 103.
38. Kennedy, *Philanthropy and Science in New York City*, 156.
39. NYT, 6 January 1932, 23.
40. NYT, 6 February 1932, 19.
41. H.F. Osborn to W.B. Scott, 22 May 1908, quoted in Kennedy, *Philanthropy and Science in New York City*, 163.
42. Clark Wissler, 'Survey', first version, n.p., quoted in Kennedy, *Philanthropy and Science in New York City*, 173.
43. AMNH Annual Report 1913, 24. For Wissler's career, see S. Freed and R. Freed, 'Clark Wissler and the Development of Anthropology in the United States', *American Anthropologist* 85(4) (December 1983), 800–25.
44. See NYT, 24 April 1916, 9.
45. AMNH Annual Report 1915, 22–23, 78; A.L. Kroeber, 'Zuni Kin and Clan', *Anthropological Papers* XVIII(I) (1917), 39–204 (published 1919).
46. AMNH Annual Report 1921, 104–06; 1922, 105. See Warwick Anderson, 'Ambiguities of Race: Science on the Reproductive Frontiers of Australia and the Pacific between the Wars', *Australian Historical Studies* 40 (2009), 143–60; Anderson, 'Racial Hybridity, Physical Anthropology, and Human Biology in the Colonial Laboratories of the United States', *Current Anthropology* 53(S5) (April 2012), S95–107; Ross L. Jones and Warwick Anderson, 'Wandering Anatomists and Itinerant Anthropologists: The Antipodean Sciences of Race in Britain between the Wars', *British Journal for the History of Science* 48(1) (March 2015), 1–16.
47. Franz Boas [henceforth FB] to ECP, 28 March 1926, APS; Clark Wissler, *The Relation of Nature to Man in Aboriginal America* (New York: Oxford University Press, 1926); Wissler, *Man and Culture* (New York: Thomas Y. Crowell, 1923).
48. ALK to ECP, 23 April; 19 and 30 January 1919, APS.
49. ECP to Herbert Parsons, 12 and 28 December 1918, APS.
50. E.g. Learned Hand to ECP, 2 January 1919, APS.

51. ECP to Elizabeth Gurley Flynn, 10 December 1917, APS.
52. See FB to ECP, 20 June 1927, APS.
53. FB to ECP, 28 March 1926, APS.
54. ALK to ECP, [September] 1923, APS.
55. Sapir to White, 30 June 1926, Leslie White Papers, Bentley Historical Library, University of Michigan.
56. Charles Avery Amsden (ed.), *Prehistoric Southwesterners from Basketmaker to Pueblo*, introduction by Alfred V. Kidder (Los Angeles, CA: Southwest Museum, 1949), xi.
57. Kidder, 'Cliff Dwellers of the Painted Desert: A Seat of Ancient Culture Long before the Spanish Conquistadores', NYT, 28 December 1924, BR25.
58. Douglas W. Schwartz, 'Introduction', in Alfred V. Kidder, *An Introduction to the Study of Southwestern Archaeology* (New Haven, CT: Yale University Press, 2000), 17.
59. Givens, *Alfred Vincent Kidder*, 42.
60. ALK to ECP, 26 January 1920, APS.
61. ALK to ECP, 29 January 1922, Parsons Family Papers, Rye Historical Society, Rye, New York; ECP, 'Sex', in Harold E. Stearns (ed.), *Civilization in the United States: An Inquiry by Thirty Americans* (New York: Harcourt, Brace and Company, 1922), 309–18.
62. Kidder to FB, 31 May 1927, FB Papers, APS, quoted in Margaret Caffrey, *Ruth Benedict: Stranger in This Land* (Austin, TX: University of Texas Press, 1989), 261.
63. ECP to ALK, 26 March 1929, ALK Papers, Bancroft Library, University of California, Berkeley.
64. Sapir to ECP, 27 March 1929, APS.
65. Kidder to ECP, 30 March 1929, APS.
66. Kidder to ECP, 8 April 1929, APS.
67. ALK to ECP, 13 April 1929, APS.
68. Gladys Reichard to ECP, 25 August 1929, APS.
69. Ruth Bunzel to ECP, 16 July 1934, APS.
70. R.L. Bunzel, *Chichicastenango; a Guatemalan Village* (Locust Valley, NY: J.J. Augustin, 1952); Bunzel, 'Alcoholism in Central America', *Boletín del Instituto Indigenista Nacional* 3(1–4) (1957), 27–81; Clyde Kluckhohn, 'The Conceptual Structure in Middle American Studies', in Clarence L. Hay et al. (eds), *The Maya and Their Neighbors* (New York: Appleton-Century, 1940), 41–51, reprinted in Richard B. Woodbury, *Alfred V. Kidder* (New York: Columbia University Press, 1973), 74–81.
71. NYT, 5 January 1932, 27; 9 April 1932, 32; Annual Report 1932, 40.
72. Kennedy, *Philanthropy and Science in New York City*, 221.
73. NYT, 7 November 1935, 23.
74. Kennedy, *Philanthropy and Science in New York City*, 227–45; NYT, 8 January 1935, 23; 6 August 1941, 19; 11 November 1941, 25.
75. *Time*, 11 May 1936.

76. NYT, 10 July 1939, 14.
77. NYT, 3 June 1938, 23.
78. Kluckhohn, 'The Conceptual Structure', 74; Walter Taylor, *A Study of Archeology*, American Anthropological Association Memoir 69 (Menasha, WI: American Anthropological Association, 1948); Quetzil E. Castaneda, 'The Carnegie Mission and Vision of Science: Institutional Contexts of Maya Archaeology and Espionage', in Regna Darnell and Frederic W. Gleach (eds), *Histories of Anthropology Annual*, Vol. I (Lincoln, NE: University of Nebraska Press, 2005), 27–60.
79. Among the many books on Mead, see Lois W. Banner, *Intertwined Lives: Margaret Mead, Ruth Benedict, and Their Circle* (New York: Vintage, 2004); and the novel by Lily King, *Euphoria* (New York: Atlantic Monthly Press, 2014).
80. Gladys Reichard, *Spider Woman: A Story of Navajo Weavers and Chanters* (New York: Macmillan, 1934); and Elsie Clews Parsons, *Mitla: Town of Souls* (Chicago, IL: University of Chicago Press, 1936). See also Lessie Jo Frazier, 'Genre, Methodology and Feminist Practice: Gladys Reichard's Ethnographic Voice', *Critique of Anthropology* 13(4), 363–78; and Deacon, *Elsie Clews Parsons*, 319–50.
81. See, for example, Warwick Anderson, 'Hybridity, Race, and Science: The Voyage of the Zaca, 1934–1935', *Isis* 103(2) (2012), 229–53.
82. Martin Thomas and Margo Neale (eds), *Exploring the Legacy of the 1948 Arnhem Land Expedition* (Canberra: ANU E Press, 2011).
83. Joseph B. Birdsell, 'Review of *Records of the American-Australian Scientific Expedition to Arnhem Land, Number 2: Anthropology and Nutrition*, by Charles P. Mountford', *American Anthropologist*, N.S. 64(2) (April 1962), 410–12.

Bibliography

Amsden, Charles Avery (ed.). *Prehistoric Southwesterners from Basketmaker to Pueblo*. Introduction by Alfred V. Kidder. Los Angeles, CA: Southwest Museum, 1949.

Anderson, Warwick. 'Ambiguities of Race: Science on the Reproductive Frontiers of Australia and the Pacific between the Wars'. *Australian Historical Studies* 40 (2009), 143–60.

———. 'Hybridity, Race, and Science: The Voyage of the Zaca, 1934–1935'. *Isis* 103(2) (2012), 229–53.

———. 'Racial Hybridity, Physical Anthropology, and Human Biology in the Colonial Laboratories of the United States'. *Current Anthropology* 53(S5) (April 2012), S95–107.

Andrews, Roy Chapman. 'Across Mongolia by Motor-Car'. *Harper's Monthly*, 1 June 1919, 1.

———. 'Camps in China's Tropics'. *Harper's Monthly*, 1 June 1918, 124.

———. 'The Lure of the Mongolian Plains'. *Harper's Monthly*, 1 September 1920, 430.

———. *On the Trail of Ancient Man: A Narrative of the Fieldwork of the Central Asiatic Expeditions*. New York: Putnam, 1926.

———. 'Traveling toward Tibet'. *Harper's Monthly*, 1 December 1917, 617.

Banner, Lois W. *Intertwined Lives: Margaret Mead, Ruth Benedict, and Their Circle*. New York: Vintage, 2004.

Birdsell, Joseph B. 'Review of *Records of the American-Australian Scientific Expedition to Arnhem Land, Number 2: Anthropology and Nutrition*, by Charles P. Mountford'. *American Anthropologist*, N.S. 64(2) (April 1962), 410–12.

Bunzel, R.L. 'Alcoholism in Central America', *Boletín del Instituto Indigenista Nacional* 3(1–4) (1957), 27–81.

———. *Chichicastenango; a Guatemalan Village*. Locust Valley, NY: J.J. Augustin, 1952.

Caffrey, Margaret. *Ruth Benedict: Stranger in This Land*. Austin, TX: University of Texas Press, 1989.

Castaneda, Quetzil E. 'The Carnegie Mission and Vision of Science: Institutional Contexts of Maya Archaeology and Espionage', in Regna Darnell and Frederic W. Gleach (eds), *Histories of Anthropology Annual*, Vol. I (Lincoln, NE: University of Nebraska Press, 2005), 27–60.

Deacon, Desley. *Elsie Clews Parsons: Inventing Modern Life*. Chicago, IL: University of Chicago Press, 1997.

Frazier, Lessie Jo. 'Genre, Methodology and Feminist Practice: Gladys Reichard's Ethnographic Voice', *Critique of Anthropology* 13(4), 363–78).

Freed, S., and R. Freed. 'Clark Wissler and the Development of Anthropology in the United States'. *American Anthropologist* 85(4) (December 1983), 800–825.

Gallenkamp, Charles. *Dragon Hunter: Roy Chapman Andrews and the Central Asiatic Expeditions*. New York: Viking, 2001.

Givens, Douglas R. *Alfred Vincent Kidder and the Development of Americanist Archaeology*. Albuquerque, NM: University of New Mexico Press, 1992.

Haraway, Donna. 'Teddy Bear Patriarchy: Taxidermy in the Garden of Eden, New York City, 1908–1936'. *Social Text* 11 (Winter 1984–85), 20–64.

Jones, Ross L., and Warwick Anderson. 'Wandering Anatomists and Itinerant Anthropologists: The Antipodean Sciences of Race in Britain between the Wars'. *British Journal for the History of Science* 48(1) (March 2015), 1–16.

Kennedy, John Michael. *Philanthropy and Science in New York City: The American Museum of Natural History, 1868–1968*. Yale University, ProQuest, UMI Dissertations Publishing, 1968.

Kidder, Alfred Vincent. 'An Introduction to the Study of Archaeology; with a Preliminary Account of the Excavations at Pecos'. Papers of the Southwestern Expedition 1. Published for the Department of

Archaeology, Phillips Academy, Andover, MA. New Haven, CT: Yale University Press, 1924.

King, Lily. *Euphoria*. New York: Atlantic Monthly Press, 2014.

Kluckhohn, Clyde. 'The Conceptual Structure in Middle American Studies', in Clarence L. Hay et al. (eds), *The Maya and Their Neighbors* (New York: Appleton-Century, 1940), 41–51. Reprinted in Richard B. Woodbury, *Alfred V. Kidder* (New York: Columbia University Press, 1973), 74–81.

Kroeber, A.L. 'Zuni Kin and Clan'. *Anthropological Papers* XVIII(I) (1917), 39–204.

Osborn, H.F. 'Where Did Man Originate? The Fitness of the Central Asian Plateau for Such a Terrestrial Animal as Fossil Man'. *Asia* 24 (June 1924), 427–31, 489, 499.

Parsons, Elsie Clews. *Mitla: Town of Souls*. Chicago, IL: University of Chicago Press, 1936.

———. *Peguche: A Study of Andean Indians*. Chicago, IL: University of Chicago Press, 1945.

———. *Pueblo Indian Religion*. Chicago, IL: University of Chicago Press, 1939.

———. 'Sex', in Harold E. Stearns (ed.), *Civilization in the United States: An Inquiry by Thirty Americans* (New York: Harcourt, Brace and Company, 1922), 309–18.

Pierpont, Claudia Roth. 'The Measure of America'. *New Yorker*, 8 March 2004, 48–63.

Reichard, Gladys. *Spider Woman: A Story of Navajo Weavers and Chanters*. New York: Macmillan, 1934.

Schwartz, Douglas W. 'Kidder and the Synthesis of Southwestern Archeology', in Alfred V Kidder, *An Introduction to the Study of Southwestern Archaeology* (New Haven, CT: Yale University Press, 2000), 1–55.

Taylor, Walter. *A Study of Archeology*. American Anthropological Association Memoir 69. Menasha, WI: American Anthropological Association, 1948.

Thomas, Martin, and Margo Neale (eds). *Exploring the Legacy of the 1948 Arnhem Land Expedition*. Canberra: ANU E Press, 2011.

Wissler, Clark. *Man and Culture*. New York: Thomas Y. Crowell, 1923.

———. *The Relation of Nature to Man in Aboriginal America*. New York: Oxford University Press, 1926.

Woodbury, Richard B. *Alfred V. Kidder*. New York: Columbia University Press, 1973.

Chapter 9

WHAT HAS BEEN FORGOTTEN?

THE DISCOURSES OF MARGARET MEAD AND THE AMERICAN MUSEUM OF NATURAL HISTORY SEPIK EXPEDITION

Diane Losche

In 1931 Margaret Mead with her husband and fellow anthropologist, the New Zealander Reo Fortune, set out on the eighteen-month American Museum of Natural History Expedition to the Sepik region of New Guinea.[1] The public learned of this expedition in the newspaper headline:

> Going and Getting It for Science: White Woman Studies Ghost Ruled Savages in Melanesia[2]

Mead and Fortune worked in three communities in the Sepik River region that came to be known as the Arapesh, the Mundugumor and the Tchambuli.[3] Although this was a joint expedition, funding for the couple came from different sources. Mead was financed by the Herbert Voss Fund, a private fund within the American Museum of Natural History (AMNH), while Reo Fortune was supported by the Social Science Research Council.[4] The expedition had a number of aims but a main one for Mead was the study of the influence of culture on the acquisition of gender roles.

This expedition is not a forgotten event. Indeed, it is one of the best-known anthropological field trips of the twentieth century. The expedition resulted in significant research outcomes concerning the Sepik region as well as major statements about the cultural shaping of gender. Books and articles of major significance were published, one of which, Mead's *Sex and Temperament in Three Primitive Societies* (1935), has had numerous reprintings and is still assigned in university courses.⁵ In addition, hundreds of artefacts were collected for the museum. The expedition was particularly foundational in that it involved the first specifically anthropological 'mapping' of the Sepik region; the results set questions that determined the research agendas of many anthropologists who followed.⁶ If this field trip is a famous event in anthropological history, some aspects of the expedition, *as expedition*, have been obscured because of the particular way it was inscribed in its many afterlives. This chapter will suggest that a return to the frame of the expedition can illuminate the importance of this particular moment, for it reveals how expeditionary history is implicated in the development of professional fieldwork in anthropology. In particular, the focus here is on the politics of gender and the gendered division of labour in the collection of ethnological materials during the expedition. On this field trip, Mead refined her distinctive methodology, begun during her research in Samoa in 1923: intensive interaction with and recording of the activities of women and children in order to build a picture of the way culture influences gender roles. Her famous research in Samoa was groundbreaking in that she was the youngest woman, and one of the first, to undertake fieldwork alone.⁷ This investigation had already made a significant contribution to the methodology of fieldwork, specifically the idea that it was worth spending time with young women. The Sepik Expedition was more ambitious in that she intended to compare the development of gender roles in different parts of a single region.

While the development of field methodologies distinctive to anthropology is complex, what is crucial for this chapter is that fieldwork in the early twentieth century came to be seen as somewhat different from commonly understood ideas of expeditionary inquiry.⁸ If the model of anthropological expeditions in Melanesia, such as the Cambridge Anthropological Expedition to the Torres Straits, tended to be group events with male leaders and a military ethos of invasion and exploration, anthropological fieldwork would become configured as an often singular activity involving face-to-face immersion in one small community for long periods of time.⁹ But this emergence did not occur all at once, nor was it ever simply a question of fieldwork versus expedition. As will be seen, Mead could present her Sepik plans as more or less expeditionary depending on her audience. Nevertheless, Mead and other women of her generation were pioneers, the first to spend significant amounts of time with women and children to elicit information. Mead argued for the centrality of that information, discouraging reliance solely on what men, particularly senior men, said. During the Sepik Expedition, for example, Mead would come to disagree with

Fortune about an important kinship structure of the Mundugumor, based on material gathered while speaking with a child. The Sepik Expedition is of particular interest here for the way in which its gender politics reflected a significant transition, but its biographical framing as an event involving the famous Margaret Mead has obscured some of its notable achievements as well as its failings.

Certain events and texts from the expedition have become iconic and multiply inscribed, while others have been ignored, due to the entanglement of this particular journey in an overriding concern of metropolitan centres during the twentieth century: the power and autonomy of individual women both professionally and sexually. Mead became a mythological figure inducing anxiety as well as awe. Because of Mead's fame – she is often referred to as the first and most successful public anthropologist – one can find materials from the Sepik sojourn in novels as well as in academic articles and biographies, and across fields such as American studies, political science, the history of race, the history of anthropology and queer studies.[10] In this chapter I do not seek to overview the many texts that deploy the Sepik materials, as if to extract some coherent truth – a pursuit that has absorbed much of the energy of those who have contributed to these narratives. Rather, I delineate fault-lines and absences to account for why this narrative has its particular shape in relation to debates about gender. This chapter will suggest that structural aspects of the expedition, particularly the gendered division of labour, have been obscured by a rather circular debate around the factual 'truth' about Margaret Mead and, by implication, some elusive 'truth' about sexuality and gender in general.

The Sepik Expedition of the American Museum of Natural History

As Desley Deacon points out, by the 1920s a generation of women anthropologists, most of whom were students of Franz Boas in the Department of Anthropology at Columbia University, was changing the way in which anthropology was conducted (see Deacon, this volume). Challenging the imperial model of the expedition as masculine, military and invasive, Elsie Clews Parsons and other female students of Boas argued for a more gender-neutral, personal and cooperative form of field research. Mead was part of this talented group and, by the time of the Sepik Expedition, the most well known due to the success of *Coming of Age in Samoa*, published in 1928. From this point on, Mead was seen as an exceptional figure and she became the subject of intense media interest.[11] Her celebrity – always linked to her interest in the development of gender and sexuality, the so-called 'woman question' – would mark the discourses around the Sepik Expedition from its very beginnings, as a New York newspaper report reveals:

> DR MARGARET MEAD TO JOIN THIRD EXPEDITION
> To Find Out How Girls Learn to Be Girls, she says.[12]

If Mead was the intrepid modern woman scientist, celebrated in the popular press, the expedition was also linked in the public mind with the AMNH, the institution in New York where the notion of the expedition as an imperial and masculine undertaking, conducted for the sake of truth and science, was most firmly entrenched. It was also Mead's place of employment. When she was hired in a junior curatorial role in 1926, Mead joined a museum already famous for extravagant ventures to places such as the Gobi Desert.[13] The same newspaper article that celebrated Mead as a white woman studying ghost-ruled savages (cited above) also said of the museum:

> New Yorkers today are piercing dark jungles. They are crossing far deserts. They are facing strange hazards. It's a matter of course. They're truth hunters. They're members of expeditions of the American Museum of Natural History. They go and get odd, new facts. They bring them back and interpret them for the sake of science.[14]

The museum celebrated its links to the national history of the United States while also foregrounding the modernity of its research agenda, contrasting primitive locales with modern scientists. This juxtaposition of imperial primitivism and scientific modernity is embedded even in its architecture. The Entrance Hall's spectacular murals celebrate the life of the American expansionist President Theodore Roosevelt, while the adjacent Akeley Hall of African Mammals features extravagant dioramas in spectacular Beaux Arts architecture.[15] The modernity of its scientific agenda was often advertised in the personage of Dr Margaret Mead, a young woman heading to the South Seas with formidable energy, intelligence and bravado, to retrieve not so much artefacts, but knowledge and scientific truth. The fact that the museum, rather than a university, sponsored the expedition marked it with a more imperial aura than other field research of its time.

By the time of the Sepik venture, university anthropology, certainly in New York and particularly within the influential circle around Franz Boas at Columbia, had definitively moved from an interest in the material and evolutionary aspects of humanity – still foregrounded in the AMNH – to the immaterial aspects of culture. The eminent historian of anthropology George Stocking has pointed out that the group of anthropologists, including Ruth Benedict and Mead, who came to be known as the 'School of Culture and Personality', was seen, in the United States at least, as offering an alternative to the outmoded evolutionary concept of race. (Mead's *Sex and Temperament in Three Primitive Societies* was a key text in this regard.) Stocking suggests: '"culture and personality" became in a sense the functional anthropological equivalent of "race" explaining the same sorts of presumed psychological uniformities in very different terms, as "culture" took over the determinism that had been governed by "race"'.[16] The change from an evolutionary concept of culture, with a concomitant interest in artefacts, to a non-material one was more uneven and contradictory than Stocking credits, particularly at the AMNH where the vast collections, the practice of mounting public exhibitions and the large number of archaeologists and physical anthropologists on the staff inevitably steered ideas and policies. Mead's curatorial duties required her to collect and oversee collections and exhibitions. While she did gather many artefacts (in total about 2,600), collecting was never her forte. Her major interests were always in the non-material aspects of culture.[17]

In the 1920s and 1930s, Mead was in somewhat difficult territory in terms of her multiple and contradictory allegiances. Her intellectual loyalty was with her mentor, Boas, who had moved, under acrimonious circumstances, from the AMNH to Columbia University, dissatisfied with the museum's intellectual orientation and administration. At the same time, certain ties between the two institutions remained. Mead, who had been instructed on the museum collections by Ruth Benedict, another of her significant mentors, was hired despite the rifts. As her many writings attest, Mead developed a keen ability to adapt her language to suit different audiences and contexts. Some of this was necessitated early on by her need to keep Boas and Benedict on the one hand, and her various bosses at the AMNH on the other, reasonably happy.

The minefield of variant ideologies that made up the complex mosaic of New York institutions was exacerbated for Mead by the fact that her boss, the president of the AMNH for twenty-five years, was Henry Fairfield Osborn. A scion of one of America's wealthiest families, Osborn was a palaeontologist, a racist and sometime president of the American Society of Eugenics.[18] The work of Boas and his many students was, sometimes implicitly and sometimes explicitly, directed against the growing ascendancy of this pseudo-science that supported racist agendas of all kinds.[19] Mead seems to have attempted to deal with Osborn by keeping a very low profile within the museum. The fact that she was employed in the belly of the very beast that Boas so committedly opposed may have dictated Mead's attitude to the museum.

> I learned very early ... that I would be a cancer in any organization if anybody knew what I was doing.[20]

Avoiding Osborn may not have been difficult since the museum was marked by a routine sexism that excluded her from male networks of power, influence and funding. Mead barely knew her fellow curators, who treated her with a 'mixture of wary chivalry and neglect'.[21] She complained of being underfunded and ill paid. Most tellingly, this woman, who happened to be the most famous public anthropologist in the world, was not made a full curator until 1964.[22]

All these factors influenced the hybrid structure of the Sepik Expedition, which was both imperial and modern. Mead's agenda, the cultural shaping of gender, was undoubtedly part of the wider liberal project of cultural relativism. Nevertheless, she could also frame the expedition as an exploratory mapping of 'virgin' territory. Melanesia was posited as one of the great and as yet 'untouched' sources for anthropological exploration where the need for research was especially urgent because the area was rapidly being missionized.[23] This is most clearly seen in Mead's discussion of the choice of the second of the three sites that the Sepik Expedition covered, the community she came to call the Mundugumor on the Yuat River, a tributary of the Sepik. She and Fortune ruled out other areas on the Sepik River because of the presence of two other anthropologists, Gregory Bateson and Richard Thurnwald: 'we selected the nearest tribe that was accessible by water which was unmissionized and which seemed least likely to have been extensively influenced, either linguistically or culturally, by either the Iatmul or the Banaro'.[24] Mead would undoubtedly have defended her choice as the only sensible course of action, given that there were so few anthropologists working 'against time', as she and others saw it, to map in some way this complex cultural area. But her language reveals the notion of a culture that is both 'untouched' and the possession of particular anthropologists.

While the Sepik Expedition may have had an imperial profile because of its genesis in the AMNH, Mead could be very critical of the colonial maltreatment of the peoples of Melanesia. She articulated the developing notion of fieldwork as a somewhat cooperative activity, noting the dependence of anthropologists on the people among whom they lived.

> The ethnologist cannot march upon a native community like an invading army, for that community is going to be not only a source of labor and food, but also the very stuff of his investigation. He must slip in quietly, lower himself or herself as gently as possible into the placid waters of native life, make the unprecedented arrival of an inquiring white person as inconspicuous as possible. Most indigenous people ... had only one kind of contact with white people, as inferiors ... Into this setting stepped ethnologists who could not work unless these carefully constructed barriers for the peace of the white invader were summarily shattered.[25]

Mead's field methods reflected her commitment to this gentler approach. At their first field site, among the Arapesh, while Fortune spent much of his time moving about the region as the major collector of artefacts, Mead stayed in the village of Alitoa, with women and children as well as men. Remaining in the village was also necessary because of a weak ankle. Nevertheless, it conformed to her notions that immersion in one locale was an important methodology.

Figure 9.1 Conducting Public Flutes, Alitoa Village, Arapesh, 1932. Gelatin silver photograph by Reo Fortune. Manuscript Division, Library of Congress (147). By permission of the American Anthropological Association and the Library of Congress.

Because of Mead's celebrity status, it often seemed that she was the only person who went to the Sepik, but it was a husband and wife team. This imbalance between famous wife and shadow husband would have an enormous effect on all the narratives about the expedition, and may have set in motion some of the major conflicts between the couple. Mead herself was very careful to emphasize the role of Reo Fortune. In the planning of the expedition, a clear division of labour between the pair was envisaged. Although both anthropologists had done solo field research (Mead in Samoa and Fortune on the island of Dobu in Melanesia), as well as previous research as a couple (on Manus Island), the conditions of the Sepik were such that Mead felt fieldwork on her own would have been unviable, even if she had wanted it. She always expressed a special indebtedness to Fortune, whose presence was necessary in multiple ways.[26] The gender separation of Sepik River societies meant that only a man could collect certain kinds of data. In addition, Fortune had a background in psychology (he had already published a book on dreams), which she hoped would assist her in understanding gender and sex roles. The inaccessibility of the region and its difficult terrain made it impossible for her to navigate on her own. Mead also acknowledged Fortune's linguistic skills as being of singular importance. She clearly foregrounds his role in her preface to *Sex and Temperament*:

> My major thanks are due to Dr. Fortune, for the partnership that made it possible for me to work with peoples more savage and more inaccessibly located than I would have been able to reach alone ... and for much concrete material concerning the men's cults and all those aspects of the men's lives which a woman ethnologist is practically debarred from studying ... The division of labour between us varied from one tribe to another.[27]

If Reo Fortune became the shadow husband on the expedition, he was not without a considerable professional anthropological profile of his own when the couple set out. He was a Cambridge scholar whose fieldwork in Melanesia had resulted in a work considered groundbreaking in its time, *Sorcerers of Dobu* (1932).[28] However, his status as a New Zealander rendered him marginal in northern hemisphere metropolitan centres. Whether in Cambridge or New York, his colonial status was marked – and often remarked upon. At the time of the Sepik Expedition he was without a permanent position, despite the attempts of Mead, Benedict and Boas to rectify this situation. His marginality, coupled with Mead's celebrity, resulted in the unusual situation of a woman being positioned as the central figure and 'leader' of the undertaking – as if an expedition of only two people could not set forth without a 'leader'.

If the plan for the Sepik Expedition was to have a clear and gendered division of labour, with Fortune focusing on religion, men's cults and language, and Mead on women and children, the reality was very different. The inability to maintain gendered and separate spheres of activity caused some of the most serious rifts between the couple. Mead later commented:

> Perhaps no other endogamous marriages ... present quite as many hazards. The members of a good anthropological team in a difficult field location are as interdependent as two trapeze artists ... It is, in retrospect, quite impossible to disentangle the threads of their expert perceptions, so as to say whose insight was more significant or who got the first clue to some unsuspected aspect of culture. When marriages between anthropologists are based on marked contrasts in temperament and tempo, as is for many reasons most desirable, there is a further hazard in the way in which cultural style, the physique and habitat of a people may lock into the preferences of one of the pair and repel the other.[29]

The problems with this gendered division of labour and the relationship between the two became clearest during the Mundugumor period, as Nancy McDowell demonstrates in her reconstruction of the ethnography from that region, based on the field notes of Mead and Fortune.[30] The two had intended to follow the combined methodologies and division of labour that they had already used in Manus and Arapesh societies. In an unpublished manuscript, Mead describes how these plans were abandoned, apparently at Fortune's instigation:

> We always specialized in different aspects of the culture, after an initial period on the census and language, but in Arapesh Dr. Fortune had specialized on the language, texts of myths, trade, and the men's sacra. The Mundugumor language proved to be less interesting than Arapesh and Dr. Fortune decided that I could do the language, the children and technology while he would specialize on the social organization, kinship, warfare and religion ...[31]

This passage suggests the control that Fortune could exert in the relationship, despite being the shadow husband in public. However, it is also clear that problems within their relationship affected the data collected and their views of the society. In her autobiography, Mead explicitly refers to their differing interpretations of Mundugumor kinship and her reservations about Fortune's insistence on a rigid division of labour.

> In the middle of our stay I discovered that Reo, who had insisted that he alone would work on the kinship system, had missed a clue. The clue had come from the children's terminology, on which I

was working. I felt that if he had not drawn so rigid a dividing line between his work and mine, we would have been able to put the material together much sooner. As it was, we might have missed the clue altogether ...[32]

Mead cites other significant discrepancies between material she and Fortune were gathering. For example, their most insightful informant, a man named Omblean, tended to provide Mead with an 'ideal' view of the kinship and marriage system – how it was supposed to work – while providing Fortune with the 'real' view, the way in which people were not able to conform to the demands of the system, which in turn led to considerable social conflict.[33] If the relationship between the two had been better, these discrepancies might have provided productive paths to a greater understanding of a very unusual system of kinship exchange and marriage. But the anthropologists' failing partnership became one of several reasons for the truncation of the Mundugumor portion of their expedition. They had planned to stay in the region for eight months, but left after only three. This meant that the Mundugumor investigation remained incomplete, raising more questions than providing answers – as Mead herself was aware.[34]

The Mundugumor materials demonstrate the struggles that the couple had within the gendered framework of the expedition, where a very traditional division of labour clearly failed in at least one of the communities studied. This attempt at dividing responsibilities would also have an enormous impact on future publication. Mead's intentions for monograph publications were signalled as follows:

> when our next field choice, the Tchambuli, provided genuinely contrastive material on culturally patterned personalities of the two sexes, we decided that I would write up most of the Arapesh ethnography, and Dr. Fortune would take the Mundugumor and Tchambuli ethnography, while I would use only as much Mundugumor and Tchambuli material as was necessary for my report on my field problems of culturally established sex differences, which I did ...[35]

The demise of their marriage, and Fortune's failure to complete any monographs, has influenced the reception and interpretation of the materials from the Sepik sojourn. If the two tried, and failed, to maintain strict boundaries between the kinds of data they collected, the role of Fortune and his significant contributions to the Sepik Expedition were never clearly distinguished from those of Mead. From today's perspective, this resulted in a striking erasure of Fortune's contribution. For example, the AMNH collection that the couple brought back is designated the 'Margaret Mead Collection', although the largest part of it was collected by Fortune. It is worth asking, however, if this erasure would have been as evident if Mead had been the shadow wife on the expedition.

In addition to *Sex and Temperament*, several other works resulted from this field trip. Mead published the multivolume *Mountain Arapesh*.[36] Fortune wrote an essay on Arapesh warfare that disagreed with Mead's findings.[37] He wrote the only published material specifically on language, an article on Arapesh.[38] Mundugumor material was included in two other essays by Fortune.[39] There was also the aforementioned collection of artefacts, which makes up a tenth of the Pacific holdings at the AMNH.[40] Despite this productivity, there were the already noted absences in the results of the expedition. The lack of full-scale monographs on the Mundugumor and Tchambuli left a void of information. *Sex and Temperament in Three Primitive Societies* would stand as the only published book-length ethnography of two of the three societies visited by the Sepik Expedition until 1991, when Nancy McDowell, who had worked in an adjacent area, went into the available archives of Mead and Fortune and published *The Mundugumor: From the Field Notes of Margaret Mead and Reo Fortune*.[41]

Sex and Temperament in Three Primitive Societies became, like *Coming of Age in Samoa*, an iconic text in debates about gender. Mead contrasted the gender ethos of the three Sepik societies visited during the expedition. Her portrait of the Arapesh suggested a society where both men and women were expected to have nurturing and maternal characteristics. Among the Mundugumor, on the other hand, Mead argued that both sexes tended to be aggressive and hostile. Among the Tchambuli, men exhibited behaviours considered rather feminine, while women seemed quite masculine in theirs. As soon as it was published, *Sex and Temperament* became a bestseller, but it also drew criticism from other anthropologists who were suspicious that Mead's portrait was too neat and had involved misleading interpretations of basic field observations. In *Sex and Temperament*, the three societies become frozen images, with no temporal or spatial grounding. Tellingly, there is no map in the book. Because this volume was intended for a popular as well as academic audience, Mead's writing is at its most journalistic and generalizing, with cultures described by an apparently omniscient observer and with no allowance for multiple and conflicting perspectives within a society.[42] Mead would call *Sex and Temperament* her 'most misunderstood book'.[43]

The Discourses of Margaret Mead, Gender and Sexuality

Despite its fame, many facets of the expedition have been swallowed by the proliferating double discourses about sex and gender mentioned in the introduction. Firstly, there is an ongoing debate about the factual correctness of Margaret Mead's portrait of the gender roles of the three societies she describes in *Sex and Temperament*. Secondly, there is the personal story of events on the Sepik River when Mead and Fortune met Gregory Bateson, another Cambridge-trained anthropologist. Some of the facts around this encounter are clear. After seven months among the Arapesh and three on the Yuat River with the Mundugumor, the couple met Bateson, who was studying a group on the Middle Sepik River known as the Iatmul. Bateson suggested that Tchambuli Lake, not far from the Iatmul, would be an appropriate third site for Mead and Fortune to study. During this period, Mead and Bateson became romantically involved. Eventually, Mead would divorce Fortune and marry Bateson.[44] Mead and Bateson became a celebrated anthropological couple while Fortune disappeared from academia for many years.

The brief time that the three spent together has attained iconic status in numerous texts. In a scenario as dramatic as that of Captain Cook on the Hawaiian beach, truth seems to have given itself as a gift to fiction, more lurid than any melodrama. As Stocking describes the love triangle that resulted, if the history of anthropology were to be made into a television miniseries, one of its "great moments" would surely be set on the Sepik River early in 1933.'[45] This vignette captures what has drawn the attention of many others: anthropological fieldwork as crucible that transforms the personal lives and relationships of anthropologists themselves.

The framing of the Sepik Expedition is not one narrative but two. On the one hand, we have the attempt to render the truth of the relationship between the three anthropologists that forms the centre of Stocking's 'TV series'. On the other, there is the 'correctness' or otherwise – the truth value – of Mead's characterizations of the gender structures of the three Sepik area cultures she studied. These two narratives, though intertwined in that they both relate to events of the Sepik Expedition, are dispersed unevenly and without reference to one another. Feminist historians read the Sepik period biographically, ignoring ethnographic issues, while anthropologists tend to focus solely on the ethnography.[46] This discursive structure, while it may conform to a traditional academic division of labour, fails to note the expedition structure, which contains both individual anthropologists, their relationships and the ethnographic work.

What we know of this period is also mediated through Mead's autobiographical works and enormous archive, one of the largest relating to a single individual in the Library of Congress and a collection that includes papers relating to Bateson, Fortune and Benedict.[47] Indeed, the size and continuing revelations of Mead's archive are part of the momentum for the continued liveliness of these ongoing narratives.

Figure 9.2 Gregory Bateson, Margaret Mead, Reo Fortune, captioned as 'Group of Anthropologists Who Arrived on Macdhui'. July 1933. Gelatin silver photograph by unknown photographer. Manuscript Division, Library of Congress (139a). By permission of the American Anthropological Association and the Library of Congress.

This long story is like a palimpsest where each epoch uncovers another facet of the Sepik sojourn and where each seems to get the story it wants or needs. Here I want to examine this unfolding in its historical context.

In 1972 Mead published her autobiography, *Blackberry Winter*, which gives an 'official' version of the transformations in her personal relationships during the Sepik sojourn. This is a somewhat self-serving description of a tropical triangle – a triangle by this time so well known that it could not be avoided. A series of fairly standard roles are depicted: a dutiful but love-starved wife; a kindly, gentle man who was himself 'starved for talk'; and an unkind, jealous and aggressive husband.[48]

If *Blackberry Winter* seems self-serving and lacking in self-reflexivity, it is worth pointing out that this autobiography was written at a time when Margaret Mead was coming under more sustained criticism from her own profession than she had ever previously experienced. Because of her popular writing for magazines such as *Redbook* (a women's magazine), and her association with 'culture and personality', her work was strongly criticized by male members of the very department at Columbia University in which she was an adjunct professor. In 1968, her own work and that of Benedict were given an entire chapter of criticism by Marvin Harris in his influential history, *The Rise of Anthropological Theory*.[49]

By the 1970s, an aura of political conservatism surrounded Mead. She was ferociously attacked in a brawl about the Vietnam War at the American Anthropology Association meeting in 1972.[50] To a generation (my own) at Columbia, obsessed with the war in Vietnam, her patriotism seemed not so much right-wing as anachronistic. If she was well known for the TV series *A Rap on Race* with James Baldwin,[51] she was also known for writing features about the right way to breastfeed and raise a child, ideas not appealing to the feminism of the time.[52] Thus, the Mead who describes the events on the Sepik in *Blackberry Winter* is indelibly marked by the politics of a later period. She was trying to defend her work and behaviour against attacks from many quarters.

Fairly soon after her death, a biography was published by the journalist Jane Howard, whose account was drawn from those portions of the Mead archive available at the time and over three hundred interviews.[53] In the Howard biography we get a far more lurid picture of the heterotropic triangle. Howard calls her Sepik chapter 'The Closest I've Ever Come to Madness' – a quote from Mead herself.[54] Most significantly, the biographer points out that in contrast to Mead's tendency to portray herself as always in control and indestructible, she was far more, as Howard puts it, 'stressed'.[55] Illness, budding romance, jealousy and close physical proximity to each other caused all three anthropologists to go a little bit 'troppo'.

If Mead's autobiography directed attention to the life of the anthropologists rather than to the life of the peoples among whom the three were living, it is undoubtedly because she felt that the lives of those she studied were more appropriately discussed in her ethnographic texts. Subsequently, a number of women historians have researched the Sepik Expedition in greater detail and with an almost exclusive focus on the relations between the three anthropologists. These biographically oriented histories include book-length studies by Hilary Lapsley and Lois Banner.[56] Banner's book is based on new materials from letters that were released into the public domain by the Mead archive post 2000.[57] The timing of this release was directed by Mead and administered by her daughter, the anthropologist Mary Catherine Bateson.[58] These letters cast light on a more complex Mead who, for all her apparent openness, apparently felt it necessary to suppress her lesbianism and, in particular, that she had had a sexual relationship with Benedict as well as other women. It is also revealed that Fortune was physically violent towards Mead during their time on the Sepik. She miscarried during the expedition, perhaps as a result of his violence.

The main concern of Banner's book is to demonstrate the intense connections between Mead and Benedict, another pioneering woman who became Chair of the Department of Anthropology at Columbia and President of the American Anthropological Association. Despite her many achievements, Benedict faced constant discrimination because of her sex, well documented in her long correspondence with Mead. Banner suggests that Mead's intense relationship with Benedict, with its intellectual, sexual and emotional dimensions, was of particular significance during the Sepik Expedition, when Benedict sent her a manuscript copy of her book, *Patterns of Culture*. This was an investigation of three native American societies that attempted to delineate the way in which cultural norms shaped personality via brilliantly rendered case studies. Published in 1934, *Patterns of Culture* is still considered one of the most significant works of comparative ethnology.[59] Banner devotes an entire chapter to the Sepik period and suggests that Mead's interpretation of her field materials in *Sex and Temperament* was strongly influenced by Benedict's text, which became a topic of intense and divisive discussions between the three anthropologists on the Sepik.[60] Far from the pristine jungle to which the *New York Herald Tribune* dispatched Mead, the Sepik resembles, in the hands of Banner, an apartment on the Upper West Side of Manhattan. Benedict, as described by Banner, was a fourth (if absent) figure on the expedition, influencing all three anthropologists in different ways.

The effect of Benedict's book upon the anthropologists is most interesting in that it demonstrates how, by the twentieth century, international communications were so extensive that materials sent by mail could influence relationships within an expedition as well as the interpretation of field data. Banner's book is clearly intended to document the close personal and professional relationship between Benedict and Mead. However, in the process of making her case, she tends to render absent certain aspects of the field trip. One would hardly know that while the discussions of Benedict's book were occurring, the three anthropologists were collecting large quantities of material from very active communities. The Banner book raises interesting questions about the expedition but leaves certain issues unaddressed. In highlighting the influence of *Patterns of Culture*, she ignores Mead's pursuit of data, about which the anthropologist was almost evangelical in her fervour. The Benedict volume looms larger in its influence than it may have been.[61]

The recent focus on the personal relationships between the three anthropologists, rather than on the ethnographic labour in which they were engaged, must itself be contextualized. The meticulous studies of Banner and Lapsley have an interest in disrupting distinctions between public and private in their quest to reveal that the past was not some dismal parade of women bound to patriarchal, heterosexual norms. This task is important since many of the progressive developments of the interwar period were lost or attacked in the period after the Second World War. These recent interventions need to be placed against the background of Mead's erasure from certain discourses. Louise Newman, writing in 1996, points to the absence of Mead from many feminist discourses and cultural histories.[62]

Responses to Margaret Mead since the 1970s, whether scholarly or popular, also have to be seen against the background of an attack by Derek Freeman – himself a fieldworker with experience of Samoa – on the veracity of her fieldwork on the island. This attack and the ensuing public and acrimonious debates transformed Mead's profile and influenced the reception, both professional and public, of *Sex and Temperament*. In 1983, Freeman suggested that aspects of Mead's description of adolescence in Samoa were factually incorrect.[63] He disputed her portrait of young Samoan women as autonomous in their sexuality and engaging in casual affairs with the de facto consent of elders. On the contrary, Freeman maintained that the young women who formed Mead's cohort had made up stories about their carefree sex lives. Freeman, who worked for the most part with older males, put the view that senior men and women monitored and controlled the sexuality of young girls very carefully.

While debates in anthropology usually stay within the bounds of academic journals, this one erupted into the popular press and continued until well into the twenty-first century. Many anthropologists pointed out that Freeman's own evidence was rather flimsy. They queried his failure to debate with Mead while she was alive, since he had ample opportunity to do so. The controversy itself was part of a wider context: late twentieth-century debates about the universality of male dominance, aggression and control over female sexuality. Within this framework, Derek Freeman was an outspoken defender of the position that patriarchy was a human universal, socio-biologically determined. The logic of Freeman's position would lead to a complete negation of the type of field research that Mead had spent her life pursuing. From the socio-biological perspective, the only relevant informants were senior men, since they controlled the behaviour of others. The effect of the eruption of this debate in the popular press, and the ensuing oversimplification of notions of the correctness of one version of social processes over another, caused much despair within anthropology. But the debate left its mark on Mead's status. Before the Freeman debate she was known as the most famous woman anthropologist in the world; after his attack, she became known as the woman who had been wrong about sex. The effect of this long and entangled episode is summed up in the title of a book that covers the history of the debate: *The Trashing of Margaret Mead* (2009).[64]

The Mead-Freeman controversy is echoed in a discussion about whether or not the Arapesh had warfare at the time of the Sepik Expedition. Anthropologist Paul Roscoe, who did research near the Arapesh, made a visit to the former site of Alitoa, where Mead and Fortune were stationed. He suggested that Fortune, who maintained that the Arapesh had warfare, in contradistinction to Mead whose portrayal cited no instances of warfare, was probably correct. The subtext in this heated discussion is, once again, the discourse about the nature and limits of gender. Can men be as nurturing and lacking in aggression as Mead's portrait of the Arapesh suggested? What is of greatest concern in this more recent debate is the failure to contextualize the complexities of the notion of warfare. How does one define warfare? How does one 'read' this complex activity from a landscape, from a text, from an oral history? Such issues seem to get lost in the discussion of the veracity of particular observations. Issues of gender and aggression seem to be of such overriding concern that more fundamental issues about interpretation and context are neglected. Mead may have decided that the conflicts she recorded were minor skirmishes, of insufficient weight to constitute 'warfare', while Fortune thought the reverse. Mead was confined to a village while Fortune travelled extensively. Their perspectives would, not surprisingly, be different, but none of this was taken into account in Roscoe's essay.[65]

The essay brought forth a ferocious response from Micaela di Leonardo, who in 1998 had herself lambasted Mead and Bateson in her volume *Exotics at Home*.[66] This exchange, given that it occurred in 2003 in a major American journal, was met with utter dismay by some commentators. One complained of Roscoe's article that it

> follows in that old academic tradition of 'beating a straw man with a dead horse'. The dead horse being any of those quaint romantic fantasies of the 19th and 20th centuries about the exotic other. The 'straw man' in this case being, well, usually Margaret Mead or Ruth Benedict, those favorite targets of Postmodernist male critics. In this case Roscoe has done one better by attacking both. He blames Mead's errors on Benedict.[67]

What is striking is that a number of recent essays tend to frame the Sepik sojourn as a boxing match between staged opponents: Mead versus Fortune; women versus men; strong successful metropolitan woman versus a wounded, marginalized colonial.[68]

Conclusion: Remembered, Forgotten, Found and Lost

The Sepik Expedition legacy is largely comprised of two discourses emanating from the figure and writing of Margaret Mead. While one is about the biography of Margaret Mead and her circle, and the other about the gender and temperament of some cultures of the Sepik, both share a central concern – an obsession really – with the variability of sex and gender, the nature and limits of the 'modern woman' (in the guise of Margaret Mead) and the universality or otherwise of male dominance and warfare. It is perhaps fitting that the Sepik triangle provided material for a novel, *Euphoria* (2014) by Lily King.[69] The author deliberately eschews loyalty to the facts in that the character Nell (based on Mead) dies in mysterious circumstances around 1936. The book lends support to the notion that Mead really is the woman we love to hate – to the point of imaginary homicide!

Seen from a Foucauldian perspective, the Margaret Mead story is a discourse about modern sexuality and gender, a proliferative discourse that essentially consumes everything in its wake. In this story, the Sepik Expedition becomes a round in the twentieth-century Battle of the Sexes, with Mead as the modern Medusa, scaring the pants off the men and committing anthropological atrocities in the process. In taking anthropology to the public arena, in working with women and children, in 'simplifying' complex field data, in her commitment to cultural relativism and in her suppressed lesbianism, she somehow became the woman we love to hate. Lévi-Strauss might have called her a myth: good to think with; Foucault would say she was a pleasure to hate, in part because she was a successful woman. If recent archival revelations demonstrate anything, it is that this discourse of the mythological woman emerged from a medley of conflicts, accidents and failures, and that it required the 'forgetting' of vast quantities of material.

While many expeditions fade into obscurity until excavated from the archive, the Sepik Expedition has not so much disappeared as been swallowed whole by the iconic figure of Margaret Mead.[70] My point in this chapter has been to draw attention to the context and surroundings. This return to the expedition as a discursive site raises the question of why certain discourses came to dominate while others simply faded into the background. How, in 2003, could we return to the straw 'man', Margaret Mead, and the dead horse, 'warfare', in a major journal?

In the desire to present coherent arguments, certain information about the Sepik period is embargoed or ignored. In their attempts to present coherent and persuasive pictures of moral rectitude and ethnographic authority, commentators often ignore contradictory material. What is being preserved in this search for the truth of the events? What does remain intact, of course, is the notion of fieldwork as an idealized pursuit capable of complete transparency across space and time. Ideas of warfare, for example, can be lifted intact from their original context and inserted into universalizing and reifying discussions of an entity called 'Warfare'. The coherence and value of ethnography itself – an ethnography that sits outside its context in time and space – is being asserted.

What I want to suggest in conclusion is that the framework of the expedition has the potential to unite this fragmented discourse. The expedition unites the biographies of the ethnologists with the anthropological materials; their personal relationships with their ethnographic perceptions and observations. What becomes apparent is that this fieldwork was one of many experiments that resulted in a transformation in field techniques and field research. Attention to the dynamics of the expedition shows that Mead and Fortune's attempt to maintain a gendered division of labour profoundly influenced how they interacted with informants and how they interpreted data. At times, this division of labour, and the failure of the relationship, resulted in irremediable gaps in knowledge, as was the case with the Mundugumor. On the other hand, it generated much close detail concerning the lives of women and children, who attracted little anthropological attention prior to Mead and her generation. Mead's ethnography proved that the perspective of women and children could illuminate understandings not only of gender roles but of kinship, economics and politics. Her celebrity and notoriety has meant that some of the particularities of the Sepik Expedition have disappeared into the loud debates of the twentieth century. But attention to the grain of the field trip shows that she was indeed one of a generation of women who transformed field research from imperial venture to a more cooperative quest in which women were in every way players.

Diane Losche is an anthropologist and Honorary Associate at the University of New South Wales, Sydney, Australia. She has done field research and written many essays on the Abelam area of the Sepik River region. The Abelam people border the Arapesh, one of the sites where Margaret Mead and Reo Fortune did their research in the 1930s and the subject of Dr Losche's chapter in this collection. Dr Losche was supervised by Margaret Mead for her PhD studies at Columbia University. She is currently researching fieldwork in the Sepik region during the interwar years.

Notes

1. The nation of which the Sepik region is a part is called Papua New Guinea. However, during the 1930s, when Australia was the colonial administrator, the northern section of the country tended to be referred to, as Mead did, by the term New Guinea, while the south was referred to as Papua. In this chapter I use Mead's terminology: New Guinea.
2. William Engle, 'Going and Getting It for Science', *New York World Telegram*, 17 June 1931.
3. The commonly used term for Tchambuli is now Chambri. However, I use Mead's spelling in this chapter.

4. Margaret Mead, *Sex and Temperament in Three Primitive Societies* (London: Routledge, 1935), acknowledgements, unpaginated.
5. Ibid. Since 1935 the book has been published in many editions. In 'Margaret Mead, Reo Fortune and Mountain Arapesh Warfare', *American Anthropologist* 105(3) (2002), 581, Paul Roscoe points out that it is among her most well-known works.
6. German expeditions went through parts of the Sepik River and its environs prior to the First World War (starting in 1885 with Otto Finsch), the best-known of which is the Kaiserin-Augusta-Fluss-Expedition of 1912–13. However, these mixed expeditions collected ethnological materials along with natural history specimens and geographical information and did not produce precise anthropological mapping of this area, which is known for its complexity. The Sepik region has, for example, the most languages, per capita, of anywhere in the world, with approximately 298 known languages. There was also exploration of the Sepik River by George Dorsey in 1908 and by A.B. Lewis from the Field Museum in Chicago in 1910. See Robert Welsch, *An American Anthropologist in Melanesia: A.B. Lewis and the Joseph N. Field South Pacific Expedition 1909–1913* (Honolulu, HI: University of Hawaii Press, 1998), 295, 565–66.
7. Margaret Mead, *Coming of Age in Samoa* (New York: William Morrow and Co., 1928).
8. George W. Stocking (ed.), *Observers Observed: Essays on Ethnographic Fieldwork* (Madison, WI: The University of Wisconsin Press, 1985); and David Parkin, Wendy James and Paul Dresch, *Anthropologists in a Wider World: Essays on Field Research* (New York: Berghahn Books, 2000).
9. Anita Herle and Sandra Rouse (eds), *Cambridge and the Torres Strait* (Cambridge: Cambridge University Press, 1998); and Welsch, *An American Anthropologist in Melanesia*, 565–66.
10. Roscoe, 'Margaret Mead, Reo Fortune and Mountain Arapesh Warfare', xvi; Lily King, *Euphoria: A Novel* (New York: Atlantic Monthly Press, 2014); for a bibliography of publications about Mead, see Nancy Lutkehaus, *Margaret Mead: The Making of an American Icon* (Princeton, NJ/Oxford: Princeton University Press, 2008).
11. Lutkehaus, *Margaret Mead*.
12. 'Dr Mead to Join Third Expedition', *New York Herald Tribune*, 18 August 1931, Box 1-4, Margaret Mead Papers, Library of Congress, cited in Lutkehaus, *Margaret Mead*, 133.
13. John Perkins and AMNH, *To the Ends of the Earth* (New York: Pantheon Books, 1981).
14. Engle, 'Going and Getting It for Science'.
15. Donna Haraway, 'Teddy Bear Patriarchy: Taxidermy in the Garden of Eden, New York City, 1908–1936', in Donna Haraway (ed.), *Primate Visions: Gender, Race and Nature in the World of Modern Science* (New York: Routledge, 1989), 26–59.

16. George W. Stocking (ed.), *Malinowski, Rivers, Benedict and Others: Essays on Culture and Personality* (Madison, WI: The University of Wisconsin Press, 1986), 5.
17. Jane Howard, *Margaret Mead: A Life* (New York: Simon and Schuster, 1984), 132.
18. Lois Banner, *Intertwined Lives: Margaret Mead, Ruth Benedict, and Their Circle* (New York: Alfred Knopf, 2003), 392–93.
19. Lutkehaus, *Margaret Mead*, 155.
20. Howard, *Margaret Mead*, 132.
21. Ibid., 320.
22. Ibid., 326.
23. Ibid., 203–4.
24. Mead, *Sex and Temperament*, 165.
25. Margaret Mead, 'Living with the Natives of Melanesia', *Natural History* 31 (January–February 1931), 63.
26. Mead, *Sex and Temperament*, Preface, unpaginated.
27. Ibid., acknowledgements, unpaginated.
28. Reo Fortune, *Sorcerers of Dobu* (London: G. Routledge & Sons, Ltd, 1932).
29. Mead, cited in Peggy Golde (ed.), *Women in the Field: Anthropological Experiences* (Chicago, IL: Aldine Publishing, 1970), 327.
30. Nancy McDowell, *The Mundugumor: From the Field Notes of Margaret Mead and Reo Fortune* (Washington, DC: Smithsonian Institution Press, 1991).
31. Mead, cited in McDowell, *The Mundugumor*, 10.
32. Margaret Mead, *Blackberry Winter: My Earlier Years* (New York: William Morrow, 1972), 205.
33. McDowell, *The Mundugumor*, 11.
34. Ibid., 8.
35. Mead, cited in McDowell, *The Mundugumor*, 21.
36. Margaret Mead, *The Mountain Arapesh 1: An Importing Culture* (New York: Anthropological Papers of the American Museum of Natural History, 1938); *The Mountain Arapesh 2: Supernaturalism* (New York: Anthropological Papers of the American Museum of Natural History, 1940). Vol. 37, 315–452; *The Mountain Arapesh 3: Socio-Economic Life. 4: Diary of Events in Alitoa* (New York: Anthropological Papers of the American Museum of Natural History, 1947). Vol. 40, 159–416; *The Mountain Arapesh 5: The Record of Unabelin with Rorschach Analyses* (New York: Anthropological Papers of the American Museum of Natural History, 1949). Vol. 41, 285–390.
37. Reo Fortune, 'Arapesh Warfare', *American Anthropologist* 41(1) (1939), 22–41.
38. Reo Fortune, *Arapesh* (New York: Publications of the American Ethnological Society, 1942).
39. Reo Fortune, 'The Rules of Relationship Behavior in One Variety of Primitive Warfare', *Man* 47 (1947), 108–10; Fortune, 'Law and Force in Papuan Societies', *American Anthropologist* 49 (1947), 244–59.

40. Diane Losche, 'The Fate of the Senses in Ethnographic Modernity: The Margaret Mead Peoples of the Pacific Hall at the American Museum of Natural History', in Elizabeth Edwards, Chris Gosden and Ruth Phillips (eds), *Sensible Objects: Colonialism, Museums and Material Culture* (Oxford: Berg Press, 2006), 223–44.
41. McDowell, *The Mundugumor*.
42. Roger Ivar Lohman, 'Sex and Sensibility: Margaret Mead's Descriptive and Rhetorical Ethnography', *Reviews in Anthropology* 33 (2004), 111–30; Diane Losche, 'The Anthropologist's Voice: Margaret Mead and Donald Tuzin', in David Lipset and Paul Roscoe (eds), *Echoes of the Tambaran: Masculinity, History and the Subject in the Work of Donald F. Tuzin* (Canberra: ANU E Press, 2011), 297–313.
43. Margaret Mead, *Sex and Temperament in Three Primitive Societies*. This is from the Preface to the 1950 edition of the book, not the original edition of 1935.
44. Mead, *Blackberry Winter*.
45. Stocking, *Malinowski, Rivers, Benedict and Others*, 3.
46. Gewertz, Deborah. 'A Historical Reconsideration of Female Dominance among the Chambri of Papua New Guinea'. *American Ethnologist* 8 (1981), 94–106. For a summary of major ethnographic critiques, see David Lipset, 'Reading Sex and Temperament: Margaret Mead's Sepik Triptych and Its Ethnographic Critics', *Anthropological Quarterly* 76(4) (Autumn 2003), 693–713.
47. Margaret Caffrey and Patricia Francis (eds), *To Cherish the Life of the World: Selected Letters of Margaret Mead* (New York: Basic Books, 2006), xviii.
48. Mead, *Blackberry Winter*, 194–222.
49. Marvin Harris, *The Rise of Anthropological Theory* (New York: Thomas Y. Crowell Company, 1968), 393–421.
50. Virginia Yans, 'On the Political Economy of Mead-Bashing, or Re-thinking Margaret Mead', in Dolores Janiewski and Lois Banner (eds), *Reading Benedict/Reading Mead: Feminism, Race, and Imperial Visions* (Baltimore, MD/London: Johns Hopkins University Press, 2004), 241.
51. Micaela di Leonardo, *Exotics at Home: Anthropologies, Others, American Modernity* (Chicago, IL/London: University of Chicago Press, 1998), 93–96.
52. Howard, *Margaret Mead*, 292.
53. Ibid., 444.
54. Ibid., 154.
55. Ibid., 161.
56. Hilary Lapsley, *Margaret Mead and Ruth Benedict: The Kinship of Women* (Boston, MA: University of Massachusetts Press, 1999); and Banner, *Intertwined Lives*.
57. Banner, *Intertwined Lives*, ix.
58. Ibid.

59. Benedict, Ruth. *Patterns of Culture* (New York, Boston MA, Houghton Mifflin, 1934); Clifford Geertz, *Works and Lives: The Anthropologist as Author* (Stanford, CA: Stanford University Press, 1988).
60. Ibid., ch. 11.
61. Howard, *Margaret Mead*, 69–70.
62. Louise Newman, 'Coming of Age but Not in Samoa: Reflections on Margaret Mead's Legacy for Western Liberal Feminism', *American Quarterly* 48(2) (June 1996), 259.
63. Derek Freeman, *Margaret Mead and Samoa: The Making and Unmaking of an Anthropological Myth* (Cambridge, MA: Harvard University Press, 1983); and Freeman, *The Fateful Hoaxing of Margaret Mead: A Historical Analysis of Her Samoan Research* (Boulder, CO: Westview Press, 1998).
64. Paul Shankman, *The Trashing of Margaret Mead: Anatomy of an Anthropological Controversy* (Madison, WI/London: The University of Wisconsin Press, 2009).
65. Roscoe, 'Margaret Mead, Reo Fortune and Mountain Arapesh Warfare'; 'Commentary: A Response to di Leonardo'. *American Anthropologist* 105(4) (2003), 882.
66. Micaela di Leonardo, 'Margaret Mead and the Culture of Forgetting in Anthropology: A Response to Paul Roscoe', *American Anthropologist* 105(3) (2003), 591–95; and di Leonardo, *Exotics at Home*.
67. Niccolo Caldararo, 'War, Mead and the Nature of Criticism in Anthropology', *Anthropological Quarterly* 77(2) (Spring 2004), 311.
68. Ann McLean, 'In the Footprints of Reo Fortune', in Terence E. Hays (ed.), *Ethnographic Presents: Pioneering Anthropologists in the Papua New Guinea Highlands* (Los Angeles, CA/Oxford: University of California, 1992), 37–68; Geoffrey Gray, 'Being Honest to My Science: Reo Fortune and HJP Murray', *The Australian Journal of Anthropology* 10(1) (April 1999), 56; Caroline Thomas, 'Rediscovering Reo: Reflections on the Life and Anthropological Career of Reo Franklin Fortune', *Pacific Studies* 32(2–3) (2009), 299–324; Lisa Dobrin and Ira Baskow, 'Arapesh Warfare: Reo Fortune's Veiled Critique of Margaret Mead's *Sex and Temperament*', *American Anthropologist* 112(3) (September 2010), 370–83; Lisa Dobrin and Ira Baskow, 'The Truth in Anthropology Does Not Travel First Class: Reo Fortune's Fateful Encounter with Margaret Mead', in Regna Darnell and Frederic Gleach (eds), *Histories of Anthropology Annual*, Vol. 6 (Lincoln, NE: University of Nebraska Press, 2006), 66–128.
69. King, *Euphoria*.
70. Foucault, Michel. *Power/Knowledge: Essays and Interviews 1972–1977*. (New York: Vintage, 1980). As Foucault suggested, the power of the myth is everywhere, constricting discourse about the fieldwork.

Bibliography

Banner, Lois. *Intertwined Lives: Margaret Mead, Ruth Benedict, and Their Circle*. New York: Alfred Knopf, 2003.

Benedict, Ruth. *Patterns of Culture*. New York/Boston, MA: Houghton Mifflin, 1934.

Caffrey, Margaret, and Patricia Francis (eds). *To Cherish the Life of the World: Selected Letters of Margaret Mead*. New York: Basic Books, 2006.

Caldararo, Niccolo. 'War, Mead and the Nature of Criticism in Anthropology'. *Anthropological Quarterly* 77(2) (Spring 2004), 311–22.

Di Leonardo, Micaela. *Exotics at Home: Anthropologies, Others, American Modernity*. Chicago, IL/London: University of Chicago Press, 1998.

———. 'Margaret Mead and the Culture of Forgetting in Anthropology: A Response to Paul Roscoe'. *American Anthropologist* 105(3) (2003), 591–95.

Dobrin, Lise, and Ira Baskow. 'Arapesh Warfare: Reo Fortune's Veiled Critique of Margaret Mead's *Sex and Temperament*'. *American Anthropologist* 112(3) (September 2010), 370–83.

———. '"The Truth in Anthropology Does Not Travel First Class": Reo Fortune's Fateful Encounter with Margaret Mead', in Regna Darnell and Frederic Gleach (eds), *Histories of Anthropology Annual*, Vol. 6 (Lincoln, NE: University of Nebraska Press, 2010), 66–128.

Engle, William. 'Going and Getting It for Science'. *New York World Telegram*, 17 June 1931.

Fortune, Reo. *Arapesh*. New York: Publications of the American Ethnological Society, 1942.

———. 'Arapesh Warfare'. *American Anthropologist* 41(1) (1939), 22–41.

———. 'Law and Force in Papuan Societies'. *American Anthropologist* 49 (1947), 244–59.

———. 'The Rules of Relationship Behavior in One Variety of Primitive Warfare'. *Man* 47 (1947), 108–10.

———. *Sorcerers of Dobu*. London: G. Routledge & Sons, Ltd, 1932.

Foucault, Michel. *Power/Knowledge: Essays and Interviews 1972–1977*. New York: Vintage, 1980.

Freeman, Derek. *The Fateful Hoaxing of Margaret Mead: A Historical Analysis of her Samoan Research*. Boulder, CO: Westview Press, 1998.

———. *Margaret Mead and Samoa: The Making and Unmaking of an Anthropological Myth*. Cambridge, MA: Harvard University Press, 1983.

Geertz, Clifford. *Works and Lives: The Anthropologist as Author*. Stanford, CA: Stanford University Press, 1998.

Gewertz, Deborah. 'A Historical Reconsideration of Female Dominance among the Chambri of Papua New Guinea'. *American Ethnologist* 8 (1981), 94–106.

Golde, Peggy (ed.). *Women in the Field: Anthropological Experiences*. Chicago, IL: Aldine Publishing, 1970.

Gray, Geoffrey. 'Being Honest to My Science: Reo Fortune and HJP Murray'. *The Australian Journal of Anthropology* 10(1) (April 1999), 56.

Haraway, Donna. 'Teddy Bear Patriarchy: Taxidermy in the Garden of Eden, New York City, 1908–1936', in Donna Haraway (ed.), *Primate Visions: Gender, Race and Nature in the World of Modern Science* (New York: Routledge, 1989), 26–59.

Harris, Marvin. *The Rise of Anthropological Theory*. New York: Thomas Y. Crowell Company, 1968.

Herle, Anita, and Sandra Rouse (eds). *Cambridge and the Torres Strait*. Cambridge: Cambridge University Press, 1998.

Howard, Jane. *Margaret Mead: A Life*. New York: Simon and Schuster, 1984.

King, Lily. *Euphoria: A Novel*. New York: Atlantic Monthly Press, 2014.

Lapsley, Hilary. *Margaret Mead and Ruth Benedict: The Kinship of Women*. Boston, MA: University of Massachusetts Press, 1999.

Lipset, David. 'Reading Sex and Temperament: Margaret Mead's Sepik Triptych and Its Ethnographic Critics'. *Anthropological Quarterly* 76(4) (Autumn 2003), 693–713.

Lohman, Roger Ivar. 'Sex and Sensibility: Margaret Mead's Descriptive and Rhetorical Ethnography'. *Reviews in Anthropology* 33 (2004), 111–30.

Losche, Diane. 'The Anthropologist's Voice: Margaret Mead and Donald Tuzin', in David Lipset and Paul Roscoe (eds), *Echoes of the Tambaran: Masculinity, History and the Subject in the Work of Donald F. Tuzin* (Canberra: ANU E Press, 2011), 297–313.

———. 'The Fate of the Senses in Ethnographic Modernity: The Margaret Mead Peoples of the Pacific Hall at the American Museum of Natural History', in Elizabeth Edwards, Chris Gosden and Ruth B. Phillips (eds), *Sensible Objects: Colonialism, Museums and Material Culture* (Oxford: Berg Press, 2006), 223–44.

Lutkehaus, Nancy. *Margaret Mead: The Making of an American Icon*. Princeton, NJ/London: Princeton University Press, 2008.

McDowell, Nancy. *The Mundugumor: From the Field Notes of Margaret Mead and Reo Fortune*. Washington, DC: Smithsonian Institution Press, 1991.

McLean, Ann. 'In the Footprints of Reo Fortune', in Terence E. Hays (ed.), *Ethnographic Presents: Pioneering Anthropologists in the Papua New Guinea Highlands* (Los Angeles, CA/Oxford: University of California, 1992), 37–68.

———. *Blackberry Winter: My Earlier Years*. New York: William Morrow, 1972.

———. *Coming of Age in Samoa*. New York: William Morrow and Co., 1928.

———. 'Living with the Natives of Melanesia'. *Natural History* 31 (January–February 1931), 62–74.

———. *The Mountain Arapesh 1: An Importing Culture*. New York: Anthropological Papers of the American Museum of Natural History, 1938.

———. *The Mountain Arapesh 2: Supernaturalism*. New York: Anthropological Papers of the American Museum of Natural History, 1940.

———. *The Mountain Arapesh 3: SocioEconomic Life. 4: Diary of Events in Alitoa*. New York: Anthropological Papers of the American Museum of Natural History, 1947.

———. *The Mountain Arapesh 5: The Record of Unabelin with Rorschach Analyses*. New York: Anthropological Papers of the American Museum of Natural History, 1949.

———. *Sex and Temperament in Three Primitive Societies*. London: Routledge, 1935.

Newman, Louise. 'Coming of Age but Not in Samoa: Reflections on Margaret Mead's Legacy for Western Liberal Feminism'. *American Quarterly* 48(2) (June 1996), 233–72.

Parkin, David, Wendy James and Paul Dresch. *Anthropologists in a Wider World: Essays on Field Research*. New York: Berghahn Books, 2000.

Perkins, John, and AMNH. *To the Ends of the Earth*. New York: Pantheon Books, 1981.

Roscoe, Paul. 'Commentary: A Response to di Leonardo'. *American Anthropologist* 105(4) (2003), 882.

———. 'Margaret Mead, Reo Fortune and Mountain Arapesh Warfare'. *American Anthropologist* 105(3) (2002), 581–91.

Shankman, Paul. *The Trashing of Margaret Mead: Anatomy of an Anthropological Controversy*. Madison, WI/London: The University of Wisconsin Press, 2009.

Stocking, George W. (ed.). *Malinowski, Rivers, Benedict and Others: Essays on Culture and Personality*. Madison, WI: The University of Wisconsin Press, 1986.

——— (ed.). *Observers Observed: Essays on Ethnographic Fieldwork*. Madison, WI: The University of Wisconsin Press, 1985.

Thomas, Caroline. 'Rediscovering Reo: Reflections on the Life and Anthropological Career of Reo Franklin Fortune'. *Pacific Studies* 32(2–3) (2009), 299–324.

Welsch, Robert. *An American Anthropologist in Melanesia: A.B. Lewis and the Joseph N. Field South Pacific Expedition 1909–1913*. Honolulu, HI: University of Hawaii Press, 1998.

Yans, Virginia. 'On the Political Economy of Mead-Bashing, or Re-thinking Margaret Mead', in Dolores Janiewski and Lois Banner (eds), *Reading Benedict/Reading Mead: Feminism, Race, and Imperial Visions* (Baltimore, MD/London: Johns Hopkins University Press, 2004), 229–248.

Chapter 10

GENDER, SCIENCE AND IMPERIAL DRIVE

MARGARET MCARTHUR ON TWO EXPEDITIONS IN THE 1940s

Amanda Harris

The Australian biochemist and nutritionist Margaret McArthur was a member of two expedition teams in the late 1940s. The two journeys, to New Guinea and the Mandated Territory of Papua and to Arnhem Land respectively, represent an important stage in the trajectory of McArthur's career and her shift from science graduate to independent researcher who would later carry out fieldwork at remote sites in Papua New Guinea. Her participation in these expeditions offers an opportunity to consider the gender dynamics of large-scale, twentieth-century scientific and ethnographic expeditions of the postwar period. In this chapter, I examine how McArthur's employment in a female-dominated field with the Institute of Anatomy in Canberra provided a gateway to a public and professional career. I reflect on the institute's insistence on the necessity of female researchers in scientific expeditions, and the ways in which this impacted on the gendered space of expedition culture. I also place these two expeditions in the context of postwar Australia, and national concerns about defining and securing the nation's outermost borders. Both the Northern Territory and the region that would become the Territory of Papua and New Guinea in 1949 were significant sites for discussion of Australian national security in the immediate postwar years. The participation of women like Margaret McArthur in the large-scale public efforts towards nation building and imperialism that expeditions into these areas represented marks both a shift in women's roles in the public realm, and an intervention into expeditionary culture.

Margaret McArthur and the Institute of Anatomy

Annie Margaret McArthur (known as Margaret) was born in Victoria in 1919, and graduated from the University of Melbourne with a Master of Science degree in the early 1940s. Armed with her degree, McArthur initially worked at the Council for Scientific and Industrial Research (CSIR). Following the Second World War, she found herself in Canberra studying for a Diploma of Nutrition at the Institute of Anatomy, an organization concerned with population health among other agendas. This disciplinary shift into an institute charged with a postwar verve for improving the nutrition of Australia and its overseas territories thrust McArthur in a new direction, exposing her to the practices and traditions of people from cultures very different to her own.[1]

By 1946, McArthur, building on her skills as a biochemist, had just completed the theoretical component of a one-year postgraduate diploma, with training in cooking, nutrition and human health. The focus of the nutritional division of the Institute of Anatomy was on documenting the postwar state of Australian health and demonstrating links between diet and certain kinds of disease. The institute carried out research on white Australians, as well as Indigenous Australians, in Northern and Central Australia and residents of territories administered by Australia such as Papua New Guinea, comparing recommended dietary intakes with actual nutrient consumption. The institute's director Frederick W. Clements sought to demonstrate the direct health effects of dietary deficiency. These data were used as a basis for developing educative programmes for Australian families (specifically Australian mothers), which included instructional pamphlets, cooking classes and ideas for healthy eating on a restricted budget. The Diploma of Nutrition, founded in 1945, was created to ensure that sufficient qualified nutritionists were available to carry out this work. The Office of the Minister for Health allocated budget to the diploma that had previously been used for nutritional education and surveys, stating that 'a policy aimed at providing a number of highly-trained personnel in the community is a much more satisfactory method of stimulating an interest and knowledge in nutritional matters'.[2] This redirection of funds was clearly an attempt to improve the expertise of personnel in work already being done; the nutrition surveys did not cease, but rather became part of the diploma. Following two terms of theoretical instruction, students were to spend their third term of study on field trips carrying out surveys.

The recruitment of students for the diploma was directed at female applicants, to the extent that in 1946 only one of the forty-four scholarship applicants was male (his gender was also remarked upon in internal notes on the applicants).[3] In that year, scholarships were awarded to eleven female science graduates, of whom Margaret McArthur was one. The gender-specific recruitment of students for the course was justified by the work graduates were expected to carry out, which involved working closely with housewives. As a pathway into fieldwork and scientific expeditions, this focus on food and the domestic sphere gave women professional opportunities that were unusual in other branches of science.

At the end of McArthur's 1946 diploma year, the student group was split between two expeditions, participation in which would mark the completion of their studies. One of the groups formed the Northern Territory Nutrition Survey. The Northern Territory, situated in the far north of the continent, had a large Aboriginal population and was directly administered from Canberra, being extraneous from the six states that comprise the Federation of Australia. The other 1947 expedition, which included McArthur, was the New Guinea Nutrition Survey Expedition. Its aim was to document 'the food the people are actually eating, their methods of cooking it, and the nutritional value when cooking is completed. It should compare their unbalanced diet with a balanced diet'.[4] In the planning of this New Guinea trip, the institute's senior staff debated the arguments for and against the viability of including female field staff in the party. Clements, the institute's director, noted that the addition of women was unusual, but argued for the inclusion of a female nutritionist and anthropologist. His arguments were countered by other members of the government planning party who considered a female anthropologist unnecessary. Others thought that the expedition should also include a female medical doctor in order to assess the health of children.[5] Although McArthur and her colleagues were by no means the first women to embark on such field expeditions within or outside the Pacific region, the extent of this discussion, which continued across several meetings, indicates that women's inclusion in such a venture remained contentious, even in the late 1940s.

The Institute of Anatomy finally decided that the expedition would consist of a small group that included a medical officer, a parasitologist, a nutritionist, an agriculturalist, a sociologist and two biochemists. A dental officer and a photographer would join the company during the final part of the survey. They would visit five different villages across New Guinea and the Mandated Territory of Papua (Busama, Kaiapit,

Figure 10.1 David Cameron, Margaret McArthur and Doreen Langley with an unidentified group in New Guinea. Photograph by James (Jim) Fitzpatrick, 1947. National Archives of Australia, Canberra: A1200, L9930. Reproduced with permission.

Patep, Kavitaria and Koravagi). McArthur was one of the two biochemists while her colleague, Doreen Langley, took the role of nutritionist. This group was joined by a dental team that also included a female dentist, Barbara Sinclair; the remaining team members were male. The inclusion of *several* women in this party made it an environment where gender was not a significant delineator in lines of command or perceived suitability to perform the task at hand.[6]

Although this first expedition was, for McArthur and her colleagues, simply the necessary requirement for completing their nutrition qualification, the survey represented much more for McArthur as an individual. While her ambitions would lead her to different parts of the world – to Arnhem Land in Northern Australia, to England and to Africa – it was to New Guinea that she would return to carry out the research that would form the basis of her work as a professional anthropologist.[7] The New Guinea Nutrition Survey also became a means for a group of women to gain experience in remote fieldwork and allowed them to be part of an expeditionary configuration that had traditionally been the domain of men. The loophole that allowed women's participation in this adventurers' domain was the study of food.[8] For female scientists such as McArthur, the study of food consumption and nutrition was a niche that they could fill in preference to men. Take-up in traditional female domains, centred around the *domestic*, offered McArthur and other women a gap through which they could enter the *public* life of scientific fieldworker. In the context of post-Second World War Australia, this move between domestic and public domains was an important symbol of the changing roles of women who, as during the First World War, had been able to work in spheres often closed to them in order to make up the at-home shortfall in male personnel.[9]

Scientific Expeditions and Australian Nationhood

Roy MacLeod notes that in the twentieth century, multidisciplinary scientific expeditions continued to be a tool of empire and an instrument of research: 'the scientific expedition drew on the language of the military expedition and the heroism of the expeditionary force. For much the same reason, an active commitment to scientific exploration was, to some, the highest measure of a nation's claim to civilization'.[10] Australian scientific expeditions played a role in asserting Australia's sovereign power, in an era of renewed concern about the security of Australia's borders. Australia's postwar preoccupations are therefore an important part of unpacking McArthur's participation in a scientific expedition.

Though more generally the Australian political gaze was shifting towards the US in the period after the Second World War, the bombing of Darwin in 1942 had returned attention to the vastness of Australia's northern borders, and the potential vulnerabilities of the north, including both the Northern Territory and Papua New Guinea. With its nominal white population, the vulnerability of the Northern Territory had been a concern in Australian politics for some years, especially before the First World War.[11] The perceived threat, during the Pacific War, of Australia being invaded from the north by Japan was cause for these anxieties to resurface. Although Australia had presided over the formerly British territory of New Guinea and the formerly German territory of Papua since 1906 and 1914 respectively, its administration of these territories was relatively complacent until the Second World War. Following the events of the war, and increasing concern with national security, the Australian government looked north with a more focused gaze.[12] Science had a role to play in these efforts and the 1947 New Guinea Nutrition Survey

Expedition was framed as a scientific exercise in national security and nation building.

One of the results of the 1947 expedition was a short film, *In the South Seas* (1948), a propaganda film portraying the territory as a potential resource for Australia and the West. It depicted Australian administrators bringing the best of their imperial scientific expertise to the aid of malnourished, under-resourced New Guineans. Early drafts of the script to accompany the film had racially differentiated the scientists from their subjects, promoting 'the science of the white man' in contrast to the 'native villages'.[13] Expunged of these racial overtones, the final script still marked the efforts of the white Australian scientists as crusaders bringing their innovations to the Pacific for the benefit of all. The voice-over to the film declared that

> through the Territory the scientists make their way, studying, recording, learning, looking for clues and facts that will help the administration of Papua and New Guinea to tackle the problems of native health and diet. Science has gone to the South Seas, to help the people of the villages shape their way of life from the best of both worlds.[14]

Through this film, what was on the surface a localized nutritional and dental survey is revealed as part of the broader imperial project. While the expedition's ostensible purpose was a legitimate, if minor, contribution to the science of nutrition and dietetics, it functioned equally as a source of state propaganda.[15]

On the ground, the participant scientists focused on recording quantities and types of food consumed by villagers and consulting with village women cooking their families' meals. The nutritionist weighed all of the foodstuffs consumed and, as biochemist, McArthur's role included analysing dried samples of the foods for their nutrient content. These methods were devised in order to provide an accurate record of eating habits in non-literate societies where the onus could not be placed on the householders to keep a written record of foods consumed. This approach would carry McArthur forward into her nutritional study in Arnhem Land in 1948, where she was employed as nutritionist on a larger, interdisciplinary scientific expedition.[16]

In the published report of the New Guinea Nutrition Survey, a series of recommendations were made that aimed to improve the dietary habits of the New Guinean villagers whose intake had been recorded. These recommendations focused on the necessity of introducing more sources of protein into the diet of the people surveyed. The recommendations were the result of comparison by the research team of their model of a healthy Western diet with that of the taro, sweet potato, yam, banana and sago-based diets found in New Guinea. The researchers found that although villagers were 'able under normal conditions to obtain enough food to sustain life and health, the diet is often badly balanced according to modern standards'.[17] Conceding that the diet was adequate in calories, the researchers were concerned that the calorie intake they observed was overly dependent on carbohydrate, with insufficient fat and protein. Although these assertions were made with some conviction in the report, the researchers had to admit that 'the clinical manifestations of this peculiar food pattern are difficult to detect'.[18] In other words, although the research team was unable to identify any negative health effects resulting from the low-protein diet of New Guinea villagers, the comparison with a 'modern' diet led the team to the conclusion that the diet was deficient.

This published report, combined with the film, highlights the extent to which scientific expeditions of this kind were an exercise in *disseminating* the knowledge of imperial scientists as well as *seeking* it. We are reminded here that even in the twentieth century, journeys of this kind retained some residual traces of expeditions from earlier epochs. Definitions of the word 'expedition' include: 'the action of expediting, helping forward or accomplishing'; 'sending forth with martial intentions'; and 'a body of persons sent out for a warlike or other definite purpose'.[19] The *Oxford English Dictionary* also reminds us that 'survey' can mean not only 'the act of viewing, examining, or inspecting in detail, esp. for some specific purpose', but also 'oversight, supervision, superintendence'.[20] In the film, *In the South Seas*, the scientific expedition appears more as a method of planting the scientific flag in new territories than as a way of gathering new knowledge through rigorous scientific exploration. Scholars such as Tom Griffiths and Stephen A. Walsh have argued that the perils of expeditions into foreign territory would have been difficult to justify if they were simply flag-waving exercises. However, the case of the Institute of Anatomy's nutrition surveys suggests that even if scientific enquiry may have been the central justification for its exertions, the knowledge-gathering motives were thickly overlaid with imperial agendas.[21]

That the dissemination of knowledge was the purpose of the survey was consistent with the educative mission of the Institute of Anatomy in the 1940s, despite its role in the training of nutritionists. The acquisition of experimental skills in the field may have been the justification for the students' participation in the expedition, but this aspect of its execution became invisible in the published report and film that gave account of the work done in New Guinea. As an implementation of British/Australian imperial control over the diet of residents of occupied territories, the results of the New Guinea expedition supported the government's endeavours in imposing colonial expertise on the colony. As Alison Bashford has argued,

> A healthy empire was an ambition of colonial officials ... Medicine, public health, nursing, and the clinic were themselves instruments and sites of colonial governance ... One aim of British medicine historically, then, has been to solve health problems created by imperialism itself.[22]

McArthur's Journey from New Guinea to Arnhem Land

While McArthur was engaged in New Guinea, a group of her fellow students at the Institute of Anatomy had embarked on a parallel nutrition survey in Australia's north. Despite its title, the reach of the wide-ranging Northern Territory Nutrition Survey extended into several of the northern settlements in the state of Western Australia. A supplementary party also collected data on the Barkly Tableland, in towns in Western Queensland, and pastoral stations in the Gulf country.[23] Four nutritionists were sent on this expedition, including Lois Cherry who was McArthur's main correspondent on work carried out in the Northern Territory. The report on the data collected between April and September 1947 makes it clear that the chief focus of the study was on non-Indigenous families. As something of an aside, it seems, data were also obtained on a small group of ten 'coloured families'. Cherry, along with other colleagues from the Institute of Anatomy, noted that the data she had collected provided only an incomplete picture of the dietary intake of residents of the Northern Territory. The main reason for this was that the methodology of Cherry's study required householders to keep a food diary to be returned to the scientists, a method that excluded the large proportion of non-literate Aboriginal people in Central and Northern Australia. The team voiced concern about discrepancies in dietary trends between white households and Aboriginal families.

The investigators noted a complete lack of knowledge of the principles of nutrition among 'coloured' housewives and that a good number of them had very little interest in the acquisition and preparation of satisfactory meals. It was further noted that the standard of education among the coloured families was low, at least in the terms of reference of the investigators, who required householders to be able to read and write English in order to keep a food diary.[24]

The limited data set obtained by the nutritionists posed a serious problem to the reliability of the study, given the high proportion of Aboriginal people in the Northern Territory. This limitation led the Institute of Anatomy to form a Nutritional Unit consisting of McArthur, Kelvin Hodges (biochemist) and Brian Billington (physician), to join the 1948 American-Australian Scientific Expedition to Arnhem Land. Their mission was to survey Indigenous people living in a variety of ecological contexts. The Arnhem Land Expedition, to use its contracted title, was supported by two US sponsors, the Smithsonian Institution and the National Geographic Society. The Australian Museum, the South Australian Museum and a range of Australian government departments also contributed personnel or resources to the expedition, which, in addition to the Nutrition Team, included anthropologists, a mammalogist, a botanist, an ichthyologist, an ornithologist and various support staff. From March until November 1948, the expedition team camped across eastern and western Arnhem Land, with shorter visits to Darwin, collecting data on Aboriginal people and their ceremonies, dietary habits and customs, as well as on native plants and animals of the region. The expedition's findings were published between 1956 and 1964 in a collection of four volumes as *Records of the American-Australian Scientific Expedition to Arnhem Land*, edited by expedition leader Charles Pearcy Mountford.[25] As nutritionist, McArthur's application of techniques derived from the New Guinea expedition in an Australian context marked a ground-breaking attempt to capture nutritional data.[26]

The Northern Australia Development Committee (NADC), formed directly after the conclusion of the Second World War in 1945, recommended the Institute of Anatomy's involvement in both the Northern Territory Nutrition Survey and the Arnhem Land Expedition. The objective of this work from the perspective of the NADC was to collect data on flora, fauna and Aboriginal people's ability to live off the resources of the land. Such information, which would have benefits for both administration and defence, was, according to the committee, 'needed, but not available, during the last war'.[27] However, the Arnhem Land Expedition was also an exercise in public relations and international diplomacy, as a planning document from 1946 suggests:

> No matter what technical developments take place in the methods of warfare there can be little doubt that the development of the north can be regarded as essential to the future security of Australia and a policy should be adopted which will make it clear to the outside world that Australia is vitally interested in this area.[28]

The 1948 Arnhem Land Expedition's strategic alliance with the US can also be seen as part of the national focus on strengthening the

Australian nation state in response to the wars of the first half of the century. Kim Beazley has shown how Australian politicians from both the progressive and conservative parties actively sought an allegiance with the US in the 1940s and especially following the war. Beazley points out that the expedition 'was conducted as the Cold War intensified and it became part of a catalogue of initiatives through which Australia was slowly enmeshed in a Cold War alignment'.[29]

The expedition thus presented a public image of Australian might and scientific sophistication; it had all of the trappings of a heroic male adventure. In press releases leading up to the expedition launch and accounts in the months and years afterwards, Mountford described the mission of the expedition group in terms reminiscent of explorers of much earlier times. Mountford evoked Arnhem Land as 'country where so few white men dared to venture on foot':

> Scarcely scratched by European exploration, Arnhem Land, an aboriginal reserve about the size of Maine, lies in northern Australia ... Except for the everspreading influence of widely spaced Christian missions, it remains blackfellows' country with a Stone Age look.[30]

In spite of the fieldwork carried out by previous researchers, especially by Donald Thomson (see Beudel, this volume), Mountford promoted the mission of his Arnhem Land Expedition as covering uncharted ground, going where few white scientists had gone before and discovering uncorrupted wild tribes. As Dane Kennedy has pointed out, this kind of 'rediscovery' was a feature of expeditionary culture in the nineteenth century, and one inherited by intrepid adventurers of Mountford's ilk, who aimed to 'explore the known anew'.[31] Among McArthur's male colleagues in the Arnhem Land Expedition was a high proportion of men who had (like many of their generation) enlisted in the recent war and its promised, if not always delivered, voyages of adventure.[32] The lifestyle inculcated by Christian missionaries, and the non-nomadic practices of many Aboriginal people who interacted with the expedition, stood in stark contrast to Mountford's public representations of encounters with putatively untouched cultures.

The Unsettling of Masculine Space: Women and the Expedition

A wide-ranging historical literature has dealt with the conception of expeditions in the expansion of empire. John Tosh traces the emergence in the last decades of the nineteenth century of a new set of masculine values linked to the expansion of empire and characterized by 'stoicism ... steely self-control [and] self-reliance'. This was accompanied by a move away from family values.[33] This shift was reflected in the new adventure fiction of the 1890s, in which key fictional characters distanced themselves from women and the world of the feminine in order to freely indulge in adventure. While British cultural historians have also documented a return to masculine domesticity in the 1950s following the ravages of two world wars, exploratory missions and scientific expeditions can be seen as a vestige of this late nineteenth-century thirst for male freedom and adventure or, as Martin Francis frames it, the 'imaginative flight from domesticity that was a reaction to the significant post-war male restlessness and a yearning for the all-male camaraderie of service life'.[34]

The narrative space of the scientific expedition had much in common with pioneering explorers and their tales of adventure from the outer reaches of empire. As Lisa Bloom has written about the North Pole, these expeditions, 'far from being innocent of the tensions of empire, represented a peculiar stage of colonialism ... that integrated the desire for empire with a presumably disinterested moral and scientific imagination'.[35] Just as explorers penetrated the dark centre of the unknown in the mythologized form of Africa, the far North, South or East, or the inhospitable centre of Australia, the language of expedition propaganda involved discovery of the unknown, interrogation of the untouched, and documentation of the never-previously-encountered. Margaret McArthur's participation in the 1947 and 1948 expeditions interacted with masculinist projects that paid homage to empire. These encounters also involved her in state projects of securing borders, making strategic links and contributing data to the country's readiness for conflict.

When it was proposed that McArthur should join the Arnhem Land Expedition, the Institute of Anatomy's director, Frederick W. Clements, found himself once again arguing the case for including a female nutritionist in the party.[36] This time, McArthur was the only female scientist, although the expedition leader's wife, Bessie Mountford, was also part of the group. The difference in the two women's status can be seen in a group photograph of the expedition (Figure 10.2). McArthur is seated on the ground and differentiated from Bessie Mountford by her clothing. McArthur's outfit matches the safari suits of the male scientists while Mrs Mountford wears a floral dress that befits her role as 'honorary secretary' of the expedition. Australian Museum anthropologist Frederick McCarthy described

Figure 10.2 The American-Australian Scientific Expedition to Arnhem Land at Oenpelli, 1948. Photograph by Howell Walker. National Geographic Creative. Reproduced with permission.

McArthur in the first weeks of their acquaintance, positioning her within a set of imagined female traits:

> McArthur is an easy going type, who admits to being lazy and enjoys it, likes to swear a bit and generally exhibits a hard exterior typical of women careerists, but is really just the opposite. She is frank and has a keen mind ready to put Setzler in his place at any moment.[37]

In spite of the presence of one other non-Indigenous woman in the group, McArthur's methodological approach to her research created tension within the expedition team. The situation in Arnhem Land contrasted significantly with what she had encountered in New Guinea, where the majority of villagers maintained a traditional diet. In Arnhem Land, McArthur found large communities of people subsisting on rations of flour, rice and tea provided by missions and other settlements in exchange either for work in gardens or attendance at church services. Occasional weekend hunting trips notwithstanding, McArthur found it initially impossible to paint a picture of how people had traditionally lived on native plants and animals.

The residence of most Aboriginal people in settlements was disappointing for many of the scientists, and it prevented McArthur from documenting the nutritional value of foods endemic to the area as she had intended. Although an analysis of the actual intake of nutrients by Aboriginal people would have brought her research in line with the 1947 Northern Territory Nutritional Survey, McArthur's ambitions for the Arnhem Land research defied the directives of the Institute of Anatomy. Instead, she focused on producing significant data on the nutritive value and time spent acquiring foods that would have formed a traditional native diet.[38] As McArthur realized that it was not going to be possible to gather data on native foods while in the settlements, she actively sought opportunities to travel away from the main camps on her own or in small research groups. The idea was to camp with those remaining Aboriginal people who hunted and gathered local foods, rather than subsisting on settlement rations.

Although McArthur's methodologies used many of the techniques derived from the earlier New Guinea expedition, her approach differed in that she sought to correlate the actual content of the Arnhem Land diet with the health results derived from the medical team's tests on mission and non-mission residents, rather than against Australian dietary norms. Jon Altman has suggested that the efficacy of McArthur's attempt to measure Aboriginal native diets on their own terms was somewhat undermined by the recommendations included at the end of the nutrition report. These recommendations suggested that a means of agricultural cultivation should be implemented for the ongoing wellbeing of Aboriginal people. They were unattributed to McArthur or any of the contributing authors to the nutrition report. Altman speculates that this lack of attribution may be indicative of McArthur distancing herself from the assimilationist government agenda of her department whose policies emphasized the integration of Aboriginal people into wider Australian society.[39]

McArthur's approaches to the Arnhem Land Expedition illuminate a conflict between the adventuring, pioneer spirit of expeditioning and the expectation that a female nutritionist would remain ensconced in the imagined kitchens of local women. By the 1940s, women's access to higher education meant that McArthur was by no means unique as a female scientist. Annette Hamilton has noted the proportionately large number of women carrying out anthropological fieldwork in Australia in the early to mid twentieth century, considering the size of the population and limited budgets (including Olive Pink, Phyllis Kaberry, Ursula McConnel, Nancy Munn, Marie Reay and Catherine Berndt, to name a few).[40] And yet McArthur's inclusion in a scientific expedition, widely promoted in the media as seeking to document unstudied tribes, still challenged expectations of the appropriate place for women in the public sphere.

While many of McArthur's colleagues viewed her position in the field as legitimate, and her supervisor, Clements, advocated strongly for her to be included as an essential part of the Nutritional Unit, McArthur encountered significant tensions within the expedition party, particularly in interactions with the leader, Charles P. Mountford. McArthur's letters to Clements and those of her colleague, Brian Billington, reveal that her attempt to carry out fieldwork away from the main expedition camp was the cause of open conflict in the party.[41] The attempts of predecessors such as Elsie Clews Parsons, Gladys Reichard and Margaret Mead (discussed by Deacon in this volume) to break down the barriers preventing women and men from becoming 'unselfconscious colleagues', had clearly not trickled down to Australia in the 1940s when McArthur came face to face with the ideological conflict between women's scientific agendas and the heroic male framework of expeditionary culture.

The culmination of this conflict was Mountford's insistence that McArthur be chaperoned on the side expedition she arranged to Kunnanj in west Arnhem Land (referred to in the expedition reports as 'Fish Creek'). She planned to camp there for several weeks with a group of people who derived all their sustenance from hunting and gathering foods in the area. Mountford initially insisted that she be accompanied by a male expedition member, along with the Indigenous married couple who would act as her interpreters. However, when Frederick McCarthy volunteered to accompany her on the trip in order to carry out his own anthropological study, Mountford protested that this too was inappropriate, given that McCarthy was a married man and that he and McArthur had become good friends over the course of the expedition. After much argument, in which Clements became involved through extensive correspondence, the expedition's cook and transport officer, John Bray, was finally designated as chaperone to McArthur and McCarthy.[42] McArthur complained to Clements:

> it is obvious that the old ideas take a long time to die, with the result that every time I have gone out from the base camp there have always been complications due to the fact that I am a woman ... I am just not used to having to fight so hard to do a job![43]

The resistance and professional isolation that McArthur faced as part of the 1948 expedition were clearly contrasted with the institutional support she had received from the Institute of Anatomy on the 1947 expedition, a support that was evidenced on a daily basis by the participation of several other female colleagues and the institution's refusal to see their gender as a hindrance.

Conclusions: Expeditionary Science and Gender

In spite of the obstacles to McArthur's professional work in 1948, it is clear that these two expeditions were instrumental in providing an avenue towards independence as a researcher.[44] After completing subsequent study in anthropology in London, McArthur was supported by A.P. Elkin, Professor of Anthropology at the University of Sydney, to carry out fieldwork in Goilala subdistrict, north of Port Moresby in Central Papua New Guinea. She lived in Omu in the Kunimaipa valley for three years, and for most of the time was the only outsider resident in the village. Initially she worked with an interpreter, but after the first year she worked alone. Like her mentor Phyllis Kaberry (one of various fieldworkers who supported her), McArthur was a beneficiary of A.P. Elkin's observation that substantial knowledge was lacking from anthropological studies carried out exclusively by men. This was especially the case in areas of knowledge that were gender-specific or secret-sacred.[45] McArthur's experiences in New Guinea and Arnhem Land were given weight by Kaberry in the reference she wrote supporting McArthur's application for the Walter Mersh Strong Scholarship at the University of Sydney in 1952. Her fellowship application proposed 'a joint nutritional and anthropological research project' which combined the techniques and skills acquired on the 1947 and 1948 expeditions with the anthropology degree completed in London under the supervision of Raymond Firth.[46]

McArthur's position in the two expeditions highlights the gendered nature of how expedition cultures were constructed. It presents expeditions as, in many ways, distillations of the preoccupations of a society and of the institutions they represent. They become rhetorical constructs as much as scientific explorations. Although scientific expeditions might have represented themselves as information and knowledge-gathering missions seeking to inform the public work of the scientists who carried them out, mid-century Australian expeditions can be viewed as projects whose objectives included the dissemination of existing scientific knowledge and the assertion of intellectual dominance over colonial territory. The fact that we are able to observe expeditions through McArthur's eyes makes visible the implicitly gendered assumptions within this combination of adventure and science. For McArthur's male colleagues too, her presence (particularly on the Arnhem Land Expedition) underscored the extent to which the social space of the expedition was constructed around premises of male freedom and independence.

Amanda Harris is Senior Research Fellow at Sydney Conservatorium of Music, University of Sydney and Director of the Sydney Unit of the digital archive PARADISEC (Pacific and Regional Archive for Digital Sources in Endangered Cultures). Her book *Representing Australian Aboriginal Music and Dance 1930-70* was published by Bloomsbury Academic in 2020. Her edited book *Circulating Cultures: Exchanges of Australian Indigenous Music, Dance and Media* was published in 2014.

Notes

1. Her training as a biochemist had also concentrated on food, but this turn towards comparative cultural research was new. A. Margaret McArthur, *Theoretical Thesis: The Breakdown and Synthesis of Glycogen; Practical Thesis : 1) Analysis of the Oil of Subterranean Clover, 2) Investigation of the Breakdown of Starch in Bananas*, Master's thesis (Melbourne: University of Melbourne, 1942).
2. Letter from J.M. Fraser, Acting Director-General of Health, Minister of the State for Health (19 Dec 1945 – reference number 726/16) headed For Cabinet: Scholarships – School of Nutrition, Nutrition Proposal for the establishment of a postgraduate school of nutrition at the Australian Institute of Anatomy, A1928/726/16 SECTION 1, National Archives of Australia (NAA), Canberra, 1946–47.
3. Nutrition Proposal for the Establishment of a Postgraduate School of Nutrition at the Australian Institute of Anatomy, Section 1, Correspondence files, multiple number series (first series), A1928/726/16 SECTION 1, NAA, Canberra, 1945–46.
4. Nutrition Proposed nutrition survey in Papua New Guinea, Extract from Minutes of Advisory Committee Meeting Held at Port Moresby, 16 January 1947, A1928/726/17, NAA, Canberra, 1946–49.
5. Ibid.
6. Though notes from McArthur's colleague Doreen Langley's diary suggest that E.H. Hipsley, the leader of the expedition, assumed that McArthur and Langley would carry out the kitchen and basic administrative tasks for the group. Langley reports that all other members of the party thought this was a great joke. Doreen Langley, *Diary*, 18 and 29 June 1947, Papers of Doreen Langley, MS9550/1/2, folder 2, National Library of Australia (NLA).
7. This decision was pragmatic and the result of obtaining the scholarship on offer to carry out anthropological fieldwork in New Guinea under the remote supervision of the University of Sydney's A.P. Elkin. Nevertheless, this early experience contributed to McArthur's eligibility for this later position. Doreen Langley also documented in her diary the pull that New Guinea had for both Langley and McArthur, and their intentions to return and do further study there. Doreen Langley, *Diary*, 29 November 1947, Papers of Doreen Langley, MS9550/1/4, NLA.

8. For further discussion of the gendered nature of food production and study in expedition culture, see Amanda Harris, 'Food, Feeding and Consumption (or the Cook, the Wife and the Nutritionist): The Politics of Gender and Class in a 1948 Australian Expedition', *History and Anthropology* 24(3) (2013), 363–79.
9. Georgine Clarsen's discussion of female motorists provides a useful perspective on the nonlinear history of women working in professions traditionally regarded as masculine. Georgine Clarsen, *Eat My Dust: Early Women Motorists* (Baltimore, MD: The Johns Hopkins University Press, 2008), 11.
10. Roy MacLeod, 'Discovery and Exploration', in Peter J. Bowler and John V. Pickstone (eds), *The Cambridge History of Science: Modern Life and Earth Sciences* (Cambridge: Cambridge University Press, 2009), 39, 45. For a discussion of the shift in anthropology, see Henrika Kuklick, 'Personal Equations: Reflections on the History of Fieldwork, with Special Reference to Sociocultural Anthropology', *Isis* 102 (2011), 1–33.
11. Brigid Hains, *The Ice and the Inland: Mawson, Flynn, and the Myth of the Frontier* (Carlton South, Vic.: Melbourne University Press, 2002), 105.
12. Stuart Doran, *Full Circle: Australia and Papua New Guinea 1883–1970* (Canberra: Department of Foreign Affairs and Trade, 2007), 2–3; and Donald Denoon, *A Trial Separation: Australia and the Decolonisation of Papua New Guinea* (Canberra: ANU E Press, 2012), 3, http://www.jstor.org/stable/j.ctt24hdvs.
13. Earlier drafts of the voice-over text are contained in 'Nutrition Survey of Natives of the Territory of Papua and New Guinea', A518/C840/1/4 PART 1, NAA, Canberra.
14. James Fitzpatrick, *In the South Seas* (1948), Access no. 60842, 60862, Film Australia, National Film and Sound Archive, Sydney.
15. This expedition, while not strictly an anthropological one, could be seen as a continuation of E.W.P. Chinnery's mission as government anthropologist for New Guinea, appointed in 1924 to use anthropological research to carry out the spirit of the League of Nations Mandate for the 'moral and spiritual progress of the natives'. Chinnery maintained that through the application of anthropological knowledge the administrator could encourage 'the natives themselves ... to take an active interest and responsibility for their own progress'. Geoffrey Gray, *A Cautious Silence: The Politics of Australian Anthropology* (Canberra: Aboriginal Studies Press, 2007), 6.
16. Among McArthur's files in the University Archives of the University of Sydney is a copy of M.W. Grant's *Technique for the Dietary Section of a Nutrition Survey* (1948), which may also have influenced her approach.
17. Eben H. Hipsley and F.W. Clements (eds), *Report of the New Guinea Nutrition Survey Expedition* (Sydney: Department of External Territories, 1950), 19.

18. Ibid., 20. Hipsley was still grappling with this contradiction years later, and reported having discovered a bodily bacteria that converts nitrogen to protein in the body, explaining why New Guineans emit twice the product of protein consumption that is actually evident in their diets. See 'Air Could Be Food Source – Scientist', *Sydney Morning Herald*, 8 September 1969, 3.
19. 'expedition, n.', *OED Online*, December 2013, http://www.oed.com.ezproxy1.library.usyd.edu.au/view/Entry/66487?redirectedFrom=expedition& (accessed 24 January 2014).
20. 'survey, n.', *OED Online*, December 2013, http://www.oed.com.ezproxy1.library.usyd.edu.au/view/Entry/195089?rskey=sZwiRp&result=1&isAdvanced=false (accessed 6 February 2014).
21. See Tom Griffiths, 'A Polar Drama: The Australasian Antarctic Expedition of 1911–14', in Martin Thomas (ed.), *Expedition into Empire: Exploratory Journeys and the Making of the Modern World* (London: Routledge, 2015), 171–93; Stephen A. Walsh, 'On Slippery Ice: Discovery, Imperium, and the Austro-Hungarian North Polar Expedition (1872–4)', in Thomas, *Expedition into Empire*, 148–70.
22. Alison Bashford has discussed medicine and medical research in the hundred years between 1850 and 1950 as a common tool of empire. Alison Bashford, 'Medicine, Gender, and Empire', in Philippa Levine (ed.), *Gender and Empire* (Oxford: Oxford University Press, 2004), 112.
23. Memorandum from F.W. Clements, 10 February 1947 about two proposed nutrition surveys to NT and PNG, 1947–49, Central Office and all States Generally – Australian Institute of Anatomy – Northern Territory – Nutrition survey, A1658/1124/7/2 Correspondence files, multiple number series (second series), NAA, Canberra.
24. Report of a Food Consumption Survey of Northern Australia (April to September 1947), NADC [Northern Australia Development Committee] Nutritional Survey, A9816/1946/477, NAA, Canberra.
25. Charles P. Mountford (ed.), *Records of the American-Australian Scientific Expedition to Arnhem Land* (Melbourne: Melbourne University Press, 1956–64).
26. The importance of McArthur's study in collaboration with Frederick McCarthy was noted by Marshall Sahlins in *Stone Age Economics* (Chicago, IL: Aldine Atherton, 1972); for more recent discussion of the impact of this work, see Jon Altman, 'From Kunnanj, Fish Creek, to Mumeka, Mann River: Hunter-Gatherer Tradition and Transformation in Western Arnhem Land, 1948–2009', in Martin Thomas and Margo Neale (eds), *Exploring the Legacy of the 1948 Arnhem Land Expedition* (Canberra: ANU E Press, 2011), 113–34.
27. N.A.D.C. [Northern Australia Development Committee] – Arnhem Land Expedition, Northern Australia Development Committee Agendum 47 Arnhem Land Survey, 1947–48, A9816/1947/89 PART 1, NAA, Canberra, p. 12. See also 'Data will be collected that will be of value to

the defence authorities, giving the food available, its nutritional value, where and when it can be obtained and other relevant information. This was badly needed but was not available during the last war'. Letter from Grenfell Ruddock to Northern Australia Development Committee, 17 December 1946, NADC [Northern Australia Development Committee] Nutritional Survey, A9816/1946/477, NAA, Canberra.
28. Anon., Northern Australia Development Committee Report on the Development of North Australia Part 1, A431/1948/213 PART 1, NAA, Canberra.
29. Kim Beazley, 'Nation Building or Cold War: Political Settings for the Arnhem Land Expedition', in Thomas and Neale, *Exploring the Legacy*, 58.
30. Charles P. Mountford, 'Exploring Stone Age Arnhem Land', *National Geographic Magazine* 96(6) (1949), 745.
31. Dane Kennedy, *The Last Blank Spaces: Exploring Africa and Australia* (Cambridge, MA: Harvard University Press, 2013), 6–7.
32. War records in the National Archives of Australia indicate that John Bray, Frederick McCarthy, Peter Bassett-Smith and Kelvin Hodges were among the Australian men who enlisted during the course of the war.
33. John Tosh, *A Man's Place: Masculinity and the Middle-Class Home in Victorian England* (New Haven, CT: Yale University Press, 1999), 174.
34. Martin Francis, 'A Flight from Commitment? Domesticity, Adventure and the Masculine Imaginary in Britain after the Second World War,' *Gender & History* 19(1) (2007), 164.
35. Lisa Bloom, *Gender on Ice: American Ideologies of Polar Expeditions* (Minneapolis, MN: University of Minnesota Press, 1993), 3.
36. Memorandum from F.W. Clements, 14 January 1948 (1947–48), Survey – Arnhem Land, Correspondence files, multiple number series, Institute of Anatomy, A2644/50/11 SECTION 1, NAA, Canberra, p. 328.
37. F.D. McCarthy, 1948, Diary 1: Field Notes Groote Eylandt 1, Papers of Frederick David McCarthy, MS 3513/14/1, Australian Institute of Aboriginal and Torres Strait Islander Studies (AIATSIS), Canberra, 55.
38. The results of this work, carried out with Australian Museum anthropologist Frederick McCarthy, were published in the second volume of the Arnhem Land report and were later used by Marshall Sahlins to formulate a theory of Aboriginal people as the 'original affluent society' in his 1972 book *Stone Age Economics*. Frederick D. McCarthy and Margaret McArthur, 'The Food Quest and the Time Factor in Aboriginal Economic Life', in Mountford, *Records of the American-Australian Scientific Expedition*, Vol. 2, 145–94.
39. Altman, 'From Kunnanj, Fish Creek, to Mumeka, Mann River', 121. On assimilation, see Russell McGregor, *Indifferent Inclusion: Aboriginal People and the Australian Nation* (Canberra: Aboriginal Studies Press, 2011), 93–118; Anna Haebich, *Spinning the Dream: Assimilation in Australia*

1950–1970 (North Fremantle: Fremantle Press, 2007); and Tim Rowse (ed.), *Contesting Assimilation* (Perth: API Network, 2005).
40. Annette Hamilton, 'Daughters of the Imaginary', *Canberra Anthropology* 9(2) (1986), 5. See also Julie Marcus (ed.), *First in Their Field: Women and Australian Anthropology* (Carlton, Vic.: Melbourne University Press, 1993).
41. See also Tom Griffiths' discussion of continuing resistance to women's presence in expeditions to Antarctica, well into the 1950s and even 1980s. Tom Griffiths, *Slicing the Silence: Voyaging to Antarctica* (Sydney: University of New South Wales Press, 2007), 215.
42. For more on these conflicts, see Amanda Harris, 'Chaperoned into Arnhem Land: Margaret McArthur and the Politics of Nutrition and Fieldwork in 1948', *Lilith: A Feminist History Journal* 20 (2014), 62–75.
43. McArthur to Clements, 30 September 1948, Survey – Arnhem Land, A2644/50/11 SECTION 1, NAA, Canberra.
44. Henrika Kuklick has pointed to a tradition of scientific work in colonized territories as a testing ground for establishing careers in the metropolis in 'Science as Adventure', in Joshua A. Bell and Erin L. Hasinoff (eds), *The Anthropology of Expeditions: Travel, Visualities, Afterlives* (New York: Bard Graduate Center, 2015), 38.
45. See Elkin's introduction to Phyllis Mary Kaberry, *Aboriginal Woman: Sacred and Profane* (Farnborough, Hants: Gregg International, 1970), xix.
46. Annie M. McArthur, G3/13/8872, University of Sydney Archives.

Bibliography

Altman, Jon. 'From Kunnanj, Fish Creek, to Mumeka, Mann River: Hunter-Gatherer Tradition and Transformation in Western Arnhem Land, 1948–2009', in Martin Thomas and Margo Neale (eds), *Exploring the Legacy of the 1948 Arnhem Land Expedition* (Canberra: ANU E Press, 2011), 113–34.

Bashford, Alison. 'Medicine, Gender, and Empire', in Philippa Levine (ed.), *Gender and Empire* (Oxford: Oxford University Press, 2004), 112–33.

Beazley, Kim. 'Nation Building or Cold War: Political Settings for the Arnhem Land Expedition', in Martin Thomas and Margo Neale (eds), *Exploring the Legacy of the 1948 Arnhem Land Expedition* (Canberra: ANU E Press, 2011), 55–72.

Bloom, Lisa. *Gender on Ice: American Ideologies of Polar Expeditions*. Minneapolis, MN: University of Minnesota Press, 1993.

Clarsen, Georgine. *Eat My Dust: Early Women Motorists*. Baltimore, MD: The Johns Hopkins University Press, 2008.

Denoon, Donald. *A Trial Separation: Australia and the Decolonisation of Papua New Guinea*. Canberra: ANU E Press, 2012.

Doran, Stuart. *Full Circle: Australia and Papua New Guinea 1883–1970.* Canberra: Department of Foreign Affairs and Trade, 2007.
Francis, Martin. 'A Flight from Commitment? Domesticity, Adventure and the Masculine Imaginary in Britain after the Second World War'. *Gender & History* 19(1) (2007), 163–85.
Gray, Geoffrey. *A Cautious Silence: The Politics of Australian Anthropology.* Canberra: Aboriginal Studies Press, 2007.
Griffiths, Tom. 'A Polar Drama: The Australasian Antarctic Expedition of 1911–14', in Martin Thomas (ed.), *Expedition into Empire: Exploratory Journeys and the Making of the Modern World* (London: Routledge, 2015), 171–93.
———. *Slicing the Silence: Voyaging to Antarctica.* Sydney: University of New South Wales Press, 2007.
Haebich, Anna. *Spinning the Dream: Assimilation in Australia 1950–1970.* North Fremantle: Fremantle Press, 2007.
Hains, Brigid. *The Ice and the Inland: Mawson, Flynn, and the Myth of the Frontier.* Carlton South, Vic.: Melbourne University Press, 2002.
Hamilton, Annette. 'Daughters of the Imaginary'. *Canberra Anthropology* 9(2) (1986), 1–25.
Harris, Amanda. 'Chaperoned into Arnhem Land: Margaret McArthur and the Politics of Nutrition and Fieldwork in 1948'. *Lilith: A Feminist History Journal* 20 (2014), 62–75.
———. 'Food, Feeding and Consumption (or the Cook, the Wife and the Nutritionist): The Politics of Gender and Class in a 1948 Australian Expedition'. *History and Anthropology* 24(3) (2013), 363–79.
Hipsley, Eben H., and F.W. Clements (eds). *Report of the New Guinea Nutrition Survey Expedition.* Sydney: Department of External Territories, 1950.
Kaberry, Phyllis Mary. *Aboriginal Woman: Sacred and Profane.* Farnborough, Hants: Gregg International, 1970.
Kennedy, Dane. *The Last Blank Spaces: Exploring Africa and Australia.* Cambridge, MA: Harvard University Press, 2013.
Kuklick, Henrika. 'Personal Equations: Reflections on the History of Fieldwork, with Special Reference to Sociocultural Anthropology'. *Isis* 102 (2011), 1–33.
———. 'Science as Adventure', in Joshua A. Bell and Erin L. Hasinoff (eds), *The Anthropology of Expeditions: Travel, Visualities, Afterlives* (New York: Bard Graduate Center, 2015), 33–57.
MacLeod, Roy. 'Discovery and Exploration', in Peter J. Bowler and John V. Pickstone (eds), *The Cambridge History of Science: Modern Life and Earth Sciences* (Cambridge: Cambridge University Press, 2009), 34–59.
Marcus, Julie (ed.). *First in Their Field: Women and Australian Anthropology.* Carlton, Vic.: Melbourne University Press, 1993.
McArthur, A. Margaret. *Theoretical Thesis: The Breakdown and Synthesis of Glycogen; Practical Thesis: 1) Analysis of the Oil of Subterranean Clover,*

2) Investigation of the Breakdown of Starch in Bananas. Master's thesis. Melbourne: University of Melbourne, 1942.

McCarthy, Frederick D., and Margaret McArthur. 'The Food Quest and the Time Factor in Aboriginal Economic Life', in Charles P. Mountford (ed.), *Records of the American-Australian Scientific Expedition to Arnhem Land* (Melbourne: Melbourne University Press, 1960), 145–94.

McGregor, Russell. *Indifferent Inclusion: Aboriginal People and the Australian Nation.* Canberra: Aboriginal Studies Press, 2011.

Mountford, Charles P. 'Exploring Stone Age Arnhem Land'. *National Geographic Magazine* 96(6) (1949), 745–82.

——— (ed.). *Records of the American-Australian Scientific Expedition to Arnhem Land.* Melbourne: Melbourne University Press, 1956–64.

Rowse, Tim (ed.). *Contesting Assimilation.* Perth: API Network, 2005.

Sahlins, Marshall. *Stone Age Economics.* Chicago, IL: Aldine Atherton, 1972.

Tosh, John. *A Man's Place: Masculinity and the Middle-Class Home in Victorian England.* New Haven, CT: Yale University Press, 1999.

Walsh, Stephen A. 'On Slippery Ice: Discovery, Imperium, and the Austro-Hungarian North Polar Expedition (1872–4)', in Martin Thomas (ed.), *Expedition into Empire: Exploratory Journeys and the Making of the Modern World* (London: Routledge, 2015), 148–70.

INDEX

*References to illustrations are in **bold***

A
Aborigines. *See* Indigenous people of Australia
Alice Springs, 18, 39, 43, 44, 45, 49, 50, 51, 52, 53, 54, 56, 59; **44, 47, 50**
American-Australian Scientific Expedition to Arnhem Land (1948), 10–17, 23, 25, 46, 109, 255, 290, 298–303, 304
American Museum of Natural History, 22, 33, 56, 236, 237, 238, 239, 240, 242, 243, 244, 248, 253, 255, 263, 264, 265, 266, 267, 268, 272, 273
American Museum of Natural History Sepik Expedition (1931–32), 23, 263, 264–273, 274, 275, 276, 277, 278, 279, 280, 281, 282; **269**
American West, 127, 128, 129, 130, 131, 132, 133, 134, 135, 138, 141, 142
Andrews, Roy Chapman, 236, 238, 241, 242, 243, 247, 254, 255; **240**
anthropometry, 20, 21, 138, 139, 150, 151, 153–60, 161, 163, 164, 245
Arabs, 151, 152, 161, 164
Arapesh, 269, 271, 272, 273, 274, 279; **269**
archaeology, 20, 128, 130, 132, 133, 134, 135, 138, 139, 142, 241, 244, 247, 248, 251, 267
Arnhem Land, 10, 11, 12, 14, 15, 19, 23, 96, 98, 99, 100, 101, 102, 103, 107, 109, 110, 111, 113, 295, 297, 298, 299, 301, 302, 303, 304; **99**

Arrernte, 43, 44, 45, 48, 49, 51, 52, 54, 57, 58, 59; **44, 50**
art, 57, 58, 64, 97, 128, 129, 131, 132, 134, 137, 138, 141, 142, 223, 239, 246
artefacts, 10, 14, 18, 22, 38, 40, 43, 53, 57, 77, 96, 97, 98, 128, 132, 133, 136, 137, 140, 142, 155, 219, 264, 267, 269, 273
Australian National Research Council, 19, 102, 103, 104

B
Bateson, Gregory, 23, 274, 275, 280; **275**
Benedict, Ruth, 235, 245, 246, 267, 270, 275, 276, 277, 278, 280
Berbers, 21, 151, 152, 155, 156, 157, 158, 159, 160, 161, 164, 165
Berndt, Catherine, 109, 302
Berndt, Ronald, 109
Boas, Franz, 22, 57, 140, 142, 235, 237, 243, 244, 245, 246, 247, 250, 251, 252, 253, 254, 265, 266, 267, 268, 270
Boongaree, 209, 210, 211, 224
British Museum, 96, 206, 221, 222, 224
Bundle, 22, 209, 210, 211, 212, 213, 214, 216, 217, 224
Bureau of American Ethnology, 134, 135, 139, 140, 141, 142, 143

C
Cambridge Anthropological Expedition to Torres Straits (1898), 18, 19, 45, 46, 64, 65–85, 95, 96, 97, 98, 101, 102, 107, 221, 264; **65, 66, 71, 76**

Cape York Peninsula, 95, 96, 101, 102, 103
cartography, 9, 12, 13, 21, 105, 127, 129, 175, 178, 180, 189, 195, 264, 268
Central Asiatic Expeditions (1920s and 1930s), 239, 241, 242, 243, 244, 254; **240**
Central Australia, 17, 18, 43, 44, 45, 46, 54, 55, 56, 59, 96, 115, 291, 297
ceremony, 10, 15, 44, 45, 48, 49, 52, 53, 55, 58, 59, 67, 74, 75, 76, 77, 78, 79, 81, 103, 114, 139, 243, 246, 298; **44, 77**
  initiation, 55, 69, 76, 77
collecting, 7, 9, 24, 25, 38, 39, 40, 41, 56, 58, 59, 70, 72, 96, 102, 105, 206, 214, 216, 223, 237, 242, 278
colonialism, 7, 21, 24, 66, 67, 70, 73, 115, 141, 151, 152, 153, 157, 158, 161, 162, 164, 165, 177, 178, 181, 190, 268, 270, 280, 297, 300, 304
Columbia University, 22, 235, 237, 238, 245, 246, 265, 267, 276, 277
Coon, Carleton S., 20, 21, 150–65; **154, 156, 162**
  expeditions to the Maghreb (1920s), 20, 150–66; **154, 156, 162**

D
dance, 9, 73, 75, 76, 78, 79
data, 3, 19, 40, 41, 42, 71, 97, 98, 103, 105, 141, 158, 255, 271, 272, 278, 298
Driver, Felix, 1, 6, 98, 100, 105, 112, 206, 209, 219
Durkheim, Emile, 53, 57

E
Elkin, A.P., 19, 104, 106, 109, 113, 304
empire, 100, 209, 219, 294, 299, 300
encounter, 21, 22, 83, 114, 165, 175, 176, 177, 179, 180, 181, 184, 190, 192, 193, 194, 195, 205, 206, 207, 208, 209, 213, 214, 215, 217, 218, 219, 222, 223, 299

eugenics 239, 240, 267
expedition
  as adventure, 1, 4, 21, 98, 111, 112, 113, 239, 241, 242, 254, 300
  as form, 100, 107, 113, 235
  as performance, 9
  collective nature of, 7, 10, 22, 96, 97, 98, 206
  connection with exploration, 9, 10, 12
  definition of, 8, 24
  financing of, 6, 11, 22, 24, 48, 104, 112, 235, 241 (see also funding)
  imaginary, 3, 13, 14, 20, 25
  maritime, 3, 21, 83, 98, 175, 176, 177, 205, 221
  methodology, 21, 79
  role of Indigenous people, 7, 17, 18, 19, 20, 21, 22, 38, 48, 53, 54, 57, 72, 80, 81, 83, 114, 157, 166, 176, 208, 209, 211, 212, 213, 216, 224, 303, 304 (see also language)
  solo expeditions, 46, 97, 98
  structure of, 7, 8, 11, 13, 15, 21, 275
  terminology, 176, 177

F
Fabian, Johannes, 9, 25
feminism, 22, 235, 237, 247, 250, 252, 274, 276, 278, 281
field ('the field'), 5, 8, 17, 18, 37, 38–41, 44, 45, 46, 47, 49, 52, 54, 56, 57, 58, 59, 97, 98, 99, 112, 143, 208, 241, 247, 268, 281, 282
film, 1, 5, 10, 11, 15, 23, 38, 45, 48, 50, 51, 56, 59, 67, 77, 78, 97, 100, 113, 242, 295, 296
food, 10, 23, 44, 48, 99, 103, 160, 190, 255, 269, 303
Fortune, Reo, 23, 263, 265, 268, 269, 270, 271, 272, 273, 274, 277, 279, 280; **275**
Frazer, James, 41, 44, 47, 57, 97; **269**
funding, 5, 6, 11, 18, 22, 24, 48, 102, 104, 112, 115, 139, 235, 236, 245, 246, 247, 251, 253

G

gender, 8, 15, 16, 17, 22, 24, 25, 235, 236, 237, 242, 243, 244, 245, 246, 247, 248, 249, 250, 251, 252, 254, 255, 263, 264, 265, 266, 268, 270, 271, 272, 273, 274, 278, 279, 280, 281, 282, 290, 292, 293, 294, 299–304
Geographical Journal, 98, 103, 108, 109, 111
Gillen, Francis, 18, 39, 40, 42, 43, 44, 45, 46, 47, 48, 49, 50, 51, 52, 53, 54, 55, 56, 57, 58, 59; **47**
Guugu Yimithirr, 213, 214

H

Haddon, Alfred, 4, 64, 45, 47, 65, 67, 68, 69, 70, 71, 72, 73, 74, 75, 76, 77, 78, 79, 80, 81, 82, 83, 84, 85, 95, 96, 97, 100, 101, 102, 106, 107, 114, 115, 221; **65, 77**
Hanover Bay, 212, 213, 214, 216, 218, 219, 221, 223, 224; **219**
heroism, 5, 6, 10, 22, 113, 239, 254, 294, 299, 303
Holmes, William Henry, 20, 127, 128, 129, 130, 131, 132, 133, 134, 135, 136, 137, 138, 139, 140, 141, 142; **130, 131, 137**
Howitt, Alfred William, 42, 43
human remains, 10, 54, 55, 155, 128, 138, 187, 216
  collection, 10
  repatriation, 11, 55
Hydrographic Surveys of the Australian Coast (1817–1822), 21, 22, 205–21, 222, 223, 224

I

immersive fieldwork, 3, 4, 19, 114, 115, 265, 269
imperialism, 2, 3, 7, 13, 17, 180, 206, 208, 265, 266, 268, 282, 290, 295, 296
Indigenous people of Australia, 12, 13, 18, 19, 20, 22, 39, 42, 43, 48, 54, 58, 111, 211, 240, 255, 291, 298

K

Kennedy, Dane, 20, 98, 99, 210, 299

Kidder, Alfred, 235, 236, 247, 248, 249, 250, 251, 252, 253, 254, 255; **249**
King, Phillip Parker, 21, 22, 205, 206, 207, 208, 209, 210, 211, 212, 213, 214, 218, 219, 221, 224; **207, 220**
kinship, 41, 44, 52, 54, 55, 69, 80, 103, 106, 139, 265, 271, 272, 282
Kuklick, Henrika, 4, 45, 46, 56, 57, 97, 102, 106

L

language, 19, 38, 43, 46, 53, 54, 64, 65, 68, 70, 73, 77, 82, 84, 139, 157, 176, 182, 206, 210, 245, 256, 248, 252, 268, 270, 271, 273
  interpreting and translating, 48, 53, 54, 81, 82, 114, 157, 178, 186, 193, 303, 304
lantern slides, 1, 5, 73, 79, 83
Lévi-Strauss, Claude, 1, 5, 6, 25, 281
London Mission Society, 70, 72, 73, 75, 82, 83

M

Maghreb, 20, 21, 150, 153, 155, 166. *See also* Morocco
Malinowski, Bronisław, 4, 19, 44, 46, 66, 83, 114
material culture, 17, 24, 68, 78, 135, 139, 192, 205, 207, 215, 221, 224
McArthur, Margaret, 10, 15, 17, 23, 255, 290, 291–95, 297, 298, 299–304; **293, 301**
McCarthy, Frederick, 23, 255, 300, 303
Mead, Margaret, 5, 6, 23, 246, 247, 255, 263, 264, 265, 266, 267, 268, 269, 270, 271, 272, 273, 274, 276, 277, 278, 279, 280, 281, 282, 303; **269, 275**
Meriam-le, 18, 19, 68, 69, 70, 71, 72, 73, 74, 75, 77, 78, 79, 80, 82, 83, 84, 85; **77**
missionaries, 6, 41, 100, 178, 220, 268
missions, 11, 42, 70, 73, 77, 82, 114, 221, 301, 302
Morgan, Lewis H., 41, 42

Morocco, 21, 150, 151, 152, 154, 155, 156, 157, 158, 159, 160, 161, 162, 163, 164, 165, 166; **154**
Mountford, Bessie, 15, 17
Mountford, Charles P., 10, 11, 12, 13, 14, 16, 17, 19, 25, 46, 298, 299, 303
Mundugumor, 263, 265, 268, 271, 272, 273, 274, 282
Murray Islands, 72, 73, 79, 83
Museum Victoria (*formerly* National Museum of Victoria), 17, 55, 56, 97
museums, 2, 5, 6, 13, 14, 24, 59, 133, 136, 141, 215, 216, 238, 248, 251
music, 9, 10, 65, 73, 74, 139, 140
myth, 2, 13, 41, 68, 69, 109, 209, 246, 265, 271, 281, 300

N
National Geographic Magazine, 5, 10, 15, 46, 99, 111
National Geographical Society, 10, 11, 12, 14, 15, 298
Native Americans, 20, 127, 128, 129, 139, 134, 135, 136, 138, 139, 140, 141, 142, 143, 243
natural history specimens, 9, 10, 13, 14, 97, 98, 105, 128, 133, 142, 222, 224, 239
Navajos, 246, 247, 252, 254, 255
New Guinea Nutrition Survey Expedition (1947), 290–94, 295, 296, 297
nutrition, 10, 23, 290, 291, 292, 293, 294, 295, 296, 297, 298, 300, 301, 302, 304

O
Osborn, Henry Fairfield, 236, 237, 239, 240, 241, 242, 243, 254, 255, 267, 268

P
Papua New Guinea (formerly New Guinea *and* Papua), 3, 13, 21, 23, 183, 184, 186, 187, 188, 189, 190, 191, 192, 193, 195, 290, 291, 292, 293, 294, 295, 296, 297, 301, 302, 304; **187, 188, 189, 293**

Parsons, Elsie Clews, 22, 23, 235, 236, 244, 245, 246, 247, 248, 250, 251, 252, 253, 254, 255, 265, 303; **236**
Pasi, 70–1, 72–4, 75, 76–8, 79, 80, 81–2, 83, 85
photography, 8, 10, 15, 24, 38, 43, 44, 48, 49, 50, 51, 52, 56, 57, 58, 65, 66, 67, 71, 73, 74, 75, 76, 79, 80, 81, 84, 85, 97, 100, 103, 104, 105, 113, 115, 138, 129, 146, 150, 158, 159, 239, 241
Pitt Rivers Museum, 43, 56
Prado y Tovar, Diego de 180, 182, 183, 184, 185, 186, 187, 188, 189, 191, 192, 193, 194, 195; **182, 183, 184, 185, 186, 187, 188, 189**
psychology, 64, 65, 68, 71, 73, 74, 75, 79, 81, 82, 98, 107, 155, 246, 267, 270
public lectures, 5, 6, 10, 11, 98, 113, 238, 242
publicity, 12, 14, 25, 47, 238, 241, 242, 244, 246, 266

Q
Quirós, Pedro Fernández de, 21, 175, 177–81, 185, 190, 191, 192, 193, 195
  South Sea voyage (1606), 3, 175, 177–195

R
race, 9, 20, 21, 68, 103, 151, 152, 153, 158, 159, 160, 163, 164, 180, 192, 193, 194, 195, 240, 244, 254, 265, 267, 268, 276, 295
Radcliffe-Brown, A. R., 19, 83, 97, 100, 102, 103, 105, 106
Reichard, Gladys, 235, 245, 246, 247, 250, 251, 255, 303
rituals, 37, 51, 53, 54, 55, 151, 224; **52**
Rivers, William, 45, 46, 47, 65, 67, 68, 69, 71, 72, 73, 74, 75, 76, 78, 80, 81, 82, 83, 85, 106; **65, 71, 76**
Royal Geographical Society, 6, 19, 98, 100, 108, 111, 112, 113, 115
Royal Society, 14, 40, 218, 222

S

Seligman, Charles G. 45, 65, 67, 68, 69, 72, 73, 74, 75, 83; **65, 71**
Sepik, 23, 263, 264, 265, 266, 268, 269, 270, 271, 272, 273, 274, 276, 277, 278, 279, 280, 281, 282
settler colonialism, 2, 100, 110, 153
sexuality, 23, 247, 253, 254, 265, 266, 274, 279, 280, 281
Simpson, Colin, 11, 12, 13, 15, 16
Smithsonian Institution, 10, 11, 13, 14, 20, 128, 132, 133, 134, 135, 139, 141, 142, 298
social evolutionism, 20, 38, 40, 43, 47, 57, 103, 138, 139
songs, 73, 74, 75, 76, 77, 78, 79, 82
sound recording, 8, 10, 15, 38, 45, 48, 56, 75, 76, 77, 97, 140
South Australian Museum, 56
South Seas, 175, 177, 178, 192. *See also* Quirós, Pedro Fernández de
Southwest Society, 22, 235, 236, 244, 245, 246, 247
Southwestern pueblos, 244, 245, 246, 250
Spencer, Baldwin, 18, 39, 42, 43, 44, 45, 46, 47, 48, 49, 50, 51, 52, 53, 54, 55, 56, 57, 58, 59; **47**
   Expedition from South Australia to Northern Territory with Francis Gillen (1901–02), 18, 39, 42, 45, 46–56, 57, 58, 59, 60; **47, 50, 52**
Stocking, George W., 4, 37, 98, 106, 114, 267, 274
Survey
   geological, 20, 133, 134, 135 (*see also* US Geological and Geographical Surveys of the Territories)
   hydrographic, 21, 22, 205, 207, 210, 222 (*see also* Hydrographic Surveys of the Australian Coast)
   nutritional, 291, 292, 293, 294, 295, 297, 298, 302 (*see also* New Guinea Nutrition Survey Expedition)
   topographical, 127, 128, 129, 130, 131, 132, 133, 134, 135, 136, 141, 142, 239

T

Taussig, Michael, 9, 65, 67, 83, 84
Tchambuli, 272, 273
Thomson, Donald, 6, 8, 14, 19, 20, 95, 96, 97, 98, 100, 101, 102, 103, 104, 105, 106, 107, 108, 109, 110, 111, 112, 113, 114, 115, 299; **99, 101, 110**
   expeditions to Arnhem Land (1930s), 19, 96, 98–115
Torres, Luis Váez de, 21, 175, 179, 180, 181, 182, 183, 184, 186, 187, 188, 190, 191, 192, 193
Torres Strait, 3, 4, 18, 19, 64, 66, 67, 68, 69, 70, 72, 80, 83, 84, 85, 102, 186. *See also* Cambridge Anthropological Expedition to Torres Straits
totem, 38, 44, 49, 53, 57, 105
trade, 1, 41, 54, 70, 74, 100, 137, 177, 178, 189, 190, 191, 193, 206, 212, 223, 271
Tylor, Edward Burnett, 40, 41, 42, 43, 47

U

United States National Museum, 128, 131, 132, 134, 135, 136, 137, 139, 140, 141, 142
US Geological and Geographical Surveys of the Territories (1870s), 127, 128, 129–33, 134, 135, 136, 141, 142, 143

V

Vanuatu, 3, 175, 177, 178

W

Warumungu, 52, 53, 54, 58, 59; **52**
Wilkins, Hubert, 95, 96, 115
Worora, 22, 205, 206, 211, 212, 213, 214, 219, 221, 224

Y

Yaburara, 207, 209
Yellowstone Park, 129, 132, 133

Methodology and History in Anthropology

Series Editors:
David Parkin, Fellow of All Souls College, University of Oxford
David Gellner, Fellow of All Souls College, University of Oxford

Just as anthropology has had a significant influence on many other disciplines in recent years, so too have its methods been challenged by new intellectual and technical developments. This series is designed to offer a forum for debate on the interrelationship between anthropology and other academic fields but also on the challenge to anthropological methods of new intellectual and technological developments, and the role of anthropological thought in a general history of concepts.

Volume 1
Marcel Mauss: A Centenary Tribute
Edited by Wendy James and N.J. Allen

Volume 2
Franz Baerman Steiner: Selected Writings Volume I: Taboo, Truth and Religion. Franz B. Steiner
Edited by Jeremy Adler and Richard Fardon

Volume 3
Franz Baerman Steiner: Selected Writings Volume II: Orientalism, Value, and Civilisation. Franz B. Steiner
Edited by Jeremy Adler and Richard Fardon

Volume 4
The Problem of Context: Perspectives from Social Anthropology and Elsewhere
Edited by Roy Dilley

Volume 5
Religion in English Everyday Life: An Ethnographic Approach
By Timothy Jenkins

Volume 6
Hunting the Gatherers: Ethnographic Collectors, Agents and Agency in Melanasia, 1870s–1930s
Edited by Michael O'Hanlon and Robert L. Welsh

Volume 7
Anthropologists in a Wider World: Essays on Field Research
Edited by Paul Dresch, Wendy James, and David Parkin

Volume 8
Categories and Classifications: Maussian Reflections on the Social
By N.J. Allen

Volume 9
Louis Dumont and Hierarchical Opposition
By Robert Parkin

Volume 10
Categories of Self: Louis Dumont's Theory of the Individual
By André Celtel

Volume 11
Existential Anthropology: Events, Exigencies and Effects
By Michael Jackson

Volume 12
An Introduction to Two Theories of Social Anthropology: Descent Groups and Marriage Alliance
By Louis Dumont

Volume 13
Navigating Terrains of War: Youth and Soldiering in Guinea-Bissau
By Henrik E. Vigh

Volume 14
The Politics of Egalitarianism: Theory and Practice
Edited by Jacqueline Solway

Volume 15
A History of Oxford Anthropology
Edited by Peter Riviére

Volume 16
Holistic Anthropology: Emergence and Convergence
Edited by David Parkin and Stanley Ulijaszek

Volume 17
Learning Religion: Anthropological Approaches
Edited by David Berliner and Ramon Sarró

Volume 18
Ways of Knowing: New Approaches in the Anthropology of Knowledge and Learning
Edited by Mark Harris

Volume 19
Difficult Folk? A Political History of Social Anthropology
By David Mills

Volume 20
Human Nature as Capacity: Transcending Discourse and Classification
By Nigel Rapport

Volume 21
The Life of Property: House, Family and Inheritance in Béarn, South-West France
By Timothy Jenkins

Volume 22
Out of the Study and Into the Field: Ethnographic Theory and Practice in French Anthropology
Edited by Robert Parkin and Anna de Sales

Volume 23
The Scope of Anthropology: Maurice Godelier's Work in Context
Edited by Laurent Dousset and Serge Tcherkézoff

Volume 24
Anyone: *The Cosmopolitan Subject of Anthropology*
By Nigel Rapport

Volume 25
Up Close and Personal: On Peripheral Perspectives and the Production of Anthropological Knowledge
Edited by Cris Shore and Susanna Trnka

Volume 26
Understanding Cultural Transmission in Anthropology: A Critical Synthesis
Edited by Roy Ellen, Stephen J. Lycett, and Sarah E. Johns

Volume 27
Durkheim in Dialogue: A Centenary Celebration of The Elementary Forms of Religious Life
Edited by Sondra L. Hausner

Volume 28
Extraordinary Encounters: Authenticity and the Interview
Edited by Katherine Smith, James Staples, and Nigel Rapport

Volume 29
Regimes of Ignorance: Anthropological Perspectives on the Production and Reproduction of Non-Knowledge
Edited by Roy Dilley and Thomas G. Kirsch

Volume 30
Human Origins: Contributions from Social Anthropology
Edited by Camilla Power, Morna Finnegan, and Hilary Callan

Volume 31
The Ethics of Knowledge Creation: Transactions, Relations and Persons
Edited by Lisette Josephides and Anne Sigfrid Grønseth

Volume 32
Returning Life: Language, Life Force and History in Kilimanjaro
By Knut Christian Myhre

Volume 33
Expeditionary Anthropology: Teamwork, Travel and the 'Science of Man'
Edited by Martin Thomas and Amanda Harris

www.ingramcontent.com/pod-product-compliance
Lightning Source LLC
Chambersburg PA
CBHW072144100526
44589CB00015B/2083